JURISPRUDENCE

JURISPRUDENCE
Denise Meyerson

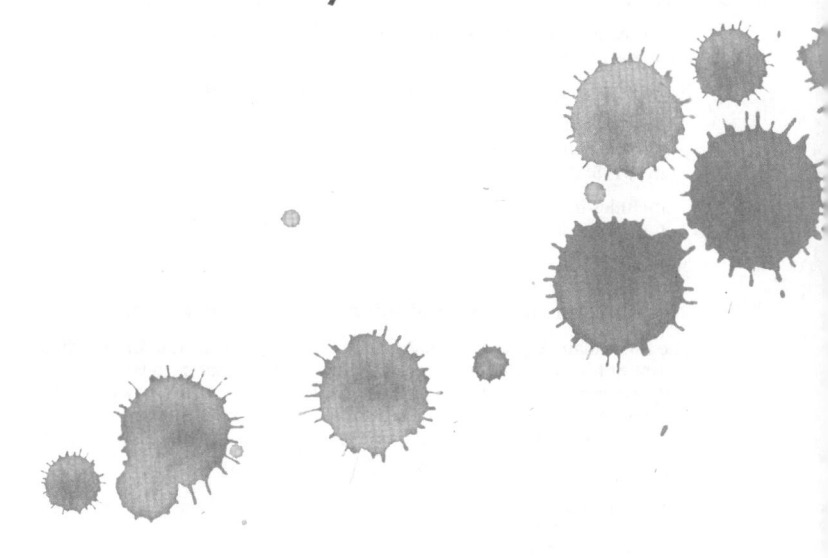

OXFORD
UNIVERSITY PRESS
AUSTRALIA & NEW ZEALAND

OXFORD
UNIVERSITY PRESS

Oxford University Press is a department of the University of Oxford.
It furthers the University's objective of excellence in research,
scholarship, and education by publishing worldwide. Oxford is a registered
trademark of Oxford University Press in the UK and in certain other
countries.

Published in Australia by
Oxford University Press
253 Normanby Road, South Melbourne, Victoria 3205, Australia

Copyright © Denise Meyerson 2011

© Oxford University Press 2013

The moral rights of the author have been asserted

First published 2011
Reprinted 2013

All rights reserved. No part of this publication may be reproduced, stored in a retrieval system, or transmitted, in any form or by any means, without the prior permission in writing of Oxford University Press, or as expressly permitted by law, by licence, or under terms agreed with the appropriate reprographics rights organisation. Enquiries concerning reproduction outside the scope of the above should be sent to the Rights Department, Oxford University Press, at the address above.

You must not circulate this work in any other form and you must impose this same condition on any acquirer.

National Library of Australia Cataloguing-in-Publication data

> Meyerson, Denise.
> Jurisprudence/Denise Meyerson.
> 9780195568714 (pbk.)
>
> Includes index.
> Jurisprudence—Australia.

349.94

Reproduction and communication for educational purposes

The Australian *Copyright Act 1968* (the Act) allows a maximum of one chapter or 10% of the pages of this work, whichever is the greater, to be reproduced and/or communicated by any educational institution for its educational purposes provided that the educational institution (or the body that administers it) has given a remuneration notice to Copyright Agency Limited (CAL) under the Act.

For details of the CAL licence for educational institutions contact:

Copyright Agency Limited
Level 15, 233 Castlereagh Street
Sydney NSW 2000
Telephone: (02) 9394 7600
Facsimile: (02) 9394 7601
Email: info@copyright.com.au

Edited by L. Elaine Miller, Otmar Miller Consultancy Pty Ltd, Melbourne
Typeset by diacriTech, Chennai, India
Indexed by Puddingburn Publishing Services
Printed in China by Sheck Wah Tong Printing Press Ltd.

Links to third party websites are provided by Oxford in good faith and for information only. Oxford disclaims any responsibility for the materials contained in any third party website referenced in this work.

Contents

Table of Cases ix
Preface x

1 Introduction 1
1.1 What is jurisprudence? 1
1.2 Outline of chapters 3
1.3 Labels, categories and schools of thought 4
1.4 What is the point of studying jurisprudence? 7

Part A Law

2 Law as Command 13
2.1 Chapter overview 13
2.2 Austin's command theory of law 13
2.3 Can threats place us under obligations? 17
2.4 Can Austin account for certain familiar features of legal systems? 19
2.5 Positivism: some preliminary points 23

3 Law as Social Practice 35
3.1 Chapter overview 35
3.2 The concept of a social rule 36
3.3 Law as a combination of primary and secondary rules 41
3.4 Hart's account compared to Austin's 48
3.5 Law as a 'remedy' 50
3.6 Legal versus moral normativity 52
3.7 Some criticisms of Hart 55
3.8 Judicial decision-making 60

4 Law as What Is 69
4.1 Chapter overview 69
4.2 Some misconceptions about the positivist separation of law and morality 70
4.3 Dworkin's attack on positivism 76
4.4 Inclusive positivism 80
4.5 Is inclusive positivism an acceptable theory of law? 84
4.6 Raz's exclusive positivism 87
4.7 Some criticisms of Raz 98
4.8 Ethical positivism 101

5 Law as Morally Valuable — 107
- 5.1 Chapter overview — 107
- 5.2 The natural law tradition — 108
- 5.3 Finnis and the central case of law — 113
- 5.4 Some criticisms of Finnis — 122
- 5.5 Fuller and the moral standards internal to law — 124
- 5.6 Some criticisms of Fuller — 127
- 5.7 Natural law in the courts — 129

6 Law as Interpretive — 135
- 6.1 Chapter overview — 135
- 6.2 Fuller's theory of meaning — 136
- 6.3 Law as spirit, not letter — 141
- 6.4 Should judges follow clear rules? — 144
- 6.5 Dworkin's challenge to Hart's doctrine of discretion — 148
- 6.6 Dworkin's distinction between rules and principles — 150
- 6.7 Theoretical disagreement — 153
- 6.8 Jurisprudence as interpretation — 156
- 6.9 Conventionalism — 161
- 6.10 Law as integrity — 163
- 6.11 The objectivity of interpretation — 171
- 6.12 Some criticisms of Dworkin — 174

7 Law as Myth — 183
- 7.1 Chapter overview — 183
- 7.2 The law is what the courts say it is — 183
- 7.3 The indeterminacy of the law — 188
- 7.4 How judges decide cases — 190
- 7.5 The pragmatic model of adjudication — 194

8 Law as Wealth-Maximising — 201
- 8.1 Chapter overview — 201
- 8.2 Posner's pragmatism — 201
- 8.3 The normative dimension of law and economics — 204
- 8.4 The descriptive dimension of law and economics — 210

9 Law as Oppressive — 217
- 9.1 Chapter overview — 217
- 9.2 The main themes of CLS — 217
- 9.3 Postmodernism — 219
- 9.4 Marxism and law — 224

9.5	Contradictions, incoherencies and law as ideology	227
9.6	Rejecting liberal values	230
9.7	CLS versus constructive interpretation	231

Part B Justice

10 Rights — 239

10.1	Chapter overview	239
10.2	The concept of human rights	239
10.3	What does respect for rights involve?	240
10.4	Which of our interests deserve the status of rights?	246
10.5	Why should governments respect rights?	248
10.6	Are rights selfish?	255
10.7	Are rights an instrument of oppression?	256
10.8	Are rights a threat to the value of community?	258
10.9	Are rights ethnocentric?	259
10.10	Bills of rights	261
10.11	Socio-economic rights	266

11 Freedom — 271

11.1	Chapter overview	271
11.2	Possible reasons for state coercion	271
11.3	Mill's harm principle	272
11.4	The concept of state neutrality	277
11.5	Lord Devlin's conservative version of legal moralism	279
11.6	Some criticisms of Devlin	281
11.7	Perfectionism, liberalism and legal moralism	284
11.8	Pornography	286
11.9	Abortion	290
11.10	Voluntary euthanasia and assisted suicide	295

12 Inequality — 303

12.1	Chapter overview	303
12.2	Utilitarianism and distributive justice	303
12.3	Rawls's two principles of justice	306
12.4	The original position	311
12.5	Are the conditions of choice in the original position justifiable?	315
12.6	Would it be rational to choose Rawls's principles in the original position?	318
12.7	Does the Difference Principle unfairly subsidise people's choices?	320
12.8	Political liberalism	321

12.9	Dworkin's equality of resources theory	328
12.10	Some criticisms of Dworkin's theory	331
12.11	Nozick's libertarianism	334
12.12	Liberty and patterns	338
12.13	The principle of self-ownership	339

13 Difference — 345

13.1	Chapter overview	345
13.2	Feminist legal theory	345
13.3	Formal equality	346
13.4	Formal equality and the male norm	348
13.5	Formal equality, liberalism and individualism	351
13.6	Difference feminism	353
13.7	Criticisms of difference feminism	355
13.8	Dominance and subordination	359
13.9	Postmodern feminism, essentialism and intersectionality	361
13.10	Postmodernism and feminist politics	364
13.11	The family as a political institution	366
13.12	Rights, justice and care	371
13.13	Feminism and multiculturalism	372
13.14	Critical race theory	374
13.15	Sexuality and the law	378

Index — 385

Table of Cases

Adelaide Co. of Jehovah's Witnesses, Inc. v Commonwealth (1943) 67 CLR 116   268

Bradwell v Illinois, 83 US 130 (1873)   346, 347

Dr Bonham's Case (1610) 8 Co Rep 107a   131

Eckert v Long Island Railroad, 43 NY 502 (1870)   212
EEOC v Sears, Roebuck & Co., 839 F 2d 302 (7th Cir 1988)   356

Fardon v Attorney-General (Qld) (2004) 223 CLR 575   268
Federal Commissioner of Taxation v Westraders Pty Ltd (1979) 38 FLR 306   146

Harris v McRae, 488 (US) 297 (1980)   369
Henningsen v Bloomfield Motors, Inc., 32 NJ 358 (1960)   78, 79, 80, 84

Leeth v Commonwealth (1992) 174 CLR 455   131
Lochner v New York, 198 US 45 (1905)   188

McLoughlin v O'Brian [1983] 1 AC 410   190
Milirrpum v Nabalco Pty Ltd (Gove Land Rights case) (1971) 17 FLR 141   9, 15

National Socialist Party of America v Village of Skokie, 432 US 43 (1977)   299

Oppenheimer v Cattermole [1976] AC 249   131

Paris Adult Theatre I v Slaton, 413 US 49 (1973)   290, 295
Practice Statement [1966] 3 All ER 77   104
President of the Republic of South Africa v Hugo 1997 (4) SA 1 (CC)   9, 358, 359
Prohibitions del Roy (1607) 12 Co Rep 63   98

R v Butler (1982) 89 DLR (4th) 449   288
R v Dincer [1983] VR 460   382
Riggs v Palmer, 115 NY 506 (1889)   78, 79, 82, 84, 151, 153, 154, 155, 159, 163, 168
Roe v Wade, 410 US 113 (1973)   262, 295, 369

Soobramoney v Minister of Health, Kwazulu-Natal 1998 (1) SA 765 (CC)   342
Steel v Houghton (1788) 126 ER 32   235
Sturges v Bridgman, 11 Ch D 852 (1879)   204

Preface

Jurisprudence is not an easy subject to cover in a way that both accurately and accessibly conveys the current state of research in the discipline. The theoretical debates in jurisprudence are complicated and deep. This means that the author has to tread a fine line between obscurity, on the one hand, and oversimplification, on the other. A further difficulty is that the point of the debates is sometimes hard to grasp, for those new to them. Ideally, the issues should therefore be brought to life by showing their relevance to everyday issues and more familiar concerns. Jurisprudence is also a 'movable feast': contemporary theorists working in the area constantly modify and refine their views in reply to objections made by other writers, making it difficult to provide snapshot accounts of particular theorists' views.

I have tried in this book to do justice to the complexities of jurisprudence in a way that is nevertheless intuitive, accessible and stimulating. Avoiding a compartmentalised approach, in which a particular theorist is dealt with in a single chapter, never to be heard of again, I have attempted to present the subject in a way that integrates, synthesises and comments on the material, so as to bring the different theorists into dialogue with each other throughout the book. I also explain the views of different theorists in the context of evolving debates, so that readers can see how objections are made, responses are provided, and new issues emerge. The idea is to convey a sense of the subject as an ongoing and dynamic enterprise. Some of my interpretations and commentary will, no doubt, be contested, but that is only to be expected, as part of the territory.

I do not want readers to come away thinking that jurisprudence is about a series of 'schools' to be learnt and mastered. The focus is on the problems to which the theorists are responding and the attractions and difficulties of their competing positions, rather than on 'schools' per se. This book is written in the belief that while categories are useful in imposing structure and calling attention to similarities and differences between the views of different theorists, it is more important to focus on the issues at stake and different theorists' responses to those issues, than on the way in which we should categorise or label their theories. I am also keen to stress that jurisprudence should not be confused with the study of the history of ideas about law. Although the history of philosophising about law is relevant to jurisprudence, this book does not explore the ideas and writings of past philosophers of law for their own sake. Instead, it assumes that the importance of past as well as contemporary thinkers lies in helping us to confront ideas in a critical way, so that the influence of what we retain is integrated with the rest of what we believe, according to our own judgment. Finally, I draw on legal cases, statutes, constitutional provisions and international human rights instruments and I apply jurisprudential theories to topical legal controversies with the aim of illustrating the interest and relevance of jurisprudence. My overall hope is that readers of this book will use the ideas presented here as a foothold in critically and reflectively developing positions of their own.

In 2006, I published a book on jurisprudence called *Essential Jurisprudence* and I have drawn on and developed some of that material in this book. This book, however, has a different purpose and focus. It is a much longer work, and its aim is to treat the subject in more depth and to reflect to a much greater extent the current state of scholarly research in the discipline. It therefore seeks to meet the needs of those who wish to grapple with the issues in a more sustained way and at a higher level.

I would like to thank a number of people who read various parts of the manuscript or assisted me in other ways. Carlos Bernal made many acute observations, which enabled me to improve the manuscript at a number of points. Aleardo Zanghellini provided very useful comments, which helped me to clarify some of the material. Paul Taylor pointed out many gaps in the arguments, where I had assumed too much. OUP's anonymous reviewers provided very constructive criticisms and suggestions. Experience in teaching jurisprudence led Roy Baker to call my attention to some common confusions, which I have been at pains to avert. David Bilchitz's perceptive comments, in a review of *Essential Jurisprudence*, assisted me in developing and rethinking the material. Charlotte Frew provided assistance with the preparation of the footnotes. I would also like to thank Katie Ridsdale, for her generous advice and support throughout the process of writing this book, as well as the production team at OUP and especially Elaine Miller for her meticulous editing of the manuscript. Finally, I am grateful to Macquarie University for granting me a period of research leave, which enabled me to write this book, and to the Gilbert and Tobin Centre of Public Law at the University of New South Wales, which hosted me for this period as a Visiting Professorial Fellow.

1

Introduction

This chapter briefly explains what jurisprudence is and what the point is of studying it. It also provides an overview of the contents of the book and introduces in a preliminary way some of the theories that will be discussed.

1.1 What is jurisprudence?

Jurisprudence is generally conceived of as the attempt to understand the social institution of law from the perspective of philosophy, and this is the conception that will be assumed in this book. But what is involved in taking a philosophical perspective? In order to understand this, let us start with our everyday involvement with the law. In our everyday lives, we operate with an unarticulated and unreflective conception of what law is. When someone appeals to the law to settle a dispute, they do not, for example, reflect on what they mean by legal 'validity', or legal 'rights', or wonder whether legal reasoning is a distinctive kind of reasoning. Similarly, lawyers practise law for the most part without thinking about very general questions, such as what sets law apart from other areas of life. They rely on an intuitive or unreflective grasp of what makes an issue a legal issue, as opposed, say, to a moral, religious or political issue.

Studying jurisprudence involves stepping back, reflecting on and, if necessary, rejecting the buried ideas and assumptions about law that are made in everyday and professional life. In contrast to the study of areas of substantive law, such as criminal law or constitutional law, jurisprudence studies law in a much more general way, and asks much more abstract and theoretical questions about law as such. A legal system provides norms with which we are supposed to comply—but what is the difference between these norms and the norms prescribed by morality or by a religion? What makes a particular rule a law? Where does law fit into our lives and our society viewed as a whole? Why is law important? What would a society be like without it? Does law have a function? Is it morally valuable? Can we be under a moral obligation to obey the law just because it is the law? Where does the authority of a legal system come from? Is there a connection between law and justice? Is the rule of law intrinsically desirable? Is legal reasoning different from the reasoning of political decision-makers? Are there determinate answers to legal questions, which can be found within the law? Are judges necessarily reaching outside the law when they draw on moral principles? Everyone implicitly has ideas about these matters but most people have not subjected them to reasoned and rigorous evaluation. This is the task of jurisprudence. It is in search of satisfactory answers to these questions, answers that can withstand an examination of their presuppositions and implications, in this way assisting us to arrive at a more disciplined and therefore deeper understanding of the nature of law.

Another way in which jurisprudence contributes to a deeper understanding of law is by providing the tools to determine what laws are desirable, and to engage in rational criticism of existing laws. Here we are interested in the shape the law should take or the standards that good law should meet. When we engage in this enterprise we use philosophy to evaluate legal institutions and practices, and the policies served by actual and potential legal rules. Examples of questions focusing on the evaluation and criticism of law are as follows. What role should the state play in our lives? What is the right balance between individual and collective interests? Are there any moral limits on the authority of government over us? Are there certain objectives that it is not legitimate for government to pursue, and certain limits on the way it should pursue its legitimate objectives? Are there certain goods that government is under a duty to provide for us? And how should the law deal with 'difference'? Should the law be blind to differences such as race, gender and sexuality or should it be sensitive to them? How can the law be made to speak for everyone, given the large differences in people's social circumstances? The answers to questions such as these are to be found in an understanding of rival moral and political theories. As we will see, these theories generate powerful resources for criticism of actual legal rules and policies. On some conceptions of jurisprudence, they may also help us to understand the nature of law itself. This last point is discussed further in 1.3, where the difference between analytical and normative conceptions of jurisprudence is explained.

I have explained the types of issues that will be discussed in this book. Questions of this kind may seem bewildering or so hard to deal with that you might think no one could come up with rationally persuasive answers to them. But when approached systematically, and with the right philosophical tools, they can come to seem less daunting. There is also a long and luminous tradition of philosophical debate on the central issues of jurisprudence on which to draw—a tradition which has produced a rich and helpful literature. The purpose of this book is to enable readers to develop their own views on philosophical issues about the law, by becoming acquainted firsthand with the methods of philosophical analysis and argumentation and with some of the most important contributions philosophers have made to the central questions of jurisprudence.

A final preliminary point relates to the terms 'jurisprudence', 'philosophy of law' and 'legal theory'. Although there have been attempts to draw fine distinctions between these terms, there is no need to enter into this debate here. I will use the terms interchangeably to refer to theoretical reflection on the nature of law and justice.

1.2 Outline of chapters

The book is divided into two parts, the first part of which deals with questions about law, whereas the second part explores questions about justice, and in particular, the moral and political principles that should govern our laws and legal institutions. The first three chapters of Part A deal with theories and arguments in the positivist tradition of legal theory: John Austin's command theory of law (Chapter 2), H L A Hart's social practice account of law (Chapter 3), and the debate between inclusive and exclusive positivists, with particular attention to Joseph Raz's views about the authoritative nature of law (Chapter 4). The next two chapters deal with the natural law tradition. Chapter 5 explores classical natural law theory in the tradition of St Thomas Aquinas and especially the work of John Finnis, who is currently the key exponent of this tradition. It also deals with Lon Fuller's procedural version of natural law. Chapter 6 investigates Fuller's and Ronald Dworkin's beliefs about the nature of legal interpretation. The following two chapters turn to more sceptical and pragmatic views about the law. Chapter 7 deals with the work of the American realists and Chapter 8 deals with the economic approach to law, especially as exemplified in the work of Richard Posner. Chapter 9 introduces critical perspectives on the law, with reference to the Critical Legal Studies (CLS) movement and to the Marxist and postmodernist influences on this movement.

Part B of the book is organised around the discussion of four connected issues: rights, freedom, inequality and difference. Chapter 10 asks whether it is morally and legally desirable to insist on respect for rights as constraints on the exercise of state power. Chapter 11 investigates whether it is legitimate for the law to prevent conduct that is immoral even if the conduct does not cause harm to anyone. Chapter 12 explores the question of whether the state is under an obligation to alleviate poverty. Finally, Chapter 13 focuses on the law's treatment of those who are 'different', whether in terms of gender, race, culture or sexuality, and asks whether and how law can be made more inclusive. These four questions are explored through the lens of different theories, which can then be seen as providing rival answers to them.

It is worth saying something about the fact that the issue of difference has been placed in Part B of the book. This issue might have been explored in a follow-up chapter to the chapter on CLS, since the theorists concerned with difference—for instance, feminists, critical race theorists (CRT) and gay and lesbian theorists—also take a critical approach to the law. On the other hand, they are in general more strongly focused than CLS on the moral and political implications of the way in which the law is systematically biased against particular groups in society, and their critique of the law is frequently aimed at overcoming disadvantage and disempowerment in a much more concrete and practical way. They speak about their experience of the law as members of 'outsider' groups. This is not a characteristic of CLS. Although all such choices are to some extent artificial, I have therefore chosen to explore the issue of difference in Part B.

1.3 Labels, categories and schools of thought

It is also necessary to say something about the labels I used in 1.2, in describing the content of the chapters—labels such as 'positivism', 'natural law', 'sceptical and pragmatic theories' and 'critical theories'. The debate between positivism and natural law has traditionally been regarded as central to jurisprudence, although the moment one tries to pin down what the debate is about, two difficulties must be confronted. First, 'positivism' and 'natural law' are broad churches and this means that there is no single positivist position in the debate and no single natural law position. For instance, while Austin, Hart and Raz are all key positivist figures, their versions of positivism are very different. Leslie Green writes that 'Raz controverted so many of Hart's central ideas that legal positivism ... will never be the same again'.[1] The same can be said about Hart's devastating attack on Austin's version of positivism.

Secondly, the boundaries between the two schools have become less clear-cut, as theorists on both sides have refined their positions and found common ground with their opponents.[2] Thus, while the debate between positivists and natural law theorists is sometimes presented as a debate between those who think that unjust laws can be valid and those who think that they cannot be valid, there are in fact very few contemporary natural law theorists who maintain that unjust laws cannot be valid. Finnis, Fuller and Dworkin, for instance, expressly deny this view. Likewise, while positivism is sometimes identified with the view that there are no necessary connections between law and morality, many contemporary positivists reject this claim.

Furthermore, it is not possible to distinguish between positivists and natural law theorists in terms of their beliefs about the nature of jurisprudence or legal theory. There is an important debate in contemporary jurisprudence about the nature of legal theory, but positivists and natural law theorists are to be found on both sides of the debate. The question at issue is whether jurisprudence is an analytical enterprise or a normative enterprise. On the former view, an analysis of the concept of law does not presuppose or commit the theorist to any claims about the value or moral justifiability of law. On the latter view, we cannot understand law without understanding that law has, by its nature, a moral purpose and without understanding what this purpose is. The important point for present purposes is that some positivists believe that conceptual inquiry into the nature of law is a morally neutral enterprise, whereas others disagree. The same is true of natural law theorists. Some defend their views about law on normative grounds, while others defend them on non-normative grounds. This means that positivists and natural law theorists do not necessarily hold different views about the methods of jurisprudence.

These difficulties in categorisation have led some legal theorists to argue that the distinction between positivism and natural law is no longer relevant

---

1 L Green, 'Three Themes from Raz' (2005) 25 *Oxford Journal of Legal Studies* 503, 503.
2 For a discussion of the boundary lines between legal positivism and natural law theory, see B Bix, 'On the Dividing Line between Natural Law Theory and Legal Positivism' (2000) 75 *Notre Dame Law Review* 1613.

or useful. Jules Coleman, for instance, argues that the old distinctions have 'worn out their welcome'.[3] I would not go quite so far. In my view, these labels are useful in organising the material and in revealing broad similarities and differences between the views of different theorists, as long as one realises that their usefulness should not be exaggerated.

Thus we can say that positivists put the social aspects of law centre-stage and that they believe that moral reasoning is not necessarily needed to ascertain the existence and content of the law. Austin, Hart and Raz all affirm these theses, as we will see. This is, of course, very general and it is no substitute for engaging with the details of their different positivist theories, but it does pick out a recognisably distinct position. Again, we can say that natural law theorists believe that law and morality are necessarily linked, while acknowledging that the way in which, for instance, Dworkin, Finnis and Fuller spell out the nature of this connection is very different. Likewise, while it is important to appreciate that there are large differences between realism and the law and economics movement, it is nevertheless true that they share some very general commitments. Both believe that judicial decisions are less constrained by law than is commonly believed, and both discount the desirability of judicial decisions being constrained by law. Furthermore, both believe that law should be understood from the perspective of other disciplines—the social sciences in the case of the realists and economics in the case of the law and economics movement—and in this way both challenge the autonomy of law. They can therefore be described as movements that aim to 'demythologise' law. Finally, critical theories take scepticism about the law one step further. These are more radical theories, which aim to delegitimise law by revealing that it does not speak for everyone, but functions to exclude and marginalise certain groups in the interests of those who have power. Once again, however, it is important to note that there are many variants of critical theory. For instance, CLS, CRT and feminist legal theory are very different movements and even within these movements, there are many variants.

The key point that should be stressed is that the shared general commitments of the kind explained in the previous paragraph are no more than a useful starting point. Jurisprudence is not fundamentally about schools of thought, and it is not particularly fruitful to ask whether a particular theorist is 'really' a positivist or 'really' a natural law theorist or whether the law and

---

3   J Coleman, 'Beyond Inclusive Legal Positivism' (2009) 22 *Ratio Juris* 359, 392.

economics movement and CLS are 'really' the heirs of realism. It is more important to focus on what the different theorists tell us about law than to wonder what we should call them. Even the categorisation I offered when I said that Part A of the book is about law and Part B of the book is about justice is just a rough-and-ready way of imposing structure on the material. It is not meant to preclude the possibility that the concept of law may be a normative concept and that theories of justice may have a bearing on our understanding of the nature of law and of its correct interpretation.

1.4 What is the point of studying jurisprudence?

There is a difference between education and vocational training. As John Bell explains:

> Training is concerned with providing a person with the knowledge and skills to undertake a specific and immediate task. It is focused and utilitarian. Education is concerned with enabling an individual to understand and reflect upon knowledge and processes and to be able to act in a critical and responsible manner. It is concerned with critical self-awarenesss.[4]

Jurisprudence plays a key role in educating lawyers. First, it provides a broader perspective on the law than that typically found in the legal profession. For instance, in asking questions about the nature of law and its purpose, it gives us a general understanding of the relation of law to the other institutions that make up our society and its significance in relation to these institutions. Jurisprudence also alerts us to a variety of external perspectives on law, such as those offered by feminists, Marxists and critical race theorists. These critical perspectives aim to expose the biases of law, the interests it serves, the way in which it masks inequality and the injustices it does. Another kind of external perspective to which jurisprudence alerts us is that offered by other disciplines, such as economics and political science. Some legal theorists claim that the law is best understood not according to its own self-image, that is, as an autonomous body of rules, which is capable of yielding determinate answers to legal questions. Rather, they claim that the logic of the law is 'really

---

4   J Bell, 'Legal Education', in P Cane and M Tushnet (eds), *The Oxford Handbook of Legal Studies*, Oxford University Press, Oxford, 2003, p 901.

economics' or that judges frequently make their decisions for political reasons, not legal reasons.

An understanding of critical and extra-disciplinary perspectives on the law promotes awareness of the historical, social and economic context in which law operates, and fosters the critical cast of mind that typifies the educated lawyer. In calling attention to the fact that law is an important social practice, and not just a set of rules, jurisprudence shows that there is more to understanding the law than the legal professional perspective on it.

Second, jurisprudence requires us to think in a self-consciously reflective way about concepts that we normally use unthinkingly and take at face value. For instance, everyone thinks they know what law is: law is whatever we find in the statutes and the reports of judicial decisions. But is law really to be identified with these rules? If it is, what are we to say about cases in which the rules are unclear? Are we to say that in these cases there is no law on the matter and that judges are free to impose their own personal views? If so, does that make sense of how judges see their task? Does it show the law in a good light? And if the answer to these last two questions is 'No', does this matter? Should we reconsider the way in which we think about law? This kind of critical and ultimately disruptive questioning goes back to Socrates, who had a famous method of encouraging his listeners to spell out their own views and the presuppositions and the implications of their views, until a point was invariably reached where it became obvious that their views were internally contradictory or flawed in some other way. In forcing us critically to examine our assumptions in this way, jurisprudence encourages us to take nothing for granted. It requires us to look deeper and to aim for a more fundamental understanding. This is, of course, another distinguishing characteristic of the educated lawyer.

Third, the aim of jurisprudence, as with all philosophical inquiry, is 'wisdom', not knowledge. Jurisprudence does not ask students to learn and reproduce different theories, but shows students how to use these theories in critically and reflectively developing positions of their own. It is not interested in the history of legal philosophy for its own sake and it does not treat the great legal philosophers of the past as authorities. Instead it focuses on the reasons why these great figures held the views they did, and it uses their work as a doorway into the subject so that students of the subject can begin engaging with the issues for themselves. Jurisprudence therefore empowers students to go on by themselves, independently of teachers and of other authority figures.

Fourth, lawyers have a responsibility to promote justice and fairness in the legal system, and jurisprudence gives lawyers the skills to detect the ways in which the law may fail to reflect the demands of justice and therefore to fulfil this responsibility. An understanding of philosophical theories about justice alerts lawyers to the questions that need to be asked in evaluating proposed laws or undertaking law reform. It enables them to debate the issues in an informed, critical and analytical way, in full knowledge of the alternative views on offer.

Fifth, an understanding of moral and political theory is not only a prerequisite to evaluating the law and reforming it. Moral and political reasoning is also frequently required when judges decide legal cases. This fact, which is acknowledged in one way or another by virtually all legal theorists, means that an understanding of moral and political theory is often indispensable to the resolution of legal cases. The most obvious examples, though not the only ones, come from jurisdictions in which moral rights are translated into law using the mechanism of a bill of rights. The protections granted by bills of rights are usually framed in a very abstract and general way which can be unpacked only by moral and political theorising. For instance, in 13.7 we will discuss the South African case of *President of the Republic of South Africa v Hugo*.[5] In this case, the court had to interpret a provision in the South African Bill of Rights, which forbids 'unfair discrimination' on the ground of sex but gives no clue as to when such discrimination will be unfair. The court had to decide whether it was unfairly discriminatory for President Mandela to pardon mothers in prison who had children younger than 12 years old, but not fathers of such children. A question such as this can be resolved only by appeal to moral and political arguments of the kind discussed in this book.

The resolution of legal cases can also depend on an understanding of conceptual issues. For instance, in *Milirrpum v Nabalco Pty Ltd*,[6] an Australian case that will be discussed in 2.2, Aboriginal claims to land were questioned on the basis that the customary rules of Indigenous Australians cannot be described as legal rules. The court was forced, as a result, to explore the distinguishing characteristics of law as a social institution. A conceptual issue was also raised in the East German Border Guards cases (see 5.7).[7] In these cases, German courts

---

5 *President of the Republic of South Africa v Hugo* 1997 (4) SA 1 (CC).
6 *Milirrpum v Nabalco Pty Ltd* (1971) 17 FLR 141.
7 Discussed in R Alexy, 'A Defence of Radbruch's Formula', in D Dyzenhaus (ed), *Recrafting the Rule of Law: The Limits of Legal Order*, Hart Publishing, Oxford, 1999, pp 19–22.

were required to consider whether an East German law, which allowed soldiers to kill innocent and unarmed civilians attempting to escape from East Germany to the West, was so iniquitous as not to provide a defence on a charge of manslaughter. The courts therefore had to consider the nature of the connection between law and morality. It should therefore be obvious that jurisprudential issues are not tangential to the law. On the contrary, the perspective provided by jurisprudence is an indispensable prerequisite to an adequate understanding of the law.

Part A
Law

2

Law as Command

2.1 Chapter overview

Law is a way of guiding human conduct, but it is not the only way. Our lives are also governed by other standards, such as those of morality, religion and etiquette. What, then, is distinctive or special about law? What differentiates law as a type of social institution from other social institutions? This question is at the heart of many of the jurisprudential debates that will be discussed in this book.

This chapter will explore the 'command theory' of law as articulated by the nineteenth-century British jurist John Austin. This is the theory that law is distinguished from other social standards, such as morality and religion, by the exercise of force. Although Austin was not the first theorist to defend the command theory—Jeremy Bentham and, before him, Thomas Hobbes had spoken of law in similar terms—Austin is generally acknowledged as having provided its most influential exposition.

This chapter will also examine the criticisms of the command theory put forward by H L A Hart, who is a key figure in contemporary legal philosophy. Hart argues that Austin's account of law is incapable of explaining some central features of legal systems. Notwithstanding their differences, both Austin and Hart are positivists. The chapter will conclude with a discussion of some key positivist claims.

2.2 Austin's command theory of law

In proposing the command theory of law, Bentham and Austin were reacting in part to natural law ideas, which at this point can loosely be defined as maintaining that law is necessarily linked to justice. William Blackstone, who wrote an influential eighteenth-century treatise on the common law, was a particular target of their criticism. Blackstone tended to present the common law as the embodiment of reason and Christian moral principles, whereas Bentham and Austin were legal reformers who wished to demystify law by providing an accurate description of law with all its imperfections. This, they thought, would provide the best basis for criticising and improving the law.

Whereas Blackstone had blurred the line between dispassionate analysis and moral evaluation, Bentham made a clear distinction between what he called 'expository jurisprudence' and 'censorial jurisprudence'. Expository jurisprudence is concerned with analysing the law as it actually exists, without regard to its justice or injustice. Censorial jurisprudence is a critical and moral enterprise designed to improve or reform the law. Austin made a similar distinction between 'general jurisprudence' and 'the art of legislation'.[1] Conceptualising law as the exercise of power was an important plank in this overall project. Obviously, if law is the exercise of power, law is not guaranteed to be the embodiment of reason, for power can be exercised for both good and bad ends.

In his set of lectures entitled *The Province of Jurisprudence Determined*, published in 1832, Austin begins by distinguishing 'laws properly so called' (laws intended to guide behaviour) from 'laws by analogy' (such as the laws of fashion or honour) and 'laws by metaphor' (these being the laws of science).[2] He then turns in more detail to the category of laws properly so called. All laws properly so called are commands, claims Austin, a command being an order backed up by a 'sanction' (a threat of harm) in the event of non-compliance with the command.[3]

Some commands, Austin tells us, are general. These are commands that prescribe types of conduct, directed to classes of persons. Other commands are directed to individual people.[4] But all commands issue from a superior, that is, a person or group of persons possessing the power to inflict harm. Austin writes: '[T]he term *superiority* signifies *might*: the power of affecting others with evil or pain, and of forcing them, through fear of that evil, to fashion their conduct to one's wishes.'[5] Austin then goes on to draw a further distinction between commands that issue from God and commands that issue from humans. Of those that issue

---

1 For discussion, see H L A Hart, *Essays in Jurisprudence and Philosophy*, Clarendon Press, Oxford, 1983, pp 271–2.
2 J Austin [1832], *The Province of Jurisprudence Determined*, W E Rumble (ed), Cambridge University Press, Cambridge, 1995, p 20.
3 Ibid pp 21–2.
4 Ibid p 25.
5 Ibid p 30, Austin's emphasis.

from humans, some, he says, are laid down by the sovereign in a state, while others, such as the commands of a father to his child, are not.[6]

Who or what is the sovereign in the state? The sovereign, Austin explains, is that person (such as an absolute monarch) or body of persons (such as a democratically elected parliament) whose orders are habitually obeyed by the bulk of society and who does not habitually obey any other person or body.[7]

Austin goes on to say that only those general commands that emanate from the sovereign in a state are laws 'strictly so called' or 'positive laws', and it is these laws that constitute the subject matter of jurisprudence.[8] This is Austin's simple answer to the question with which this chapter began, namely: how can we distinguish legal standards from the many other kinds of standards that regulate and govern human conduct? Legal standards, on Austin's view, are the commands of a supreme political superior or sovereign, which are backed up by the threat of sanctions. Here we have what Austin calls 'the key to the science of jurisprudence'.[9] Hart explains that, on Austin's view, 'in every human society where there is law, there is ultimately to be found ... [a] simple relationship between subjects rendering habitual obedience and a sovereign who renders habitual obedience to no one'.[10] Where this vertical structure is not present, we cannot, according to Austin, speak of law.

Austin's views about the nature of law are not of only abstract interest. Consider the Australian case of *Milirrpum v Nabalco Pty Ltd* (the *Gove Land Rights* case),[11] in which Austin's account of law was directly relevant to the legal issues and the court therefore had to confront the question of its adequacy. The plaintiffs were certain Aboriginal clans who claimed that a mining company had unlawfully interfered with rights they had under Aboriginal customary rules to occupy and enjoy certain areas of land in the Gove Peninsula in the Northern Territory. Blackburn J found that the clans in question had a religious basis and a connection with the land. They did not, however, have an internal organisation, were not ruled over by a chieftain, and were not in control of a definable territory. This raised the question whether in their world there was anything recognisable *as law*, because, if not, their relationship to their land could not amount to a proprietary right and their argument would have floundered at the first hurdle.

6　Ibid pp 18–19.
7　Ibid p 166.
8　Ibid p 19.
9　Ibid p 21.
10　H L A Hart, *The Concept of Law*, 2nd edn, Clarendon Press, Oxford, 1994, p 50.
11　*Milirrpum v Nabalco Pty Ltd* (*Gove Land Rights* case) (1971) 17 FLR 141.

On Austin's view, the answer would be 'No', since there was no identifiable sovereign authority with a capacity to enforce the clans' claims to land. In fact, the defendants implicitly relied on Austin's view, arguing that, in the absence of any machinery for enforcement, the clans' customs could not be described as legal rules and therefore that no invasion of legal rights had taken place. But is Austin correct that force applied by the state is the defining characteristic of law? The Federal Court rejected his view, and as we will see, there are powerful arguments in favour of the position it took. In fact, there are few contemporary legal theorists who accept the command theory of law.

In order to understand why this is so, we need to take note of an important distinction: that between normative statements and descriptive statements. Normative statements tell us what we have a right to do, what we ought to do and what we ought not to do. They aim to guide our conduct and to provide a standard for its appraisal. They are therefore 'practical' or 'prescriptive' in the sense that they prescribe how we should behave. Normative statements can be contrasted with descriptive statements, which do not tell us what we *ought* to do but instead describe the way the world actually *is*.

Austin's analysis of law treats propositions of law, such as propositions about the legal validity of a rule and propositions about legal rights and duties, as descriptive or predictive statements about the empirically observable behaviour of the sovereign and the sovereign's subjects. In other words, Austin thinks that statements of what individuals are legally required to do can be reduced to non-normative, factual statements about the giving of orders, habits of obedience, and the likelihood of being punished. Austin therefore sees legal concepts as ordinary factual concepts, not normative concepts. His account makes no reference, for instance, to the lawmaker as the person or body with the *authority* or *entitlement* to make laws, or to statements of law as statements that tell people what they *ought* to do, or to breaches of legal duties as *justifying* sanctions. Instead, he analyses statements of what individuals are legally required to do in non-normative, descriptive terms, namely, in terms of the factual likelihood of being harmed and facts about commands and obedience.[12]

Austin took this approach because he wished to extend the methods of science to the study of social phenomena such as law. This led him to analyse law from the outside, in terms of empirically observable regularities in behaviour, rather than from the inside, by reference to the role played by legal rules in the

---

12 J Raz, 'The Purity of the Pure Theory of Law', in R Tur and W Twining (eds), *Essays on Kelsen*, Clarendon Press, Oxford, 1986, p 83.

internal reasoning processes of those who are committed to legal institutions and practices. H L A Hart is the theorist who is best known for exposing the difficulties in Austin's behaviourist approach. As we will see, although both Hart and Austin are legal positivists, their versions of positivism are very different. Let us begin with Hart's reasons for objecting to Austin's approach.

2.3 Can threats place us under obligations?

On Austin's picture, as Hart points out, law is to be found in the 'gunman situation writ large'.[13] A gunman who accosts you, saying 'your money or your life', achieves what he wants by threatening to kill you. We say that you have been coerced or forced to hand over your money. Law, for Austin, is coercive in the same way. The only points of difference are that the gunman's orders are directed temporarily at a particular individual and the gunman is not the supreme source of commands in the society, whereas for Austin, laws are general, are obeyed over time, and issue from the sovereign. Nevertheless, both the gunman's command and the dictates of the law can be seen as orders backed up by a threat of harm. For Austin, force or coercion is the essence of law: the state is a gunman on a large scale.

Hart objects to this picture on a number of grounds. For one thing, he argues that threats are not capable of giving rise to obligations. Hart draws a distinction between 'being obliged' and 'being under an obligation'. If the threat of being killed leads me to hand over my money to a gunman, then we would say that I am obliged to hand over the money, in the sense of having no real choice. But, says Hart, we would not say that I was under an obligation to do so or was duty-bound to do so.[14] Nor would we say that the gunman has authority to tell me what to do.[15]

The notion of authority will be considered in detail in 4.6, but for the moment it will be sufficient to make the following slightly simplified points. Authority is a normative matter. Someone who has authority over me has the normative capacity to bind me by issuing directives with which I am under a duty to comply just because of the person's status as an authority, and no matter what I may think of the merits of the directive.[16] The gunman exercises control over me, not authority. His threats do not impose a duty on me and I am not bound to obey him. He merely influences my actions by making it prudent for me to do as

---

13 Hart, above n 10, p 7.
14 Ibid p 82.
15 Ibid p 20.
16 J Raz, *The Morality of Freedom*, Clarendon Press, Oxford, 1986, pp 24–6.

he orders, and if someone were to disarm him, I would have no further incentive to give him my money. Furthermore, if for some reason I were to resist the gunman, while this would no doubt lead to my suffering a harm, no one would suggest that the harm was justified by my resistance. It makes no difference whether it is the state or a lone villain who plays the role of gunman. Threats backed up by sanctions may affect my actions, but they cannot create an obligation for me to comply or make it justifiable to punish me for failure to comply.

The law, by contrast, does speak in the normative language of rights and obligations. Although both law and threats are intended to make certain forms of conduct non-optional, and although law may be backed up by threats of harm, law's primary intention is that we should take its directives as authoritative.[17] Law claims, in other words, that it has authority to tell us what to do. It tells us that we are *bound* to obey its directives. When, for instance, judges order someone to pay money as compensation for wrongdoing, they claim, as bank robbers do not, that the person is under an *obligation* to comply. We are supposed to obey the law not because we will be punished if we fail to do so but just because it is *the law*.

But what are these obligations that law purports to impose on us and what sort of authority to create obligations does the law claim to have? Hart argues that they are legal obligations, not necessarily moral obligations, and that the law need not claim morally legitimate authority. Joseph Raz, by contrast, thinks that law's claim to authority is a claim to morally legitimate authority and that the law therefore claims to impose moral obligations on us. He thinks that the law asserts that we are under a *moral* obligation to obey the law just because it is the law. We will examine the dispute between Hart and Raz in 3.7. At this point, however, we should take note of the fact that, although Raz thinks that the law necessarily claims moral authority, he also thinks that its claim to such authority is frequently unwarranted. We will examine his reasons for saying this in 4.6. For the moment we simply need to be aware of the difference between saying that the law necessarily *claims* moral authority and saying that it necessarily *has* moral authority. Raz makes the former assertion about the law, not the latter.

Finally, to say that the law claims authority is not to say that everyone who obeys the law accepts the claimed authority of the law. Some people may obey the law because it happens to coincide with what they independently think is right. Mark Murphy explains this point as follows:

---

17 Hart, above n 10, p 20.

[T]he person who acts under authority goes along with what the authority demands. If one is told to do something, and then deliberates about what to do, then one is not acting as someone under authority, even if one ends up doing just what the authority told one to do. (If I tell my daughter to clean her room, and she thinks about how messy her room is, and why now is a good time to do it, and then decides to go ahead and do it, she is not acting as someone under my authority—she is just making up her mind that, on the merits, cleaning her room is the thing to do.)[18]

Others may obey the law out of fear of sanctions. In this case, as Hart says, sanctions are intended to provide a motive for conformity for those who refuse to accept the authority of the law. But sanctions merely function as a back-up in cases where the system has failed and the law's directives are not accepted as giving rise to a duty to obey.[19]

2.4 Can Austin account for certain familiar features of legal systems?

Even if commands backed up by threats were capable of imposing obligations, Austin's account of law is too simple, according to Hart. It ignores the variety of laws and therefore imposes on law a 'spurious uniformity'.[20] In particular, it is not the case that all laws order people to do or not to do certain things on pain of a sanction. Austin's picture comes closest to describing criminal laws, which in some ways resemble commands backed up by a threat of punishment. But even criminal laws cannot be seen as analogous to a gunman's threats, because a gunman's orders do not apply to himself, whereas criminal laws have to be obeyed even by those who make them.[21] Thus it is not appropriate to conceptualise even criminal laws as Austin's account would.

Furthermore, Hart argues that there are many laws that are even more difficult to force into Austin's duty-imposing model. Consider laws that confer powers, whether on private individuals or officials. Such laws do not impose duties or demands that require us to behave in certain ways, whether we wish to do so or not. Rather, they provide the means to realise our wishes, and they enable officials to act in certain ways. Far from reducing our freedom, they enlarge it.

---

18 M C Murphy, *Philosophy of Law*, Blackwell Publishing, Malden, MA, 2007, p 185.
19 H L A Hart, *Essays on Bentham*, Clarendon Press, Oxford, 1982, p 254.
20 Hart, above n 10, p 49.
21 Ibid pp 24, 26, 42.

There are, for instance, laws that empower us to make a will, or to enter into a contract or a marriage. And there are laws that confer power on courts to hear certain matters and on legislatures to make laws. Failure to observe the requirements laid down by these laws leads to legal invalidity, not a sanction. If, for instance, I fail to sign my will, I will not be punished. I will merely have failed to make a valid will. Likewise, if there is a law conferring power on a legislative body to pass laws in accordance with certain procedures, an attempt to pass a law that does not comply with the procedures will not be punished. It will merely be ineffective. Nor, according to Hart, can it be said that legal invalidity is a kind of penalty, for the purpose of sanctions is to *discourage* certain conduct, whereas legal invalidity is not used for that purpose. Hart concludes that the command theory of law is incapable of adequately accounting for private and public power-conferring rules.[22]

Hart turns next to Austin's account of sovereignty in terms of habits of obedience, and argues that there are other typical features of legal systems that it cannot explain. One such feature is that legal systems make provision for the uninterrupted continuity of lawmaking power when one lawmaker succeeds another. When a new set of legislators take their seats in parliament, the first bills they pass are laws. When an absolute monarch's son succeeds him, the son's first orders are laws. But, for Austin, we can talk of law only when there is a habit of general obedience. It follows that when one lawmaker succeeds another there is, for Austin, no law until the populace has acquired the habit of generally obeying the new lawmaker. There will, in other words, be an in-between period in which law cannot be made. Hart concludes that Austin's account therefore cannot explain a central feature of legal systems. This is the fact that there is a seamless transfer of authority to the successor lawmaker: the first law made by the new lawmaker is *already* law, despite the fact that the new lawmaker has not yet received habitual obedience.[23]

Another familiar characteristic of legal systems for which Austin's concept of sovereignty cannot account, according to Hart, is the fact that laws that were made by an earlier lawmaker, now dead, can *still* be valid law even though that lawmaker is, by definition, no longer habitually obeyed. When one lawmaker replaces another there is no reason to fear that all the old laws have disappeared. A law enacted 100 years ago can still be law today.[24] Yet Austin's theory has

---

22   Ibid pp 27–35.
23   Ibid pp 53–4.
24   Ibid pp 61–2.

obvious difficulty in explaining this phenomenon. How can the orders of previous lawmakers still be law when those lawmakers are no longer habitually obeyed? The only way in which Austin can attempt to account for this phenomenon is to say that if the new lawmaker has not expressly repealed the old statute, then this amounts to 'tacitly' commanding it. In particular, by not interfering when the courts enforce the old statute, the new lawmaker has given a tacit order that the old law should be obeyed. The trouble with this response, though, as Hart points out, is that it implies that the old law is not law until it is actually applied by the courts during the tenure of the new sovereign. But this is false. A statute does not become law only *after* it is applied by the courts. It is *already* law before any cases arise to which it may be applied.[25]

Other features of Austin's concept of sovereignty to which Hart objects are the indivisibility of the sovereign's power (the fact that, for Austin, there can be only one sovereign body or one sovereign individual) and the sovereign's legally illimitable status (the fact that the sovereign is outside the law). Insofar as the latter is concerned, since Austin's sovereign by definition does not habitually obey any other person or body, there can be no legal limits on what the sovereign can command and no laws that the sovereign cannot make. According to Austin, this must be the case in all societies in which there is law: it is a necessary condition of law. Austin writes: 'Supreme power limited by positive law, is a flat contradiction in terms ... Every supreme government is legally despotic.'[26]

As Hart points out, however, there are many legal systems in which we do not find a sovereign who is above the law. Austin's definition of sovereignty may seem to fit British constitutional arrangements, in which there is no written constitution limiting the legislative powers of the Westminster Parliament and (leaving aside certain complications arising from British membership of the European Union) the doctrine of unlimited parliamentary sovereignty has long been regarded as a fundamental rule. But there are many other countries in which the legal situation is different. Furthermore, there are many systems in which sovereign power is divided among different organs.[27]

In both the United States and Australia, for instance, there is a written constitution, which not only divides power between the federal parliament and the legislatures of the states, but also prevents legislative interference with certain individual rights and entrenches the separation of powers. To give

---

25 Ibid p 64.
26 Austin, above n 2, pp 212, 225.
27 Hart, above n 10, p 72.

just one example, s 116 of the Australian Constitution prohibits the federal parliament from interfering with the free exercise of religion. This means that if the federal parliament attempted to pass a law with such a purpose, the High Court would strike it down as invalid. In such a case, the parliament would have failed to make a valid law. But although the power of the federal sovereign is subject to this and other legal limitations, it is obvious that Australia has a legal system.

At this point, someone sympathetic to Austin's view might point out that in his later work Austin did not identify the sovereign in a democracy with the legislature, but with the *body of electors*—a body perhaps more plausibly thought of as necessarily free of legal limitation. Thus, if we consider the Australian Constitution again, we find that it contains a provision, s 128, that provides for alterations to the Constitution. Leaving aside certain special cases in which proposed amendments must pass an additional hurdle, the normal rule under s 128 is that a proposed amendment has to be approved by a majority of voting electors in a majority of the states and by an overall majority of voting electors. This seems to suggest that the true sovereign in Australia is the people—not, as we first assumed, their elected representatives in parliament. And if it is the people who are sovereign—the people who issue the commands that provide for the legislative powers of the federal and state parliaments and for the limits on those powers—have we not found a body whose power is legally illimitable, in which case Austin would be vindicated, at least in this respect?

Hart's reply is to argue that if it is the people who are sovereign, then it is impossible to understand their sovereignty on Austin's original model of commands issued by a political superior and backed up by sanctions. After all, who is doing the commanding and who is doing the obeying? It seems that if the people are sovereign, and if Austin's account of sovereignty is correct, then the people must be issuing commands to themselves, which they themselves habitually obey. They must, in effect, be holding a gun to their own heads—an idea that is hard to comprehend.[28]

In summary, Hart argues that Austin's theory of law as the will of a sovereign ruler is too crude. An adequate theory of the nature of law must explain the central features of legal systems, but there are many features of legal systems that Austin's theory lacks the resources to explain. It cannot, for instance, account for the fact that there are many rules of law that do not have

---

28 Ibid pp 75–6.

their source in a lawmaker's will; that a lawmaker's powers are conferred by law and can be limited by law; that legal powers may be used in ways that are not equivalent to prohibiting conduct; and that, when powers are used in such ways, what has been done can be assessed for legal validity or invalidity.

Hart does not deny that, in practice, some degree of coercion is needed to sustain a legal system and that many people do, in fact, comply with legal demands out of fear of sanctions. He insists, however, that coercion does not play a central role in a theoretical account of law. As we will see in the next chapter, Hart thinks that law is not a matter of mere regularities in behaviour, but a matter of rules. Hart argues that once we see that law consists in rules, we will be able to explain the features of legal systems that Austin cannot explain.

2.5 Positivism: some preliminary points

Both Austin and Hart are legal positivists. The debate between legal positivists and those who are, broadly speaking, in the natural law tradition, will be a recurring theme in the chapters that follow. It is nevertheless necessary to introduce some relevant concepts at this stage, in order to lay the foundation for subsequent discussion. It needs to be appreciated at the outset, however, that there are many versions of positivism and this makes it difficult to single out certain elements as the 'defining' features of positivism. In what follows, I will therefore speak of 'central' doctrines or 'key ideas' associated with the positivist tradition without necessarily suggesting that all positivists accept all of these ideas or give them equal prominence in their theories. I will also highlight some of the differences between positivist theories.

One such key positivist idea is the idea, as Leslie Green puts it, that law is a 'social construction'.[29] On this view, law is ultimately a matter of 'social facts'. Social facts are facts about the behaviour, beliefs and attitudes of people in their social interactions.[30] For instance, the fact that the sovereign has issued a command on pain of punishment is a social fact. Social facts are non-normative. They can be contrasted with normative facts, such as moral facts. Moral facts are facts about what is morally right and wrong.[31] For instance, the fact that slavery is wrong is a moral fact. It should be emphasised that moral facts are not

---

29 L Green, 'The Concept of Law Revisited' (1996) 94 *Michigan Law Review* 1687, 1687.
30 Murphy, above n 18, p 30.
31 M Greenberg, 'How Facts Make Law', in S Hershowitz (ed), *Exploring Law's Empire: The Jurisprudence of Ronald Dworkin*, Oxford University Press, Oxford, 2006, pp 225, 234.

facts about what people *believe* is right and wrong but facts about what is *really* right and wrong. In some societies, slavery may be thought morally acceptable. This does not, however, make slavery acceptable. Facts about what social groups find acceptable or unacceptable are non-normative, social facts. Facts about what is really acceptable or unacceptable are moral facts.

The view that moral judgments can be true and that they are true when they correctly report facts is called 'moral realism' or 'cognitivism'.[32] There is obviously much more that could be said about this view. For our purposes, however, it will be sufficient to note that we do generally think of our moral views as purporting to report facts and that we make an intuitive distinction between non-normative facts (among which are social facts) and normative facts (among which are moral facts). It is beyond the scope of this book to counter the sceptical doubts of those who think that the idea of objectivity in morality is mistaken.[33]

For Austin, law owes its existence to the social facts of commands, habits of obedience and punishment. Laws are the orders of those who have power. What the law requires will therefore be an empirical and contingent matter, depending on what has been ordered by those in power. It is perhaps worth mentioning that Austin's view explains the origins of the label 'legal positivism'. Another way of saying that rules owe their status as law to the sovereign's deliberate acts of will is to say that law is put in place or 'posited' by the sovereign. And a theory which stresses the posited nature or 'positivity' of law is naturally called a 'positivist' theory.

Although Hart agrees with Austin that law owes its existence to social facts, he has a different view, as we will see in 3.3, about the nature of the social facts to which law owes its existence. For Hart, law is a social practice. Social practices, as Matthew Noah Smith explains, are things that people do together, in the sense that there is some sort of systematic unity to their activity.[34] For Hart, law owes its existence to official agreement on the criteria for identifying valid laws and to the fact that members of the population generally obey the rules that are valid according to the criteria of legal validity. Hart puts this by saying that legal officials follow a 'social rule' in identifying and applying the law, and he calls this rule the 'rule of recognition'. A particular norm will

---

32 G Sayre-McCord, 'Moral Realism', in D Copp (ed), *The Oxford Handbook of Ethical Theory*, Oxford University Press, New York, 2006, p 40.
33 For a useful discussion of this issue, see D Lyons, *Ethics and the Rule of Law*, Cambridge University Press, Cambridge, 1984, Chapter 1.
34 M N Smith, 'The Law as a Social Practice: Are Shared Activities at the Foundations of Law?' (2006) 12 *Legal Theory* 265, 269.

therefore be a law if it conforms to certain criteria found in a special kind of rule accepted by legal officials.

The 'social rule' account is widely accepted among contemporary positivists, although there is disagreement as to what exactly a social rule is. One well-known answer is that a social rule is a convention, although not all positivists agree with this answer. Here the word 'convention' is being used in a technical sense, which will be explained in 3.3. But whatever the exact nature of social rules, the main point for present purposes is that Hart takes the view that the law of a jurisdiction is the set of norms that satisfy the criteria of legal validity accepted by officials in that jurisdiction. This means that what the law requires is for Hart, as it is for Austin, ultimately an empirical and contingent matter, depending on what criteria of validity officials happen to agree upon.

Natural law theorists oppose the view that the existence of legal rights and duties is simply a matter of social fact or social practice. The natural law view is that the existence of law or 'genuine' law is in some way tied to morality. Although most natural lawyers do not deny that law has an institutional, human dimension, they believe that law is not a 'mere man-made artifact'.[35] It is something less dependent on arbitrary or optional human choices and social practices. Law (or 'true' law) derives its authority not from human choices, or not solely from human choices, but from being reasonable: it 'comes to [us] from something outside and bigger than [ourselves]'.[36]

Another key doctrine associated with the tradition of legal positivism relates to the relationship between law and morality. It is obvious that there are many *contingent* connections between law and morality, or connections that hold as a matter of fact. Law is, for instance, frequently morally defensible: consider laws prohibiting murder and assault. Positivists, however, deny certain (and even, in the case of some positivists, any) *necessary* or conceptual links between law and morality—links, in other words, deriving from the *nature* of law. Positivists therefore say that law and morality are conceptually 'separable'. This view is for obvious reasons called the 'separability thesis'.[37]

Some positivists adhere to the separability thesis because they believe that law is objective and that moral standards are subjective and relative. Most contemporary positivists, however, believe in the objectivity of moral

---

35 This is Hart's phrase: see above n 1, p 146.
36 L L Fuller, *Anatomy of the Law*, Penguin Books, Harmondsworth, 1971, p 82.
37 This phrase was coined by J Coleman in 'Negative and Positive Positivism' (1982) 11 *Journal of Legal Studies* 139, 140–1.

standards—they believe in what I called 'moral facts'—and they therefore have different reasons for adhering to the separability thesis. These positivists make a distinction between 'critical morality' and 'popular morality'. 'Popular morality' refers to the moral beliefs of a particular group or society. It is, in Hart's words, the 'accepted morality of [a] group ... even though this may rest on superstition or may withhold its benefits from slaves or subject classes'.[38] Popular morality therefore refers to whatever beliefs a particular group happens to think are right, whether or not these beliefs are sound. 'Critical morality', by contrast, refers to 'the general moral principles used in the criticism of actual social institutions including [popular] morality'.[39] Critical morality therefore refers to sound moral principles, whether or not these are accepted by a particular group or society. These sound principles can be used to evaluate popular morality.

Most positivists think that *popular* morality is necessarily connected with law, law being one way in which the *mores* of the group are expressed.[40] The more interesting question, and the one to which positivists and natural law theorists give different answers, concerns the nature of the connection between law and *critical* morality. From now on all references to morality should therefore be understood as references to 'critical morality', unless otherwise stated.

Although all positivists hold that law and morality are conceptually separable, it would be wrong to exaggerate the uniformity in the positivist tradition. There is, in fact, considerable disagreement among positivists as to the exact extent of the separability, and by implication, about the significance to be attached to the separability thesis in the overall positivist project. In particular, although positivism is sometimes said to be committed to the thesis that there are *no* necessary connections between law and morality, there are many contemporary positivists who do not accept so expansive a claim.[41]

All positivists are united, however, in taking a narrower view. This is that there is nothing in the nature of law that requires laws to pass moral tests to be valid, or that requires moral facts to play a role in determining the content of the law. The tests in a particular jurisdiction for determining whether a rule is 'law' and for identifying the content of legal rules may refer only to social or

---

38 Hart, above n 10, p 205.
39 H L A Hart, *Law, Liberty and Morality*, Oxford University Press, Oxford, 1963, p 20.
40 N MacCormick, 'The Normativity of Law', in R Gavison (ed), *Issues in Contemporary Legal Philosophy: The Influence of H L A Hart*, Clarendon Press, Oxford, 1987, p 110. However, for a contrary view, see M H Kramer, *In Defense of Legal Positivism: Law without Trimmings*, Oxford University Press, Oxford, 1999, pp 212–15.
41 See, for example, J Raz, 'About Morality and the Nature of Law' (2003) 48 *American Journal of Jurisprudence* 1, 2–3; J Gardner, 'Legal Positivism: 5½ Myths' (2001) 46 *American Journal of Jurisprudence* 199, 223.

non-moral facts, such as the rule having been declared by a court or enacted by a legislature. It follows from this view that legal rules are not necessarily just. For positivists, therefore, the 'law as it is' is not necessarily the 'law as it ought to be'.

As explained, all positivists take the view that law and morality are separable, in the sense that there is nothing in the nature of law that requires laws to pass moral tests to be valid or that requires moral facts to play a role in determining the content of the law. There are, however, two versions of this view. At a minimum, it implies that law may be identifiable without recourse to moral reasoning. Some positivists, however, assert a stronger claim, namely, that law not only *may* but *must* be identifiable without recourse to moral reasoning. We will examine this issue in detail in Chapter 4. We will see that some positivists, who are called 'inclusive positivists', take the view that it is *possible* (although, of course, not necessary) for laws to be identified using moral tests. Thus, in particular jurisdictions, the accepted tests for legal validity might require judges to make reference to matters of moral merit in deciding whether a law is valid or determining its content. Exclusive positivists, by contrast, take the view that this is *impossible*. They say that law must be identifiable without recourse to moral standards. They say that, necessarily, there cannot be moral tests for law.

Austin expressly affirmed the view that laws do not have to pass a moral test, saying: 'The existence of law is one thing; its merit or demerit is another. Whether it be or be not is one enquiry; whether it be or be not conformable to an assumed standard, is a different enquiry. A law, which actually exists, is a law, though we happen to dislike it.'[42] It is easy to see why Austin took this view. For Austin, in order to determine whether a rule is a valid law and what its content is, we have to find out what commands have been issued by the sovereign and whether people are likely to be punished for disobeying them. But the fact that a sovereign has commanded something does not guarantee the moral soundness of what has been commanded. Hence law is not necessarily good law. Furthermore, since ascertaining the law's requirements involves an empirical inquiry into the sovereign's will, rather than a moral inquiry into the acceptability of the commands, identifying the law is, for Austin, a different kind of enterprise from investigating whether the law is just or ought to be obeyed. The first is a matter of non-moral or social facts. The second is a matter of moral facts. Although both questions have objective answers for Austin, different considerations are relevant to answering them. Austin thought, in particular, that the justice of

---

42 Austin, above n 2, p 157.

the law is tested by its conformity to utilitarian principles of the general good. (For discussion of utilitarianism, see 10.3.) Bentham's distinction between expository and censorial jurisprudence, mentioned in 2.2, rests on the same distinction between identifying the law and evaluating it, and he too thought that utilitarian morality was a measure of the justice of law.

We have seen that all positivists take the view that the law as it is does not necessarily coincide with the law as it morally ought to be. Some positivists believe, however, that the conceptual independence of law from morality goes further. These positivists deny additional necessary connections between law and morality. Their view is that law has no intrinsic moral value but is rather a 'morally neutral instrument which is as serviceable for evil as for good'.[43] They say that there is *no* role morality must play in law and that *any* moral value or moral merit that law in general or individual laws may have is contingent rather than necessary, depending on the content of the law or the use to which the law is put in a particular system. This is sometimes expressed by saying that there are *no* necessary connections between law and morality—a slightly hyperbolic formulation which lays itself open to various objections, such as the objection that both law and morality consist of norms.[44] The thesis is not, however, intended quite as literally as the objections assume. When it is claimed that there are 'no necessary connections between law and morality', what is meant is that there are no *interesting* necessary connections.[45] The 'no necessary connections' thesis should therefore be understood as a rough or shorthand way of rejecting all of the supposedly necessary connections which have been proposed by other legal theorists.[46]

In subsequent chapters we will examine a number of possible necessary connections between law and morality, which have been denied by some (though, as noted, not all) positivists. Positivists have argued, for instance, that legal systems do not secure anything of moral value merely by virtue of complying with the principles of the rule of law; that legal officials such as judges do not have to believe (or even profess to believe) that the rules that they apply and enforce are morally legitimate or have moral authority; and that normative terms such as 'obligations' and 'rights' have different meanings in legal and

---

[43] N E Simmonds, *Law as a Moral Idea*, Oxford University Press, Oxford, 2007, p 38.
[44] Gardner, above n 41, 223.
[45] See Hart, above n 1, p 6: Hart is careful to say that there are no 'important necessary connections between law and morality'.
[46] M H Kramer, *Where Law and Morality Meet*, Oxford University Press, Oxford, 2004, pp 225-7.

moral contexts. We will examine these claims as well as various criticisms of them in Chapters 3 and 5.

So far, we have been dealing with positivist views about the nature of law. Such views fall under what is called 'substantive' legal positivism. There is, however, also another kind of positivism, which is called 'methodological' positivism. Whereas substantive legal positivism involves claims about the nature of *law*, such as the claim that law and morality are conceptually distinct, methodological legal positivism is a claim about *legal theory* or jurisprudence. It is the view that theorising about the law can be a *morally neutral* enterprise, which aims merely to *describe* what is distinctive about law as a special form of social organisation. On this view, we can give an illuminating and fully adequate account of the nature of law without being committed to any moral views and without attempting to provide a moral justification of law. This is a methodological form of positivism because it is a claim about the *method* of jurisprudence or how it should be done. Methodological debates have been a feature of much recent work in jurisprudence.[47]

Methodological positivists do not take the implausible view that theorising about the law can be entirely value-free. They concede that legal theorising, like all theorising, is an *evaluative* activity, in the sense that there are certain desiderata or norms of theory construction, such as simplicity, clarity and coherence, by reference to which theorists are guided and the adequacy of their theories judged. Methodological positivists are at pains to point out, however, that values such as simplicity and coherence are not *moral* values.[48]

Methodological positivists also concede that a descriptive account of law will inevitably be based on only some facts about law, namely, those facts that the theorist considers central or important to law. A description of law is, as Green explains, a *selection* of facts about it, which are taken to be interesting and important.[49] This means, as Raz notes, that 'any good theory of [law] is based on evaluative considerations in that its success is in highlighting important social structures and processes, and every judgment of importance is evaluative'.[50] Furthermore, such evaluative judgments of importance will need to relate to the

---

47 S R Perry has been influential in highlighting the issues about the methodology of jurisprudence. See S R Perry, 'Hart's Methodological Positivism', in J Coleman (ed), *Hart's Postscript: Essays on the Postscript to* The Concept of Law, Oxford University Press, Oxford, 2001, pp 311–54.
48 W J Waluchow, *Inclusive Legal Positivism*, Clarendon Press, Oxford, 1994, pp 19–21; J Dickson, *Evaluation and Legal Theory*, Hart Publishing, Oxford, 2001, pp 32–5.
49 Green, above n 29, 1713.
50 J Raz, 'Authority, Law and Morality' (1985) 68 *The Monist* 295, 320.

judgments of importance made by those who are subject to the law, because, as Raz says, 'unlike concepts like "mass" or "electron", "the law" is a concept used by people to understand themselves'.[51] Julie Dickson explains Raz's point as follows: '[A]ny explanatorily adequate legal theory must, in evaluating which of law's features are the most important and significant to explain, be sufficiently sensitive to, or take adequate account of, what is regarded as important or significant, good or bad about the law, by those whose beliefs, attitudes, behaviour, etc. are under consideration.'[52]

Thus, no doubt Austin highlighted sanctions in his account of law because the fact that we are punished for failing to obey the law is a fact we find significant, in contrast to other facts about law, such as the fact that judges may wear robes, which is of less or no significance to us. Other theorists, such as Raz, highlight the way in which law asserts the authority to tell us what to do, regardless of whether we think the law's demands are justifiable or not. It is likely that those who find this feature of law important do so because they are concerned about a possible conflict between law and the value of autonomy, that is, the value of not subjecting our will to the will of another person.[53]

Once again, however, methodological positivists maintain that we should not confuse *evaluative* judgments of importance with *moral* judgments of merit. In their view, the identification of the important features of law does not rest on *moral* judgments concerning the moral attractiveness or justifiability of those features.[54] For instance, in saying that law claims ultimate authority over how we should behave, Raz merely wishes to report on an important way in which law as a social institution invariably operates and impinges on us, without in any way suggesting that it is a good thing (or a bad thing) that the law should make such a claim.[55]

Analysing law is therefore, in the view of methodological positivists, like analysing other concepts, such as knowledge. No one supposes that an account of knowledge requires moral argument or must seek to justify knowledge. Similarly, methodological positivists claim to provide a morally neutral, conceptual account of law as a distinctive form of social organisation. Such an account does not tell us whether law's central features are good or bad. Nor does it tell us why and when law ought to be obeyed. Legal theory

---

51 Ibid 321–2.
52 Dickson, above n 48, p 43.
53 Waluchow, above n 48, p 22.
54 Dickson, above n 48, p 9.
55 J Raz, *Ethics in the Public Domain: Essays in the Morality of Law and Politics*, Clarendon Press, Oxford, 1994, pp 236–7.

is an essential precursor to answering these latter questions, but legal theory cannot itself answer them. These questions are moral and political questions and it is therefore the disciplines of moral and political philosophy that provide the answers to them. This, then, is the specific sense in which methodological positivists aim to offer a 'descriptive' as opposed to a 'normative' account of law.

John Finnis and Ronald Dworkin are vigorous opponents of this kind of approach to legal theory, as we will see in Chapters 5 and 6. For them, law is a morally charged concept and they believe that an account of the nature of law therefore has moral implications for how citizens and officials ought to behave. Consider, as an analogy, the concept of 'democracy'. Can we arrive at a view about what democracy is without considering the moral point, function or purpose of democracy? Must anyone who wishes to participate in the conceptual debate about the nature of democracy have a view about the values which democracy is meant to serve? If you answer 'yes' to this question, you will believe that 'democracy' is a morally charged concept. This is what Dworkin and Finnis believe about the concept of 'law'. They believe that explaining what law is involves explaining its value. They therefore ascribe a morally valuable purpose to law, with a view to showing how its serving this purpose can give citizens and officials reasons to obey it. In the case of Finnis, law's morally valuable purpose is the coordination of conduct for the common good. In the case of Dworkin, the purpose of law is to limit and morally justify the use of state force. Either way, their conception of jurisprudence is entirely different from that of methodological positivists, insofar as they believe that a theoretical account of what law is must be governed by the need to show what is morally valuable about law, such that it is capable of generating moral obligations to enforce and obey it. For Dworkin and Finnis, in other words, analysing the concept of law is not a descriptive project but a morally engaged project, and on their view, articulating a theory of law necessarily involves making moral arguments.

Both Finnis and Dworkin deploy their normative methodology in the service of defending anti-positivist theories of law, but it should be noted that moral arguments can also be used to support substantively positivist theories of law, and that there are, indeed, some positivists who do use them in this way. Once again, we need to be alert to the variety of different views that make up the positivist tradition. Just as there are substantive differences among positivists (for example, the difference between inclusive and exclusive positivism mentioned above), there are methodological differences. Thus some positivist theorists, as we will see in 4.2, argue that there are good *moral* reasons to *conceptualise* law as different from morality because, for instance, such a conceptualisation makes it more likely that we will resist unjust laws. Dworkin goes so far as to suggest that a theory that ties law to social facts for moral and political reasons is the only plausible form of positivism (see 6.9).

There is also, as we will see in 4.8, a prescriptive form of legal positivism. This is a theory that *recommends* a rule-based form of governance, which minimises the need for citizens and officials to rely on moral judgments in identifying and applying the law. These theorists argue that laws should be framed as clearly and precisely as possible and that judges should interpret and apply legal rules according to their clear meaning because this is a way of securing certain benefits. The benefits include public guidance and predictability, and ensuring that disputed moral questions are resolved by majoritarian decision-making rather than by judicial decision.

We have distinguished between substantive positivism and methodological positivism. It remains to mention a third kind of positivism, which is called 'sociological positivism'. Roger Shiner describes sociological positivism by saying that it '[regards] the legal system and its operations as an inanimate machine'.[56] Shiner gives the example of the work of Donald Black, a contemporary sociologist of law who takes an empiricist or scientific approach to law. Black writes: 'Law consists in observable acts, not in rules ... law is not what lawyers regard as binding or obligatory precepts, but rather, for example, the observable dispositions of judges, policemen, prosecutors, or administrative officials.'[57] The behaviourist character of Austin's account of law puts him in the sociological positivist camp. As we have seen, Austin thought that social phenomena such as law should be approached in the way that we approach natural phenomena, using the methods of science. It was for this reason that Austin attempted to reduce normative legal statements to non-normative, factual statements about observable regularities in human behaviour.

Austin's command theory is positivist in all of the three ways considered above: it is substantively, sociologically and methodologically positivist. However, as indicated above, it represents just one contribution to the positivist school of thought. Thus, as we will see, Hart is not a sociological positivist. Although he is a methodological positivist, who does not seek to justify law but rather to describe and explain it in a way that carries no moral commitment to its

---

56 R A Shiner, *Norm and Nature: The Movements of Legal Thought*, Clarendon Press, Oxford, 1992, p 54.
57 Ibid.

institutions, he does not believe law lends itself to being understood in scientific or naturalistic terms, that is, in terms of regularities in observable behaviour. Nor does Hart adhere to the command theory of law. In both these ways, his version of positivism is more sophisticated than Austin's. We turn to Hart now.

Questions

1. What are the defining features of Austin's positivism?
2. Can the rules of contract law be explained on a coercive model of law?
3. Can Austin explain the duty of a judge to apply the law?
4. Roger Cotterrell writes: 'Writers who have argued forcefully against [Austin's account of law] have usually wanted to see the legal system as being governed by rules, even in its highest regions of authority, rather than—as Austin's theory so starkly claims—governed by *people*, mere human decision-makers with all their frailties and potential for arbitrary or tyrannous exercise of human power ... Austin's is not a theory of the Rule of Law: of government subject to law. It is a theory of the 'rule of men': of government using law as an instrument of power. Such a view may be considered realistic or merely cynical. But it is, in its broad outlines, essentially coherent' (R Cotterrell, *The Politics of Jurisprudence: A Critical Introduction to Legal Philosophy*, 2nd edn, LexisNexis UK, London, 2003, p 70). Discuss.
5. Are the rules of customary societies—rules that do not derive their obligatory force from the existence of a state—law?

Further reading

J Austin [1832], *The Province of Jurisprudence Determined*, W E Rumble (ed), Cambridge University Press, Cambridge, 1995, Lectures I, V and VI.

B Bix, 'Legal Positivism', in W A Edmundson and M P Golding (eds), *Blackwell Guide to Philosophy of Law and Legal Theory*, Blackwell, Oxford, 2005, pp 29–49.

J L Coleman and B Leiter, 'Legal Positivism', in D Patterson (ed), *A Companion to Philosophy of Law and Legal Theory*, Blackwell, Oxford, 1996, pp 241–60.

R Cotterrell, *The Politics of Jurisprudence: A Critical Introduction to Legal Philosophy*, 2nd edn, LexisNexis UK, London, 2003, Chapter 3.

J Dickson, *Evaluation and Legal Theory*, Hart Publishing, Oxford, 2001, Chapter 1.

H L A Hart, *The Concept of Law*, 2nd edn, Clarendon Press, 1994, Chapters II–IV.

R N Moles, *Definition and Rule in Legal Theory: A Reassessment of H L A Hart and the Positivist Tradition*, Blackwell, Oxford, 1987, Chapters 1–2.

W L Morison, *John Austin*, Edward Arnold, London, 1982.

F Schauer, 'Critical Notice of Roger Shiner, *Norm and Nature: The Movements of Legal Thought*' (1994) 24 *Canadian Journal of Philosophy* 495.

N Stavropoulos, 'The Relevance of Coercion: Some Preliminaries' (2009) 22 *Ratio Juris* 339.

3

Law as Social Practice

3.1 Chapter overview

This chapter considers Hart's account of the way in which law regulates our conduct, as well as his views about adjudication. Hart offers a more sophisticated account of the nature of law than Austin's, one which rejects the reductionist model of law as brute power. Hart does not deny that some or even most individuals may view the law from an external perspective, complying with law's demands not because the law requires compliance but because they fear sanctions. He observes, however, that an account built entirely around the external viewpoint or extrinsic motivations of such individuals leaves out the fact that at least the officials of a legal system, and especially judges who have to apply the law, treat law as authoritative. They are *guided* by legal rules, which is to say that they follow them *because* they are the rules. They conform to legal rules not because they fear the consequences of not doing so but because they willingly accept them. They therefore speak the normative language of obligations and rights. Hart's theory of law seeks to make this feature of legal discourse intelligible. Furthermore, such commitment to the system on the part of officials is, for Hart, a conceptual condition of the existence of law: it is impossible to explain law without making reference to the internalisation of legal rules by officials, or their voluntary cooperation in maintaining the rules. Hart is at the same time a positivist. He wishes to gives an account of law that makes its use of normative language intelligible while preserving the conceptual independence of law from morality. His answer is that law's normativity is grounded not in morality but in contingent matters of social fact. The relevant facts, according to him, are facts about the social practices or 'customs' of officials. In Hart's view, it is these practices that are the ultimate source of law's normativity. Hart goes further: he thinks that although officials must internalise the rules of law, they do not have to believe that the rules are morally legitimate.

3.2 The concept of a social rule

We have seen that Austin aspired to provide a scientific theory of law. He sought to characterise law from the outside, in terms of regularities in observable behaviour. Thus he unpacks the concept of legal authority in terms of habitual behaviour: the lawmaker is that person or body of persons whose orders most people are disposed to obey. Similarly, what it means to be under a legal obligation is, for Austin, to be likely to suffer a punishment for failing to do what the lawmaker has commanded. In general, he makes no reference to the mental states and attitudes of those who participate in legal institutions or the way in which they understand their own conduct. In short, he provides a behaviourist account of law.

For Hart, by contrast, it is impossible to analyse concepts such as legal obligation and legal authority in 'flatly descriptive' terms.[1] Hart argues that if we are successfully to elucidate the concepts that 'constitute the framework of legal thought'[2]—concepts such as obligation, duty, authority and validity—we need to take into account the point of view of those who take an *internal* view of the practice of law, a view whose character is essentially normative or prescriptive, as we will see. Law looks different to those who take such a view and if we ignore their viewpoint on law, as Austin did, our account of law will, according to Hart, be distorted and incomplete.

Hart was influenced by an approach to social science that, in contrast to Austin's sociological positivism, emphasises the differences between understanding human behaviour and understanding the physical world. On this approach we cannot explain and understand social phenomena such as law by modelling our explanations on the natural sciences, which view human behaviour purely 'in terms of observable regularities of conduct, predictions, probabilities and signs'.[3] Instead, we need to attend to the perspective of those who are committed to the relevant institutions. This is not to say that we should *adopt* or *share* their internal perspective. But we do need to understand and report on the meaning and significance to them of their regular behaviour. Such an approach,

---

1   H L A Hart, *Essays on Bentham*, Clarendon Press, Oxford, 1982, p 253.
2   H L A Hart, *The Concept of Law*, 2nd edn, Clarendon Press, Oxford, 1994, p 81.
3   Ibid p 89.

which stresses the difference between the ways in which we understand natural and social phenomena, is often called 'hermeneutic'.[4]

Hart was also influenced by mid-twentieth-century developments in analytical philosophy, and especially by the linguistic philosophy of Gilbert Ryle and J L Austin. This way of doing philosophy focuses on the way in which we talk about social phenomena, not because of an interest in words but rather as a means of enhancing our understanding of the realities our language describes. Hart draws attention to his use of this method in the Preface to *The Concept of Law*, in which he states: 'Many important distinctions, which are not immediately obvious, between types of social situation or relationships may best be brought to light by an examination of the standard uses of the relevant expressions and of the way in which these depend on a social context, itself often left unstated.'[5]

Hart is interested in language, in other words, not because he is in search of a 'definition' of law, and not because he thinks the test for a successful theory of law is whether it matches our linguistic intuitions about when the word 'law' has been correctly used. Instead, by analysing how we use the concept of law, he wants to uncover the distinctive features of law as a social institution. He thinks, in other words, that attention to the way in which we use legal concepts can help to cast light on the central characteristics of the institution of law.[6] The converse is also true: Hart believes that an improved understanding of the central features of a legal system can help to clarify our pre-theoretical grasp of the concept of law, for instance by revealing what it implicitly presupposes or by giving us reason to revise it. In this way, Hart gave a distinctively philosophical slant to inquiries into the nature of law, which up until that point had been largely atheoretical and undertaken by legal scholars who had little knowledge of philosophy as a professional discipline.[7]

Taking the points about conceptual analysis and Hart's hermeneutic method together, we can see that Hart seeks to illuminate the nature of law by analysing the way in which those who have internalised the rules of law conceptualise legal practice. We have already seen this approach at work in Hart's critique of Austin. Think, for instance, of how Hart gives us insights into the nature of law—in particular, into the difference between law and force—by

---

4   N MacCormick, *H L A Hart*, Edward Arnold, London, 1981, pp 29–30.
5   Hart, above n 2, p vi.
6   Ibid, pp 13–17.
7   W Twining, 'General and Particular Jurisprudence—Three Chapters in a Story', in S Guest (ed), *Positivism Today*, Aldershot, Dartmouth, 1996, p 130; F Schauer, 'Book Review of N Lacey, *A Life of H L A Hart: The Nightmare and the Noble Dream*' (2006) 119 *Harvard Law Review* 852, 858–9.

referring to the fact that we would not describe a gunman's threats as placing us under *obligations* but only as *obliging* us.

We need to turn now to another crucial distinction Hart draws: the distinction between a habit and a social rule. Once again, his aim is to show us how this distinction helps us to understand the nature of law. Both habits and social rules involve convergent behaviour, but a habit, even one that is common to many people, is *only* a matter of convergent behaviour. Kenneth Himma gives as an example of a habit the fact that most people put on both their socks before putting on their shoes.[8] This is a fact about observable behaviour and the statement that describes the habit is an 'is'-statement or a statement of fact. There is no rule requiring the behaviour. The habit does not justify the behaviour and if particular people were to put a sock and shoe on one foot before dressing the other foot, they would not be criticised for their deviation from the habit.

By contrast, if putting a sock and shoe on one foot before dressing the other foot were to come to be regarded as *wrong*, then we would say that there is a social *rule* requiring that both socks be put on first. This is because, as Hart explains, when behaviour is required in terms of a social rule, it is a matter not merely of regular or convergent behaviour but of regular behaviour that is *perceived* in a certain way. The behaviour is treated by most of the members of a group 'as a general standard to be followed by the group as a whole'.[9] This means that most of the members of the relevant social group see the general behaviour as proper, an attitude that they manifest by *criticising* and *exerting pressure* on those who disobey it. Rules prescribe conduct, rather than describing it, and rules are therefore expressed in normative vocabulary, such as 'ought', 'must', 'should', 'right' and 'wrong'.[10]

Social rules therefore involve not only external conformity or regular conduct but also 'a distinctive attitude to that conduct as a standard'.[11] Hart calls this the 'internal aspect of rules'[12] and he says that members of the group who accept and use social rules as a guide to conduct are concerned with the rules from 'the internal point of view'.[13] For Hart, the social rules of a group are therefore created by a form of social practice. Social practices, as defined in 2.5,

---

8   K E Himma, 'Inclusive Legal Positivism', in J Coleman and S Shapiro (eds), *The Oxford Handbook of Jurisprudence and Philosophy of Law*, Oxford University Press, Oxford, 2002, p 130.
9   Hart, above n 2, p 56.
10 Ibid p 57.
11 Ibid p 85.
12 Ibid p 56.
13 Ibid p 89.

are things that people do together in the sense that there is some sort of systematic unity to their activity.[14] Social rules are that form of social practice that involves the majority of the members of a group regularly following a certain pattern of conduct and adopting the internal point of view towards that conduct, which is to say that they take the regular pattern as a guide to behaviour and a standard of criticism.[15] It is therefore adoption of the internal point of view that turns regular conduct into a social rule. Obvious examples of practice rules are customary rules, the rules of games and rules of etiquette.

In later writing, Hart realised that there is more to being guided by a rule than thinking that one ought to act in a certain way: there is something distinctive about rule-based decision-making. Rules are, as Hart later called them, 'content-independent' reasons for action. Furthermore, we are required to comply with rules, even if compliance is contrary to our own best judgment. Rules are therefore also 'peremptory' reasons.[16] These notions play a much larger role in Joseph Raz's theory than in Hart's, and elucidation of them will therefore be deferred until a later chapter (see 4.6).

Hart believes that an adequate account of the nature of law will need to be built around the concept of rules rather than habits of obedience. In 3.3, we will examine in detail the role rules play in Hart's account, but it will be helpful to start with a short summary first.[17] First, Hart makes a point about people's *motivations*. He points out that many people do not conform to the law out of unreflective habit any more than they conform out of fear. Although some people may obey out of 'inertia',[18] and some may reject the legal rules, being interested in the rules only insofar as they are likely to be punished for violating them,[19] others view their own and others' behaviour in terms of the rules. They accept the legal rules as supplying general standards of conduct and they comply with them willingly.

This is not necessarily to say that such people accept the rules for *moral* reasons. Hart repudiates this idea, as we will see in 3.6 and 3.7. He thinks that people can be disposed to evaluate conduct in terms of legal rules for a range of reasons. But, whatever their reasons for doing so, the key point is that some

---

14 M N Smith, 'The Law as a Social Practice: Are Shared Activities at the Foundations of Law?' (2006) 12 *Legal Theory* 265, 269.
15 Hart, above n 2, p 255.
16 Hart, above n 1, pp 253–5.
17 I am indebted to Scott Shapiro for this way of conceptualising the matter. See 'What is the Internal Point of View?' (2006) 75 *Fordham Law Review* 1157, 1158.
18 Hart, above n 2, p 115.
19 Ibid p 90.

participants in the legal system do accept the rules, and a theory of law that stays at the level of external behavioural regularities misses this fact. According to Hart, such a theory accounts at most for the way in which law functions in the lives of those who obey the law out of fear of punishment. But it obscures the point of view of those who take the internal point of view, and consequently misses an important dimension of social life.[20] A complete theory of law will not only describe the perspective of the 'bad man', who does not see the law as a set of rules that ought to be followed and talks simply in descriptive terms of being 'obliged' and of liability to punishment. It also needs to describe the perspective of those who willingly do what the law requires.[21]

Secondly, Hart believes that it is not possible to *make sense* of the distinctive nature of legal discourse without making reference to rules. As we noted in 2.3, legal discourse is normative or prescriptive in character. Propositions of law, such as statements of legal rights and obligations, are concerned with how we *should* behave. When judges, for instance, refer to people's legal obligations, they are prescribing a certain form of conduct. Habits of obedience, by contrast, are merely facts about how people *do* behave, and no normative significance can be attached to them. Therefore when judges speak of someone as being under a legal obligation, this can no more be analysed in terms of facts about habitual behaviour than it can be analysed in terms of facts about what the sovereign has commanded. It is the fact that they regard the law as laying down rules that leads judges to speak of legal rights and obligations.[22] Once again, however, we should not assume that such normative legal judgments are a kind of *moral* judgment: as we will see in 3.6 and 3.7, Hart rejects this idea as well.

Thirdly, Hart thinks that social rules are a *precondition* for the existence of law. He argues, in particular, that at the foundation of all legal systems is a particular kind of social rule, namely, one that is used by law-applying officials to identify all the other legal rules of the system. Hart calls this rule the 'rule of recognition'. Hart believes that although private citizens *may* take the internal point of view, legal officials *must*. This is a necessary condition for the existence of law, according to Hart, and Austin's failure to appreciate this explains, in Hart's view, many of the failures in his account of law.

---

20 Ibid pp 89–91.
21 Ibid p 40.
22 Ibid p 89.

3.3 Law as a combination of primary and secondary rules

In the previous section, a brief outline of the role played by rules in Hart's account was provided. In this section we examine Hart's arguments in more detail. The first point to note is that Hart does not believe that all legal rules are social rules. As we have seen, social rules are rules that exist because they are practised or accepted. Hart says that most legal rules exist not because they are accepted but because they are 'valid'. He explains the concept of validity in the following way.

Most legal rules are what Hart calls 'primary' rules. Primary rules impose duties and permit people to behave in certain ways. They directly regulate our conduct by telling us what we may do and what we are under a duty to do and not to do.[23] For instance, primary rules may tell us that we are under a duty to refrain from violence or to keep our promises. Clearly, not all primary rules are legal rules. Some primary rules are, for instance, moral rules. What, then, makes a primary rule a legal rule and not a moral rule? What makes the rule about paying taxes, for instance, a legal rule, while the rule about not jumping queues is non-legal? What allows us, in other words, to talk of a 'valid legal rule'? Hart's answer is that a primary rule will be a valid legal rule if it was made in a way that conforms to certain criteria of validity laid down in a secondary or higher-order rule. This higher-order rule is the 'rule of recognition'. The rule of recognition tells us what counts as law in a particular society by providing authoritative criteria for identifying primary legal rules.[24] Jules Coleman describes it as 'the signature of a legal system'.[25] The existence of a rule of recognition therefore underpins our concept of legal validity and is a key element of a legal system.

The rule of recognition in a particular society might pick out valid sources of law by reference to how a rule *originates*, stating, for instance, that a primary rule is a valid law if and only if it is an unrepealed enactment of parliament or if it is contained in a judicial decision. We can call these facts about the rule's pedigree. In this hypothesised society, if a rule can be found in the statute books or the reports of judicial decisions, it is a legal standard. If it cannot be found in the statute books or the law reports, it is not a legal standard. Such a complex

---

23 Ibid p 81.
24 Ibid p 100.
25 J Coleman, *The Practice of Principle: In Defence of a Pragmatist Approach to Legal Theory*, Oxford University Press, Oxford, 2001, p 76.

rule of recognition, which refers to more than one source of law, would also have to rank the sources, for instance by providing that precedent is subordinate to statute in that it can be overridden by legislation.[26]

In Chapter 4, we will canvass the possibility that the rule of recognition might also license recourse to *moral* standards in determining whether a particular rule is a valid legal rule. But for present purposes, it is necessary only to note that, in whatever way the rule of recognition tests validity, it enables us to speak of a legal rule as valid by providing us with authoritative criteria for determining whether a particular rule or norm is part of the society's law. It thereby enables us to distinguish valid legal rules from rules that are incorrectly argued to be rules of law, and also to distinguish legal rules from other social standards.

Another typical feature of legal systems is the ability of lawmakers to make new legal rules and abolish old ones. To explain this ability, we once again, according to Hart, have to invoke the concept of a secondary rule, in this case a 'rule of change'. Rules of change make it possible to change the primary rules. Such rules specify who or what body has the power to create new legal rules and specify any procedures that must be followed by such a person or body. There is obviously a close connection between the rule of recognition and the rules of change. For instance, if a society has a rule of change to the effect that parliament can amend or repeal laws, then the rule of recognition will state that what parliament enacts is the law. Rules of change also allow private persons to change their own legal position. For instance, by making a will, an individual can opt out of the law of intestacy. It will be remembered that one of Hart's criticisms of Austin (see 2.4) was precisely that that he did not recognise the different social functions that laws can have, including the fact that some laws do not impose duties on individuals but rather provide them with the means of realising their wishes.[27]

Finally, Hart argues that we need to invoke secondary rules to account for the fact that legal systems have mechanisms that enable disputes about whether a primary rule has been broken to be conclusively resolved. These are 'rules of adjudication'. In our society, such disputes are resolved by courts, which are constituted in certain ways and given jurisdiction to hear certain matters, according to the rules of adjudication. Since a judge's authoritative finding on a matter will be a source of valid law, there will once again be a close connection between the rule of recognition and the rules of adjudication. Additional

---

26 Hart, above n 2, p 101.
27 Ibid pp 95–6.

secondary rules give judges, at least in developed systems of law, the exclusive power to impose penalties for violation of the rules, thereby centralising the imposition of sanctions, in contrast to systems of 'self-help'.[28]

Having explained that particular legal rules get their authority from having been created in a way that satisfies the criteria in the rule of recognition, Hart needs to explain what gives the rule of recognition *its* authority. Obviously, the most fundamental rule could not owe its existence to yet another rule. That would lead to an infinite regress of rules.[29] To what, then, does the rule of recognition owe its existence? It is at this point that Hart relies on the notion of a social rule. He argues that the rule of recognition is a social rule and social rules, as we know, are not created in terms of other rules but are social practices. This solves the regress problem. Let us examine Hart's solution more closely.

Unlike other legal rules, which exist as a result of formal law-making and law-interpreting activities, and which are laws because they are valid and not because they are practised, the rule of recognition is not itself valid. It exists simply because it is practised and its existence is therefore a matter of social fact.[30] It is brought into existence by being accepted from the internal point of view as the appropriate standard for deciding legal disputes, by the officials who are charged with applying and enforcing the law. Although law-applying officials rarely expressly invoke the rule of recognition, they adopt it as a guide to their own and others' behaviour. They see it as obligating them to assess conduct in terms of the primary rules that it validates, and they criticise any deviations from it.[31] This normative attitude is manifested in the making of internal statements about the law, such as 'It is the law that ...'.[32] Judges may, for instance, accept that they are bound to apply the rules made by the legislature. If so, their 'custom' *creates* the rule that legislative provisions are a source of law, in the same way that our custom of eating with a knife and fork creates the social rule that we should eat with a knife and fork. What gives the legislature authority to make law is therefore, according to Hart, not habits of obedience, and not the moral legitimacy of the legislature's directives, but a judicial customary rule constituted by the social facts of a regular form of behaviour and an attitude of acceptance.[33]

---

28 Ibid pp 96–8.
29 S Shapiro, 'On Hart's Way Out', in J Coleman (ed), *Hart's Postscript: Essays on the Postscript to The Concept of Law*, Oxford University Press, Oxford, 2001, pp 150–1.
30 Hart, above n 2, p 109.
31 Ibid pp 100–2.
32 Ibid p 102.
33 Ibid p 256.

We have seen that Hart argues that judges view the rule of recognition as binding and that they regard themselves as under a duty to apply it. But, it may be asked, how does the mere existence of a common practice give rise to reasons, let alone duties, to follow the practice? As Leslie Green says: 'The fact that most people ø and expect others to do likewise does not generally give one a reason for ø-ing. Typically, one should do likewise only if there is some further reason for conformity.'[34]

Green goes on to point out, however, that in some special cases, the fact of common practice does give rise to reasons for action. This is, for instance, the case when we are dealing with conventions.[35] Here the word 'convention' is being used in a technical sense. To understand this technical sense, we need to understand the concept of a coordination problem. A coordination problem arises when there is more than one way in which we can coordinate our behaviour in our mutual interest. For instance, it is arbitrary as to which side of the road we should drive on. We do, though, all have an interest in driving on the same side so as to avoid accidents. We therefore need to coordinate our behaviour. The convention of driving on one side rather than the other solves this problem by giving everyone a reason to drive on that side. As Green says, '[t]he existence of a convention makes salient one of the alternative possible ways of coordinating action; it makes it the one to follow'.[36] A convention therefore exists when a shared practice of following a certain rule is *part of the reason* why individuals accept the rule as binding and follow it. Dworkin explains the concept of a convention as follows:

> A convention exists when people follow certain rules ... for reasons that essentially include their expectation that others will follow the same rules ... and they will follow rules for that reason when they believe that ... having some settled rule is more important than having any particular rule ... Our reason for driving on the right in America and on the left in Britain is just our expectation that this is what others will do, coupled with our further belief that it is more important that there be a common rule than that it be one rather than the other.[37]

Let us return now to the rule of recognition and the question asked by Green, namely: why do judges have reason to follow the practice of identifying

---

34 L Green, 'Positivism and Conventionalism' (1999) 12 *Canadian Journal of Law and Jurisprudence* 35, 38.
35 Ibid.
36 Ibid. David Lewis's analysis of conventions underlies this account. See D Lewis, *Convention: A Philosophical Study*, Harvard University Press, Harvard, 1969.
37 R Dworkin, *Law's Empire*, Belknap Press of Harvard University Press, Cambridge, MA, 1986, p 145.

certain rules as valid law? The fact that the behaviour of those who follow conventions can provide reasons for action for others has encouraged some positivists to answer this question by saying that the rule of recognition is a coordination convention. On this view, judges have reason to follow the rule of recognition because it resolves officials' coordination problems in settling on the criteria of validity to be applied. Gerald Postema defends this position. He writes:

> [G]iven that the activity of law-identifying has all the characteristics of a complex and continuous coordination problem, and that there are significant professional pressures to seek coordination, the fact that there is a regularity which focuses the expectations of the parties generates a (prima facie) obligation on the part of the judge to follow the practice.[38]

This is a simplified explanation of Postema's views. There are also other positivist accounts of how the shared practice of officials can be reason-giving, which unfortunately cannot be dealt with here.[39] Nor is it possible to deal with the views of those theorists who criticise the idea that the rule of recognition is best understood as a coordination convention.[40] We should, though, briefly attend to Hart's views on this difficult matter.

In the Postscript to the second edition of *The Concept of Law*, Hart suggests that he believes that the rule of recognition is a convention. He writes: '[T]he rule of recognition is treated in my book as resting on a conventional form of judicial consensus ... for surely an English judge's reason for treating Parliament's legislation ... as a source of law having supremacy over other sources includes the fact that his judicial colleagues concur in this.'[41] On the other hand, as Julie Dickson points out, in the original edition of *The Concept of Law*, Hart appears to be uninterested in explaining *why* judges treat the rule of recognition as binding. As we will see in 3.7, Hart says that judges must have some reason for accepting the rule of recognition, but he also says there are many such reasons. For the purposes of elucidating the central features of a legal system, he seems to suggest, all we need to know is that common judicial practice is necessary for the rule of recognition to *exist* and that such practice enables us to identify

---

38 G Postema, 'Co-ordination and Convention at the Foundations of Law' (1982) 11 *Journal of Legal Studies* 165, 198.
39 See, for instance, A Marmor, *Social Conventions: From Language to Law*, Princeton University Press, Princeton, 2009, who takes the view that the rule of recognition is a convention but not a coordination convention. A different kind of account may be found in the work of Scott Shapiro. See, for instance, his 'Law, Plans and Practical Reason' (2002) 8 *Legal Theory* 387.
40 See, for instance, Green, above n 34, 52; J Coleman, above n 25, pp 94–5.
41 Hart, above n 2, pp 266–7.

the content of the rule. We do not need to know why officials accept the rule of recognition. Mostly, then, Hart is not concerned to explain how the shared practice of officials can be reason-giving, but confines himself to explaining how the rule of recognition comes into existence and therefore how law comes into existence.[42] Consequently, it is not clear whether we should read Hart as subscribing to a conventionalist account of the rule of recognition.

Summing this discussion up, we can say that there are difficult questions about how social practices can give rise to reasons. Hart's own view on this matter is unclear and contemporary positivists are divided. It is generally accepted among contemporary positivists that the existence of law depends on a shared or social practice among officials, but there are many different ways of understanding this idea and the matter is a subject of continuing debate.

Let us move on now to further aspects of Hart's theory. Hart makes clear that it is only legal officials who need to be guided by the rule of recognition in order for a legal system to exist. He argues that the law must be *obeyed* by most individuals in society for a legal system to exist (in contrast, for instance, to a legal system that has become defunct). To be a system of legal rules, in other words, the system must be effective. Hart says that it is not necessary, however, that such obedience be accompanied by acceptance of the criteria of legal validity on the part of ordinary citizens. They need not think of their conforming behaviour in normative terms, as obligatory or right behaviour.[43] This is one of the features that distinguishes a legal regime from a regime of customary rules, according to Hart. In the latter situation, the rules must be generally accepted because there are no officials to resolve disputes and enforce the rules.[44] When it comes to a legal regime, however, ordinary citizens may obey not because they accept the rules but rather out of fear of sanctions or unthinkingly. In fact, Hart says:

> [I]n an extreme case, the internal point of view with its characteristic normative use of legal language ('This is a valid rule') might be confined to the official world ... The society in which this was so might be deplorably sheeplike; the sheep might end in the slaughter-house. But there is little reason for thinking that it could not exist or for denying it the title of a legal system.[45]

---

42 J Dickson, 'Is the Rule of Recognition Really a Conventional Rule?' (2007) 27 *Oxford Journal of Legal Studies* 373, 380–1, 383.
43 Hart, above n 2, pp 115–16.
44 Ibid p 117.
45 Ibid.

Officials, by contrast, *must* accept the system's rule of recognition and its rules of change and adjudication. They must, in other words, regard the secondary rules from the internal point of view, having internalised them as standards of obligatory official behaviour. Thus judges must, for instance, regard the fact that parliament enacted a provision as a reason for them to apply the provision. If this were not the case—if only some judges respected the rule of recognition and if deviations from the rules were not regarded with disapproval—we would not be able to speak of the existence 'of a single legal system'.[46] This would, in fact, be a situation of such unpredictability and chaos that we would be hard-pressed to find words with which to describe it.[47] Certainly, it would not be a legal system.

Hart's aim in *The Concept of Law* is to provide a general theory about the institution of law—an institution which has, he says, 'in spite of many variations in different cultures and in different times ... taken the same general form and structure'.[48] As noted in 3.2, Hart makes clear that he is not concerned to define law, that is, to provide a rule for the correct use of the word. Rather, he wishes to 'advance legal theory by providing an improved analysis of the distinctive structure of a municipal legal system'.[49] This is what he calls the 'central case' of law[50] and we now know what he takes the central case of law to be, and therefore how he answers the question posed at the beginning of Chapter 2: what distinguishes law from related social phenomena?

We can sum up Hart's answer in the following way. Non-legal norms such as moral norms are not institutionalised, nor are they related systematically to each other. Moral rules are not created, abolished or amended at specific times as a result of prescribed people or bodies acting in prescribed ways. Law, by contrast, is an institutional system of rules. It is a system of primary rules that are authoritatively identified, created, interpreted and enforced by special institutions, such as the legislature and the judiciary. These institutions are created by secondary rules, of which the rule of recognition is the most fundamental. In order for a legal system to exist, legal officials must accept the rules defining validity as common public standards. Furthermore, the members of the population must generally obey the rules that are valid according to the

---

46 Ibid p 116.
47 Ibid.
48 Ibid p 240.
49 Ibid p 17.
50 Ibid p 81.

criteria of legal validity. This set of circumstances, which combines what Hart calls the 'relatively passive' behaviour of ordinary citizens with the more active 'law-making, law-identifying and law-applying operations of the officials', is what, in Hart's view, centrally characterises law and distinguishes it from related social phenomena.[51]

3.4 Hart's account compared to Austin's

Hart argues that his characterisation of the social practice of law, as consisting in and founded on rules, has the power to 'elucidate the concepts that constitute the framework of legal thought'.[52] As we have seen, we talk about the law using concepts such as obligation, duty, legislation, jurisdiction, validity and legal powers. Hart argues that once we analyse law in terms of rules, we are able to explain this distinctive type of discourse. In particular, reference to the internal point of view in its simplest form—namely, that of using primary rules as standards for evaluating behaviour—assists us in understanding the basic concepts of obligation and duty. And the addition of the notion of secondary rules explains more complex concepts, such as legislation, jurisdiction, validity and legal powers.[53] All of these notions are, Hart concludes, logically dependent on a rule-based analysis and this is the reason why Austin's austerely behaviourist characterisation of law fails.

Let us examine in more detail how an analysis of law in terms of rules is able to explain the features of law that Austin's analysis could not explain. It will be remembered that Hart argued that threats of punishment and habits of obedience cannot explain the characteristic concepts of legal discourse. There is a difference between saying that X does Y as a matter of habit, or saying that X is likely to be punished for not doing Y, and saying that X is under a legal obligation to do Y. Whereas Austin's account cannot explain this difference, Hart has a ready explanation. For him, the difference emerges once we pay attention to the perspective of those who adopt the internal point of view and make internal statements about the law. To say that X is under a legal obligation to do Y involves invoking a legal rule as a standard with which X should comply. The endorsement of rules—rules that pick out certain conduct as a standard to be

---

51   Ibid p 61.
52   Ibid p 81.
53   Ibid pp 98–9.

followed—and the application of these rules to particular cases therefore provide an explanation of the normative character of statements of the law.[54]

An account of law in terms of rules can also account for the other features of legal systems that Austin's account lacks the resources to explain. These are, as we saw, the existence of power-conferring rules, the continuity of the authority to make law, the persistence of law, the existence of legal limitations on sovereign power and the exercise of sovereign power by the electorate.

The reason why lawmaking authority survives a change in individual lawmakers is because the authority to make law is conferred on persons in virtue of their occupation of an 'office'. But 'office' is not a concept that can find a place in Austin's theory. 'Office' is the legal source of sovereignty. For Austin, however, sovereign status is not conferred by law. Rather, the sovereign is the person or persons with the power to impose their will, not the person or persons entitled to make law by virtue of occupying the office of lawmaker. Hart, by contrast, has no such difficulty explaining the concept of 'office'. For Hart, it is law, and in particular, a secondary, power-conferring rule, which establishes the office of lawmaker and prescribes what the lawmaker must do in order to make law. This rule explains the continuity of the authority to make law. In an absolute monarchy, for instance, there might be a rule specifying that the new ruler shall be the first-born son of the previous monarch. If so, the first-born son has the legal right to make law on his father's death and this explains why the laws he makes are already law before the bulk of the population has shown any disposition to obey him. Secondary rules, on Hart's picture, also define the scope of the office-holder's power, which explains how sovereignty can be subject to legal limitations: any attempt to make rules that breach these accepted restrictions would be regarded by officials as invalid. Hart's account of the power to make law, as conferred by higher-order legal rules that qualify a person or body to make law, is therefore superior to Austin's factual account of sovereignty in terms of commands and habits of obedience.[55]

Again, the concept of a secondary rule is able to explain the fact that laws that were made by an earlier lawmaker, now dead, can still be valid law. For Hart, the reason why unrepealed statutes passed by a previous lawmaker are still law is that they were enacted by a person or body of persons whose enactments are accepted as authoritative under secondary legal rules. Officials accept a

---

54 Ibid pp 85, 88.
55 Ibid p 54, pp 59–60, 68–9.

fundamental rule of what is to count as law that embraces, as Hart says, 'past as well as present legislative operations'.[56]

Finally, while it is impossible to understand how the electorate can exercise sovereign power by reference to habits of obedience—after all, how can the people be in the habit of obeying orders issued by themselves?—Hart can explain this in terms of a secondary legal rule. The rule defines what the members of society must do in order to function as an electorate and therefore in order to speak as a sovereign body. Hart explains: '[T]heir qualifications under certain rules, and their compliance with other rules ... define what is to be done by them to make a valid election [of a representative] or a law.'[57] Sovereign status is therefore, on Hart's account, underpinned by legal rules. Such rules tell us what *counts* as the sovereign body's will and therefore pre-exist and authorise any 'commands' that body may issue or impose. It follows that if the people are sovereign, they are no more outside the law than the elected legislature: it is the law that gives both their power.[58]

3.5 Law as a 'remedy'

At one point in *The Concept of Law*, Hart suggests that complex societies require the regime of primary and secondary rules that constitutes law because a regime consisting only of primary rules or customs is not as effective a form of 'social control' as law.[59] He says that only a very small, close-knit community in a stable environment could live successfully by customary or unofficial rules alone. Hart asks us to imagine a society in which the only rules are primary rules of obligation accepted from the internal point of view. These rules do not exist because they are valid, but only because they are practised. This is more in the nature of a thought-experiment than a description of an actual society, because, as Hart says in a note to his discussion, few such societies have existed.[60] Hart argues that this society would be beset by numerous problems.

First, although we can suppose that the people living in this hypothetical society generally wish to act according to their customs, they would be unable to resolve disagreements about whether a particular rule is or is not a rule of their

---

56   Ibid p 65.
57   Ibid p 76.
58   Ibid pp 76–7.
59   Ibid p 92.
60   Ibid p 291.

society. Suppose such a difference of opinion has arisen. If they had a master rule that told them how to recognise valid rules of their society, they would be able to settle this doubt. If, for instance, they had 'an authoritative list or text of the rules ... in a written document or carved on some public monument',[61] they could resolve the question. The acknowledgment of such an *authoritative* list or text involves a secondary rule—a rule for identifying valid primary rules. But we have hypothesised that the only rules they have are primary or duty-imposing rules. They would therefore be unable to ascertain whether a putative rule is really one of their rules or has been falsely said to be one.

Let us now suppose that the people living in this society wish to abolish one of their primary rules or introduce a new one. If they had a rule that told them how to achieve such a change, this would be easy. Once again, such a rule would be a secondary rule. Such a rule might say 'whatever the king enacts is law'. But, as we know, the only rules they have are rules for regulating their behaviour. They do not have rules for validly making *deliberate* changes to their rules.

Finally, let us suppose that a dispute has arisen in this society about whether one of their rules has been violated. They have, let us suppose, a rule against killing, but it is not clear whether this rule also applies to acts of killing in self-defence. If they had a rule that gave power to a certain body to determine authoritatively how their rules should be interpreted, the dispute could be settled. Such a rule would be another kind of secondary rule. But they do not have rules for conferring such powers. The only rules they have are rules that impose duties. They would therefore be unable to resolve disputes about the meaning and application of their rules.

Such a society—a society that has only primary rules of obligation, the rules of which do not exist as rules by virtue of their relationship to a master rule and are not systemically interconnected with other rules—would therefore suffer from certain 'defects' insofar as the ability to control conduct is concerned. The defects are uncertainty, the static character of the rules and the inefficiency of the diffuse social pressure by which they are maintained.[62] The acceptance of secondary rules as binding by judges and other legal officials remedies these defects and makes the system into a legal system.

Stephen Perry argues that in offering this account, Hart betrayed his methodological positivism. We encountered the notion of methodological

---

61   Ibid p 94.
62   Ibid pp 92–3.

positivism in 2.5. It is the claim to offer a morally neutral, descriptive theory of law. Such a theory does not appeal to moral arguments in defending its conclusions. Perry thinks, however, that one reason why Hart emphasises the centrality of secondary rules in an adequate account of law is because he ascribes moral value to the way in which secondary rules assist in guiding conduct.[63] Hart has therefore, in Perry's view, 'abandoned the goal of offering a description of social practices that in no way depends on normative argument'.[64]

This does not seem quite accurate, however. Perry seems to assume that Hart's talk of 'defects' implies that a legal system is *morally* superior to a system of primary rules. In fact, Hart's attitude to the law is best described as 'unromantic'.[65] Hart expressly states that a system of law may be more unjust than a system of primary rules, in creating 'the risk that the centrally organised power may ... be used for the oppression of numbers with whose support it can dispense, in a way that the simpler regime of primary rules could not'.[66] This shows that Hart does not think societies that enjoy the efficiencies in social control which law brings are necessarily better societies. It all depends on the use to which the efficiencies are put. Hart's view is, as Green explains, that '[law] is just one way in which a complex society copes when the direct, transparent form of social order no longer works very well'.[67] On Hart's view, therefore, '[l]aw may be beneficial, but only in some contexts and always at a price, at the risk of grave injustice; our appropriate attitude to it is therefore one of caution rather than celebration'.[68]

3.6 Legal versus moral normativity

It is important to emphasise that when Hart talks about the normativity of law, he does not mean moral normativity. It is tempting to think that if there is a difference between power and law—a difference between a gunman and a tax official—the difference must be that the tax official's demands differ from the gunman's in being morally legitimate and therefore that they morally justify sanctions against those who do not comply. It is also natural to suppose

---

63 S R Perry, 'Hart's Methodological Positivism', in J Coleman (ed), *Hart's Postscript: Essays on the Postscript to* The Concept of Law, Oxford University Press, Oxford, 2001, pp 323-4.
64 Ibid p 346.
65 J Raz, 'Authority, Law and Morality' (1985) 68 *The Monist* 295, 295.
66 Hart, above n 2, p 202.
67 L Green, 'The Concept of Law Revisited' (1996) 94 *Michigan Law Review* 1687, 1699-1700.
68 Ibid 1687.

that when Hart talks about legal officials accepting the rule of recognition he must mean that they morally approve of it and of the laws that the rule of recognition identifies.

In fact, however, Hart makes neither of these claims. His adherence to the separability thesis leads him to draw a very sharp distinction between legal obligations and moral obligations. First, Hart says merely that the tax official's demands are legally justified and that the tax official has legal authority to make them. Whether legal requirements are morally legitimate is an entirely separate question for Hart. For Hart, there can be legal rights and duties which have, as he says, 'no moral justification or force whatever',[69] not even of a prima facie kind. A prima facie moral right or duty is one that can be overridden by more powerful moral considerations. But Hart thinks that there are not necessarily even *weak* moral grounds for the assertion of legal rights and obligations, that is, grounds that may be outweighed by countervailing considerations. For Hart, in other words, legal rights and obligations may deserve no moral respect whatsoever. Let us examine this aspect of his theory more closely.

Moral standards are like legal standards in functioning as practical guides to conduct. Both morality and law are normative practices. The criteria for moral and legal validity are, however, different. What makes something morally right is not a matter of social facts or facts about people's behaviour, attitudes or beliefs. It will be remembered that we are concerned with critical morality, not popular morality. Although what is right in terms of *popular* morality depends on facts about what people believe is right—beliefs that may or may not be sound—standards that are morally valid from the perspective of critical morality must be *genuinely* meritorious. There must be a sound justification for complying with them. We can put this by saying that (critical) morality is not a matter of what is socially accepted.

By contrast, for Hart, it is a social matter as to what the criteria of legal validity are. As we have seen, he thinks that the foundation of all legal systems is a rule of recognition, which is used to identify valid legal rules. Furthermore, the existence and content of the rule of recognition are matters of social fact to be established by empirical investigation of the practices of legal officials. No moral judgment is required. The criteria of legal validity can therefore have any content, depending on what the social practices of legal officials happen to be. As a result, valid laws can, unlike valid moral standards, be unmeritorious and unjust.

---

[69] Hart above n 2, p 268.

This is what leads Hart to conclude that there can be legal rights and duties that are 'devoid of moral justification'.[70] It follows, also, that the 'bare fact' that a rule is a valid rule of law does not tell us whether the law ought to be obeyed.[71] It all depends on the content of the law as to whether it is morally justifiable for legal officials to enforce the law and whether citizens are under a moral duty to comply with it.

The second way in which Hart attempts to sever legal and moral normativity is by insisting that officials' statements of legal obligation do not presuppose even the *belief* that what is legally obligatory is morally obligatory. Hart thinks, in other words, that the internal attitude of acceptance that legal officials take towards the legal rules when they speak of the law as conferring rights and duties need not involve *moral* acceptance. Officials *may* believe that the legal rules are morally binding but it is not *necessary* that they should do so. According to Hart, therefore, 'the dichotomy of "law based merely on power" and "law which is accepted as morally binding" is not exhaustive'.[72] Hart seeks, in other words, to carve out a middle road between the view that a legal system rests on mere power and the view that it rests on beliefs about the system's moral value on the part of legal officials. As we have seen, he thinks that Austin was wrong in treating propositions of law as descriptive. Officials' statements of legal obligation are internal statements. They are, in Hart's view, prescriptive. When officials make internal statements, they use the law as a standard by which to evaluate conduct and they express a willingness to be guided by legal standards. Hart insists, however, that these statements do not necessarily express an attitude of moral approval.[73] The law's normativity is therefore something *sui generis*.

A final point worth emphasising is that although Hart believes that any adequate theory of law must make reference to the fact that law is a normative practice, he also believes that this is consistent with his theory being descriptive and morally neutral. In the Preface to *The Concept of Law*, Hart describes the book as an essay in 'descriptive sociology'.[74] Although the phrase is somewhat obscure, it seems that one thing Hart meant by it is that the task of the legal theorist is merely to describe or report on the fact that official participants in legal

---

70 Ibid.
71 H L A Hart, 'Positivism and the Separation of Law and Morals' (1958) 71 *Harvard Law Review* 593, 618.
72 Hart, above n 2, p 203.
73 J Raz, 'The Purity of the Pure Theory of Law', in R Tur and W Twining (eds), *Essays on Kelsen*, Clarendon Press, Oxford, 1986, p 86.
74 Hart, above n 2, p v.

institutions take the law to have normative force. Legal theorists do not have to adopt the internal point of view themselves or endorse the participants' view that the law provides a standard that should be followed.

In this respect as well, then, Hart attempts to occupy the middle ground. On the one hand, there are those who think that legal theorists must themselves take up the committed, insider viewpoint of those who accept the rules and use them as guides to conduct. This is Finnis's view and Dworkin's view, which we will explore in Chapters 5 and 6. On the other hand, there is Austin's 'extreme external point of view',[75] which does not refer to normative attitudes at all but only to regularities in behaviour.

Hart's view is different from that of both Finnis and Dworkin, on the one hand, and that of Austin, on the other. Hart thinks that the legal theorist must occupy the point of view of someone who 'without accepting the rules himself, assert[s] that the group accepts the rules, and thus may from outside refer to the way in which *they* are concerned with them from the internal point of view'.[76] 'Such an observer', as Roger Shiner says, 'both observes from a position of non-commitment and pays due regard to the internal point of view'.[77] Thus, although both Hart and Austin are methodological positivists in that they describe law from what Shiner calls 'a position of non-commitment', Hart's account is different from Austin's in including a *description* of the fact that participants in legal institutions view law as standards with which they *should* comply. We will return in Chapters 5 and 6 to Hart's views about the descriptive character of jurisprudence, when we explore Finnis's and Dworkin's rejection of the possibility of a morally neutral theory of law.

3.7 Some criticisms of Hart

Hart's views have been the subject of many criticisms by Dworkin, Fuller and Finnis. Their criticisms will be considered in later chapters. At this point we will focus on a set of criticisms made by a different set of theorists, who disagree with Hart's views about legal normativity. As we saw in 3.6, Hart maintains that when legal officials make statements from the internal point of view—such as 'X is under a legal obligation to ...' or 'The rule that ... is legally valid'—their endorsement of the rule of recognition, and the legal rules which it requires them

---

75 Ibid p 89.
76 Ibid, Hart's emphasis.
77 R A Shiner, *Norm and Nature: The Movements of Legal Thought*, Clarendon Press, Oxford, 1992, p 55.

to apply, is not necessarily moral endorsement. Many theorists are critical of this claim.

Austin's theory of legal obligations, in terms of liability to punishment for failure to comply, is obviously compatible with official indifference to the moral defensibility of the demands made by law. But is Hart's theory, which stresses the normative attitude that officials must take to the legal rules, compatible with such indifference? Hart's critics argue that it is not. They think that if, for instance, judges regard the fact that parliament enacted a provision as a *good reason* to apply the provision (as Hart tells us they must), then such judges must also believe in the moral legitimacy of the legislature. The critics maintain, in other words, that once the intrinsically normative character of the internal point of view is recognised, it is impossible to stop short of attributing moral commitment to officials: officials who make statements of legal obligation from the internal point of view must believe that law's demands are morally legitimate and give rise to a moral obligation to obey them. Although the critics do not say that the officials' beliefs are necessarily *correct*, their argument nevertheless implies that there is an important conceptual connection between law and moral beliefs, which follows from recognising the normative character of statements of legal obligation. This view therefore poses a problem for Hart insofar as he denies that there are any necessary connections between law and morality.

Raz provides a sophisticated argument along these lines. The foundation of his argument is what Hart calls a 'reason-based' explanation of legal normativity.[78] Raz argues as follows. When officials say that I am under a legal obligation to act in a certain way, they are implying that I *ought* to act in that way, and this is the equivalent of saying that I have *reasons* to act in that way. Furthermore, since the legal obligation that I am under may require me to do something that is contrary to my own interests, my reason to comply cannot be a *prudential* reason. My reason cannot, in other words, be dependent on performance of the duty being personally advantageous. But if my reason is not a prudential reason, it must be a moral reason. Hence when officials say that I am under a legal obligation, they must be asserting that I have an *objective* or *moral* reason to behave in the required way. The assertion may be false, and the officials may not themselves sincerely believe it, but to say that someone is under a legal obligation is the equivalent of saying that that person is morally bound to comply with the law.[79] Hart summarises Raz's position as follows:

---

78 Hart, above n 1, p 157.
79 J Raz, 'Hart on Moral Rights and Legal Duties' (1984) 4 *Oxford Journal of Legal Studies* 123, 130–1.

[A] judge who accepts and applies laws imposing [legal] duties and in the course of doing so makes statements of legal duty must either believe that there are such objective moral reasons for complying with the law or must at least pretend to do so. So ... normative statements of duty made by a judge in the course of applying the law are moral claims, sincere or insincere.[80]

Hart points out that even if Raz's view is correct, the 'moral component in the judge's acceptance [is] very small indeed'.[81] Not only may the judge's beliefs about the moral duty to comply with the law be mistaken; they may even be insincere. Hart nevertheless argues that even so minimal a moral component need not be present.

For one thing, he believes that Raz's reason-based explanation of statements of legal obligation is incorrect. Hart says that even if *moral* judgments of duty provide objective reasons to act, this is not true of *legal* judgments of duty. For Hart, the judge's statement that 'X has a legal duty to ...' does not mean that 'there is an objective reason for X to ...'. Instead, the statement means that the 'action can be properly demanded or extracted from him according to legal rules or principles'.[82] Statements of legal obligation do not, in other words, express conclusions about what the duty-bearer has reason to do. They merely express conclusions about the applicability of legal rules and what may be enforced against the duty-bearer without presupposing that the application of the rules is morally justified. Thus when judges offer a 'justification' for their decisions, the justification in question can be a purely 'technical' one, which is merely relative to the rules.[83] Judges *may* combine moral judgment with this 'technically confined' way of speaking, but such moral judgments are not *entailed* by judgments of legal duty.[84] Hart calls this a 'non-cognitive' theory of legal duty.[85] As Neil MacCormick explains, Hart's thesis is that 'the judicial statement of the citizen's legal obligation ... is only a statement of the reasons the *judge* has for holding the citizen to a certain line of conduct, not a statement of reasons the judge supposes there to be for the *citizen* to do something'.[86]

Furthermore, according to Hart, there are many reasons why judges may accept the rule of recognition, which tells them what they are legally justified

---

80 Hart, above n 1, p 157.
81 Ibid p 158.
82 Ibid p 160.
83 N E Simmonds, *Law as a Moral Idea*, Oxford University Press, Oxford, 2007, pp 134, 139.
84 Hart, above n 1, p 266.
85 Ibid p 159.
86 N MacCormick, 'The Normativity of Law', in R Gavison (ed), *Issues in Contemporary Legal Philosophy: The Influence of H L A Hart*, Clarendon Press, Oxford, 1987, p 111, emphasis added.

in doing. They must have a 'standing disposition'[87] to be guided by the rule of recognition but this normative attitude or disposition to treat the rule of recognition as action-guiding does not need to be supported by moral reasons. Judges must have *some* reason for guiding their conduct by reference to the law, but the range of possible reasons is diverse.[88] Thus Hart states that there are many reasons why people may willingly accept a social rule, whether this be the rule of recognition or any other social rule. They may regard the social rule as morally sound. However, 'some rules may be accepted simply out of deference to tradition or the wish to identify with others or in the belief that society knows best what is to the advantage of individuals. These attitudes may coexist with a more or less vivid realization that the rules are morally objectionable.'[89]

Suppose, for instance, that judges accept the rule that they are obliged to apply legislative provisions. As we know, this means, for Hart, that the judges must regard the fact that parliament enacted a provision as a *good reason* to apply the provision. But he says that this does not mean that they must believe in the moral legitimacy of the legislature. Hart concedes that it would be 'extraordinary' if judges could give *no* answer as to why they accept legislative enactments as determinants of the standards of correct judicial behaviour. He believes, however, that as long as they have a 'comprehensible motive' for accepting the legislature's authority, this will be sufficient.[90] Hart explains:

> [I]ndividual judges may explain or justify their acceptance of the legislator's enactments by saying that they simply wish to continue in an established practice or that they had sworn on taking office to continue it or that they had tacitly agreed to do so by accepting the office of judge. All this would be compatible with judges either having no belief at all concerning the moral legitimacy of the legislature or even with their believing that it had none.[91]

Hart concludes that judges can internalise the rules of law and regard them as authoritative without believing or even pretending to believe that they have a moral right to demand obedience.

On Hart's account, therefore, judges could apply the law in a wicked legal system in full awareness of its morally objectionable nature and without seeking to conceal this. This would be possible because judges do not have to think of

---

87 Hart, above n 2, p 255.
88 Simmonds, above n 83, p 122.
89 Hart, above n 2, p 257.
90 Hart, above n 1, p 265.
91 Ibid.

their judgments of legal obligation as giving those to whom they are addressed moral reasons to obey the law, and because judges do not themselves have to have moral reasons for treating the rule of recognition as a standard that guides their conduct. Hart therefore claims to have accounted for law's normativity without any recourse to moral values.

Hart says, of course, that most legal systems are not like this, and he concedes that such a system would be likely to be unstable.[92] He insists that it would nevertheless be a legal system. It will be remembered that Hart thinks that ordinary citizens do not have to *accept* the law but only have to *obey* it in order for us to say that a legal system exists. He talks about the possibility of law being used for oppressive purposes and says that 'for those thus oppressed there may be nothing in the system to command their loyalty but only things to fear'.[93] That such a system is possible, however undesirable, shows, in Hart's view, that Raz is wrong and there can be legal systems for which their officials do not claim moral authority.

It might be wondered whether Hart's picture, on which legal norms do not necessarily give ordinary citizens genuine reasons to act and may therefore be nothing but coercive insofar as citizens are concerned, has not collapsed back into Austin's picture with its attendant difficulties. Hart insists, however, that his picture is entirely different from Austin's because Austin overlooked the 'official side to law'.[94] Austin's single-minded focus on factual obedience 'only caters', Hart says, 'for what we may term the "end product" of the legal system, where it makes its impact on the private citizen; whereas its day-to-day existence consists also in the official creation, the official identification, and the official use and application of law'.[95] Here, when it comes to the perspective of officials, Hart says it does not make sense to talk of 'obedience'. Instead, when we describe the officials' relationship to the secondary rules, we cannot do without the normative (albeit not necessarily moral) notion of acceptance or allegiance.[96] It is the voluntary cooperation of officials, Hart tells us, which creates authority and explains the difference between coercion and law.[97] There are many difficulties here which Hart himself admitted he was not able satisfactorily to

---

92 Ibid pp 160–1.
93 Hart, above n 2, p 201.
94 Ibid p 113.
95 Ibid pp 112–13.
96 Ibid pp 113–15.
97 Ibid p 201.

resolve.[98] His analysis of statements of legal obligation continues, nevertheless, to be influential.[99]

3.8 Judicial decision-making

So far we have been concerned with Hart's views about the identification of legal standards. We turn now to his views about the application of these legal standards in legal disputes, and in particular to his views about the extent to which the legal standards once identified provide objective and determinate answers to these disputes. As we will see, the idea of general agreement plays a role not only in Hart's views about the identification of law but also in his views about its correct application. Both, according to him, are social.[100]

On what can be described as a traditional view about law, there are right answers to legal questions, which can be found within the law. When individuals reason in a legal way it is therefore the law that determines the answer, even if the law on the matter is not one with which they personally agree. Judges reason legally when, for instance, they apply the clear provisions of a statute or refuse to depart from a settled precedent, even though they think the precedent is mistaken or the statute misconceived. Such judges decide according to the law, not according to the way they personally think would be best. Legal reasoning is therefore very different, on the traditional picture, from the reasoning of political decision-makers or legislators. Legal reasoning involves the application of pre-existing law, not the creation of new law. Politicians, by contrast, are entitled to try to shape society on the basis of their own beliefs about the form the law ought to take. Although such beliefs may be rationally justifiable, they are nevertheless 'subjective' in the sense that they express the politicians' own judgments as to what would be the best outcome. The task of politicians is to create new legal rules that they believe to be socially desirable. Theirs is not the legal task of working out what pre-existing law objectively requires.

There are significantly different versions of the traditional view, as we will see. These turn partly on the question, to be discussed in Chapters 4 and 6, as to whether morality can be relevant to deciding what the law is on some matter. For

---

98 Hart, above n 1, p 267.
99 See, for instance, M H Kramer, *In Defense of Legal Positivism: Law without Trimmings*, Oxford University Press, Oxford, 1999, Chapter 4, for a defence of Hart's position against Raz's arguments. See also K E Himma, 'Law's Claim of Legitimate Authority', in J Coleman (ed), *Hart's Postscript: Essays on the Postscript to* The Concept of Law, Oxford University Press, Oxford, 2001, pp 271–309.
100 N Stavropoulos, 'Objectivity', in M P Golding and W A Edmundson (eds), *The Blackwell Guide to the Philosophy of Law and Legal Theory,* Blackwell Publishing, Oxford, 2005, pp 318–19.

some defenders of the traditional view, such as Raz, legal reasoning is necessarily non-moral. For Raz, the world of the law is very narrow and contains only positive or enacted rules. By contrast, other defenders of the traditional view, such as Dworkin, believe that moral reasoning is necessary to determine what the law requires. This makes their respective conceptions of what is involved in finding the law very different. For Dworkin, judges are required to reflect on controversial matters of political morality when deciding cases. Dworkin can, however, still be classified as a defender of the traditional view because he believes that there are right answers to legal questions and that these answers can be found within the law. Judges are, in his view, not in the business of making law. This is because they are constrained by the need to decide in a way that makes moral sense of the legal materials and because there are objective answers to such questions, which may differ from the answers judges would give if they simply consulted their own views as to what ought to be the law on the matter.

The traditional view is also compatible with different conceptions of what makes it the case that there are determinately correct answers to questions about what the law requires. Some theorists believe that the law is determinate to the extent that it generates generally agreed upon answers. We will shortly see that this is Hart's position. For Hart, the traditional picture of legal reasoning as an objective form of reasoning that determines a uniquely correct outcome is therefore accurate only in uncontroversial or 'easy' cases.

Others, however, maintain that the law can be determinate even in the presence of considerable disagreement about the answers to legal questions. They believe that there can be right answers to legal questions even if these answers cannot be proved to everyone's satisfaction. This is Dworkin's view. The traditional view is therefore accurate, for Dworkin, in a much wider range of legal cases—indeed in all or virtually all of them. What makes it possible for Dworkin to take this view is his belief, mentioned above, that controversial moral reasoning underpins legal reasoning. Once legal reasoning is conceptualised in this way, it becomes more plausible to say that all legal disputes can be decided according to the law. We will explore Dworkin's views in Chapter 6. It should also be noted that there are many theorists who are sceptical about the traditional view. They attack the distinction between law and politics, arguing that law is indeterminate and incapable of generating uniquely correct answers to legal disputes. Their views will be discussed in Chapters 7 and 9.

Let us now examine Hart's views about the extent to which law provides objective and determinate answers to disputes. In a nutshell, Hart believes that the legal standards determine correct answers to *some* legal questions but not *all*. It follows that, for Hart, it is not always possible for judges to reason legally: the resolution of cases may sometimes require judges to reason as politicians do. In order to understand this answer, we need to understand the distinction Hart draws between a core of clear application had by legal rules and what he calls their 'penumbra' of uncertainty. Consider, Hart says, the rule 'No vehicles in the park'. There are obvious cases that the rule clearly covers. It is clear, for instance, that the general term 'vehicle' applies to motor cars and trucks. Hart says that in the plain cases, the general terms 'seem to need no interpretation and ... the recognition of instances seems unproblematic or "automatic"'.[101]

The reason why, in Hart's view, 'vehicle' clearly applies to motor cars and trucks is by virtue of general agreement in the way we ordinarily use language. However, Hart makes clear in later work that agreement that a case falls within the scope of a rule can also be based on other factors. For instance, the meaning of words can sometimes be clear by virtue of special conventions relating to the legal use of words.[102] As Frederick Schauer points out, even if legal terms do not have an ordinary meaning, or have a legal meaning that differs from their ordinary meaning, they can still have a *plain* meaning for those who are legally trained.[103] Where the meaning of terms, whether legal or everyday, is plain, there will be no doubt that a case falls within or outside the scope of a legal rule. Furthermore, Hart thinks that the meaning of a rule can sometimes (though not always) be 'clearly controlled' by the purpose of the rule, which is not a linguistic matter at all.[104] What unites all such cases, for Hart, is the fact that everyone in the relevant community will agree that the rule is applicable to the facts. As with the criteria for identifying valid law, it is a matter of agreement, but in this case, in respect of the applicability of terms.

Notice that Hart's claim is not that judges always *do*, in fact, apply clearly applicable rules. Such an empirical claim is obviously false, as judicial decisions biased by the race, class, gender or ideology of the judge attest. Rather, Hart is making the conceptual claim that some legal cases *can* be resolved objectively, in the sense that there are legal rules which conclusively settle the dispute in virtue of general agreement about the applicability of the words used to the situation at hand.

---

101 Hart, above n 2, p 126.
102 H L A Hart, *Essays in Jurisprudence and Philosophy*, Clarendon Press, Oxford, 1983, p 106.
103 F Schauer, 'A Critical Guide to Vehicles in the Park' (2008) 83 *New York University Law Review* 1109, 1122-3.
104 Hart, above n 102, p 106.

Hart does not even say that judges *should* always apply such clearly applicable rules. For Hart, the fact that something is the law does not necessarily mean it should be applied. This is because positivism is a theory about the nature of law and not a theory of adjudication or a theory about how judges should decide cases. Positivism tells us, as David Lyons explains, that 'if the meaning of the law is clear, determinate and uncontroversial ... then there is only one way to act within the law, which is by following the law's directions'.[105] Positivism is not, however, committed to the view that law's clear directions should always be followed. Most obviously, valid laws may be too iniquitous to be enforced.[106] Whether judges should always apply clearly applicable laws is a *moral* matter, not a conceptual matter, which is properly dealt with under a moral theory of how judges should adjudicate. We will return to the issue of positivism and the moral issues surrounding adjudication in 4.2.

We have seen that there are cases, for Hart, in which the legal rules clearly apply to the situation at hand. There are, however, also cases in which it is *not* clear whether the rule applies because 'no firm convention or general agreement dictates its use, or, on the other hand, its rejection by the person concerned to classify'.[107] Such cases are in what Hart calls the 'penumbra'. Furthermore, there are, as Schauer points out, different kinds of penumbral problems.

First, some terms—such as 'vehicle'—have a clear core but an area of vagueness at their edges. The term 'vehicle' obviously applies to motor cars, but does it apply to bicycles, roller skates and electrically propelled toy vehicles? There are reasons both for and against subsuming these under the general term 'vehicle', for they are like standard cases of vehicles in some ways but not in others. Secondly, some terms—such as 'reasonableness' and 'fairness'—are more pervasively vague (although judicial decisions will gradually pin down their meaning for future courts bound by the doctrine of precedent). Finally, there is the phenomenon of 'open texture'. With some terms, such as 'after dark', the drafters of rules will be aware even at the time of drafting that there will be cases where we are not sure whether the term applies. But open texture refers to the fact that even *non-vague* terms are potentially vague. In support of this point, Hart quotes the philosopher Friedrich Waismann, who asked: 'Suppose I come across a being that looks like a man, speaks like a man, behaves like a man, and

---

105 D Lyons, *Ethics and the Rule of Law*, Cambridge University Press, Cambridge, 1984, p 87.
106 Hart, above n 2, p 208.
107 Ibid p 127.

is only one foot tall, shall I say it is a man?'[108] Waismann's example shows that even the most precise term can become vague when an unanticipated situation arises. This means that no rule, however precisely we attempt to frame it, can eliminate the possibility of future uncertainty about its application. Unforeseen fact situations may crop up, which possess some of the features of the plain case but not all, and in which even reference to non-linguistic aids, such as canons of statutory interpretation and the purpose of the rule, will not be capable of settling the issue because the guidance provided by these aids is itself unclear.[109]

Since the rules that make up a legal system are necessarily vague—whether at their edges, or more comprehensively, or potentially—there will inevitably be borderline or debatable cases in which 'plain meaning' will not settle the matter because there is no general agreement that the statute or precedent applies. Thus Hart writes: '[H]owever smoothly [precedent and legislation] work over the great mass of ordinary cases, [they] will, at some point where their application is in question, prove indeterminate.'[110]

Since Hart *identifies* the law with plainly applicable legal rules, whether contained in statutes or in judicial precedents, it follows that where a rule does not plainly or unambiguously cover a particular situation, there is *no law*. The law has here run out or has 'gaps': there is no legal answer to the question that has cropped up. In such cases Hart says that judges are empowered to make a choice between alternative answers: they have discretion whether to subsume the case under the rule or not. And in exercising that discretion, they have to rely on considerations that lie *outside* the currently existing law, such as moral considerations and policy considerations.

In hard cases, it is therefore not possible for judges to reason in a legal way. In hard cases, courts are empowered to perform a law-making rather than a law-applying function. They may not make arbitrary or irrational choices, to be sure.[111] They must make a reasonable decision. And they make the law only in the 'interstices' created by the open texture of legal rules. Thus they are not able to undertake far-reaching law reform.[112] But it remains true that, within these confines, they are creating new legal rights, not applying pre-existing legal standards. If, for instance, they decide that bicycles fall under the prohibition

---

108 Hart, above n 102, p 275.
109 Schauer, above n 103, 1125–7; Hart, above n 2, p 128; Hart, above n 102, p 103.
110 Hart, above n 2, p 128.
111 Ibid p 273.
112 Ibid.

on vehicles, they are playing a role that is like the role played by legislators when they enact legislation. They are making a decision which is, in their own personal opinion, the best decision, all things considered. They are, as a result, deciding what the law ought to be, not what it is. Of course, in the process of deciding what the law ought to be, they will authoritatively settle the issue for subsequent judges: from now on bicycles will be clearly covered by (that is, within the core of) the newly made rule and subsequent courts bound by the doctrine of precedent will be obliged to apply the rule to bicycles.[113]

Scott Shapiro argues that Hart's doctrine about the inevitability of judicial discretion follows from his view about the nature of law. Because, for Hart, a legal rule is a standard that exists as a result of some social act, such as a legislative enactment or a judicial decision, and because it is impossible for social acts to provide standards that resolve in advance every conceivable question that may crop up (due to indeterminacies of language and intention), judicial discretion is inevitable. The reason why the law can run out, in other words, is because there are limits to the guidance that social acts can provide.[114] As we will see in Chapter 6, Dworkin disagrees strongly with Hart's views about the non-legal nature of adjudication in hard cases. This is because Dworkin does not identify legal norms with norms that have been posited for the purposes of social guidance.[115]

One possible misconception should be warded off at this point: it would be wrong to assume that *any* recourse to moral and political reasons must, on Hart's account, be an appeal to reasons that lie outside the legal system, and therefore must constitute an act of judicial lawmaking. Raz believes that law must be identifiable in a morally neutral way (see 4.6), but although Hart does not say so, it would not make sense for him to limit clear cases to cases in which the law is identifiable in a morally neutral way. This is because Hart believes, as we will see in 4.4, that judges might be required by the rule of recognition to use moral tests in deciding legal questions. And since moral questions can have uncontroversial answers, it follows that a rule that contains moral terms can clearly cover a particular fact situation.

Suppose, for instance, that a judge has to decide whether a constitutional provision outlawing unfair discrimination applies to apartheid-style laws that reserve particular jobs for white people. Presumably, everyone will agree that

---

113 Ibid.
114 S Shapiro, 'The "Hart-Dworkin" Debate: A Short Guide for the Perplexed', in A Ripstein (ed), *Ronald Dworkin*, Cambridge University Press, New York, 2007, p 30.
115 Ibid pp 30–1.

the provision rules out such laws. If so, Hart's account implies that judges who found to this effect, though reasoning morally, would be objectively applying rather than making the law. They would not be exercising discretion or consulting their own views on the matter, since it is obvious that such laws discriminate unfairly. Of course, in other cases, the moral standards contained in the law may not clearly determine the answer to the legal dispute and in such cases Hart's account implies that judges will be forced to make law on the matter. But the main point is that for Hart, the dividing line between clear and hard cases must be understood as a line between cases in which there is general agreement that a legal rule applies, whether it contains moral terms or not, and cases in which there is no such agreement. It cannot be understood as a line between cases in which judges consult 'hard facts' for the answers and cases in which they reason morally.

Some critics of positivism associate it with the view that the legal system is a 'closed logical system',[116] in which judging is simply a matter of mechanical decision-making, judges having to do nothing but apply the rules of law to the facts of legal cases, and in which the answer to every legal case is deductively dictated by rules whose meaning is not in doubt. We have seen that this is not Hart's view, and in fact he describes it as one of two 'great exaggerations'.[117] We will examine this view further in 7.2. The second great exaggeration, according to Hart, is the sceptical view that the rules dictate the answer to no legal cases, a view which will be discussed in Chapters 7 and 9. Hart occupies a position that is midway between these two extremes: that of 'slot-machine' or 'mechanical' jurisprudence and what he calls the 'nightmare' in which the rules of law do not constrain at all.[118]

It should be clear why Hart rejects the view that judging is a mechanical enterprise. As we have seen, he believes that there will always be what he calls 'legally unregulated cases' at the margins of the law.[119] These are cases in which the law does not dictate an answer. When they are confronted by such cases, judges are entitled to consult their own views about what is right and wrong, in effect exercising political power. Raz agrees with Hart on this point, but Dworkin, as we will see in Chapter 6, disagrees. For Dworkin, although judging is not a mechanical matter and judges have to reason morally, they are always in

---

116 Hart, above n 2, p 302.
117 Ibid p 147.
118 Hart, above n 102, p 126.
119 Hart, above n 2, p 272.

the business of identifying the law, not making it or exercising political power. For Dworkin, all of the standards that judges are required to apply in deciding cases should be viewed as 'legal standards'.

Questions

1. Does Hart's account of law imply that the law is whatever judges say it is?
2. 'Whatever the problems with Hart's rule of recognition may be, one of its great values is that it identifies law with a kind of coordinated social activity ... [Hart] has an insight in thinking that we do not grasp what law is ... if we fail to identify the distinctively social aspects of it. The relevant social aspects of law are those at its foundation' (J Coleman, 'Beyond Inclusive Legal Positivism' (2009) 22 *Ratio Juris* 359, 381–2). In what way does Hart put the social aspects of law centre-stage? Do you agree with Coleman that Hart was right to do so?
3. Are moral rules social rules?
4. Hart sets out to provide a descriptive and morally neutral account of law. Do you think he succeeds? Do you think it is possible for a theory of law to be morally neutral?
5. Neil MacCormick points out that we have legislation under the name 'Administration of Justice Act' but never under the name 'Administration of Injustice Act' (N MacCormick, 'A Moralistic Case for A-Moralistic Law?' (1985) 20 *Valparaiso University Law Review* 1, 28). Does this prove that Hart is wrong when he says that the law does not necessarily claim moral legitimacy?
6. Does Hart's account of judicial decision-making authorise retrospective judicial legislation? If it does, is this a defect in his account?

Further reading

J Coleman, *The Practice of Principle: In Defence of a Pragmatist Approach to Legal Theory*, Oxford University Press, Oxford, 2001, Lectures 6–7.

J Coleman (ed), *Hart's Postscript: Essays on the Postscript to* The Concept of Law, Oxford University Press, Oxford, 2001.

H L A Hart, *Essays on Bentham*, Clarendon Press, Oxford, 1982, Chapters VI, X.

H L A Hart, *The Concept of Law*, 2nd edn, Clarendon Press, 1994, Chapters V–VII.

R Gavison (ed), *Issues in Contemporary Legal Philosophy: The Influence of H L A Hart*, Clarendon Press, Oxford, 1987, Part 1.

R P George (ed), *The Autonomy of Law: Essays on Legal Positivism*, Clarendon Press, Oxford, 1996.

L Green, 'The Concept of Law Revisited' (1996) 94 *Michigan Law Review* 1687.

M H Kramer, *In Defense of Legal Positivism: Law without Trimmings*, Oxford University Press, Oxford, 1999, Chapter 4.

N MacCormick, *H L A Hart*, Edward Arnold, London, 1981.

J Raz, 'Hart on Moral Rights and Legal Duties' (1984) 4 *Oxford Journal of Legal Studies* 123.

F Schauer, 'A Critical Guide to Vehicles in the Park' (2008) 83 *New York University Law Review* 1109.

S Shapiro, 'What is the Internal Point of View?' (2006) 75 *Fordham Law Review* 1157.

4

Law as What Is

4.1 Chapter overview

A central positivist doctrine is the conceptual separability of law and critical morality. Although there is dispute among positivists as to how far the separability extends, all positivists hold that law does not have to pass moral tests to be valid law: the law 'as it *is*' is therefore not necessarily the law 'as it *ought* to be'. This thesis is often mischaracterised or misunderstood by the critics of positivism. This chapter will examine some of these misconceptions.

The chapter will also explore an important current debate among positivists as to the exact meaning of the thesis that law does not have to pass moral tests to be valid law. This debate relates to whether the rule of recognition can make reference to moral criteria in stipulating the conditions that must be met for a norm to count as legally valid. The so-called 'inclusive positivists', such as Jules Coleman and Wilfred Waluchow, think that although the identification of law is not *necessarily* dependent on matters of moral merit, it *may* be dependent on such matters. This is because, in their view, the rule of recognition can include moral tests for ascertaining the existence and content of valid laws, thereby incorporating morality into law.

Other positivists, the 'exclusive positivists', believe that the identification of law *cannot* depend on matters of moral merit. The most prominent defender of exclusive positivism is Joseph Raz. He argues that only exclusive positivism is compatible with law's claim to be authoritative.

This chapter will also examine the views of ethical positivists such as Tom Campbell and Jeremy Waldron. Ethical positivists argue that a legal system that separates law from morality is morally desirable.

4.2 Some misconceptions about the positivist separation of law and morality

Notwithstanding their disagreements on other matters, Austin and Hart both affirm the thesis that laws do not have to pass moral tests to be valid. 'A law which actually exists', said Austin, 'is a law, though we happen to dislike it'.[1] Hart maintains that 'it is in no sense a necessary truth that laws reproduce or satisfy certain demands of morality'[2] and he also states that 'there are no necessary conceptual connections between the content of law and morality'.[3] We need, though, to be clear on exactly what it is that Austin, Hart and other positivists are claiming, because their view tends to be caricatured in a number of ways.

One misconception is to confuse legal positivism with non-cognitivism about morality.[4] Non-cognitivism about moral judgments is the theory that all moral judgments are subjective and that there are no right and wrong answers to moral questions. The philosopher David Hume famously defended non-cognitivism. He argued that there is a fundamental difference between moral 'ought' statements and factual 'is' statements. Moral statements, he said, express our subjective attitudes of approval and disapproval, whereas factual statements describe the way the world objectively is. Thus a statement such as 'Many countries have the death penalty' is a factual statement that tells us something objective about the world. It is, according to Hume, fundamentally different in kind from a statement such as 'The death penalty is wrong', which tells us something about the speaker's subjective feelings about the death penalty. Objective facts cannot dictate subjective attitudes. Moral statements therefore cannot be derived from factual statements and are incapable of rational defence.

The so-called 'logical positivists'—who held that only empirically verifiable statements are meaningful—were led by their epistemological beliefs (beliefs about what is required for a person to have knowledge) to an extreme form of non-cognitivism in ethics. Since, they argued, moral statements are not empirically verifiable, they must be meaningless.[5] In jurisprudence, this can give

---

1   J Austin [1832], *The Province of Jurisprudence Determined*, W E Rumble (ed), Cambridge University Press, Cambridge, 1995, p 157.
2   H L A Hart, *The Concept of Law*, 2nd edn, Clarendon Press, Oxford, 1994, pp 185–6.
3   Ibid p 268.
4   H L A Hart, 'Positivism and the Separation of Law and Morals' (1958) 71 *Harvard Law Review* 593, 626.
5   For a classic statement of this position, see A J Ayer, *Language, Truth and Logic*, Penguin Books, Harmondsworth, 1971, pp 136–50.

rise to confusion. We may make the mistake of thinking that *legal* positivism is the same as *logical* positivism and its associated non-cognitivist ethics.

The temptation to make this mistake has two sources. First, there is the coincidence in terminology: the fact that both help themselves to the label 'positivism'. Secondly, legal positivism and non-cognitivism make apparently similar claims: legal positivism insists on the distinction between the law as it is and the law as it ought to be, while non-cognitivism asserts that what ought to be the case cannot be derived from what is the case. These sound like similar claims but in fact they are very different.

Legal positivism is a theory about the nature of *law*, not about the nature of *moral judgments*. It is a 'positivistic' theory because it takes the view that all law is 'posited'—that law owes its existence ultimately to human decisions or practices. This is different from the non-cognitivist or logical positivist view that moral standards do not have a rational basis. Legal positivists may be non-cognitivists, but they do not have to be.

Bentham and Austin, for instance, accepted cognitivism, or as it is also sometimes called, 'moral realism' (see 2.5). They believed that the standards of justice are universal and objective. The particular moral theory which Bentham and Austin took to be objectively true was utilitarianism. We will discuss this theory in 10.3. It states that the standards of right conduct are to be found in the 'greatest happiness principle'. Laws that do not serve the end of maximum human happiness are therefore objectively unjust, according to Bentham and Austin, but their injustice is no barrier to their enjoying legal status. Bentham and Austin therefore combine cognitivism about ethics with legal positivism. On their view, it is an objective moral fact that the law *ought* to conform to utilitarian standards, but laws that fail to do so do not lose their character as laws.

A second misconception is to suppose that positivists believe that there is no *need* for laws to meet moral standards—that they believe, as Leslie Green puts it, that 'law and morality should be *kept separate* (as if the separation of law and morals were like the separation of church and state)'.[6] The truth, of course, is that positivists are not indifferent to the justice or injustice of law. On the contrary, they believe that although laws may not be just, they *should* be just, and that unjust laws should be criticised and reformed.

---

[6] L Green, 'Positivism and the Inseparability of Law and Morals' (2008) 83 *New York University Law Review* 1035, 1035–6, Green's emphasis.

A third mistake is to think that positivists claim that law and morality are necessarily *separate* or must *diverge*.[7] Apart from recognising that law is shaped by popular morality, positivists also believe that many legal systems are morally legitimate and that many laws are morally defensible from the perspective of critical morality. For instance, the actions that law prohibits are usually those that morality also condemns. They point out, however, that this does not disprove the thesis that law and morality are *separable*, because such overlap between law and critical morality is a purely contingent, not a necessary, matter. In fact, even if all the legal systems we happen to have come across were morally acceptable, this would not disprove the positivist thesis, because positivism does not say that law and morality *cannot* coincide. It says only that there is nothing in the nature of law that *necessitates* such convergence.

Hart even argues that the separability thesis is compatible with the recognition that a *viable* legal system will have to include rules whose content overlaps with moral rules. Hart believes that a legal system will be unable to serve the 'minimum purpose of survival which men have in associating with each other'[8] unless it includes rules that, for instance, restrict the use of violence and protect property. If a legal system did not punish violence and theft, society would soon degenerate into a state of anarchy. And since rules prohibiting violence and protecting property are of benefit to those whom they protect, Hart concludes that every viable legal system must contain some rules of moral value.[9] He makes the point, however, that such inevitable overlap between law and morality is not a conceptual truth. It is the result of contingent facts about the human situation, such as our vulnerability to attack, the limits on our altruism and the scarcity of resources. The overlap is also very minimal, being geared to survival only. It is therefore compatible with great iniquity and discrimination in the law. Hart states that 'though a society to be viable must offer some of its members a system of mutual forbearances, it need not, unfortunately, offer them to all'.[10] Thus slave-owning societies that protect the slave-owners but not the slaves from violence and theft will meet the minimum standard.[11]

Fourthly, positivists do not deny that judges should sometimes decide cases on moral grounds. Although positivism is frequently associated with the

---

7 M H Kramer, *In Defense of Legal Positivism: Law without Trimmings*, Oxford University Press, Oxford, 1999, p 2.
8 Hart, above n 2, p 193.
9 Ibid pp 193–200.
10 Ibid p 201.
11 Ibid p 200.

belief that judges should never have regard to the merits of cases when deciding them, this is another misconception.[12] As we saw in 3.8, Hart believes (as do other positivists) that there are situations that are not covered by the existing law. In order to resolve such cases, positivists say, judges have to exercise discretion. And in so doing they are permitted to rely on moral and policy considerations, and therefore to choose what the law ought to be. Of course, the new rule created in the course of resolving such a dispute will become part of the law, which later judges in lower courts are bound by the doctrine of precedent to apply, but it is the fact that it can now be found in a judicial decision which gives it its legal status, not its moral acceptability.

Even in easy cases, positivists do not necessarily adhere to the formalistic view (to be discussed in 6.4) that judges should always apply legal rules without regard to the merits of doing so.[13] This is because positivism is a theory with a limited scope: it is a theory only about the nature of law or the conditions necessary for the existence of law. It does not set out to provide answers to other philosophical questions about law, including questions about the circumstances in which judges or citizens are under a moral obligation to comply with the law. Views about such matters are prescriptive, whereas the aims of positivism are descriptive. It aims to tell us what law is, not whether it ought to be obeyed or applied. As John Gardner explains: 'To show that valid legal norms are ever worth having or following, and in what way, always requires a separate argument, regarding which [positivism] is in itself entirely agnostic.'[14]

Yet many critics of positivism miss this point. It is a common misconception that positivism is an immoral approach that legitimises the laws of the state and demands blind obedience to those laws, however tyrannical they may be. Hobbes is probably the positivist who comes closest to taking this view, although even Hobbes thinks that there are circumstances in which disobedience to the law is justifiable. And Hart expressly rejects the idea that officials are under a duty to apply and enforce the law and citizens under a duty to obey it, regardless of the law's merits. Hart thinks that we should not place too much value on 'the bare fact that a rule may be said to be a valid rule of law, as if this, once declared, [were] conclusive of the final moral question: "Ought this rule of law to be obeyed?"'[15] On the contrary, Hart thinks that

---

12 J Gardner, 'Legal Positivism: 5½ Myths' (2001) 46 *American Journal of Jurisprudence* 199, 211–12.
13 Ibid 213.
14 Ibid 225.
15 Hart, above n 4, 618.

officials may be justified in refusing to enforce grossly unfair or unjust laws and that citizens may be justified in refusing to obey them. Their moral obligations in such cases trump their legal obligations.

In a well-known debate between Hart and Lon Fuller on the separability thesis, Fuller claimed that even if positivism does not, strictly speaking, entail the thesis that we are obliged to obey all laws no matter how tyrannical they may be, in practice its effect is to encourage blind obedience. This led him to conclude that the willingness to call evil dictates 'laws' is dangerous, because merely calling something 'law' leads judges and others to believe that they ought to obey it. Referring in particular to the Nazi regime, Fuller argued that positivism played a role in Hitler's rise to power because it made German lawyers and judges 'peculiarly prepared to accept as "law" anything that called itself by that name'.[16] Hart responded by arguing that in fact the opposite is the case. Hart claimed that citizens and officials who accept the positivist view that law is conventional and that ascription of legal status to a rule does not convey automatic moral approval of the rule—those who see the law for what it is, rather than through rose-tinted spectacles—will be *more* rather than less likely to resist tyrannical laws.[17]

In maintaining that positivism encourages an appropriately critical attitude to the law, Hart is claiming that the distinction between legal and moral validity has desirable moral consequences. This interest in the practical consequences of positivism goes back to the early positivists, such as Bentham. They thought that the distinction between the law as it is and the law as it ought to be facilitates a demystifying and reforming attitude to the law, and Hart finds positivism morally attractive for similar reasons. Instead of venerating the law, positivism, in Hart's view, encourages individuals to rely on their own conscience when confronting a powerful state. Hart tells us that the law does not automatically deserve our respect but must *earn* it:

> What surely is most needed in order to make men clear-sighted in confronting the official abuse of power, is that they should preserve the sense that the certification of something as legally valid is not conclusive of the question of obedience, and that, however great the aura of majesty or authority which the official system may have, its demands must in the end be submitted to a moral scrutiny.[18]

---

16 L L Fuller, 'Positivism and Fidelity to Law—A Reply to Professor Hart' (1958) 71 *Harvard Law Review* 630, 659.
17 For a detailed critique of the plausibility of Fuller's claim that positivism was causally connected to the rise of Nazism, see S L Paulson, 'Lon L Fuller, Gustav Radbruch, and the "Positivist" Theses' (1994) 13 *Law and Philosophy* 313.
18 Hart, above n 2, p 210.

It should be noted that Hart's suggestion that the separability thesis is beneficial in encouraging us to see the law as it is, warts and all, is a somewhat more speculative claim than the more familiar arguments that the separability thesis is theoretically correct, deepens our understanding of the nature of law and clarifies our reasoning. Furthermore, it is not clear whether Hart is arguing that the beneficial consequences of a belief in the separability thesis are a *reason* to believe it or whether he is merely saying that the separability thesis is true and that good consequences would flow from the recognition of its truth.

Some legal theorists have embraced the first of these approaches, arguing for the acceptance of the distinction between legal and moral validity on the 'practical-political' ground that those who accept it are more likely to resist unjust laws. Thus Liam Murphy argues that 'the best place to locate the boundary of law [and morality] is where it will have the best effect on our self-understanding as a society, on our political culture'.[19] But how can the fact that it would have good consequences if we were to accept the separability thesis have any bearing on whether the thesis is true? As Wilfred Waluchow says, true theories can have undesirable practical consequences and having good consequences does not make a theory true.[20]

Murphy responds to this objection by saying that there is no truth of the matter about where the boundary between law and morality lies, and that this frees us to draw the boundary in the way that positivists do, with a view to discouraging uncritical acceptance of the law.[21] Hart would not, however, agree that there is no truth about this matter. It is therefore more plausible to interpret Hart's response to Fuller not as an argument for the separability thesis on moral and political grounds, but rather as making the claim mentioned above: that the separability thesis is true and the general recognition that it is true would have good moral and political consequences.[22]

A fifth mistake is to identify positivism with the view that the existence and content of law can always be ascertained in a morally neutral way and that moral judgments therefore have no role to play when judges identify the law or say what it is. Although this is the view of some positivists, it is not the view of all of them. As we will see in 4.4, inclusive positivists believe that moral reasoning may be required not only when the law does not cover a particular situation, but

---

19 L Murphy, 'Concepts of Law' (2005) 30 *Australian Journal of Legal Philosophy* 1, 9.
20 W J Waluchow, *Inclusive Legal Positivism*, Clarendon Press, Oxford, 1994, pp 88–90.
21 Murphy, above n 19, 9.
22 A Marmor, 'Legal Positivism: Still Descriptive and Morally Neutral' (2006) 26 *Oxford Journal of Legal Studies* 683, 684.

even to determine what the *existing* law requires. They believe that moral validity *can,* though need not, be a condition for legal validity because moral criteria of legal validity can be included in the rule of recognition. This view was developed in response to points made by Dworkin in his very important early articles, 'The Model of Rules I' and 'The Model of Rules II'. Dworkin's work contains a sustained challenge to positivism, to which it offers a highly sophisticated alternative. We will return in Chapter 6 to Dworkin's own theory of law, but our focus in this chapter will be on the way in which the views Dworkin expressed in these early articles led to an important debate as to the core commitments of positivism.

4.3 Dworkin's attack on positivism

In 'The Model of Rules I', Dworkin states that one of the central propositions to which positivists are committed is the view that 'the law of a community … can be identified and distinguished by specific criteria, by tests having to do not with their content but with their *pedigree* or the manner in which they were adopted or developed'.[23] Dworkin characterises positivism, in other words, as taking the view that the criteria of legality contained in the rule of recognition must refer exclusively to social or institutional sources: what makes a standard a legal standard is the fact that it has, for instance, been authoritatively posited in legislation or a judicial decision and not the fact that it is just or fair. It is a matter of conforming to certain *formal* or *pedigree* or *non-moral* criteria.

In later work, Dworkin puts forward a similar characterisation of positivism, now saying that positivism takes a 'plain-fact' view of the law. By 'plain facts', Dworkin means social facts (see 2.5). He distinguishes between 'propositions of law' and 'grounds of law'. Propositions of law are statements about the law's requirements, whereas the grounds of law are what make propositions of law true. Thus 'no one may drive over 55 miles an hour in California' is a proposition of law, whereas the fact that the Californian legislature enacted this rule is what makes this proposition true.[24] The plain-fact view holds that the grounds of law are always historical facts. Dworkin writes:

> The law [on the plain-fact view] is only a matter of what legal institutions, like legislatures and city councils and courts, have decided in the past. If some body of that sort has decided that workmen can recover compensation for

---

23   R Dworkin, *Taking Rights Seriously*, Duckworth, London, 1977, p 17, Dworkin's emphasis.
24   R Dworkin, *Law's Empire*, Belknap Press of Harvard University Press, Cambridge, MA, 1986, p 4.

injuries by fellow workmen, then that is the law. If it has decided the other way, then that is the law. So questions of law can always be answered by looking in the books where the records of institutional decisions are kept.[25]

Thus, on the plain-fact view, the grounds of law are never moral: 'law is always a matter of historical fact and never depends on morality'.[26]

Having characterised positivism in this way, Dworkin goes on to reject it, arguing that it is incompatible with the role played by moral arguments in actual legal cases. Dworkin makes three points in this regard. First, he points out that judges often resort to *moral principles* to resolve hard cases when the rules of law do not seem to generate an answer. He observes that the identification of these principles is controversial, as is their weight, and that they are not necessarily to be found in the discrete set of explicit rules laid down by institutional office-holders. They may be part of the much larger set of moral and political norms that are recognised in society more generally. Principles, he concludes, are not special standards that can be said to count as 'legal standards' by virtue of meeting certain criteria of validity contained in a rule of recognition. Secondly, Dworkin argues that the appeal to such principles is not discretionary, as suggested by Hart, when he said that judges may exercise their discretion by appealing to moral principles in hard cases. Dworkin says that judges think of themselves as *legally obliged* to follow them when they apply, and he thinks that this makes it plausible to infer that moral principles are legally binding on judges. Dworkin's third point is that judges take these principles to be *present in the law*, despite the fact that they may lack a pedigree in a written or black-letter source of law and therefore do not owe their legal authority to the fact that they satisfy conditions laid down by the rule of recognition. It is, according to Dworkin, their truth as principles of critical morality which makes them part of the law.[27] There is therefore no sharp line to be drawn between legal standards and moral standards: principles of morality may be relevant to determining people's legal rights.

We will return to some of these points in 6.5 and 6.6, when we will discuss in more detail Dworkin's distinction between rules and principles and his attack on Hart's notion of discretion. For present purposes, however, our interest is confined to Dworkin's claim that positivism cannot account for the role of moral principles in the law. In order to support this claim, Dworkin makes reference to

---

25 Ibid p 7.
26 Ibid p 9.
27 Dworkin, above n 23, p 40.

two United States cases. In *Riggs v Palmer*,[28] the question was whether a grandson who had poisoned his grandfather so as to prevent him from changing his will could inherit under the will. The court noted that on a literal reading of the relevant statute the grandson was entitled to take his inheritance. But it went on to say: '[A]ll laws as well as all contracts may be controlled in their operation and effect by general, fundamental maxims of the common law. No one shall be permitted to profit by his own fraud, or to take advantage of his own wrong, or to found any claim upon his own iniquity, or to acquire property by his own crime.'[29] The court found that the grandson therefore could not inherit. Dworkin sees this as an example of a court invoking moral standards so as to create a previously unknown exception to an unambiguous rule, while also holding that its decision was somehow already prefigured in the law.

In *Henningsen v Bloomfield Motors, Inc.*,[30] the question was whether a manufacturer of motor cars could escape liability for the expenses of persons injured in an accident due to defects in a car, by invoking a clause in the contract that excluded such liability. There was no explicit rule of law authorising the court to ignore the clause. The court nevertheless held that the manufacturer could not rely on it, invoking several principles of fairness which outweighed, in its view, the competing principle of freedom of contract. It held that car manufacturers are under special obligations in connection with the construction, promotion and sale of their products, in contrast to other manufacturers; that courts will not allow themselves to be used as instruments of inequity and injustice; and that courts will seek to protect those who are economically vulnerable. Dworkin writes: 'The origin of [the *Riggs* and *Henningsen* principles] as legal principles lies not in a particular decision of some legislature or court, but in a sense of appropriateness developed in the profession and the public over time.'[31] They are part of the law, in other words, by virtue of their moral content or moral merits and they can therefore be discovered only via the use of moral reasoning.

Dworkin's analysis of cases such as *Riggs* and *Henningsen* has three components. He argues that the judges are not relying on plain facts but rather on moral principles, which are not to be found in the law reports or in statutes. He also argues that the judges are finding the law, not making it. Thirdly, he assumes that positivism must be committed to exclusively source-based criteria

---

28 *Riggs v Palmer*, 115 NY 506 (1889).
29 *Riggs v Palmer*, 115 NY 506, 511 (1889).
30 *Henningsen v Bloomfield Motors, Inc.*, 32 NJ 358 (1960).
31 Dworkin, above n 23, p 40.

of legal validity—that, according to positivists, law must be a matter of social facts and never moral facts. If *all* of these points are true, positivism has indeed been presented with an insuperable problem. If judges frequently draw on moral considerations in the process of determining what the existing law requires, and if positivism is committed to the plain-fact view of law, positivism must be rejected.

Positivists responded to Dworkin's challenge by accepting the truth of his observation that judges are often obliged to apply moral principles in deciding legal cases, but arguing that this does not refute positivism. There are two versions of this response, which differ according to the explanation they provide of how positivism can explain Dworkin's observation.[32] One response involves rejecting Dworkin's characterisation of positivism. Dworkin assumes that when positivists say that law is distinguishable from morality, they must mean that moral soundness *cannot* be a source of law. If this is what they do mean, and if moral principles are sometimes legally determinative, Dworkin would be right that positivism is false. Inclusive positivists argue, however, that Dworkin has misinterpreted the separability thesis. They agree with Dworkin's claim that moral principles can be part of the law, but they say that the separability thesis is compatible with moral tests for identifying law: they argue that the criteria contained in a rule of recognition do not have to refer only to the pedigree or social source of rules. The rule of recognition might include moral principles, such as the *Riggs* and *Henningsen* principles, as criteria for valid law.

Exclusive positivists, on the other hand, do take the plain-fact view of law. They think that it is impossible for moral principles to be valid law by virtue of their merits or moral content. At the same time, they agree with Dworkin that judges often appeal to moral principles in deciding cases, and indeed, that judges may be obliged to do so. They explain this in the following way. First, they argue that moral principles can be part of valid law in the same way that rules are part of valid law, namely, because of their pedigree or social source. In such cases, the status of the moral principles as law depends on the fact that they have, for instance, been recognised in the past by courts.[33] While this answer might cover the case of *Riggs*, inasmuch as the majority argued that the principle that no one may profit from his or her own wrongdoing had been previously invoked by courts, it does not

---

[32] J Coleman, 'Incorporationism, Conventionality and the Practical Difference Thesis', in J Coleman (ed), *Hart's Postscript: Essays on the Postscript to* The Concept of Law, Oxford University Press, Oxford, 2001, pp 125–7.

[33] J Raz, 'Legal Principles and the Limits of Law' (1972) 81 *Yale Law Journal* 823, 848.

cover cases such as *Henningsen*, because no court had previously enunciated the principle that car manufacturers should be held to higher standards than other manufacturers. Yet the court felt obliged to apply the principle.

In response to cases such as *Henningsen*, the exclusive positivists concede that in hard cases judges may be under an obligation to apply non-pedigreed moral principles, but they deny that such principles are *legal* principles. In their view, judges are in such cases under an obligation to apply *non-legal* norms. It follows that, regardless of whether judges are obliged to apply a moral principle that lacks a pedigree or whether they invoke such principles in the exercise of their discretion, they are, according to exclusive positivists, deciding not what the existing law is but what it ought to be. Their decision may be correct in terms of moral standards but it is not correct in terms of legal standards and it acquires the status of law only once it has been handed down. We turn to examine these different schools of positivism now.

4.4 Inclusive positivism

Inclusive positivists, such as Hart (who embraced the theory in his later work, referring to it as 'soft' positivism), Jules Coleman and Wilfred Waluchow, reject the view that what the law is on some matter necessarily depends only on empirically discoverable historical facts, such as legislation and judicial decisions. Inclusive positivists say that the rule of recognition is whatever rule happens to be accepted by judges in a particular society as setting out the criteria of legality. There is nothing in this picture, they say, requiring that the criteria provided by the rule of recognition must be restricted to non-moral, historical facts, such as Acts of Parliament and precedents. 'There is', Hart says, 'no logical restriction on the content of the rule of recognition'.[34] Since what makes a norm a legal norm is simply a matter of variable social practice, judges may be required by such practice to make reference to matters of moral merit in deciding questions of legal validity. In such cases, moral principles would be part of the law in virtue of their merits. David Lyons sums up the argument like this:

> Hart seems to place no limits on the sort of test that might be employed by officials and the reason is simple: unlike other legal rules, the rule of recognition may be said to exist only by virtue of the actual practice of officials. Nothing else determines the content of this rule. The tests for law in

---

34 H L A Hart, *Essays in Jurisprudence and Philosophy*, Clarendon Press, Oxford, 1983, p 361.

a system are whatever officials make them—and Hart suggests no limits on the possibilities.[35]

Thus a particular rule of recognition might specify that morality is *necessary* for legal validity in that legal system, and some inclusive positivists hold that a rule of recognition might even specify that morality is *sufficient* for validity in the system.

Let us begin with the weaker possibility that morality may be a necessary ground for legal validity in terms of a rule of recognition. In some countries, such as the United Kingdom, judges accept the conventional rule that parliament is sovereign (leaving aside certain issues arising from British membership of the European Union). In these countries there are no legal restrictions on parliament's lawmaking power that derive from moral (or any other) principles. By contrast, in countries such as the United States, according to Hart, 'the ultimate criteria of legal validity ... explicitly incorporate besides pedigree, principles of justice or substantive moral values'.[36]

Hart is here referring to the fact that in countries such as the United States, we find constitutions with bills of rights expressed in abstract moral language. For instance, the US Constitution grants rights to the 'equal protection' of the laws and to 'due process'. All laws must respect these moral principles and judges in the United States are consequently not confined to investigating whether a law has been duly enacted or adopted (Dworkin's matters of 'pedigree') but are frequently required to engage in political and moral theorising. For instance, they have had to decide whether laws that allow for affirmative action violate the right to be treated equally, or whether the procedures stipulated by a law are fair or unfair. These are questions of political morality. They require investigation of the justice or the merits of the law.

The inclusive positivists explain this in the following way. They say that by virtue of the rule of recognition in the United States (and in other systems which either expressly or as a matter of practice measure legislation against moral standards), compliance with whatever aspects of critical or sound morality have been included in the law is a threshold condition of validity, which any law must meet to be considered a law. In these legal systems, courts are obliged to consider the moral merits of law because it is impossible for valid laws to breach certain moral principles and any attempt by the legislature to pass laws

---

35 D Lyons, 'Principles, Positivism and Legal Theory' (1977) 87 *Yale Law Journal* 415, 423–4.
36 Hart, above n 2, p 247.

in conflict with them will be struck down by the courts as invalid. (For further discussion of invalidation of legislation under a bill of rights, see 10.10.) Morality is therefore, according to inclusive positivists, a necessary condition for legal validity in these systems.

Dworkin's critique of positivism, however, revolved around common law cases in which morality was apparently a sufficient ground of legal validity, with the decisions in these cases seemingly justified solely on the basis that they were required by morality. Thus, according to Dworkin, the moral correctness of forbidding the grandson in *Riggs* to inherit was a sufficient condition for its status as a legal norm. Some inclusive positivists—who are sometimes called 'Incorporationists'—respond by agreeing with Dworkin that morality can be a sufficient condition for legal validity, but they claim that this is not incompatible with positivism. They say that there is nothing to stop a rule of recognition from specifying that moral correctness is, in some or perhaps even all circumstances, sufficient to make a norm a legal norm. On such a rule of recognition, rules would be law only *because* they are just or fair. Coleman takes this view. Matthew Kramer explains the Incorporationist view as follows:

> An Incorporationist theorist maintains that moral principles regularly regarded by officials as legally determinative are indeed legal norms, notwithstanding that they have perhaps never been laid down in any explicit sources such as legislative enactments or judicial rulings. When officials do regularly engage in a practice of treating the moral soundness of norms as a sufficient condition for the norms' legal authoritativeness, they have thereby incorporated moral principles into the law of their system of governance.[37]

Dworkin is therefore wrong to claim that positivism is committed to the view that law is necessarily a matter of non-moral facts. On the contrary, inclusive positivists believe that there is nothing in the nature of law that rules out the relevance of matters of moral value to legal validity. This is because the rule of recognition is whatever judges accept as the standard that they are bound to follow. In some legal systems, the practice of judges may be to identify legal norms and determine their content without recourse to moral tests. In other systems, however, their practice may be to test putative legal norms by reference to their moral merits or even to apply moral principles as binding laws, as in Dworkin's examples. If so, moral principles will be part of that community's law.

---

37 M H Kramer, *Where Law and Morality Meet,* Oxford University Press, Oxford, 2004, p 3.

This allows inclusive positivists to agree with Dworkin's argument that judges frequently regard moral considerations as part of the law.

If law is not necessarily a matter of non-moral facts but may depend on morality, it might be wondered how inclusive positivists can affirm the two key positivist theses that were outlined in 2.5: the social constructivist thesis that law owes its existence to contingent social facts and the separability thesis that law and morality are conceptually distinct (that the existence of law is one thing and its merit or demerit another). The answer to this is as follows. First, inclusive positivists maintain that whether morality has been made part of the law is a matter of social fact. When morality has been made part of the law that will be by virtue of a social rule, the rule of recognition, whose existence is a matter of acceptance by legal officials and is therefore a matter of social fact. The *existence* of such a rule of recognition, one that includes moral tests for legal validity, is therefore purely a matter of social fact, even though the question of whether a particular rule *satisfies* the criteria of legal validity contained in the rule of recognition may not be. So the positivist view of law as a social construction is retained. Although the validity of particular laws may depend on their moral merits, it is a social or customary practice that makes the merits of laws relevant to their validity and therefore, on the inclusive positivist picture, law depends *ultimately* on social facts alone.[38] The social constructivist thesis remains intact.

Secondly, inclusive positivists argue that since it is an empirical or factual matter as to whether judges in a particular system use moral tests in deciding questions of legal validity, if this kind of connection between law and morality happens to exist, it is just another contingent connection of the kind that the separability thesis does not deny. The separability thesis, inclusive positivists say, is about what *need not* be the case rather than about what *cannot be* the case. Thus the separability thesis, as they interpret it, states merely that morality is not *necessarily* a criterion of legal validity, not that it is *impossible* for morality to play a role in identifying valid law.[39] Or, as Kramer formulates the separability thesis: 'no legal system *has* to include moral principles among its criteria for ascertaining the law', but 'any legal system *can* include moral principles among those criteria'.[40] And since it is quite possible that the rule of recognition in a particular system might refer only to non-moral or pedigree criteria of legality, inclusive

---

38 J D Goldsworthy, 'The Self-Destruction of Legal Positivism' (1990) 10 *Oxford Journal of Legal Studies* 449, 452-3.
39 J Coleman, 'Negative and Positive Positivism' (1982) 11 *Journal of Legal Studies* 139, 141-2.
40 Kramer, above n 7, p 152, Kramer's emphasis.

positivism is compatible with the separability thesis: morality as a condition of legal validity is not inherent in the very nature of law.

4.5 Is inclusive positivism an acceptable theory of law?

Is inclusive positivism an acceptable theory of law? Dworkin thinks not, and this view is shared by some positivists—positivists of the exclusive kind. Let us begin with Dworkin's objections to inclusive positivism. For one thing, he rejects the view that moral reasoning plays a role in legal argument only as a contingent matter, namely, if it happens to be recognised as relevant by a particular legal system. As we will see in Chapter 6, Dworkin thinks that the identification of the law is an interpretive enterprise, which *necessarily* involves sound moral judgment.

Secondly, faced with the inclusive positivist argument that positivism is not committed to the plain-fact view of law, Dworkin counter-argues that there are inconsistencies between inclusive positivism and other key positivist commitments and hence that inclusive positivism is positivism only in a 'Pickwickian' sense: '[I]t is not positivism at all, but only an attempt to keep the name "positivism" for a conception of law and legal practice that is entirely alien to positivism.'[41] Dworkin provides two arguments for his belief that inclusive positivism is really a surrender of positivism.

Dworkin's first argument is that it is impossible to accept the inclusive positivist thesis that moral principles of the sort invoked in *Riggs* and in *Henningsen* can count as law while simultaneously holding the view that in every legal system there is a social rule supplying the standards of legal validity. This is because we speak of social rules only where there is regular behaviour or *agreement* about how to behave. But morality is inherently *controversial* and judges will therefore inevitably disagree about what morality requires. Dworkin argues, in other words, that positivists cannot accept moral criteria of legal validity, which are in their nature controversial, while also conceptualising law as ultimately based on an agreed-upon test for determining which standards count as law. A rule of recognition that directs judges to have recourse to moral considerations therefore cannot be a social rule.[42]

---

41 R Dworkin, *Justice in Robes*, Belknap Press of Harvard University Press, Cambridge, MA, 2006, p 188.
42 Ibid p 190.

Inclusive positivists attempt to answer this challenge by distinguishing between controversy or disagreement about the *content* of a rule and disagreement about its *applicability*. They maintain that the disagreements to which Dworkin refers are merely disagreements about application, not about content, and that such disagreements do not threaten the social status of the rule of recognition. Inclusive positivists concede that if there were widespread controversy about the content of the rule of recognition—if, for instance, judges disagreed as to whether there is a duty to apply moral principles in adjudication—then the rule of recognition could not be a social rule. If judges were unsure as to what rule they were supposed to be following, there could not be a social practice of following the rule. But, they say, the disagreements to which Dworkin refers are disagreements about what the rule requires in particular cases. They are disagreements about what the requirements of morality are in a particular case and therefore about which norms satisfy the conditions of legality set out in the rule of recognition. Such 'application' disagreements *presuppose agreement about the content of the rule.* They are therefore compatible with its social status.[43] Hart makes the same point in the *Postscript* to *The Concept of Law*, saying:

> [T]he function of the rule [of recognition] is to determine only the general conditions which correct legal decisions must satisfy in modern systems of law ... Of course in particular cases judges may disagree as to whether such tests are satisfied or not ... Judges may be agreed on the relevance of such tests as something settled by established judicial practice even though they disagree as to what the tests require in particular cases.[44]

Dworkin finds the distinction between the content of the rule and its applicability 'doubtful',[45] but quite apart from these doubts (which cannot be considered here), he also has another reason for thinking that inclusive positivism is incompatible with other key positivist commitments. He argues that a rule of recognition that directs judges to have recourse to controversial moral considerations is incompatible with the positivist view of law's *function*, namely, that of providing reliable public standards of conduct.[46] If moral argument

---

43 J Coleman, *The Practice of Principle: In Defence of a Pragmatist Approach to Legal Theory*, Oxford University Press, Oxford, 2001, p 116.
44 Hart, above n 2, pp 258–9.
45 R Dworkin, 'A Reply by Ronald Dworkin', in M Cohen (ed), *Ronald Dworkin and Contemporary Jurisprudence*, Rowman and Allanheld, Totowa, New Jersey, 1984, p 252; Dworkin, above n 41, pp 191–4.
46 R Dworkin, 'A Reply by Ronald Dworkin', in M Cohen (ed), *Ronald Dworkin and Contemporary Jurisprudence*, Rowman and Allanheld, Totowa, New Jersey, 1984, p 248.

were required to ascertain the validity or content of laws, the law would not be able to pick out in an uncontroversial way the patterns of behaviour that are required of us. Hence inclusive positivism is incompatible with the positivist view of law's function.

Inclusive positivists have two responses to this point. One is to deny that positivism is committed to the view that law's primary or overriding function is to resolve social issues in ways that are certain and determinate. Thus Hart points out that values such as certainty and determinacy compete with values such as flexibility, and he says he does not believe that it is an essential feature of law that it should always choose to resolve disputes certainly rather than flexibly. Indeed, Hart takes the view that a margin of uncertainty is not only *inevitable*—he believes, as we saw in 3.8, that no rule, including the rule of recognition, can be entirely clear—but actually *desirable*. It is desirable because it leaves room for judges to make appropriate choices when unanticipated cases arise, instead of 'blindly prejudging what it is to be done in a range of future cases, about whose composition we are ignorant'.[47] Hart therefore thinks that even if the vagueness in ordinary legal rules could be eliminated, or at least reduced, to do so would be undesirable. In his view, legal rules should sometimes deliberately be framed loosely, using vague terms such as 'reasonable' and 'fair', so as to allow judges the latitude to arrive at sensible results in unforeseen future cases. For the same reason, a rule of recognition that makes reference to moral values that are in some respects indeterminate may serve a valuable purpose. Hart writes:

> [T]he exclusion of all uncertainty at whatever costs in other values is not a goal which I have ever envisaged for the rule of recognition … Only if the certainty-providing function of the rule of recognition is treated as paramount and overriding could the form of soft positivism that includes among the criteria of law conformity with moral principles or values which may be controversial be regarded as inconsistent.[48]

A second response to Dworkin's argument against inclusive positivism is to question whether rules whose validity depends on meeting moral tests are necessarily incapable of providing reliable public standards of conduct. After all, some moral questions are uncontroversial and easily resolved. As Waluchow says, they may indeed be easier to resolve than some of the controversies which attend the interpretation and application of rules whose validity depends only

---

47 Hart, above n 2, p 130.
48 Ibid, pp 251–2.

on matters of pedigree.[49] Waluchow points out that in Canada, where there is a constitutional bill of rights (called the 'Canadian Charter of Rights and Freedoms'), 'normally it is clear that no Charter right is unreasonably infringed, and so the validity and content of Canadian law is seldom challenged on these grounds. Everyone knows that almost all Canadian law satisfies the Charter and acts accordingly.'[50] Hart argues along these lines as well, saying that we should not 'exaggerate ... the uncertainty which will result if the criteria of legal validity include conformity with specific moral principles or values'.[51]

4.6 Raz's exclusive positivism

We turn now to exclusive positivism. As we have seen, inclusive positivists say that there can be moral criteria of legal validity. They claim that this is consistent with the separability thesis because in their view the separability thesis asserts merely that morality is not necessarily a condition of legality. Exclusive positivists disagree. They say that, necessarily, morality is not a condition of legality.[52] They say, in other words, that the morality of a norm *cannot* be a condition of its legality, not even as a contingent matter: moral criteria of legal validity are conceptually impossible. They therefore take the plain-fact view of law: what the law is on any matter can be determined solely by a non-moral inquiry concerning the enactment or declaration of legal rules in parliaments and courts.

It will be obvious that exclusive positivism offers a much more stringent version of the separability thesis than inclusive positivism. It insists, as Frederick Schauer says, on the 'actual not just conceptual separation of law and morality'.[53] On the exclusive positivist view, law is a 'limited domain of plainly pedigreed legal materials'.[54] Exclusive positivists therefore draw a very sharp line between law and non-law, seeing law as a necessarily autonomous or 'sealed off' domain—one in which only certain kinds of arguments are valid.[55] They distinguish the narrow domain of legal norms from the much larger set of norms—moral, social, conventional and political—which are recognised more generally in society and on which non-legal decision-makers legitimately draw.[56]

---

49 Waluchow, above n 20, p 122.
50 Ibid p 186.
51 Hart, above n 2, p 251.
52 Coleman, above n 43, pp 151–2.
53 F Schauer, 'The Limited Domain of the Law' (2004) 90 *Virginia Law Review* 1909, 1948.
54 Ibid 1942.
55 Ibid 1943.
56 Ibid 1951.

I will focus on the writings of Joseph Raz, who provides a powerful defence of exclusive positivism. (Other important exclusive positivists are Andrei Marmor and Scott Shapiro.) Raz argues that law necessarily consists only of source-based or pedigreed standards: the fact that a standard has moral value can never be a criterion of legal validity. The tests for determining whether a rule is 'law' must, in other words, refer only to facts concerning its institutional source or social source in, for instance, legislation, a past judicial ruling or custom. Furthermore, the tests for identifying the content of legal rules must refer only to facts about human beings—for instance, their intentions in enacting legislation and deciding cases—that once again can be described in value-free terms.[57]

Raz does not think that these facts are necessarily easy to discover. On the contrary, he thinks that they may depend on very complex reasoning and that attributing views or intentions to legal institutions may be a controversial matter.[58] Such attribution is, nevertheless, in Raz's view, based on non-moral, factual criteria. Social facts therefore figure twice in Raz's theory of law. Raz agrees with the inclusive positivists that the criteria of legal validity are accepted by officials as a matter of common practice and therefore owe their existence to social facts. However, in contrast to the inclusive positivists, he also asserts that it must be possible to establish the validity and content of particular legal rules by reference only to social facts, concerning matters such as events that have taken place in parliament, decisions made by judges, and the morally neutral meaning of the terms of legal rules.[59] For Raz, therefore, the criteria for identifying valid laws owe their existence to social facts and the identification of law in terms of those criteria involves purely factual, non-moral reasoning. Law is therefore not only *ultimately* but also *exclusively* a matter of social facts.[60] Raz takes this view, which he calls the 'sources thesis',[61] because he believes that moral tests for identifying the content of the law and determining its existence are inconsistent with law's claim to be a practical authority.

What is a 'practical authority'? Let us begin with the concept of a 'theoretical authority', on which the concept of a practical authority is modelled. A theoretical authority is an authority on matters of belief. As Hart explains, if a scientist is regarded as an authority on some subject, then the fact that he or

---

57 J Raz, *The Authority of Law: Essays on Law and Morality*, Clarendon Press, Oxford, 1979, pp 39–40, 47–8.
58 J Raz, 'Authority, Law and Morality' (1985) 68 *The Monist* 295, 316.
59 K E Himma, 'Inclusive Legal Positivism', in J Coleman and S Shapiro (eds), *The Oxford Handbook of Jurisprudence and Philosophy of Law*, Oxford University Press, Oxford, 2002, pp 127–8.
60 For this distinction, see Goldsworthy, above n 38, 452.
61 Raz, above n 57, p 47.

she believes something is a reason for me to believe the same thing. If scientists believe that hydrogen is the lightest gas, that is a reason for me to believe this as well, without any need for independent investigation on my part. The scientists' belief therefore provides me with a 'content-independent' reason for my belief. It is content-independent in the sense that my reason for believing it is a function of the fact that the scientists believe it and has nothing to do with my being persuaded by the content or substance of the scientists' arguments.[62]

By analogy, a practical authority has authority over us in what Hart calls 'matters of conduct'.[63] A person has practical authority when the fact that that person has told me to do something provides a content-independent reason for me to act in that way. The reason is a function of the fact that someone or some institution that has authority has told me to behave in a certain way. It is a function of the person's or institution's status as an authority—not, as Hart says, a function of 'the nature or character of the action to be done'.[64] Schauer gives the example of a parent's exasperated yell, 'Because I said so!', as an example of an authoritative order. Children who treat their parents as an authority accept that the sheer say-so of the parent gives them a reason to do as told. It is the source of the directive, not its content, that makes it into a reason for them.[65]

Raz explains the notion of content-independence as follows:

> A reason is content-independent if there is no direct connection between the reason and the action for which it is a reason. The reason is in the apparently 'extraneous' fact that someone in authority has said so, and within certain limits his saying so would be reason for any number of actions, including ... for contradictory ones. A certain authority may command me to leave the room or to stay in it. Either way, its command will be a reason.[66]

Authoritative directives are therefore content-independent reasons for action. Furthermore, authoritative directives *require* our obedience. The fact that the recipient thinks the order or instruction is unwise or wrong is not a reason to disobey the order.[67] This means that authoritative instructions are capable of making a 'practical difference',[68] where a practical difference is a difference

---

62 H L A Hart, *Essays on Bentham*, Clarendon Press, Oxford, 1982, p 261.
63 Ibid.
64 Ibid p 254.
65 F Schauer, *Thinking Like a Lawyer: A New Introduction to Legal Reasoning*, Harvard University Press, Cambridge, MA, 2009, pp 62–3.
66 J Raz, *The Morality of Freedom*, Clarendon Press, Oxford, 1986, p 37.
67 Schauer, above n 65, pp 62–3.
68 Coleman, above n 32, p 101.

in people's deliberations about what they should do. Authoritative instructions make such a difference because they give us an obligation to do something despite our believing that there are good reasons not to act in the required way. Someone who accepts authority therefore treats the authority's directive as a reason to comply just because the authority has so decreed and in the face of reasons to the contrary.

It is one thing to say that a practical authority makes a practical difference. Raz, however, has a distinctive view of the way in which authoritative directives affect our practical reasoning. On one conception of authority, authoritative directives affect our reasoning by providing especially powerful reasons for action, that is, reasons that override competing reasons in all or at least the majority of cases. Raz's conception of authority is different. For him, authoritative directives provide what he calls 'exclusionary reasons' for action.

Raz explains the concept of an exclusionary reason in the following way. When I am deciding whether to do something—go to the cinema, say—all sorts of reasons, whether moral or prudential, will be relevant to this matter, some of these for going to the cinema, some against. These reasons may also have different weights. We can call these my first-order reasons. Suppose that, taking into account all the relevant considerations and their weight, I ought to go to the cinema. Raz calls this the conclusion of 'right reason'. Right reason is whatever I ought to do on the basis of all the first-order reasons that apply to me. It might seem to follow that in deciding whether I ought to go to the cinema, I should rely directly on my own assessment as to what right reason requires. But Raz argues that this is not necessarily the case. For I might have a second-order reason for *not* acting on the balance of my first-order reasons as they appear to me. Such a second-order reason is an 'exclusionary' reason. It is a reason to disregard or not to act on my own assessment of what ought to be done on the balance of reasons.[69] Hart captures a similar thought with the notion of 'peremptory reasons', which he defines as reasons that are 'intended to *preclude* or *cut off* any deliberation … of the merits pro and con of doing the act'.[70] A peremptory reason is not the strongest or dominant reason for acting in a certain way, because the strongest reason is a reason that plays a role in first-order deliberations.[71] Instead, a peremptory reason is a 'deliberation-excluding' reason.[72]

---

69 Raz, above n 57, p 17.
70 Hart, above n 62, p 253, emphasis added.
71 Ibid.
72 Ibid p 255.

Raz illustrates the notion of an exclusionary reason with the example of a soldier who is ordered to do something by his commanding officer. The soldier would not have acted in this way had he been reasoning on the balance of first-order reasons, but he obeys the order just because it is the officer's order. Although the officer's order does give the soldier a new first-order reason for doing the action he was ordered to perform (because one ought to obey the commands of one's commanding officer), Raz argues that this new reason is not added to the existing ones, thus tipping the balance in favour of doing the action. Rather, the order functions to *exclude* consideration of the soldier's first-order reasons for *not* following the order, leaving only the new one in the field. His competing first-order reasons (which Raz calls his 'dependent' reasons) have been banished from his deliberations, so that there is nothing to be balanced against the new first-order reason.[73] The soldier, in other words, treats the order as giving him reasons for acting which *replace* the reasons he would otherwise have acted on in deciding what to do. He is from now on 'blind' to those considerations.

This special way of affecting our practical deliberations is, for Raz, a defining feature of an authoritative directive. Raz says: 'The fact that an authority requires performance of an action is a reason for its performance which is not to be added to all other relevant reasons when assessing what to do, but should replace some of them.'[74] Raz calls this the 'Preemption Thesis'. He also argues that authoritative directives should be based on the subject's dependent reasons, calling this the 'Dependence Thesis'.[75] Finally, Raz argues for the 'Normal Justification Thesis'. This thesis aims to explain why some person's say-so should give me a reason to comply, without deliberating on the merits of the instruction. When, in other words, do we have reason to subject ourselves to authority?

Raz's answer is that the normal argument for the justification of authority is an instrumental one. In particular, authority will be justified if we are more likely to comply with the dependent reasons that apply to us by obeying the authority than by trying *directly* to comply with our dependent reasons.[76] I might, for instance, be more likely to do what ought to be done on the balance of reasons if I rely on the opinion of an expert rather than my own opinion as to what the balance of reasons requires. Thus I am more likely to get well if I follow

---

73   J Raz, *Practical Reason and Norms*, Hutchinson, London, 1975, pp 41–3.
74   Raz, above n 58, 299.
75   Ibid.
76   Ibid.

my doctor's instructions rather than my own idea of a cure.[77] Authorities can also solve coordination problems by establishing conventions. We saw in 3.3 that a coordination problem exists when there is more than one way in which we can coordinate our actions in our mutual interest. It is arbitrary whether we drive on the left or the right but we have a mutual interest in driving on the same side. By designating one of the options as the one to be followed by everyone, authorities give us a reason to act that did not previously exist. Authorities can therefore help us to comply with our dependent reasons because we may not be able to coordinate our behaviour without assistance from an external agent.[78] In this way, as Scott Shapiro explains, Raz secures the possibility of rational obedience to legitimate authority: 'If an agent believes that he will do better in terms of the reasons that apply to him by deferring to directives issued than by deliberating, he is rationally required to defer to each directive irrespective of his judgments about the balance of dependent reasons.'[79]

Raz calls this a 'service conception' of authority because the authority performs a service for us. We hand over to the authority the task of weighing up the pros and cons of different courses of action and making a decision as to what we should do, the authority being better placed to do this than we are. The service conception therefore regards authorities as 'mediating between people and the right reasons which apply to them, so that the authority judges and pronounces what they ought to do according to right reason. The people on their part take their cue from the authority, whose pronouncements replace for them the force of the dependent reasons.'[80]

Having examined Raz's analysis of the nature of practical authority, let us now return to law. Raz believes that an important function that law is meant to serve is to settle in a determinate way what ought to be done in the face of serious and pervasive disagreements about this matter. We cannot expect to resolve our moral disagreements, but we do need to live together. Law attempts to settle our disputes at a practical level by issuing directives about what ought to be done, which claim to be binding on everyone just by virtue of their status as laws, and which we are obliged to obey whether we agree with the directives or not.[81]

---

77 J E Penner, 'Legal Reasoning and the Authority of Law', in L H Meyer, S L Paulson and T W Pogge (eds), *Rights, Culture and the Law: Themes from the Legal and Political Philosophy of Joseph Raz*, Oxford University Press, Oxford, 2003, p 72.
78 Raz, above n 66, pp 30–1.
79 S Shapiro, 'Authority', in J Coleman and S Shapiro (eds), *The Oxford Handbook of Jurisprudence and Philosophy of Law*, Oxford University Press, Oxford, 2002, p 407.
80 Raz, above n 58, 299.
81 Raz, above n 57, pp 50–1.

It is therefore a necessary truth about law, in Raz's view, that individuals such as judges, lawmakers and administrative officials issue directives that claim to be authoritative. This is one of the features of law that, in Raz's view, characterises it as a distinctive form of social organisation: it is of the essence of law that it claims priority over all other beliefs as to what we ought to do, a claim that it enforces with sanctions if individuals do not comply. Raz further believes that law's claim to be authoritative is a claim to *morally legitimate* authority. He writes: 'No system is a system of law unless it includes a claim of legitimacy, of moral authority. That means that it claims that legal requirements are morally binding, that is that legal obligations are real (moral) obligations arising out of the law.'[82] It might therefore seem that Raz is not putting forward a positivist view at all, but rather a view on which laws necessarily give rise to moral obligations. But, as we will now see, this is not the case.

First, saying that the law necessarily *claims* to possess morally legitimate or genuine authority is not the same as saying that it necessarily *has* such authority. In fact, Raz rejects the idea that law necessarily has moral authority.[83] He does not believe, in other words, that law necessarily gives us a content-independent, moral obligation to obey its directives just because they have the status of law. Raz tells us that no exercise of authority is legitimate 'if the moral or normative conditions for one's directives being authoritative are absent'.[84] In particular, his service conception implies that law's claim to authority will be warranted only if we are more likely to make the best choices if we defer to law's directives—something that is not guaranteed to be the case. Raz indeed goes further than this, for he believes that the law's claims to legitimate authority are frequently *unwarranted* and that we seldom have even a prima facie obligation to obey the law.[85] As Vincent Wellman explains:

> [A]pplying this notion of justification leads quickly to the conclusion that law lacks the authority that it claims for itself. Law claims authority generally. It demands that all its subjects obey all its directives, not just those which are likely to be wise. Law's claim of authority will therefore outrun any reasonably persuasive claim of its justification. To begin with, only just governments, with well-reasoned legal systems, could claim that obeying the norms of law will more likely lead its citizens to act in ways that will fulfill their practical deliberations than they would achieve by reasoning for themselves about how

---

82 J Raz, 'Hart on Moral Rights and Legal Duties' (1984) 4 *Oxford Journal of Legal Studies* 123, 131.
83 Raz, above n 58, 301.
84 Ibid 302.
85 Raz, above n 57, pp 233–49.

to act. And, even if the government is just and the legal system well reasoned, it is implausible that the system's decrees will, in fact, satisfy the criteria of normal justification for each citizen in every arena that is regulated by law.[86]

Law must, however, *claim* to be a legitimate authority—in the absence of such a claim, we would not be in the presence of law, according to Raz—and therefore law must purport to play the distinctive role in our practical reasoning which, according to him, legitimate authorities play. In particular, legal rules, such as statutes and judicial decisions, must claim to mediate between us and our dependent reasons. And this means, as we have seen, that legal rules must purport not just to provide us with powerful reasons to act in certain ways but to *replace* any reasons that would otherwise be relevant with an overriding or exclusionary directive. Law, in short, according to Raz, consists in standards that purport to provide us with exclusionary reasons for action, and those who accept the authoritative status of the rules will therefore see them not as outweighing their ordinary or dependent reasons but as making those reasons *irrelevant* to what they should do.

It might be wondered what this has to do with exclusive positivism. The answer to this is as follows. We have seen that Raz believes that it is part of the concept of law that it claims to be a legitimate authority and therefore to mediate between people and the reasons that apply to them by providing exclusionary reasons for action. Raz goes on to argue that certain constraints on the criteria of legality follow from this fact. He argues, in particular, that if law claims legitimate authority, that must be a claim that *could* be true. Since the claim could be true, law must be *capable* of possessing legitimate authority—it must be capable of assisting us to act in accordance with right reason—and in order to be the sort of thing that could be a legitimate authority, legal directives must possess two important features. First, they must be presented as the lawmakers' view of how their subjects ought to behave. Second, it must be possible to identify the directives without relying on considerations on which the directives purport to adjudicate, which include moral considerations.[87] This means that the existence and content of the rules must be established only by reference to their sources in empirically discoverable historical facts, such as legislation and judicial decisions, and therefore without reference to moral argument.[88]

---

86 V A Wellman, 'Authority of Law', in D Patterson (ed), *A Companion to Philosophy of Law and Legal Theory*, Blackwell Publishers, Malden, MA, 1996, p 578.
87 Raz, above n 58, 303.
88 Ibid.

Why does Raz think that rules capable of possessing legitimate authority must have these features? His answer is as follows. First, if individuals are more likely to conform to right reason by following the law rather than their own judgments, that must be because the law reflects *someone else's* superior or more reliable judgment. Secondly, if it were necessary to investigate the moral merits or defensibility of a rule in order to ascertain whether it is law, or to determine its content, then the rule could not function *as an authority*. For one would then be obliged to revert to the dependent reasons on which the legal rule has already purported to adjudicate and which it was meant to replace.

Let us examine the second point in more detail. Remember that, for Raz, authoritative directives replace our own judgments as to the reasons that apply to us, on the basis that we are more likely to satisfy the demands of right reason by following the directives than by following our own judgments. This, as we have seen, is the service authorities perform for us. Their function is to guide our conduct by replacing our personal judgments. It follows, says Raz, that if we could not identify a valid legal directive without first determining whether the directive *really* reflects the demands of right reason, law would not be able to perform this service. We would be inquiring into what the rule should be—evaluating its merits by consulting our dependent or background reasons—whereas the concept of an authority is of something that is meant to pre-empt our own independent deliberation, replacing the reasons on the basis of which we would otherwise decide, and therefore of something that *saves* us from having to resolve practical matters for ourselves. Think of the doctor example again. It would be of no use to you if the doctor instructed: 'Do whatever will make you well.' If you knew what would make you well, you would not need a doctor. Similarly, if we were capable of complying with the requirements of right reason without help we would not need law. Raz explains: '[T]he whole point of recognising the authority was that its judgment should be trusted rather than mine.'[89]

Raz concludes that both Dworkin and the inclusive positivists are wrong in thinking that there can be moral criteria of legal validity, because their view erases the very point and purpose of law, namely, the service it claims to perform for us. Standards that do not have a social source cannot count as law because it is only social sources of law, such as legislation and judicial decisions, which are capable of mediating between our actions and the precepts of morality in the

---

89   J Raz, 'Facing Up' (1989) 62 *Southern California Law Review* 1153, 1193.

way required if law is to discharge its intended function of settling what we ought to do. As Raz says:

> Since it is of the very essence of the alleged authority that it issues rulings which are binding regardless of any other justification, it follows that it must be possible to identify those rulings without engaging in a justificatory argument, i.e. as issuing from certain activities and interpreted in the light of publicly ascertainable standards not involving moral argument.[90]

Or, as Raz also puts it, we can benefit from law's decisions only if we 'can establish their existence and content in ways which do not depend on raising the very same issues which the authority is there to settle'.[91] For instance, the identification of a tax law cannot depend on determining what a just tax law would be, because those are the very issues that the tax law was supposed to have authoritatively settled.[92] In order to determine the existence and meaning of such a law, one need simply 'establish that the enactment took place, and what it says. To do this one needs little more than knowledge of English (including technical legal English), and of the events which took place in Parliament on a few occasions.'[93] Raz concludes that Dworkin and the inclusive positivists include in law standards that are inconsistent with the fact that law purports to be an authority, because moral tests for law are incapable of replacing our dependent reasons for acting. On Raz's view, 'to establish the law we engage in factual reasoning',[94] by which he means non-moral reasoning.

We have seen that Raz thinks that law is necessarily a limited domain and that standards that are not source-based cannot count as law. What, then, does he say about the fact that bills of rights contain moral language, and about Dworkin's claim that moral principles, such as the principle that no person should profit from his or her own wrongdoing, are binding on courts as law in virtue of their merits, not their social source? Although Dworkin's point can be accommodated by the inclusive positivists, it may be wondered how a plain-fact positivist like Raz can explain the role played by moral argument in legal practice.

Raz's response is to agree with Dworkin that judges often appeal to moral principles, and indeed, that they can be bound to do so. However, he claims that when this is so, morality only *appears* to be a test for law. Dworkin has

---

90 Raz, above n 57, pp 51–2.
91 Raz, above n 58, 304.
92 Ibid 310.
93 Ibid 306.
94 J Raz, *Between Authority and Interpretation*, Oxford University Press, Oxford, 2009, p 115.

therefore, in Raz's view, mistaken appearance for reality. Raz argues that where the law requires judges to apply moral standards, either by virtue of the rule of recognition itself, or by virtue of legal rules that the rule of recognition validates, these standards have not been incorporated into the law and are not part of it. Rather, judges are legally bound in such cases to apply an *extra-legal* or *non-authoritative* standard.

Suppose that a statute requires employers to pay a 'fair' wage. In determining what is fair, the judge, says Raz, is not answering a question to which the law provides the answer. Instead the statute places judges under a legal obligation to go beyond the law. The statute obliges judges to seek guidance from *non-legal* norms, namely, the norms of morality.[95] The statute therefore empowers judges not to determine what the *existing* law requires but rather to *make* law on the matter of what constitutes a fair wage, thereby creating new legal rights. The matter will then be settled for future courts, which will now be able to apply the decision of the previous court. Furthermore, insofar as bills of rights are concerned, Raz says that they do not require conformity with moral norms as a threshold condition of legal validity. Instead, they empower judges to eliminate immoral law, by invalidating law that was perfectly valid before the judge struck it down.[96]

Raz compares morality to the law of a foreign legal system. There are situations in which the law requires judges to apply the rules of a foreign legal system in deciding cases that have arisen in their own system. The rules of the foreign system are not, however, thereby incorporated into the municipal system: they do not become the law of the municipal system.[97] Moral standards are likewise 'foreign' to the law, according to Raz: though judges may be obliged *by* the law to apply them, this does not mean that they are thereby converted into *legal* standards. Not all of the standards that judges may have a legal obligation to apply are necessarily legal standards. Or, put otherwise: reasoning *according* to law is not necessarily the same as legal reasoning or reasoning *about* the law. The former may involve moral reasoning; the latter is always source-based.[98] In this way, by seeing law as an 'open normative system',[99] which can oblige

---

[95] Waluchow, above n 20, pp 83, 157.
[96] W J Waluchow, 'Legality, Morality and the Guiding Function of Law', in M H Kramer, C Grant, B Colburn and A Hatzistavrou (eds), *The Legacy of H L A Hart: Legal, Political, and Moral Philosophy*, Oxford University Press, Oxford, 2008, p 88.
[97] Raz, above n 57, p 46.
[98] J Raz, *Ethics in the Public Domain: Essays in the Morality of Law and Politics*, Clarendon Press, Oxford, 1994, p 332.
[99] Raz, above n 73, pp 152–3.

judges to apply standards that are not necessarily legal standards, Raz is able to explain the fact that morality plays a role in legal practice without giving up his plain-fact positivism.

4.7 Some criticisms of Raz

Most legal theorists agree with Raz that the law presents itself as a practical authority, in the sense that law's say-so is intended to give us a reason to do things we might not otherwise have done. As Dworkin says, it is a common assumption that 'law can compete with morality and wisdom and, for those who accept law's authority, override these other virtues in their final decision about what they should do'.[100] The assumption goes back to classical common law theory of the sixteenth and seventeenth centuries, which made a distinction between 'natural' reason, which every individual possesses, and 'artificial' or legal reason. The latter, said Chief Justice Coke in the famous case of *Prohibitions del Roy*, requires 'long study and experience'.[101]

    This is not to say that all theorists accept the idea that legal decision-makers ought to reason 'artificially'. As we will see, the legal realists reject this idea (see 7.5), as do theorists in the law and economics school (see 8.2). However, the majority of theorists take the view that legal reasoning is artificial in the sense that individuals who accept the authority of law may be under a duty to reach a decision that is different from the one they would otherwise think best. Schauer uses the related concept of 'counterintuitiveness' to describe the way in which legal reasoning can be 'a path *away* from what had otherwise seemed to be the right decision',[102] 'forc[ing] us away from our own best judgment in favor of someone else's'.[103]

    Raz, however, goes further than this. He argues that it is *impossible* for moral reasoning to play a role in the identification of law. This is because the Preemption Thesis holds, as we have seen, that if a legal rule is accepted as authoritative, it must *altogether* or *entirely* replace the moral assessments of those who accept it. Dworkin regards this as 'Ptolemaic dogma', by which he means that Raz is led to embrace an eccentric conception of authority so as to

---

100 Dworkin, above n 24, p 429, n 3.
101 *Prohibitions del Roy* (1607) 12 Co Rep 63, 65.
102 Schauer, above n 65, p 7, Schauer's emphasis.
103 Ibid p 61.

preserve his dogmatic faith in the truth of the sources thesis.[104] Why, Raz's critics ask, should law's authority have to be understood in such an all-or-nothing, exclusionary way? Might law's authority not sometimes be a matter of degree?[105]

Why should precedents, for instance, necessarily give rise to exclusionary reasons for action that totally preclude judges from revisiting the contested moral questions that the precedent has taken into account and on which it has adjudicated? As Stephen Perry points out, this may be true in the case of lower courts, which can plausibly be said to be bound, in Raz's exclusionary sense, not to depart from the decisions of higher courts.[106] But is the same true in the case of courts that are under an obligation to treat their own earlier decisions as authoritative? Does the authoritative nature of their earlier decisions require them to treat their current moral views about those decisions as having *no* weight, as Raz's view implies? Or is it rather the case that, in particular circumstances, the authority of their own precedents may merely give them reason to ascribe *less* weight to their current moral views than they would if the precedent did not exist and they were simply required to consider the matter on its merits?[107] If so, the precedent would provide a genuine constraint on their reasoning, without constraining them to the full extent suggested by Raz.[108] There would, in other words, be a halfway house between the exclusionary account of precedents and what Schauer calls 'unconstrained substitution of judgment'.[109]

Perry argues along these lines. We have seen that Raz's analysis of authority implies a very strong conception of precedent, on which a court will always regard a past decision decided on the balance of first-order reasons as giving rise to a rule that prevents the court from making a fresh evaluation of the strength of the relevant arguments. Perry argues, however, that this is not the only possible approach to precedent that is compatible with the authoritative nature of law. Although the authoritative nature of law is incompatible with judges overruling a precedent merely because they believe the case was wrongly decided, it *is* compatible, Perry argues, with an approach on which judges

---

104 Dworkin, above n 41, pp 188, 209.
105 Waluchow, above n 20, pp 136–7.
106 S R Perry, 'Judicial Obligation, Precedent and the Common Law' (1987) 7 *Oxford Journal of Legal Studies* 215, 257.
107 Ibid 222–3.
108 Ibid 234–5.
109 F Schauer, 'Formalism' (1988) 97 *Yale Law Journal* 509, 545.

are permitted to overrule a precedent for an *exceptionally strong reason*, such as the need to avoid gross injustice. Perry explains: '[On] this conception of precedent ... one needs more than just *a* reason to overcome the binding force of a precedent, but at the same time it differs from the exclusionary model in that no relevant first-order reasons are excluded from consideration as a matter of course.'[110] Perry's approach therefore allows judges to revisit the balance of reasons but only in rare cases, when the reasons to do so are exceptionally weighty. In the normal course of events, 'the judge is ... not free ... to ignore the past and to decide the case presently before him in the way that he now happens to think is correct'.[111]

Perry's account shows that there does not have to be a stringent, exclusionary prohibition on overruling precedents in order for us to explain how precedents can be authoritative or have priority over judges' background moral beliefs. As long as precedents are capable of making a difference to judges' practical reasoning—as they do on a model such as Perry's, on which judges can be under a duty to make a decision they believe to be mistaken—they will enjoy the special status of an authoritative decision. In the absence of very strong countervailing reasons, judges are bound to follow the previous decision *just because* it was decided in that way in the past, ignoring their own best judgment. This means that they have to attribute extra weight to the decision, 'beyond the weight which [it is] thought to carry on purely moral grounds'.[112] This is artificial reasoning of the kind we associate with authoritative directives.[113]

Of course, if we take this less stringent view about law's authority, then law would not be able *conclusively* to settle how we should behave. But why should we accept Raz's view that the function of law is always conclusively to settle disputes, no matter what the cost to competing values such as flexibility? We have already canvassed the considerations relevant to this matter in 4.5, where we saw that inclusive positivists take the view that it is not an essential feature of law that it must always opt for certainty over flexibility.

Raz's critics also argue that his account of how moral argument plays a role in legal practice does not make sense of the way in which participants in

---

110 Perry, above n 106, 222, Perry's emphasis.
111 Ibid 240.
112 S R Perry, 'The Varieties of Legal Positivism' (1996) 19 *Canadian Journal of Law and Jurisprudence*, 361, 376.
113 See also W Waluchow, 'Authority and the Practical Difference Thesis' (2000) 6 *Legal Theory* 45 for further defence of the view that the authority of law does not necessarily consist in its power to exclude or replace *all* moral reasons for action.

legal institutions understand legal practice. Thus it does not fit the way in which judges describe their task when they are, for instance, engaged in applying and interpreting the moral standards contained in a bill of rights. Judges do not see themselves as stepping outside the law when they adjudicate such moral matters (except to the extent that the standards are indeterminate or incapable of providing a uniquely correct answer). They see the moral constraints on legislation contained in a bill of rights as the source of *legal* rights, not extra-legal rights. The same is true of the judges in the common law cases described by Dworkin. They claim that they are in the business of *finding* the law, not making it. For Raz, however, such judicial activity is not based on law.

Of course, Raz is not alone in holding that that there are legally unregulated cases. Hart also adheres to this view, as we saw in 3.8. It will be remembered that Hart believes that some of the questions which judges are called upon to decide (those in the penumbral area of uncertainty) do not have a legal answer. And there is something illuminating about Hart's and Raz's view because the contrary view, that law is *everything* that judges do, is, as Schauer points out, 'too simple, for we need to differentiate the distinctively legal part of such roles and activities from the parts that are shared with other agents, other institutions, and other functions'.[114] There is, however, also an important difference between Hart and Raz. In particular, Hart does not narrow the domain of the law to the same extent as Raz. This is because Hart is an inclusive positivist, and although Hart does not say this in so many words, his account of law implies that moral reasoning can be a way of identifying existing law when the moral standards contained in the law are clear and capable of determining a uniquely correct answer to the question at hand. For Raz, on the other hand, moral reasoning can never amount to reasoning about the law and there are therefore large chunks of apparently legal activity that are not legal for him. This must inevitably raise the question whether exclusive positivism 'explain[s] too little of legal practice and too little of the process by which conclusions are reached in legal argument and judicial decision'.[115]

4.8 Ethical positivism

There is one last version of positivism to which we should attend. It goes under the name of 'ethical positivism' and its key thesis is that an exclusivist-type

---

114 Schauer, above n 53, 1949–50.
115 Ibid 1950.

separation of law and morality is morally desirable. Prominent ethical positivists are Tom Campbell and Jeremy Waldron. Ethical positivists hold that moral criteria of legal validity are *conceptually possible*, as inclusive positivists say they are, but that they are not *morally desirable* and that they should therefore be avoided in practice. Legal systems, they say, should be designed so as to minimise the role moral standards can play in determining the existence of law or its content.

Ethical positivism is therefore what Campbell calls a 'prescriptive separation thesis',[116] in contrast to the conceptual versions of positivism we have been considering up until now. It is not a *descriptive* theory about the *nature* of law but a *moral recommendation* or prescription as to the form a legal system *should* take. The aim of ethical positivists is to prescribe what should be the case. They argue, in particular, that someone trying to design the ideal legal system should keep law and morals separate. Ethical positivists claim that 'the values associated with law, legality and the rule of law ... can best be achieved if the ordinary operation of such a system does not require people to exercise moral judgment in order to find out what the law is'.[117] Ethical positivism is therefore a 'political theory of law'.[118] Instead of focusing on what law is, it focuses on what sort of law it is desirable to have.

Ethical positivism has its source in democratic values and it is therefore also sometimes called 'democratic positivism'. As David Dyzenhaus explains, it is a movement that puts more faith in legislatures than courts: 'It seeks to reverse a trend from an era in which judges are thought to be more trustworthy than politicians and in which there is a world-wide experiment taking place as both old and new democracies give ever more authority to judges by constitutionalizing human rights.'[119] Ethical positivism seeks to reverse this trend in maintaining that, for democratic reasons, only the people's representatives in parliament should make controversial moral choices for society. We will see in 10.10 how Waldron draws on these ideas to criticise judicially enforceable bills of rights. The same worry about political legitimacy may also lead ethical positivists to attack the common law as being too uncertain, leaving too much to the

---

[116] T D Campbell, *The Legal Theory of Ethical Positivism*, Aldershot, Dartmouth, 1996, p 3.
[117] J Waldron, 'Normative or Ethical Positivism', in J Coleman (ed) *Hart's Postscript: Essays on the Postscript to The Concept of Law*, Oxford University Press, Oxford, 2001, p 421.
[118] Campbell, above n 116, p 2.
[119] D Dyzenhaus, 'The Genealogy of Legal Positivism' (2004) 24 *Oxford Journal of Legal Studies* 39, 62.

subjectivity of judges, and opening the door to judicial usurpation of lawmaking power.

Some of the inspiration behind ethical positivism goes back to Bentham, who thought that common law judges are in the business of making law with retrospective effect, thus treating us like dogs by punishing us after the event, rather than for conduct that has been prohibited in advance. 'Whenever your dog does anything you want to break him of', Bentham wrote, 'you wait till he does it, and then beat him for it. This is the way you make laws for your dog: and this is the way the judges make law for you and me.'[120] In place of political power surreptitiously, retrospectively and capriciously exercised by conservative judges, Bentham wished to substitute a rational, codified legal system enacted by the legislature, so that people might know in advance what conduct is permitted and what is prohibited. In this way, judicial lawmaking would be minimised. Such a rational system would, for Bentham, be based on utilitarian principles of the general good (see 10.3).

In contrast to Hart, who believes that law should be loosely framed to allow judges to arrive at sensible results, ethical positivists believe that legislatures should assume full responsibility for the making of moral and policy choices, drafting legislation in precise and unambiguous language that reduces to the greatest possible extent the opportunities for judges to rely on their own disputed political and moral views in determining the existence and content of the law. Law *ought* therefore to be a system of rules drafted in such a way as to allow us to 'recognise without controversy whether actual conduct does or does not conform to the rule[s]'.[121]

Furthermore, because ethical positivists stress the moral values served by rule-based governance, they are attracted to the 'mechanical' or formalistic theory of adjudication that judges are under a duty to apply clear legal rules. We saw in 3.8 and 4.2 that Hart rejects this approach, but other theorists argue that there are virtues in it. We will return to this issue in 6.4. In Chapters 7 and 9, we will also examine the views of those who think that law is incapable of speaking with a clear voice and that it is therefore impossible for legal rules to restrict the discretionary power of judges.

---

120 Quoted in G J Postema, *Bentham and the Common Law Tradition*, Clarendon Press, Oxford, 1986, p 277.
121 Campbell, above n 116, p 64.

Questions

1. Are Hart's views about the inevitable overlap between law and morality compatible with his positivism?
2. Dworkin claims that inclusive positivism is really 'anti-positivism' (*Justice in Robes*, Belknap Press of Harvard University Press, Cambridge, MA, 2006, p 198). Do you agree?
3. Raz describes a view on which legitimate authority is impossible. According to this view, '[i]t is of the nature of authority that it requires submission even when one thinks that what is required is against reason. Therefore submission to authority is irrational. Similarly the principle of autonomy entails action on one's own judgment on all moral questions. Since authority sometimes requires action against one's own judgment, it requires abandoning one's moral autonomy … All practical authority is consequently immoral' (J Raz, *The Authority of Law: Essays on Law and Morality*, Clarendon Press, Oxford, 1979, p 3). Do you agree that authority is incompatible with rationality and moral autonomy and therefore that legitimate authority is impossible?
4. In 1966, the House of Lords issued a Practice Statement, which modified the Lords' previous practice of treating their past decisions as absolutely binding. The Statement declared: 'Their lordships recognise that too rigid adherence to precedent may lead to injustice in a particular case and also unduly restrict the proper development of the law. They propose therefore to modify their present practice and, while treating former decisions of this House as normally binding, to depart from a previous decision when it appears right to do so' ([1966] 3 All ER 77). Does this mean that the House of Lords no longer regards its previous decisions as authoritative?
5. Dworkin writes: 'Suppose a nation's legislature adopts a law declaring that henceforth, on pain of severe criminal punishment, subjects must never act immorally in any aspect of their lives. That is an exceptionally silly statute, and life in that nation will thereafter be repulsive as well as dangerous. According to Raz, however, it would be a conceptual mistake to describe the statute as law at all. Even in this extreme example, his claim seems too strong. The statute, after all, has normative consequences for those disposed to accept its authority. They now have an additional reason to reflect carefully on the moral quality of everything they do and to act punctiliously,

not only because they are now subject to official sanction but also because their community has declared ... the cardinal importance of moral diligence. They would not be making a conceptual mistake if they said they were behaving differently out of deference to the authority of the new law' (*Justice in Robes*, Belknap Press of Harvard University Press, Cambridge, MA, 2006, p 207). Do you agree with Dworkin that such a statute can be treated as authoritative? If Dworkin is right, does this undermine Raz's arguments for exclusive positivism?

Further reading

T D Campbell, *The Legal Theory of Ethical Positivism*, Aldershot, Dartmouth, 1996.

J Coleman (ed), *Hart's Postscript: Essays on the Postscript to* The Concept of Law, Oxford University Press, Oxford, 2001.

J Coleman, *The Practice of Principle: In Defence of a Pragmatist Approach to Legal Theory*, Oxford University Press, Oxford, 2001, Lectures 8–10.

R Dworkin, *Taking Rights Seriously*, Duckworth, London, 1977, Chapters 2–3.

R Dworkin, *Justice in Robes*, Belknap Press of Harvard University Press, Cambridge, MA, 2006, Chapter 7.

L L Fuller, 'Positivism and Fidelity to Law—A Reply to Professor Hart' (1958) 71 *Harvard Law Review* 630.

J Gardner, 'Legal Positivism: 5½ Myths' (2001) 46 *American Journal of Jurisprudence* 199.

H L A Hart, *The Concept of Law*, 2nd edn, Clarendon Press, Oxford, 1994, Chapter IX and Postscript.

H L A Hart, 'Positivism and the Separation of Law and Morals' (1958) 71 *Harvard Law Review* 593.

M H Kramer, *Where Law and Morality Meet,* Oxford University Press, Oxford, 2004, Parts I and II.

L H Meyer, S L Paulson and T W Pogge (eds), *Rights, Culture and the Law*: Themes *from the Legal and Political Philosophy of Joseph Raz*, Oxford University Press, Oxford, 2003.

J Raz, 'Authority, Law and Morality' (1985) 68 *The Monist* 295.

J Raz, *The Authority of Law: Essays on Law and Morality*, Clarendon Press, Oxford, 1979.

J Raz, *Ethics in the Public Domain: Essays in the Morality of Law and Politics*, Clarendon Press, Oxford, 1994, Part II.

J Raz, *Between Authority and Interpretation: On the Theory of Law and Practical Reason*, Oxford University Press, Oxford, 2009, Part II.

S Shapiro, 'Authority', in J Coleman and S Shapiro (eds), *The Oxford Handbook of Jurisprudence and Philosophy of Law*, Oxford University Press, Oxford, 2002, pp 382–439.

W J Waluchow, *Inclusive Legal Positivism*, Clarendon Press, Oxford, 1994, Chapters 4–5.

5

Law as Morally Valuable

5.1 Chapter overview

This chapter explores views about law whose central claim is that law has, by its nature, moral value and that there is therefore a much more intimate connection between law and morality than positivists suppose. These are traditionally called 'natural law views'. The natural law school of thought is, like the positivist school, a complex one: there are different ways of arguing that law has an essentially moral dimension and there are correspondingly different versions of natural law theory. This chapter will examine two different kinds of natural law theory: *substantive* theories, which focus on the content or substance of legal rules (the *ends* or objectives that the rules pursue) and *procedural* theories, which focus on the formal and procedural aspects of law (the *means* by which law is made and applied). Substantive natural law theories hold that in order to be law, or 'genuine' law, the content of rules must meet certain tests of moral acceptability. Procedural natural law theories hold that legal forms and processes necessarily have moral value. It is, of course, possible to hold both of these views, and some theorists do.

    It should be noted that plausible versions of these theories accept that law is *partly* a matter of social facts. They claim merely that law depends on *more* than social facts: in addition to having the appropriate pedigree, official directives or systems of directives must also pass the requisite tests of moral content and/or form. If they do not pass these tests, they will either fail to be legal or they will be legally defective. The focus of this chapter will mainly be on the theories of John Finnis and Lon Fuller.

5.2 The natural law tradition

Although the focus of this chapter will be on contemporary natural law theories, it is necessary to start with some brief comments about the history of such theories. These comments must inevitably be incomplete. This is partly because natural law thinking spans thousands of years, from ancient Greek thought until the present, and it is impossible to summarise such a long and rich history in a few pages. It is also because, traditionally, natural law thinking is concerned with much more than analysing the nature of law. Its account of law is typically embedded in a much broader project, which is concerned with such matters as the possibility of moral knowledge, with laying down moral principles to guide conduct, and with the nature of legitimate government and the source of the obligation to obey the law. For instance, a central theme in natural law thinking is the belief that there are moral truths, which are connected in some way with human nature or with human flourishing and which are discoverable by the use of reason. Indeed, when thinkers in the natural law tradition speak of natural 'law', it is actually, and perhaps somewhat confusingly, these *moral* truths to which they are referring. Natural law is, in other words, 'moral law'.

This chapter will say very little about the details of natural law moral theory and natural law ethics. It will concentrate instead on natural law legal theory—the way in which natural law theory has been applied to questions about law—since this is more directly relevant to our concerns, particularly insofar as natural law views about law compete with positivist views about law. With respect to jurisprudential matters, past thinkers in the natural law tradition focused on the relationship between law and morality (or, to put it in their terms, the relationship between human law and natural law). They defended the view that putative legal rules whose content does not meet certain moral tests of acceptability are either not laws at all or are not laws in the true sense of that word. The difference between these versions of the claim will be explained in 5.3, but the distinction will be left without comment for the moment since it is not clearly drawn by the thinkers in question.

As indicated above, this view has its origins in ancient Greek thought, beginning with thinkers such as Plato and Aristotle and becoming more identifiable in the writings of the Stoics. These Greek philosophers believed that a rational order exists in nature, which is discoverable by human reason. They thought of this rational order as the source of universal and objective moral standards, which are 'higher' than merely conventional or enacted human standards.

Sophocles' play, *Antigone*, dramatises this way of thinking. Antigone has to decide whether to obey a command of the king, Creon, that her brother's body should not be buried but left to be devoured by the beasts. The Greeks thought that such a fate would lead to horrible suffering in the afterlife. Antigone scatters earth on her brother's body, is arrested and is brought to Creon. She defends herself by saying that she was fulfilling a higher obligation than obedience to merely human laws:

> These laws were not ordained of Zeus,
>
> And she who sits enthroned with gods below,
>
> Justice, enacted not these human laws.
>
> Nor did I deem that thou, a mortal man,
>
> Couldst by a breath annul and override
>
> The immutable unwritten laws of heaven.
>
> They were not born today nor yesterday;
>
> They die not; and none knoweth whence they sprang.[1]

Stoic thinking in turn influenced Roman thought. Cicero, a Roman writer of the first century BCE, was particularly influential in conveying Greek ideas to a Roman audience and in his writings we find the first systematic statements of the natural law position as well as the appearance of the phrase 'natural law' for the first time.[2] Cicero famously stated the natural law position in *De Re Publica*:

> True law is right reason in agreement with nature; it is of universal application, unchanging and everlasting ... It is a sin to try to alter this law, nor is it allowable to attempt to repeal any part of it, and it is impossible to abolish it entirely. We cannot be freed from its obligations by senate or people ... And there will not be different laws at Rome and at Athens, or different laws now and in the future, but one eternal and unchangeable law will be valid for all nations and for all times, and there will be one master and one ruler, that is, God, over us all, for he is the author of this law, its promulgator and its enforcing judge.[3]

Here we see Cicero identifying the universal, unchanging and objective moral standards that the Greeks thought were present in nature and discoverable by reason as a form of law—'natural law'. It is 'law' in the sense

---

1   J M Kelly, *A Short History of Western Legal Theory*, Clarendon Press, Oxford, 1992, p 20.
2   L L Weinreb, *Natural Law and Justice*, Harvard University Press, Cambridge, MA, 1987, p 39.
3   Cicero, *De Re Publica*, C W Keyes (trans), Harvard University Press, Cambridge, MA, 1928, III, xxii, 33.

that it provides standards for human conduct. It is 'natural' in the sense that it is not 'man-made': it is discovered rather than created. Since this form of law owes its existence and authority to nature/reason (no clear distinction is drawn between them) rather than to human choices, its status as law does not depend on official recognition by positive or human legal systems and it is impossible for it to be abolished by human enactments. Cicero also defended the idea that human standards that breach this 'true' or 'higher' law are of no legal force. He said that a legislature could not, for instance, make theft lawful: such a rule would no more deserve to be called law than the rules made by a band of robbers.[4] The natural law therefore serves as a constraint on what human lawmakers can validly enact *as law*.

These ideas passed subsequently into Christian thought. Natural law was now understood as the law of God and the idea of a normative order in nature receded in importance. Lloyd Weinreb states that natural law became 'a specifically theological concept and much more concrete than the natural law of the Stoics'.[5] St Augustine was a key figure in these early Christian developments and it is to him that the natural law slogan, '*Lex iniusta non est lex*', is usually attributed. This slogan, translated literally, means 'an unjust law is not a law at all'. However, until the Middle Ages, natural law was a vague doctrine, with little concrete application to human institutions.[6] It was only in the thirteenth century that it became fully developed in the highly influential writings of Saint Thomas Aquinas. In his *Summa Theologiae*, Aquinas synthesised classical Graeco-Roman ideas of natural law as discoverable by human reason with the teachings of Christianity. In Weinreb's view, '[n]othing approaching the dimension and coherence of Aquinas' statement [of natural law] has appeared since'.[7]

Aquinas distinguished four types of law: eternal law, natural law, human law and divine law. The first three of these are the most important for our purposes. Aquinas took over from Aristotle the idea that everything has its own nature or end, which it is necessarily good to attain. To be an oak tree, for instance, is the optimal state of existence towards which an acorn tends. Aquinas fused this Aristotelian idea with Christian thinking, saying that it is God

---

4   Cicero, *De Legibus*, C W Keyes (trans), Harvard University Press, Cambridge, MA, 1928, II, v, 13.
5   Weinreb, above n 2, p 47.
6   Ibid p 55.
7   Ibid p 2.

who directs everything in nature towards its end. 'Eternal law' was the phrase Aquinas used for this divine plan.

Insofar as natural law is concerned, Aquinas thought that reason allows us to discern the ends that are natural for us and therefore the good we should pursue and the evil we should avoid, as directed by God. 'Natural law', for him, was therefore that part of the eternal law that humans are capable of discerning with human reason: 'the natural law', Aquinas wrote, 'is nothing else than the rational creature's participation of the eternal law'.[8] In other words, natural law consists in rational standards for guiding human conduct.

Finally, human law is the translation of these rational standards into temporal or positive standards, which are promulgated by human lawmakers and reinforced with sanctions. It follows, for Aquinas, that positive directives which have been enacted or declared by officials who have lawmaking authority, but which deviate from the ideal or rational standards of natural law, are not genuine law but a 'perversion' of law:

> As Augustine says, 'that which is not just seems to be no law at all': wherefore the force of a law depends on the extent of its justice. Now in human affairs a thing is said to be just, from being right, according to the rule of reason. But the first rule of reason is the law of nature ... Consequently, every human law has just so much of the nature of law, as it is derived from the law of nature. But if in any point it deflects from the law of nature, it is no longer a law but a perversion of law.[9]

Aquinas made the same point by saying that unjust laws are 'acts of violence rather than laws'.[10]

We are now in a position to understand Aquinas' answer to the question posed at the beginning of Chapter 2, namely: what are the distinguishing characteristics of law? Law, Aquinas tells us, is necessarily 'an ordinance of reason for the common good, made by him who has care of the community, and promulgated'.[11] The idea of the common good is at the heart of the natural law theory of Aquinas and those influenced by him. They believe that it is of the essence of law that it gives us reasons to comply with it. Rules that we are not morally obliged to obey do not, in their view, have the full quality of law. These reasons to comply with law are explained, according to these thinkers, by

---

8   T Aquinas, *Summa Theologiae*, Benziger Brothers Inc, New York, 1947, IaIIae 91.2.
9   Ibid IaIIae 95.2.
10 Ibid IaIIae 96.4.
11 Ibid IaIIae 90.4.

the role law plays in securing the common good of the political community.[12] We will return to the common good in 5.3, when we examine John Finnis's conception of it, but at this point it is enough to say, following Jonathan Crowe, that '[t]he common good ... is both *good* and *common*; it is a state of affairs that is *good for everyone* (or, at least, for all members of the political community)'.[13] Rules that fail to serve the common good are unjust, and since injustice is one kind of unreasonableness for Aquinas, unjust laws do not deserve the description of 'law'. They are 'acts of violence', not laws.

It follows that although Aquinas recognised that human laws have a social or institutional dimension, in that they are made or posited by persons with lawmaking authority, such social facts are not enough to guarantee them the status or character of law. Official directives that have the appropriate pedigree but are unjust or otherwise unreasonable are not genuine laws, and Aquinas thought that there is no obligation to obey them, unless disobedience would have worse social consequences than obedience. Disobedience would not be justified, for instance, if it would undermine respect for a system that is generally just. Aquinas put this point by saying that unjust laws are not binding on a person in conscience 'provided he avoid giving scandal or inflicting a more grievous hurt'.[14]

Natural law thinking took a more secular and individualistic turn in the seventeenth and eighteenth centuries. Many trace these modern developments to Hugo Grotius, who announced that natural law would retain its validity even if God did not exist.[15] Here we see the seeds of the idea that the law of nature can be elaborated without reference to theological presuppositions. Furthermore, it was not long before the problem of the legitimacy of government began to loom large and emphasis came to be placed not so much on natural *law* as on natural *rights*, or rights possessed by individuals in virtue of their nature as human beings. (Chapter 10 contains a detailed discussion of such rights—now generally called 'human rights'.) Thus John Locke saw the 'law of nature', which he also described as the 'law of reason', as decreeing that 'no-one ought to harm

---

12 M C Murphy, *Natural Law in Jurisprudence and Politics*, Cambridge University Press, New York, 2006, pp 1–2.
13 J Crowe, 'Natural Law in Jurisprudence and Politics' (2007) 27 *Oxford Journal of Legal Studies* 775, 778, Crowe's emphasis.
14 Aquinas, above n 8, IaIIae 96.4.
15 H Grotius [1625], *De Jure Belli ac Pacis*, F W Kelsey (trans), Bobbs-Merill, Indianapolis, 1925, para 11.

another in his Life, Health, Liberty, or Possessions'.[16] Locke also argued that it is the primary function of the state to respect the rights to life, liberty and property to which the law of nature gives rise. For Locke, therefore, natural rights impose moral limits on governmental power to interfere with our freedom, and laws are justified, in his view, only insofar as they respect these limits.

The doctrine of natural rights would come to justify the American and French Revolutions, as expressed in the American Declaration of Independence of 1776:

> We hold these truths to be self-evident, that all men are created equal, that they are endowed by their Creator with certain unalienable Rights, that among these are Life, Liberty and the pursuit of Happiness. That to secure these rights, Governments are instituted among Men, deriving their just powers from the consent of the governed. That whenever any form of Government becomes destructive of these ends, it is the Right of the People to alter or to abolish it.

Although natural law thinking receded in importance in the nineteenth century, the atrocities of World War II reinvigorated the tradition.

5.3 Finnis and the central case of law

In the previous section, we considered the work of historical thinkers who, in one way or another, defend the substantive natural law thesis that the moral content of rules is relevant to their legal validity or their legal character. On this view, it is not enough for legal rules to have the appropriate source or pedigree in, for instance, legislation or adjudication. Putative legal rules that do not pass certain substantive moral tests lack the status or character of 'law', even if they have been enacted or declared by officials who have lawmaking authority. We turn now to contemporary defences of this thesis.

A key thinker here is Finnis, whose important work *Natural Law and Natural Rights* makes him the leading contemporary theorist writing in the classical natural law tradition. Finnis is deeply influenced by Aquinas in particular, although it should be appreciated that the version of natural law for which Finnis argues is nuanced and that his account of law is in certain respects compatible with positivist legal theory—a point that Finnis himself is keen to stress.[17]

---

16 J Locke [1690], 'An Essay Concerning the True Original, Extent, and End of Civil Government', in P Laslett (ed), *Two Treatises of Government* , Cambridge University Press, Cambridge, 1970, s 6.
17 J Finnis, 'The Truth in Legal Positivism', in R P George (ed), *The Autonomy of Law: Essays on Legal Positivism*, Clarendon Press, Oxford, 1996, pp 195–205.

Some distinctions made by Mark Murphy will help us to understand Finnis's theory. Murphy points out that there are different ways of reading the substantive natural law thesis that, in order to be law or 'genuine' law, rules must meet certain moral tests of acceptability insofar as their content is concerned. Consider St Augustine's slogan, 'An unjust law is not a law at all', or Aquinas' claim that human laws that deviate from the natural law are a 'perversion' of law or 'acts of violence'. What exactly do these claims mean? We did not directly address this question in the previous section but we now need to think about it more carefully.

Murphy argues that there are three possible interpretations of such claims. First, they can be read as saying that some laws are so unjust that there is no *moral* obligation to *obey* them. Secondly, they can be read as saying that unjust rules cannot be *legally valid*. They are, in other words, not laws at all. Thirdly, they can be read as saying that unjust rules are legally valid but are not laws in the *true* sense of that word. They are not merely morally defective but also *legally defective* or defective *as law*.[18] Murphy elaborates on the notion of a defect as follows:

> To say that something is defective is to say that it belongs to a certain kind, and there are certain standards of perfection that are internal to it (that are intrinsic to, that necessarily belong to) members of that kind. To be an alarm clock just is, in part, to be the sort of thing that if it cannot sound an alarm when one wishes to be awakened, is defective. But something can be an alarm clock even if it cannot sound an alarm: it might be broken, or poorly constructed, or whatever.[19]

Thus on the third reading of the natural law thesis, law has certain standards of perfection that are internal to it and unjust laws are defective in failing to measure up to these standards, which are internal to being law.

Which of these is the most plausible reading of the natural law thesis? By this I do not mean 'which reading did thinkers like Aquinas actually have in mind?' The interesting question for our purposes is rather: 'which reading makes the best philosophical sense of the belief in natural law?' The first reading, which Murphy calls the 'Moral Reading', trivialises the natural law thesis. As Murphy observes, the natural law claim, when understood as a claim about the justifiability of disobeying unjust laws, 'is excruciatingly uninteresting, a claim that almost everyone in the history of moral and political philosophy has accepted, and thus

---

18 Murphy, above n 12, pp 9–12.
19 M C Murphy, *Philosophy of Law*, Blackwell Publishing, Malden, MA, 2007, p 44.

is not much worth discussing'.[20] Since, as we saw in 4.2, positivists can and do accept the Moral Reading, the Moral Reading cannot be what distinguishes natural law from its rivals. The real contenders are therefore the second and third readings, which Murphy calls the 'Strong Natural Law Thesis' and the 'Weak Natural Law Thesis' respectively.

There are certainly theorists who defend the Strong Natural Law Thesis, at any rate in the case of extremely unjust laws. The German jurist Gustav Radbruch famously did so in response to the atrocities of the Nazi regime, in terms that have come to be known as Radbruch's 'formula'. Radbruch wrote:

> The conflict between justice and legal certainty may well be resolved in this way: The positive law, secured by legislation and power, takes precedence even when its content is unjust and fails to benefit the people, unless the conflict between statute and justice reaches such an intolerable degree that the statute, as 'flawed law', must yield to justice.[21]

This formula has been recently embraced by Robert Alexy, who agrees with Radbruch that although unjust laws can still be laws, there is an 'outermost limit' governing what can count as law, and that extreme injustice, such as the destruction of a racial minority, is not law.[22] Alexy accepts the Strong Natural Law Thesis in the case of extremely unjust rules and the Weak Natural Law Thesis in respect of laws that suffer from lesser 'moral defects'.[23] Philip Soper also argues for the Strong Natural Law Thesis in 'extreme cases of wicked law'.[24] He says that law must pass through what he calls a 'moral filter' in order to count as law.[25] Soper argues that 'one begins the process of identifying what is to count as law by employing empirical tests of "pedigree" or validity that can be traced to social sources or social facts. But ... these officially identified directives cannot count as law if they are too unjust.'[26] This is because, in Soper's view, the recognition that law must meet minimum requirements of justice is part of what we mean by law.[27]

The critics of the Strong Natural Law Thesis, however, find it implausible to suppose that rules which meet all the acknowledged criteria of legal validity

---

20 Murphy, above n 12, p 10.
21 G Radbruch, 'Statutory Lawlessness and Supra-Statutory Law (1946)', S L Paulson and B Litschewski Paulson (trans) (2006) 26 *Oxford Journal of Legal Studies* 1, 7.
22 R Alexy, *The Argument from Injustice: A Reply to Legal Positivism*, S L Paulson and B Litschewski Paulson (trans), Clarendon Press, Oxford, 2002, p 54.
23 R Alexy, 'On the Concept and the Nature of Law' (2008) 21 *Ratio Juris* 281, 287-8.
24 P Soper, 'In Defence of Classical Natural Law in Legal Theory: Why Unjust Law is No Law at All' (2007) 20 *Canadian Journal of Law and Jurisprudence* 201, 213.
25 Ibid 202.
26 Ibid 205.
27 Ibid 204.

in a legal system and are taken to be law by officials in that system could fail to be laws. They say that there are obvious examples of flagrantly unjust laws. Consider the rules of the apartheid regime in South Africa. The critics argue that it confuses matters to say that these rules, grotesquely unjust as they were, were legally invalid. This is obviously a point that is pressed by positivists, but some natural law theorists, including Finnis, agree with the criticism. Finnis writes: '[H]uman law is artefact and artifice, and not a conclusion from moral premises'.[28] Finnis also says that if the slogan 'An unjust law is not a law' is intended literally, then it is 'pure nonsense, flatly self-contradictory'.[29] After all, how can something both be and not be a law? Finnis thinks that the strong reading is a caricature of the natural law tradition, which is not, according to him, concerned with questions of legal validity but rather with the morally obligatory force of law.[30] He therefore rejects the strong reading and defends a position that fits what Murphy calls the Weak Natural Law Thesis.

In order to understand Finnis's views on this matter we need to start with his methodological approach. Finnis believes that theorising about law cannot be a morally neutral enterprise. He says that 'any plausible theory of law that results from an effort to describe law ... has not been and will not be normatively inert'.[31] He argues, in particular, that because law is a human affair, which arises as a result of human choices, a plausible theory of law and its necessary features must be designed to show why law is something there is *reason* to create and maintain.[32]

In explaining why this is the case, Finnis takes Hart's approach to legal theory as his starting point. As we know, Hart was not in search of a definition of law. Instead he focused on explaining what he called the 'central case' of a legal system, maintaining that 'the diverse range of cases of which the word "law" is used are not linked by ... simple uniformity, but by less direct relations—often of analogy of either form or content to a central case'.[33] Hart also thought that an adequate account of the central case of law cannot remain at the level of external regularities in behaviour, but must make reference to the insiders' point of view. In particular, it must make reference to the practical viewpoint of those who treat the legal rules as standards by which it is proper to guide their conduct.

---

28 Finnis, above n 17, p 205.
29 J Finnis, *Natural Law and Natural Rights*, Clarendon Press, Oxford, 1980, p 364.
30 Ibid pp 364–5.
31 J Finnis, 'Law and What I Truly Should Decide' (2003) 48 *American Journal of Jurisprudence* 107, 119.
32 Ibid.
33 H L A Hart, *The Concept of Law*, 2nd edn, Clarendon Press, Oxford, 1994, p 81.

Finnis agrees with Hart on both of these points but he rejects Hart's view that the internal point of view can be adopted for a range of reasons that need not be moral reasons. As we saw in 3.7, Hart believes that officials may follow the law for reasons such as 'calculations of long-term interest; disinterested interest in others; an unreflecting inherited or traditional attitude; or the mere wish to do as others do'.[34] For Finnis, by contrast, the perspective of those who adopt the internal point of view for non-moral reasons cannot be the central internal perspective. Finnis describes these as 'manifestly deviant, diluted or watered-down instances of the practical viewpoint that brings law into being'.[35] He elaborates on this in later work by saying that '[t]he internal viewpoint has a central case that is not the viewpoint of careerists, or conformists, or traditionalists'.[36] The central participant point of view, according to Finnis, is that of the person who believes that the law is worth establishing and maintaining as a distinctive form of social order, and who therefore treats the law as giving rise to moral obligations to obey it. If officials do not have this attitude, the legal system will be unstable.[37] It is therefore this morally committed point of view that legal theory must seek to explain, in his view.

Furthermore, Finnis thinks that it will not be possible to analyse these beliefs without assessing whether they are *correct*.[38] This means that theorists will not be able to confine themselves merely to recording the beliefs of those who think there is reason to create and maintain law, but will have to draw on their *own* views about the moral value of law. Finnis puts this point by saying that there is an 'inherent ... dependence of descriptive general social theory ... upon the conscientious evaluations of the person who is ... theorizing (describing, explaining, analyzing)'.[39]

Consider, for instance, the role that power-conferring rules play in Hart's account of the distinctive features of law. Power-conferring rules give us the power to do such things as bequeath our property or enter into contracts. In explaining the importance of power-conferring rules, Hart gives reasons for rejecting the view of Hans Kelsen. Kelsen's way of explaining such rules was to reduce them to rules creating duties on officials to impose sanctions. Hart

---

34 Ibid p 203.
35 Finnis, above n 29, p 14.
36 J Finnis, 'Grounds of Law and Legal Theory: A Response' (2007) 13 *Legal Theory* 315, 336.
37 Finnis, above n 29, p 14.
38 J Dickson, *Evaluation and Legal Theory*, Hart Publishing, Oxford, 2001, p 46.
39 J Finnis, 'Natural Law: The Classical Tradition', in J Coleman and S Shapiro (eds), *The Oxford Handbook of Jurisprudence and Philosophy of Law*, Oxford University Press, Oxford, 2002, pp 16–17.

concedes that, with sufficient ingenuity, legal rules that confer powers can be rewritten as directions to officials to apply sanctions. For instance, the rule that states that two witnesses are required for the making of a valid will can be seen as a mere fragment of a more complete, coercive rule, stating (among other conditions): 'if there has been a will witnessed by two witnesses, and signed by the testator, and if the executor has not given effect to the provisions of the will, then the court ought to apply sanctions to the executor'.[40] Hart argues, however, that such a view of power-conferring rules is inadequate because it leaves out the perspective of those on whom the power is conferred. To those persons, the rules appear as conferring a 'huge and distinctive amenity' in providing them with the means to realise their wishes.[41]

Finnis seeks to press this further, arguing that Hart could not have made this theoretical claim about the 'practical point'[42] of power-conferring rules unless he himself saw the need for such rules or the reasons for having them. A valuable 'amenity' cannot, Finnis says, be normatively inert.[43] Thus, although Hart claimed to be merely *describing* the fact that people regard certain aspects of law as valuable, in fact, according to Finnis, he does *not* confine himself to merely reporting on this fact but implicitly shares their moral viewpoint. Indeed, Finnis argues, had Hart confined himself to a bare report, it would have been impossible for him to explain why he had chosen to report on *these* attitudes rather than others.[44]

Finnis therefore concludes that the concepts necessary for an adequate account of law are 'dependent on standards of assessing *importance* that ... track the standards of practical judgment we discern and employ in our truly practical deliberations toward choice and action in our own lives'.[45] In this way, Finnis's methodology is fundamentally opposed to the methodological positivism of thinkers such as Hart. It is impossible, according to Finnis, to give an explanatory account of law that is morally neutral, because it is impossible to come to a proper understanding of the nature of law without appreciating its moral point.

What, then, is the moral point of law, according to Finnis? Finnis's starting point in answering this question is the claim that there are certain goods that are self-evidently and objectively good for all human beings. They

---

40 Hart, above n 33, p 36.
41 Ibid p 41.
42 Finnis, above n 29, p 7.
43 Finnis, above n 31, 120.
44 J Finnis, 'On Hart's Ways: Law as Reason and as Fact' (2007) 52 *American Journal of Jurisprudence* 25, 42.
45 Finnis, above n 36, 319, Finnis's emphasis.

are goods for the reason that they make life worthwhile and contribute to human flourishing. In *Natural Law and Natural Rights*, Finnis lists the following as basic human goods: life, knowledge, play, aesthetic experience, sociability, religion (in a broad sense) and practical reasonableness.[46] He defines 'practical reasonableness' as the 'basic good of being able to bring one's own intelligence to bear effectively (in practical reasoning that issues in action) on the problems of choosing one's actions and life-style and shaping one's own character'.[47] He also describes it as 'reasonableness in deciding, in adopting commitments, in choosing and executing projects, and in general in acting'.[48]

Finnis thinks there is no sharp line to be drawn between pursuing one's own good and pursuing the good of others. For instance, sociability is part of our own flourishing, but the pursuit of sociability will lead us to be concerned with the common good of the political community. To be concerned with the common good is therefore part of what it is to flourish as a human being. By the common good of the political community, Finnis does not mean a utilitarian concern with the greatest good of the greatest number (see 10.3), but rather the securing of conditions 'that tend to favour the realization, by each individual in the community, of his or her personal development'.[49]

This notion of the common good leads Finnis to his account of law. Since the common good consists in the conditions that allow the members of a community to lead good lives and to pursue their own form of human flourishing, we need to live in a stable and orderly society in which people's conduct is coordinated. However, as we saw in 3.3, there may be more than one way in which we can coordinate our actions in our mutual interest. Reasonable people may disagree about which scheme of promoting the common good is best. The purpose of law, according to Finnis, is to solve this problem by authoritatively designating which course of action we should follow, thereby giving everyone a reason to conform to the same standard. Law is, in other words, an indispensable way of securing the basic goods and satisfying the requirements of practical reasonableness, because authoritative directives are the only way to solve the coordination problems that inevitably arise when efforts are made to secure the basic goods. This morally valuable purpose is intrinsic to law.[50]

---

46 Finnis, above n 29, pp 86–90.
47 Ibid p 88.
48 Ibid p 12.
49 Ibid p 154.
50 Ibid pp 276–7.

Finnis's account of the moral function of law enables him to explain how law can make a normative difference in the way discussed in 4.6—how it can create obligations to obey it, which did not exist prior to its enactment. Finnis's discussion here is based on a distinction made by Aquinas. There are two ways, for Aquinas, in which human laws can be based on natural law. They may be *deduced* from natural law principles, in which case they merely replicate the requirements of reason or morality. An example of such a law is the law forbidding murder. In such cases, we have a reason not to do what the law forbids, a reason that is independent of the legal prohibition. But some natural laws require *fleshing out* by human laws, and when this is the case human laws *fix* or *make determinate* what it is reasonable to do. Aquinas gives the example of a law providing for one type of punishment rather than another. It is a principle of natural law that an evildoer should be punished, but this principle is to some extent indeterminate and when deciding 'that [an evildoer] be punished in this way or that way',[51] there is a range of permissible punishments from which legislators may choose. Finnis makes the same point with reference to the rules of property law. He thinks that it is a principle of justice (that is, natural law) that there should be a regime of private property but he adds that 'precisely what rules should be laid down in order to constitute such a regime is not settled ("determined") by this general requirement of justice'.[52]

Finnis's claim that the requirements of reason are under-determined leads him to his explanation of the authority of law. Although legal rules must be *consistent* with the requirements of natural law in order to be genuinely authoritative, there is generally a *range* of such consistent rules. Therefore the rules actually chosen by the lawmaker to achieve the common good need not coincide with the rules that the individuals subject to them would themselves have chosen.[53] The persons subject to the rules need not even regard them as 'sensible'.[54] For reasons of stability and coordination, however, everyone has a content-independent reason to comply with these rules once they have been posited by the lawmaker. We are, in other words, obliged to obey the scheme of coordination selected by the law just because it has been selected by the law.

---

51 Aquinas, above n 8, IaIIae 95.2.
52 Finnis, above n 29, p 286.
53 Ibid p 289.
54 Ibid p 290.

Hence positive laws can create moral obligations that did not exist prior to their enactment: law is not otiose.[55]

We have seen that, according to Finnis, law serves a morally valuable purpose by virtue of its nature. The essential purpose of law is to promote the common good. This does not mean, of course, that the law will always be oriented towards justice and the common good. What, then, should we say about cases where the law is unjust? At this point Finnis takes two further steps. Once again drawing on the central case methodology, he claims, first, that the central case of law is law that serves its purpose successfully, and secondly, that laws which are not oriented towards the common good are defective as laws.[56]

For Hart, as we know, the central case of a legal system is to be found in the combination of primary and secondary rules. For Finnis, however, the central case of law is law that serves the moral ideals which are, according to him, intrinsic to the nature of law. He says that this is law in its 'focal' meaning.[57] Such law gives rise to moral obligations to obey it.

Unlike the adherents of the Strong Natural Law Thesis, Finnis does not say that unjust laws are invalid. As we know, the central case approach does not seek to provide a definition of law, but only to identify the paradigmatic cases of law. Hence Finnis is not led to define unjust laws out of existence, and in this respect his views are compatible with positivism. Instead of saying that unjust laws are invalid, he distinguishes the focal or primary meaning of the term 'law' from its secondary meanings and he argues that unjust laws are 'laws' in a secondary or derivative sense. When we are dealing with unjust laws, according to Finnis, we are talking about instances of law which are 'undeveloped, primitive, corrupt, deviant or other "qualified sense" or "extended sense" instances of [law]'.[58] Hence unjust laws are not 'really' laws, or are not laws 'in the fullest sense'. They are defective *as laws* and consequently, judged from the perspective of law's focal meaning, 'less' legal than laws that are just.[59] This means that, apart from considerations about weakening a generally just system, unjust laws do not create moral obligations to obey them.[60]

---

55 Finnis, above n 39, pp 20–23.
56 J Dickson, 'Is Bad Law Still Law? Is Bad Law Really Law?', in M Del Mar and Z Bankowski (eds), *Law as Institutional Normative Order*, Ashgate, Surrey, 2009, p 171.
57 Finnis, above n 29, p 276.
58 Ibid p 11.
59 Ibid p 279.
60 Ibid pp 361–2.

When we are concerned with law in such a secondary sense—when we are concerned with what is merely 'in a *sense*' law—Finnis says that we may fall back on the technical, lawyer's use of language, which for practical purposes must treat any standard that meets the acknowledged social-fact criteria of validity in a particular legal system as valid.[61] Finnis writes: 'It is not conducive to clear thought, or to any good practical purpose, to smudge the positivity of law by denying the legal obligatoriness *in the legal or intra-systemic sense* of a rule recently affirmed as legally valid and obligatory by the highest institutions of the "legal system".'[62] This technical or intra-systemic viewpoint therefore sits alongside and coexists with the very different viewpoint of practical reasonableness, which uses what Finnis calls the 'focal, moral sense of "legal validity"'[63] and which is geared towards a very different task. This is the task of 'describing and explaining the role of legal process within the ordering of human life in society, and the place of legal thought in practical reason's effort to understand and effect real human good'.[64]

In later work, Finnis sheds light on this argument by comparing the concept of law to the concepts of medicine and arguments. He observes that invalid or fallacious arguments are not really arguments, 'even though these non-arguments ... are still, in a secondary or watered down sense, arguments'.[65] Futile or lethal medicines are likewise not really medicinal, even though they may be sold as medicines or listed as such in histories of medicines.[66] What law, arguments and medicine have in common, according to Finnis, is that they have to be understood in terms of their normative point, and putative instances of them that do not serve this point are not really instances of law, arguments and medicine at all.[67]

5.4 Some criticisms of Finnis

Discussion of Finnis's normative conception of jurisprudence will be deferred until the next chapter, where we will consider Hart's response to comparable claims made by Dworkin (see 6.12). In this section we will consider two other

---

61 Ibid pp 279–80.
62 Ibid p 357, Finnis's emphasis.
63 Ibid p 27.
64 Ibid p 280.
65 Finnis, above n 31, 108.
66 Ibid 114.
67 Ibid.

criticisms. First, granting for the sake of argument that law has by its nature a distinctive moral purpose, and therefore conceding that we cannot understand it without reference to the moral objectives it is meant to serve, some theorists ask whether Finnis is entitled to conclude that laws which fail to serve those objectives are less than fully laws or are laws only in a secondary sense. Julie Dickson argues along these lines. She argues that the reason why we are troubled so much by unjust laws and unjust legal systems is precisely because they are *genuine* laws. She writes:

> [I]f it turned out that the thing doing the failing was not law at all, or was not really law, then why should it be held to the particular standards that *law* ought to live up to, and why would it trouble us if it failed to attain those particular standards? ... It only makes sense to regard instances of morally bad law as subject to those standards, and to be concerned about their failure to be as law ought to be when they do not attain them, if they are indeed instances of law.[68]

Hart makes a different point. He is sceptical about the idea that there is something in the *nature* of law which could help us to distinguish just from unjust laws, and he doubts that the most illuminating perspective for understanding legal systems is the ideal law or form of law that serves the common good. He thinks that in order to understand the central features of a legal system, we do not have to have a view about the form law ideally ought to take. He also thinks that identifying the 'central case' of law with the ideal form of law is likely to cause confusion rather than to bring clarity. Hart writes:

> [T]he identification of the central meaning of law with what is morally legitimate, because orientated towards the common good, seems to me in view of the hideous record of the evil use of law for oppression to be an unbalanced perspective, and as great a distortion as the opposite Marxist identification of the central case of law with the pursuit of the interests of a dominant economic class.[69]

Matthew Kramer reasons along similar lines. He rejects Finnis's claim that the central case of the internal or legal viewpoint is the perspective of someone whose allegiance to the law is based on moral reasons. On the contrary, in Kramer's view, the self-interest of tyrannical officials can be a solid basis for a fully functioning legal system, and there is therefore no reason to say that a legal system founded on the rulers' self-interest rather than the achievement of the

---

68 Dickson, above n 56, p 176.
69 H L A Hart, *Essays in Jurisprudence and Philosophy*, Clarendon Press, Oxford, 1983, p 12.

common good is not a straightforward instance or 'central case' of a legal system.[70]

5.5 Fuller and the moral standards internal to law

We turn now to procedural natural law theories, and in particular, to Lon Fuller's theory. Fuller was an American legal scholar of the mid-twentieth century who made an important contribution to jurisprudence, although, as has often been noted, his work is not quite as philosophically rigorous as that of later legal theorists. Fuller's theory is more narrowly focused on questions specifically about law than traditional natural law theories, which, as we have seen, are first and foremost moral theories. A further difference is that Fuller is not concerned with the substantive aims of particular legal rules and their possible conflict with a law 'higher' than positive law—a concept that he rejects.[71] Instead, he is concerned with the conditions for the existence of a legal system, particularly with the ways in which, according to him, rules must be made and administered if we are to talk of a legal system. For this reason, he describes his theory as a 'procedural natural law theory'.[72] Fuller attempts to show that there are certain forms that legal norms must take, and certain procedures that must be used in their application. He also argues that these forms and processes have intrinsic moral value. This leads him to conclude that there is a necessary connection between law and morality.

Fuller's starting point is the claim that law is an activity with a distinctive purpose. In contrast to other forms of social ordering or social control, law is, in his view, 'the enterprise of subjecting human conduct to the governance of rules'.[73] This enterprise contains a 'certain inner logic of its own',[74] imposing demands that must be met if it is to succeed in attaining its objectives. First, if legislators were to decide issues on an ad hoc and therefore unpredictable basis, they would not be able to guide behaviour in the desired direction. Guidance requires some degree of generality. Furthermore, if legislators did not promulgate

---

70 M H Kramer, *In Defense of Legal Positivism: Law without Trimmings*, Oxford University Press, Oxford, 1999, pp 236–8.
71 L L Fuller, *The Morality of Law,* revised edn, Yale University Press, New Haven, 1969, p 96.
72 Ibid.
73 Ibid p 106.
74 Ibid pp 150–1.

their rules, the rules would again be incapable of guiding conduct. The same would be true if legislators were to make frequent use of retrospective rules, or to use incomprehensible language in drafting the rules, or to enact contradictory rules or rules with which it is impossible to comply, or to change the rules so frequently that those subject to them do not have time to adjust to the changes, or if those who apply the rules were to misinterpret the rules and depart from the law as enacted.[75]

Because, in Fuller's view, nothing can count as law if it cannot be followed, and because it is not possible for citizens to follow rules suffering from formal and procedural defects such as these, he concludes that these defects would be 'routes to failure' in the enterprise of creating law.[76] And a total failure in all of these ways would result in something that is not simply bad law but not law at all. Just as we would not describe something that is totally incapable of cutting as a 'knife', we would not describe a system of rules that is totally incapable of guiding conduct as a 'legal system'.

For Fuller, there are therefore certain formal and procedural principles without which a system of laws cannot exist. Laws must be general: that is, they must refer to classes of people and circumstances, not individuals. Laws must be public. They must also be clear, non-contradictory, possible to obey, relatively constant and prospective. Finally, there must be congruence between official application and declared rule: officials must faithfully apply the rules that have been enacted. Fuller calls these principles the 'principles of legality'. A government that observes them can also be said to be based on the 'rule of law' because compliance with the principles serves as a restraint on the exercise of governmental power. Although Fuller concedes that legal systems do not need to comply *perfectly* with these principles, he thinks that they must comply with them on the whole if a set of standards is to amount to a legal system.[77] It is therefore a *necessary* truth, according to Fuller, that law consists of standards which by and large satisfy the principles of legality. Jeremy Waldron summarises Fuller's position as follows: 'Observance of the principles of legality is among the necessary criteria for the application of the concepts *law* and *legal system*. There comes a point in a system's failure to observe the principles of legality where we

---

75   Ibid pp 46–91.
76   Ibid p 41.
77   Ibid.

would have to say that it does not really count as a legal system or a system of law at all.'[78]

What, it might be wondered, does this have to do with a necessary connection between law and morality? Although Fuller's answer is sketchy, it seems that he believes that observance of the principles of legality has inherent moral value. He argues that the principles of legality speak to our dignity by respecting us as responsible agents who are capable of making free choices. Rules that satisfy the principles make it clear what we are free to do and not to do. They therefore provide a predictable and secure framework within which we can plan and lead our lives, confident that we will not be punished as long as we obey the rules. Conversely, departure from the principles of legality strikes at our powers of self-determination by unfairly holding us to standards with which we could not have complied. Thus, for instance, retrospective laws, which punish us for conduct that was not unlawful at the time it was undertaken, convey 'indifference to [our] powers of self-determination'.[79] The same is true of rules that breach the other principles of legality: they all constitute a similar affront in making no attempt to *guide* our behaviour. Because Fuller thinks that the principles of legality are morally significant in this way, in showing respect for us as rational agents, and in 'furnish[ing] a baseline for self-directed action',[80] he describes them as constituting law's 'inner morality' or as 'the morality which makes law possible'.[81]

Since Fuller believes that a system cannot count as a legal system unless it substantially conforms to the principles of legality, and since he also believes that these principles embody certain moral standards, he concludes that the criteria for the existence of law include moral criteria and that there is therefore a necessary connection between law and morality. There is consequently, on his view, no sharp conceptual separation between inquiries into the existence of law and inquiries into its moral value, because breaches of the principles of legality simultaneously make rules both *morally worse* (because they do not respect our dignity as self-determining agents) and *less legal* (because they are less capable of guiding conduct). Fuller concludes that law is not an 'amoral datum'[82] but an

---

78 J Waldron, 'Positivism and Legality: Hart's Equivocal Response to Fuller' (2008) 83 *New York University Law Review* 1135, 1141, Waldron's emphasis.
79 Fuller, above n 71, p 162.
80 Ibid p 210.
81 Ibid p 42.
82 L L Fuller, 'Positivism and Fidelity to Law—A Reply to Professor Hart' (1958) 71 *Harvard Law Review* 630, 656.

achievement worthy of respect, at least to some extent. Since the ideal of legality, which is a moral ideal, is built into the very concept of a legal system, anything that is recognisable as law has an inbuilt claim on our moral allegiance.

Fuller applies his theory to the Nazi regime, arguing that it departed so far from the principles of legality as to cease to be a legal system. He writes as follows about the formal and procedural perversions of the Nazi system:

> When a system calling itself law is predicated upon a general disregard by judges of the terms of the laws they purport to enforce, when the system habitually cures its legal irregularities, even the grossest, by retroactive statutes, when it has only to resort to forays of terror in the streets, which no one dares challenge, in order to escape even those scant restraints imposed by the pretence of legality—when all these things have become true of a dictatorship, it is not hard for me, at least, to deny to it the name of law.[83]

Thus, although Fuller believes that Nazi statutes were not law, this is not because he believes they were in breach of a 'higher' law—one above human law, existing independently of human legal institutions. Nor does Fuller put the emphasis on the odious ends pursued by the Nazis and the murderous means they used to achieve them. These matters fall under what he calls the 'external morality' of the law. Instead, he emphasises the way in which Nazi statutes violated the principles of legality or the moral principles that are, in his view, internal to the concept of law. Fuller does, however, think that form (internal morality) and content (external morality) are connected, because he thinks that if lawmakers respect the principles of legality, they will be more likely to respect the external morality of law and therefore to enact substantively just laws. He takes the view, which he concedes might seem naïve, 'that coherence and goodness have more affinity than coherence and evil'.[84] He thinks, in other words, that rulers who obey the principles of legality are more likely to pursue justice and human welfare.[85]

5.6 Some criticisms of Fuller

Criticism of Fuller's views has mainly concentrated on his claim that the principles of legality (and therefore governance by law) have intrinsic moral value. Hart, for instance, argues that compliance with the principles of legality

---

83 Ibid 660.
84 Ibid 636.
85 Fuller, above n 71, p 154.

does not necessarily confer moral value on a legal system. According to Hart, the principles of legality are merely efficient ways for lawmakers to achieve their aims, and the principles will possess moral value only if the lawmakers' aims are good. Thus if racist lawmakers, for instance, wish to achieve their racist objectives, they will need to make sure that their laws are capable of being obeyed and they will therefore be well advised to enact laws that satisfy the principles of legality. Such a racist system is not, however, morally improved by the fact that its laws are clear, possible to obey, consistently applied, and so on. Hart compares the principles of legality to the principles of carpentry, which are useful regardless of whether the carpenter is making hospital beds or torturers' racks.[86] The principles of legality are likewise just a recipe for making effective laws, whether good or bad. They are no more a 'morality' than a recipe for effectively poisoning people is a 'morality of poisoning'.[87]

It is not possible to pursue this criticism here, except to note that the issue continues to be debated. Nigel Simmonds, for example, has recently argued that while it is logically possible for a wicked regime to pursue its goals through meticulous observance of the rule of law, the principles of legality are not morally neutral. They are not, in other words, neutral as between the pursuit of good aims and of bad aims.[88] Simmonds maintains that a wicked regime would have less reason to govern by law than a good regime. He concedes that wicked rulers would have good reason to publish rules and enforce them. He argues, however, that it would not be in the interests of wicked rulers to confine punishment to people who have broken the law, because punishing people who have not breached any rules is a highly effective way of suppressing opposition.[89] By contrast, a just regime, which regards restraints on government power as *morally* desirable, would have a good reason not to resort to extra-legal violence, even though such violence might help to achieve governmental goals. It is therefore, in Simmonds' view, only concern for the *moral* value of governing by law which can provide governments with a reason to confine punishment to those who have broken the rules.[90] It should be clear that Simmonds' argument for the moral value of the principles of legality puts the emphasis on the way in which they curb government power, rather than on their efficacy in guiding conduct.

---

86 Hart, above n 69, p 347.
87 Ibid p 350.
88 N E Simmonds, *Law as a Moral Idea*, Oxford University Press, Oxford, 2007, p 62.
89 Ibid pp 84–8.
90 Ibid pp 88, 187.

5.7 Natural law in the courts

The kinds of conceptual issues discussed in this chapter are of practical as well as theoretical significance. For instance, courts have been confronted with them after the collapse of totalitarian regimes when the question of the validity of the laws passed by the previous government has been raised. Faced with these problems of 'transitional justice'—the need for a new liberal democratic regime to respond to human rights abuses perpetrated in the past—domestic courts have sometimes resorted to natural law reasoning, even referring on occasion to Radbruch's formula (see 5.3).

Alexy describes one such case, decided by a German court. The court had to decide whether a Jewish lawyer had forfeited his German citizenship by fleeing to Amsterdam shortly before the outbreak of World War II. Under a Nazi Ordinance, emigrant Jews had been stripped of their German citizenship on the ground of race. The Federal Constitutional Court stated that not every instrument that emanates from the lawmaker is law. It held that the Ordinance was null and void or legally invalid from the outset because it violated 'fundamental principles of justice so evidently that the judge who elected to apply them or to acknowledge their legal consequences would be administering lawlessness rather than law'.[91] The lawyer had therefore never lost his citizenship.

A less clear-cut but nonetheless informative example is discussed by Hart and Fuller. It also involves a post-World War II case: the prosecution of a woman who had deliberately exploited the oppressive laws of the Nazis in order to get rid of her husband. She had denounced him to the authorities, reporting that he had made critical comments about Hitler and the Nazi Party. The making of such comments was illegal under Nazi law and the husband was sentenced to the death penalty, although he was not in fact executed but sent to the front. After the war ended, the wife was prosecuted for the offence of illegally depriving a person of his freedom. She defended herself by saying that since her husband's conduct was illegal under the law existing at the time, she could not have been guilty of a crime. She had merely taken steps to ensure that the law was enforced. How, then, could she have committed an offence?

The Court of Appeal found that she *had* committed an offence. According to Hart and Fuller, this was because the court took the view that the Nazi law in question violated natural law. As Hart and Fuller describe the case, the court

---

91 Quoted in Alexy, above n 22, p 6.

held that, although the statute under which the husband was sentenced to death was valid in terms of all the standard criteria of validity for Nazi laws, it was so evil as not to be a law. In informing on her husband, the wife had therefore acted not merely immorally but also, despite appearances, illegally. She was therefore guilty of the offence with which she had been charged.

Some later scholars have, however, cast doubt on this interpretation of the case.[92] It seems that the original reporting of the case, on which Hart and Fuller had relied, was unclear. The Court of Appeal did not, in fact, invalidate the statute for reasons of its incompatibility with 'higher law' or natural law. Instead, it relied on rather implausible legal reasoning to the effect that, although the court-martial judges were under a legal duty to find the husband guilty, his wife had illegally deprived him of his liberty because she had no legal duty to inform on him and she had used the court-martial as an instrument, in much the same way as one might set a dog on someone.[93] It is true that this is not, on the face of it, an appeal to natural or suprapositive law. However, it could be argued that the Court of Appeal would not have been driven to such implausible reasoning except as a disguise for the natural law belief that the woman's actions were so reprehensible that they could not be supported by anything we would be prepared to describe as law. Since openly stating this might have been too controversial, the court instead may have sought to conceal the real, natural law basis for its decision by searching for a 'legal' justification for finding the woman guilty—a justification which it hoped would be, however unconvincing as a piece of legal reasoning, at least less philosophically controversial.

Other interesting cases are the East German Border Guards cases. These were trials held after the collapse of the Berlin Wall in an attempt to deal with human rights abuses by the former socialist regime of East Germany. Approximately 200 fugitives, who had done nothing more than attempt to escape from East Germany to the West, had been shot at the border. Some of the guards who were responsible for these killings, as well as their superiors who had given the orders, were convicted of manslaughter, notwithstanding the fact that their actions were apparently licensed by East German law—in particular, by a defence under the *Border Act*. In a case affirming the guilt of some of the border guards, the Federal Court of Justice made express reference to Radbruch's

---

[92] H O Pappe, 'On the Validity of Judicial Decisions in the Nazi Era' (1960) 23 *Modern Law Review* 260, 263.

[93] D Dyzenhaus, 'The Grudge Informer Case Revisited' (2008) 83 *New York University Law Review* 1000, 1009.

formula and then stated that 'in judging deeds done at the command of the state one has to take into account whether the state has crossed the outer limits which are ordained to it by general convictions in any country'.[94] The court found that the *Border Act* offended against justice by allowing soldiers to kill innocent and unarmed civilians. It was therefore invalid and the soldiers did not have a defence.[95]

There are also some well-known English cases from the seventeenth century in which judges invoked the common law as a proxy for natural law, appearing to suggest that there were certain moral principles, inherent in the common law, which could not be abrogated by Acts of Parliament or by the monarch. The most famous of these is *Dr Bonham's Case* of 1610, in which Chief Justice Coke said: '[W]hen an Act of Parliament is against common right and reason, or repugnant, or impossible to be performed, the common law will controul it, and adjudge such Act to be void.'[96]

After the Glorious Revolution, it was assumed that the principle of the sovereignty of parliament had triumphed and that the courts could not invalidate Acts of Parliament. Yet traces of the notion of fundamental moral principles higher than parliamentary sovereignty survive. Thus the atrocities of Nazi Germany invited a reappearance of natural law thought not only in Germany but also in England. In *Oppenheimer v Cattermole*, a majority of the House of Lords indicated that it would refuse to recognise a Nazi law depriving Jewish citizens of German nationality (despite the fact that the law met all the standard criteria of legal validity in terms of English legal rules) because it was morally iniquitous. Lord Cross of Chelsea said: '[L]egislation which takes away without compensation from a section of the citizen body singled out on racial grounds all their property ... and ... deprives them of their citizenship ... constitutes so grave an infringement of human rights that the courts of this country ought to refuse to recognise it as a law at all.'[97]

In Australia, the minority judgment of Deane and Toohey JJ in the case of *Leeth v Commonwealth*[98] contains a controversial attempt to use common law principles as a vehicle for striking down unjust laws. The law challenged in

---

94 Quoted in R Alexy, 'A Defence of Radbruch's Formula', in D Dyzenhaus (ed), *Recrafting the Rule of Law: The Limits of Legal Order*, Hart Publishing, Oxford, 1999, p 22.
95 For a full discussion, see M J Gabriel, 'Coming to Terms with the East German Border Guards Cases' (1999) 38 *Columbia Journal of Transnational Law* 375.
96 *Dr Bonham's Case* (1610) 8 Co Rep 107a, 118a.
97 *Oppenheimer v Cattermole* [1976] AC 249, 278.
98 *Leeth v Commonwealth* (1992) 174 CLR 455.

this case made it possible for federal offenders who had committed identical offences to be subjected to differing minimum non-parole periods, depending on the state in which they happened to be convicted. This law discriminated, in Deane and Toohey JJ's view, on irrational or irrelevant grounds. There are certain limits on the legislative power of the Commonwealth Parliament, which derive from the Australian Constitution. But there is no general guarantee of equality or non-discrimination in the Constitution and for this reason the majority found that there was no legal basis on which the law could be invalidated. Deane and Toohey JJ, by contrast, found that the common law principle that all persons are equal under the law and before the courts is incorporated in the Constitution as a matter of necessary implication. This principle functions, they said, to invalidate laws that arbitrarily discriminate on irrational grounds. They would therefore have struck down the law. Some commentators, such as Leslie Zines, have argued that Deane and Toohey JJ were in reality relying on natural law reasoning: they objected to the law because of its injustice, but since that is a moral rather than a legal basis for striking down a law, they invoked a supposedly constitutionalised common law principle of equality as the justification for invalidating it. Zines writes: 'To limit governmental power by reference to fundamental principles of the common law has, at best, a tenuous link with anything in the Constitution and resembles more notions of "higher law" or "natural law", which depend very much on personal values.'[99]

Questions

1. 'The ideology does not exist that cannot be defended by an appeal to the law of nature. And, indeed, how can it be otherwise, since the ultimate basis for every natural right lies in a private direct insight, an evident contemplation, an intuition. Cannot my intuition be just as good as yours?' (A Ross, *On Law and Justice*, Stevens and Sons, London, 1974, p 261). Is this a sound criticism of natural law theory?
2. Do you agree with Finnis's list of objective basic goods? Is it possible to provide a list of objective goods?
3. Do you agree with Finnis that the central case of law is law that is oriented towards the common good and that unjust laws are not laws in the fullest sense?

---

99 L Zines, 'A Judicially Created Bill of Rights?' (1994) 16 *Sydney Law Review* 166, 183.

4   The 'Grudge Informer' cases were post-World War II German cases in which people who had exploited the Nazi reign of terror to denounce their enemies were prosecuted. One of these cases involved a woman who, wanting to be rid of her husband, had informed on him for making critical comments about Hitler and the Nazi Party. The making of such comments was illegal under Nazi law. After the war ended, the woman was prosecuted for the offence of illegally depriving a person of his freedom. How would you have decided the case if you were the judge? Would you have acquitted the woman on the ground that what she had done was not illegal under Nazi law? Would you have convicted her on the ground that the 'law' under which her husband had been convicted was so evil as not to be a valid law? Would you have conceded that the Nazi law was a valid law, but refused to apply it? Consider the arguments for and against these different courses of action.

5   Leslie Green writes: 'Hart's overall message about the relationship between law and morality is in one way similar to Hannah Arendt's in *Eichmann in Jerusalem*. What made Arendt's book so controversial was her claim that ... Eichmann was the epitome of law-abidingness. What Arendt called the "banality of evil" thus may be seen also as the lawfulness of evil. That is what is so shocking—that law may be, in a phrase that Fuller derided, "an amoral datum". Some resist this idea so strongly and are so intent to preserve the halo around the procedural virtues of law, that they are prepared to make its denial an item of faith. In his exchange with Hart, Fuller said: "I shall have to rest on the assertion of a belief that may seem naïve, namely, that coherence and goodness have more affinity than coherence and evil." That is a faith that Hart, like Arendt, could not share' (L Green, 'The Concept of Law Revisited' (1996) 94 *Michigan Law Review* 1687, 1711). Do you agree with Hart that legal forms and processes are as serviceable for evil as for good?

Further reading

R Alexy, 'On the Concept and the Nature of Law' (2008) 21 *Ratio Juris* 281.

B Bix, 'Natural Law: The Modern Tradition', in J Coleman and S Shapiro (eds), *The Oxford Handbook of Jurisprudence and Philosophy of Law*, Oxford University Press, Oxford, 2002, pp 61–103.

J Dickson, 'Is Bad Law Still Law? Is Bad Law Really Law?', in M Del Mar and Z Bankowski (eds), *Law as Institutional Normative Order*, Ashgate, Surrey, 2009, pp 161–83.

R P George (ed), *Natural Law*, Ashgate, Dartmouth, 2003.

J Finnis, *Natural Law and Natural Rights*, Clarendon Press, Oxford, 1980.

J Finnis, 'The Truth in Legal Positivism', in R P George (ed), *The Autonomy of Law: Essays on Legal Positivism,* Clarendon Press, Oxford, 1996, pp 195–214.

J Finnis, 'Natural Law: The Classical Tradition', in J Coleman and S Shapiro (eds), *The Oxford Handbook of Jurisprudence and Philosophy of Law*, Oxford University Press, Oxford, 2002, pp 1–60.

L L Fuller, *The Morality of Law,* revised edn, Yale University Press, New Haven, 1969.

L L Fuller, 'Positivism and Fidelity to Law—A Reply to Professor Hart' (1958) 71 *Harvard Law Review* 630.

H L A Hart, 'Positivism and the Separation of Law and Morals' (1958) 71 *Harvard Law Review* 593.

H L A Hart, *Essays in Jurisprudence and Philosophy*, Clarendon Press, Oxford, 1983, Chapter 16.

M H Kramer, *In Defense of Legal Positivism: Law without Trimmings,* Oxford University Press, Oxford, 1999, Chapters 2, 8.

M C Murphy, *Natural Law in Jurisprudence and Politics*, Cambridge University Press, New York, 2006, Chapters 1–4.

N E Simmonds, *Law as a Moral Idea*, Oxford University Press, Oxford, 2007.

J Waldron, 'Positivism and Legality: Hart's Equivocal Response to Fuller' (2008) 83 *New York University Law Review* 1135.

6

Law as Interpretive

6.1 Chapter overview

This chapter will explore anti-positivist theories that focus on the role of judges and the nature of adjudication. The theories to be considered see judicial decision-making as involving recourse to morality—not because the practices of officials may happen to license it in particular legal systems, nor as an extra-legal add-on when the social-fact sources of law are indeterminate. They maintain that morality plays a necessary, not a merely possible, role in identifying what the law is on some matter. Furthermore, for these theorists, it is not a matter of referring to social sources, such as legislation and judicial decisions, and then applying a 'moral filter' to exclude or downgrade as defective certain norms identified in the 'plain-fact' way. Instead, these theorists take the view that laws cannot be identified in the first place without considering the question of their moral merits. The most prominent and sophisticated defender of this view is Ronald Dworkin, and the bulk of this chapter will therefore be devoted to his work. Some attention will also be paid to the views of Lon Fuller, whose 'purposive' approach to legal interpretation prefigures Dworkin's approach in some ways, although it is not as well developed.

Dworkin takes what he describes as an 'interpretive' approach to the question of what the law is on a particular matter and he gives a central role to the political virtue of 'integrity' in explaining why this should be the case. On his approach, to ascribe meaning to a statute or a judicial decision is to undertake an interpretive exercise, which involves trying to make the law the 'best it can be' from the point of view of political morality. Indeed, for Dworkin, finding out what *law* is, as opposed to what *the law* is—in other words, explicating the *concept* of law—is also an interpretive exercise and therefore inextricably dependent on judgments about the extent to which particular theories of law show law to be a morally attractive form of governance. Both the doctrinal task of identifying the law and the philosophical task of theorising about the law are therefore inherently moral endeavours for Dworkin, locating him in the natural law tradition, on a broad understanding of that tradition.

6.2 Fuller's theory of meaning

In the previous chapter, we examined Fuller's views about the inner morality of law and the sense in which this makes him a natural law theorist. We turn now to his views about legal interpretation, which present a different kind of challenge to positivism. Generally speaking, an interest in judicial decision-making is a characteristic feature of American legal theory and it is therefore unsurprising that American anti-positivists such as Fuller and Dworkin focus on features of adjudicative practice that they believe to be inconsistent with positivism. Fuller believes that legal interpretation is a purposive activity and that legal rules must be interpreted in ways that yield just or reasonable results. In setting out this view, he presents a direct challenge to Hart's positivist account of legal reasoning and the judicial task.

We saw in 3.8 that Hart distinguishes between the core and penumbra of a rule. The core is generally determined by the plain meaning of the language in which the rule is formulated—a meaning on which everyone will agree—although Hart does not believe that agreement that a case falls within the scope of a rule is exclusively a function of the plain meaning of language. In later work, he says that such agreement can also, on occasion, be based on the explicitly stated or generally agreed purpose of the legal rule. A clear case can be clear, in other words, by virtue of knowledge of a rule's purpose.[1] Hart then goes on to identify the *law* with the core cases: when judges apply rules that are clearly applicable, whether by virtue of their plain meaning or their obvious purpose, they are applying law. Conversely, when there is disagreement about the meaning of the rule, either because the words do not uncontroversially apply or because the purpose of the rule is unclear, then there is no legal answer to the question that has been raised and the judge is obliged to go *outside* the law to resolve the issue.

It will be remembered that Hart uses the rule 'No vehicles in the park' to illustrate these points. He argues that some cases clearly fall within the scope

---

1   H L A Hart, *Essays in Jurisprudence and Philosophy*, Clarendon Press, Oxford, 1983, p 106.

of the rule by virtue of its plain linguistic meaning. It is clear, for instance, that the term 'vehicle' applies to motor cars and trucks. Hart also believes that determining the meaning of a legal rule does not necessarily involve moral reasoning. Of course, as we know, Hart embraced inclusive positivism in his later work, maintaining that moral considerations *may* enter into the law-finding process. He insists, however, that they do not do so *necessarily*. And although Hart does not say this in so many words, the straightforward application of the 'No vehicles in the park' rule to cars looks like a good candidate for legal reasoning that is morally neutral, since in determining what the law on this matter *is*, it seems that judges do not consider what it *ought to be*.[2] In penumbral cases, by contrast, judges are necessarily reasoning morally. In deciding whether the word 'vehicle' covers bicycles, for instance, judges have to make the decision that they believe to be the most reasonable one, all things considered. This is not a threat to Hart's positivism, however, because he believes that there is no law on the matter in such cases. Hence, although judges in such cases necessarily draw on their beliefs about what the law ought to be, this is not with a view to saying what the law is. It is with a view to making new law on the matter.

Fuller rejects this picture. He does not accept that on some occasions judges are determining what the law is and on other occasions they are determining what it ought to be. They are always determining what the law is, but in so doing they are also always drawing on their beliefs about what it ought to be. Let us see what he means by this rather obscure-sounding claim. In arguing for this conclusion Fuller relies, in part, on the claim that language can never be a source of legal determinacy and that we always need to know what the purpose of a rule is in order to know what it clearly covers. Fuller says: 'If the rule excluding vehicles from parks seems easy to apply in some cases, I submit this is because we can see clearly enough what the rule "is aiming at in general" so that we know there is no need to worry about the difference between Fords and Cadillacs.'[3] The clarity of a rule is, in other words, a function of the clarity of its purpose, not the clarity of its words.[4]

Fuller is making a very strong point. Although Hart thinks that the purpose of a legal rule can sometimes determine whether it is applicable, he also thinks that the plain meaning of its words can have the same effect. Fuller goes

---

2   H L A Hart, 'Positivism and the Separation of Law and Morals' (1958) 71 *Harvard Law Review* 593, 615; F Schauer, 'A Critical Guide to Vehicles in the Park' (2008) 83 *New York University Law Review* 1109, 1113–14.

3   L L Fuller, 'Positivism and Fidelity to Law—A Reply to Professor Hart' (1958) 71 *Harvard Law Review* 630, 663.

4   L L Fuller, *Anatomy of the Law*, Penguin Books, Harmondsworth, 1971, p 162.

much further. For Fuller, the *only* way to determine the meaning of a legal rule is to rely on purpose-based interpretation, because it is impossible for rules clearly to apply to factual situations merely by virtue of the meaning of the language in which they are written. For Fuller, there is no such thing as context-independent, literal meaning and there cannot therefore be a 'language-determined core'.[5] We cannot know what circumstances clearly fall under a rule without knowing the purpose of the rule. Fuller gives two examples to support his view.

Focusing specifically on Hart's claim that, whatever else the term 'vehicle' refers to, it clearly refers to cars and trucks, Fuller asks us to imagine that some local patriots want to construct a memorial by mounting a working truck used in World War II on a pedestal in the park. Fuller argues that in order to know whether 'vehicle' covers this situation we have to determine its meaning in the light of the purpose for which the rule was enacted. Since to prohibit the truck on the pedestal would be incompatible with any imaginable purpose behind the rule, Fuller concludes that 'vehicle' must have a different meaning in this context from the meaning it usually has: it does not cover trucks.[6]

Fuller's second example is a law that makes it an offence to sleep at railway stations. He asks what Hart would say about the following two cases. In the first case, a businessman, waiting for a delayed train in the early hours of the morning, nods off while sitting upright. In the other case, a homeless person has settled down for the night on the platform with blankets and pillows but has not yet actually fallen asleep. Who is 'sleeping' in terms of the rule? On the view that words have a clear core of plain meaning, the businessman would obviously be asleep while the homeless person would not. But Fuller argues that we must have recourse to the likely purpose behind the law in order to interpret the word 'sleeping'. Having regard to this likely purpose, namely, preventing homeless people from bedding down at the station, Fuller suggests that in this context, the businessman is not 'sleeping', but the homeless person is.[7]

It might be wondered what exactly Fuller means by the 'purpose' of a legal rule. Does he mean that judges should investigate the lawmakers' intentions in enacting the rule, focusing on what the lawmakers subjectively intended to say with the words they used? This view has well-known difficulties, including the fact that it is implausible to think that all those who vote for a particular piece of legislation will share the same mental states. It is implausible, in other words,

---

5   This is Schauer's phrase, above n 2, 1111.
6   Fuller, above n 3, 664.
7   Ibid.

to think they will all have the same purpose for the legislation in mind and exactly the same view about the range of factual situations that fall under the statutory words they have chosen. They may, in fact, have no clear view at all about these matters.[8]

In fact, Fuller downplays the role of the lawmakers' actual mental states in determining the purpose of the law. He says that the difficult cases are not resolved in advance by the legislator.[9] Instead, he places the emphasis on the underlying policy goals of the legislation and even on the objectives that can be imputed to rational legislators, whose purposes can be presumed to be reasonable. This view of 'purpose' is quite different from Hart's. Hart believes that the purposive interpretation of a rule is no threat to the separation of law and morality because the purpose that makes the meaning of a legal rule clear may be an evil purpose.[10] For Fuller, however, the notion of 'purpose' is more rarefied. Thus he calls attention to the virtues of a 'modest' form of natural law, whose 'fundamental tenet is an affirmation of the role of human reason in the design and operation of legal institutions'.[11] Along these lines, Fuller says that the answers to the questions courts must ask themselves—such as 'What are parks for anyway?'—'must largely be drawn from what may be called implicit sources, from the attitudes and practices of the community, and some shared conception of the most beneficial use of park areas'.[12] Fuller also tells us:

> [N]o constitutional draftsman can foresee what points of rub and friction will develop in the future as the structure he has created feels the strain of new and novel demands. The solution must be found in an interpretation of the constitution that will respect not merely its words but the implicit ideals of orderly and decent government those words attempted to express.[13]

For Fuller, language does not constrain the interpretation of legal rules at all. The meaning of words is entirely a function of the context in which they are used. Fuller seems to be saying, as Frederick Schauer observes, that 'in the *particular* context of applying a rule prohibiting vehicles from the park to a *particular* military truck used as a war memorial, the alleged vehicle may simply not be a vehicle at all'.[14] How plausible is this view about meaning?

---

8   D Lyons, 'Original Intent and Legal Interpretation' (1999) 24 *Australian Journal of Legal Philosophy* 1, 17-22.
9   Fuller, above n 4, p 85.
10 Hart, above n 2, 629.
11 Fuller, above n 4, p 163.
12 Ibid p 95.
13 Ibid pp 95-6.
14 Schauer, above n 2, 1120, Schauer's emphasis.

Schauer argues that it is implausible. He argues for the 'semantic autonomy' of language. By this he means that language can convey meaning independently of the communicative intentions of speakers. Schauer maintains that there are acontextual understandings shared by all speakers of a particular language, which enable one speaker of that language to be understood by another even if the second knows nothing about the circumstances or context in which the first spoke. Schauer does not argue that language is entirely acontextual. He acknowledges that understanding the context is likely to *increase* our understanding of what has been said. But he maintains, nevertheless, that '*some* meaning exists that can be discerned through access only to those skills and understandings that are definitional of linguistic competence'.[15] Meaning can therefore be 'acontextual' in the sense that 'it draws on no other context besides those understandings shared among virtually all speakers of [a particular language]'.[16] Schauer says: 'That we might learn *more* from considering additional factors or from more fully understanding a speaker's intentions does not mean that we learn *nothing* by consulting the language of the rules themselves.'[17]

Let us suppose—to adapt an example given by Schauer—that someone who understands English but knows nothing of the history, politics, law or culture of Australia is given the Australian Constitution to read. In Schauer's view, such a person would be able to glean just from the language of the Constitution some rudimentary idea of its content.[18] Such a person would know, for instance, from a bare reading of s 72, that an eighty-year-old is not going to be appointed as a Justice of the High Court.

Schauer also argues that the fact that language is not perfectly *precise* does not imply that it is therefore *worthless*. He agrees with Hart that language is open-textured and that every use of language is therefore potentially vague, in the sense that unforeseen situations may occur in which it is not clear whether a particular term is applicable or not. But this does not mean, he says, that there are no language-determined core cases. He calls our attention to 'the driver of a pickup truck, with family and picnic preparations in tow, who sees the "No Vehicles in the Park" sign at the entrance to the park and simply turns around'.[19] There are likewise many cases that never leave the lawyer's office because

---

15 F Schauer, *Playing by the Rules: A Philosophical Examination of Rule-Based Decision-Making in Law and in Life*, Clarendon Press, Oxford, 1991, p 58, Schauer's emphasis.
16 F Schauer, 'Formalism' (1988) 97 *Yale Law Review* 509, 528.
17 Ibid, emphasis added.
18 F Schauer, 'Easy Cases' (1985) 58 *Southern California Law Review* 399, 418.
19 Schauer, above n 2, 1134.

litigation seems futile. How can we explain this, Schauer asks, if the law does not speak with clarity at least some of the time?[20]

Schauer therefore agrees with Hart: sometimes rules lack clear meaning, in which case they produce hard cases, but some cases are easy and at least one source of their 'easiness' is that 'language can and frequently does speak with a sufficiently clear voice',[21] the answer being dictated on such occasions by a straightforward reading of the rules. Schauer does not, of course, deny that judges sometimes ignore clear language. He claims merely that legal rules are frequently *capable* of generating determinate outcomes in virtue of the language in which they are written.

It remains to address one last challenge to the idea of clear, literal meaning. This challenge is based on the fact that meaning is a human creation. Meaning, some theorists point out, depends on arbitrary human arrangements and conventions: there is no magical relationship between words and the world that is a given. Hence, they conclude, there are no objective constraints on how words may be understood. Schauer argues that this is a non sequitur. It is, of course, true that it is completely arbitrary which words we apply to which objects. We might have called dogs 'cats' and cats 'dogs'. But it does not follow that words cannot have clear literal meanings. To say that 'dog' has a clear literal meaning is merely to say that any English-language speaker will agree on a certain range of ways of using the word.[22]

6.3 Law as spirit, not letter

So far we have canvassed the disagreement between Hart and Fuller about the ability of language to constrain the interpretation of legal rules, and we have examined Fuller's view that there is no such thing as a core of plain meaning and that we always need to know what the purpose of a rule is in order to decide what it means. This is a conceptual argument about the nature of meaning. But Fuller also offers a second argument in favour of a purposive approach to the interpretation of legal rules.

Apparently conceding to Hart that words *can* be understood acontextually and that rules *do* have clear instances by virtue of the language in which they are couched, Fuller argues that judges should not necessarily follow the rules

---

20 Schauer, above n 18, 412.
21 Ibid 416.
22 Schauer, above n 16, 524.

in clear cases. He suggests, in particular, that judges should ignore the plain meaning of legal rules when the plain meaning dictates an absurd result or one that obviously defeats the rule's purpose. Another way of putting Fuller's point is to say that when something falls within the letter of the law but not its spirit, its letter—its plain meaning—should give way to the spirit. For instance, the businessman should not be found guilty of the offence of sleeping at the station despite the fact that his conduct is clearly covered by the relevant rule, because applying the literal language of the rule in these circumstances is manifestly unreasonable. This is a normative argument about what judges should do when 'language gives the wrong answer'.[23] Fuller's view is that they should ignore the language in which the rule is formulated, not only because they should always be sensitive to the purpose behind the rule but also because law in general has a purpose—the reasonable regulation of conduct—and particular legal rules should therefore be understood in ways that do not frustrate law's general purpose.[24]

Of course, as we know, positivists also believe that there are occasions on which judges should not follow clear rules. This is because they make a distinction between a theory of law and a theory of adjudication (see 4.2). As Wilfred Waluchow says, 'it does not follow from Hart's thesis that whenever an undeniably valid law applies incontestably to a case, the judge's adjudicative obligation ... points in the direction of application'.[25] I previously made this point in respect of iniquitous laws, but Waluchow also points out that there is nothing in the positivist theory of law that is incompatible with the view that certain courts should in some circumstances have the legal power to overrule undesirable or mistaken precedents.[26] How, then, is Fuller's position different from Hart's on this matter?

The answer to this question is that there is a difference between not applying a clear rule for moral reasons and letting our view as to what a rule ought to be influence our view as to what it is. The first is Hart's approach; the second is Fuller's. Hart identifies the letter or clear meaning of the law with the law and argues that judges do not necessarily have a duty to decide according to the law, since the law may be too unreasonable to be applied. Fuller, by contrast, believes that the letter of the law, clear in meaning though it may be, is not necessarily the 'real' law, and that this is why judges are not necessarily

---

23   This is Schauer's phrase, above n 2, 1124.
24   Ibid 1130.
25   W J Waluchow, *Inclusive Legal Positivism*, Clarendon Press, Oxford, 1994, p 65.
26   Ibid pp 33–6.

obliged to apply clear rules. It is, for Fuller, the spirit of the rule, not its plain meaning, which is the 'real' legal rule. On Fuller's view, in other words, even if Hart is right that rules have a language-determined core, we should not identify the *law* with the language-determined core of rules. This is because Fuller thinks it is impossible to grasp what the law requires without investigating the objectives it sought to achieve—by which Fuller seems to mean the objectives that *reasonable* legislators would have sought to achieve. In this way, what the law *ought* to be influences our view as to what it really *is*.

This is very evident in a passage from Fuller's early book entitled *The Law in Quest of Itself*, in which he explains his views about legal interpretation. He compares the interpretation of a statute or decision to the retelling of a funny story. 'If I attempt to retell a funny story', he says:

> the story as I tell it will be the product of two forces: (1) the story as I heard it, the story *as it is* at the time of its first telling; (2) my conception of the point of the story, in other words, my notion of the story *as it ought to be* ... If the story as I heard it was, in my opinion, badly told, I am guided largely by my conception of the story as it ought to be ... On the other hand, if I had the story from a master raconteur, I may exert myself to reproduce his exact words ... These two forces, then, supplement one another in shaping the story as I tell it. It is a product of the *is* and the *ought* working together.[27]

A statute or decision likewise involves two things, according to Fuller:

> a set of words, and an objective sought. This objective may or may not have been happily expressed in the words chosen by the legislator or judge. This objective ... may be perceived dimly or clearly; it may be perceived more clearly by him who reads the statute than by him who drafted it. The statute or decision is not a segment of being, but ... a process of becoming ... By becoming more clearly what it is, the rule of the case becomes what it was previously only trying to be. In this situation to distinguish sharply between the rule as it is, and the rule as it ought to be, is to resort to an abstraction foreign to the raw data which experience offers us.[28]

For Fuller, the law should therefore not be identified with the words of the law—words that may lead to an unjust or unreasonable outcome. The law is what the words would say if they were an accurate reflection of the law's presumed underlying reasonable purpose.

---

27 L L Fuller, *The Law in Quest of Itself*, Foundation Press Inc, Chicago, 1940, p 8, Fuller's emphasis.
28 Ibid pp 8–9.

It is important to emphasise that when Fuller tells us that the words in which the law is couched should not necessarily be identified with the law, this is not because he thinks that judges are entitled to ignore the law in the service of extra-legal standards of morality or justice. Judges who ignore the letter of the law are not, in Fuller's view, departing from the law or making new law. Rather, they are being *faithful* to the pre-existing law—law which is latently *in* the statute, albeit not in its words as ordinarily understood. Purposive judges demonstrate intelligent obedience to the law, in contrast to the unintelligent obedience of those who insist on rigidly applying the letter of the law.

Fuller wrote a famous fictional case, called 'The Case of the Speluncean Explorers', in which the different opinions in the case are informed by different judicial philosophies. One of the fictional judges, Foster J, whose views resemble Fuller's own views about interpretation, makes the point outlined in the previous paragraph. Foster J says:

> No superior wants a servant who lacks the capacity to read between the lines. The stupidest housemaid knows that when she is told 'to peel the soup and skim the potatoes' her mistress does not mean what she says ... Surely we have a right to expect the same modicum of intelligence from the judiciary. The correction of obvious legislative errors or oversights is not to supplant the legislative will, but to make that will effective.[29]

In summary: Fuller agrees with Hart that there are right answers to legal questions, which can be found within the law. However, he puts a natural law spin on this by identifying the 'law' not with what appears on the face of the legal materials but with the interpretation of the materials that would make the law a defensible or justifiable law.

6.4 Should judges follow clear rules?

As we have seen, Fuller believes that judges should not necessarily follow clear rules. The opposing view can be called 'formalistic'. Schauer defines formalism as the theory that judges should apply rules according to their plain meaning without regard to whether it is unjust or absurd to do so.[30] Formalism in this sense is a moral theory about how judges should decide cases. Formalistic decision-making is 'acontextual': even in contexts in which a rule is not apt

---

29 L L Fuller, 'The Case of the Speluncean Explorers' (1949) 62 *Harvard Law Review* 616, 625–6.
30 Schauer, above n 16, 521.

to achieve its underlying purpose or leads to manifestly inequitable results, formalistic decision-makers will follow the rule if its bearing on the case is clear.[31]

Formalism has obvious problems. Rules are, as we have seen, a blunt instrument for achieving legislative purpose. They cannot cater for unimagined situations. They may also be badly drafted and not capable of being given sensible meaning, even after the statute has been examined in its entirety. There is therefore no doubt that clearly applicable rules can give the wrong answers. A purposive approach holds out the hope of a more fine-grained, individualised interpretation, which avoids the more egregious errors that attend rigid adherence to rules. Why, after all, be 'enslaved by mere marks on a printed page'?[32] Where following a rule would lead to manifestly unreasonable results or results obviously at variance with the rule's purpose, what possible reason can be given for blindly applying the rule according to its plain meaning? Should judges not rather serve, as Lord Denning thought, the 'fundamental principles of truth and justice'?[33]

The appeal to truth and justice has the look of a knock-down argument, but formalists respond by pointing out the overlooked virtues of a formalistic approach. They concede that rigid rule-following is incompatible with the ideal of perfect justice. But they argue that it also has benefits. These benefits, in their view, outweigh the costs of rigidity. They say that there are moral values that compete with the ideal of perfect justice and that speak in favour of judicial deference to the plain linguistic meaning of rules. This view has become more popular in recent times.

First, formalists argue that the more willing we are to allow judges to disregard the literal meaning of rules, the more difficult it becomes to explain the sense in which law is authoritative for them. Formalism is clearly able to accommodate the idea of judges being bound by law. It requires judges to treat rules as 'authorities' in the strong, exclusionary sense we considered in 4.6: they are altogether precluded from revising the rule in the light of its suitability to the matter at hand. By contrast, the more scope we give judges to consider matters on their merits and to be guided by their own assessment of what 'right reason' requires, the more we permit them to treat legal rules not as 'proper' rules. On this approach, rules become mere provisional guides to decision-making—guides

---

31   Schauer, above n 15, p 135.
32   Schauer, above n 16, 521.
33   A T Denning, *The Discipline of Law*, Butterworths, London, 1979, p 292.

that are usually useful but that can be ignored when the circumstances are unsuitable for their application. Schauer writes:

> If every application that would not serve the reason behind the rule were jettisoned from the coverage of the rule, then the decision procedure would be identical to one applying reasons directly to individual cases, without the mediation of rules. Under such a model, rules are superfluous except as predictive guides, for they lack any normative power of their own.[34]

If the purposive approach is taken this far, it begins to approximate realism, the difficulties with which will be discussed in the next chapter. It is sufficient to note here that realism rejects the idea that law is authoritative for judges.[35]

Second, even if it is possible for those who advocate the purposive approach to draw a line preventing them from sliding into realism—by insisting, perhaps, on a presumption in favour of following clear rules, albeit one that can be overridden when the reasons to do so are very strong—formalists will argue that such an approach represents a threat to the rule of law. This is because even if the range of cases in which judges do not apply laws according to their publicly ascertainable meaning is restricted, citizens will nevertheless be uncertain as to how the rules will be applied in practice. After all, the 'spirit of the law' is a much more controversial and unpredictable matter than its plain meaning. When judges have recourse to the law's spirit, citizens will therefore be less able to plan their lives and to use the law to achieve their ends. By contrast, strict adherence to the plain, language-determined meaning of legal rules increases the likelihood that those who are subject to the law will know what conduct the law permits or prohibits. Respect for the language of the law therefore promotes predictability and certainty in the law, serving the ideal of government as 'a rule of laws, not men'.[36]

The connection of formalism with the rule of law was spelt out by Deane J in the Australian case of *Federal Commissioner of Taxation v Westraders Pty Ltd*, where, dealing with a taxation matter, he remarked:

> For a court to arrogate to itself, without legislative warrant, the function of overriding the plain words of the Act in any case where it considers that overall considerations of fairness or some general policy of the Act would be best served by a decision against the taxpayer would be to substitute arbitrary taxation for taxation under the rule of law and, indeed, to subvert the rule of law itself.[37]

---

34 Schauer, above n 16, 535.
35 Waluchow, above n 25, p 259.
36 This argument is canvassed but rejected by Waluchow, above n 25, pp 263–8.
37 *Federal Commissioner of Taxation v Westraders Pty Ltd* (1979) 38 FLR 306, 319–20.

Third, formalists argue that judges may make mistakes when trying to do justice on the basis of the purposive approach. They argue that those who support the purposive approach may have a naïve faith in the judiciary to arrive at 'the spirit of the law'. Schauer points out that there are two sources of error. There are, as we have already noted, the errors (unreasonable results) that flow from the inflexible application of rules. But errors can also be made when decision-makers attempt to rely on the purposive approach, and purposive decision-making may produce worse results on average than rigid rule-following. After all, decision-makers in the real world are imperfectly rational and not usually in possession of all the relevant information. These human imperfections may lead them to make mistakes in trying to determine whether it is desirable to depart from the plain meaning of a rule. In fact, judges following the purposive approach may reach the wrong result *more* often than formalistic judges, and therefore may be *less* successful at achieving justice than judges who simply follow the rules.[38]

This argument may be supported by pointing to the fact that judges tend to be drawn from a very narrow section of the community. As a result, their class, race and gender may perhaps skew their views about the underlying purpose of the law or what is a manifestly unreasonable result in a particular case. If so, judges may subvert legislative programs if they are given carte blanche to depart from established or clear rules under the guise of purposive interpretation.

A fourth influence on formalism is democratic theory. Formalists argue that theirs is the correct interpretive method because formalism ensures that controversial moral and political choices are made by those 'with a superior democratic pedigree',[39] namely, elected and accountable representatives, not unelected and unaccountable judges. For this reason, formalism is sometimes referred to as 'democratic formalism'. The democratic values served by formalism explain why ethical positivists find formalism attractive, as discussed in 4.8. Though Fuller claims that his approach does not amount to an activist usurpation of the legislative role, formalists disagree. They say that, notwithstanding Fuller's claims to the contrary, Fuller's purposive judge is *not* reasoning legally: the notion of purpose is indeterminate and functions as a disguise for judicial lawmaking. They believe that formalism, by contrast, promotes democratic government by requiring judges to defer to clear rules

---

38 Schauer, above n 15, pp 149–55.
39 C R Sunstein, 'Justice Scalia's Democratic Formalism' (1997) 107 *Yale Law Journal* 529, 530.

of law, even when to do so will lead to evidently undesirable results. As Patrick Atiyah explains, 'the fundamental purpose of respecting formality is that it is an important part of a system of distributing power in society'.[40] In particular, it allocates the making of laws to parliament and the application of laws to the judiciary. If the law applied according to its clear meaning leads to injustice, then it is parliament's duty to reform it. It is not, Atiyah says, the 'job [of judges] to run everything ... [O]ther participants in the political process have an important role to play.'[41]

The argument of the democratic formalists is therefore that even if a purposive approach *could* be relied on to achieve perfect justice, judges are not *entitled* to engage in the kind of reasoning that it requires. Lacking the political legitimacy enjoyed by lawmakers, they are obliged to apply pre-existing legal principles according to their clear meaning. For the democratic formalists, the democratically elected legislature should occupy centre stage in legal theory. At the other extreme from this view is Dworkin's judge-centred approach. We turn to Dworkin now.

6.5 Dworkin's challenge to Hart's doctrine of discretion

Dworkin's challenge to positivism has undergone considerable development over the years. We will start with his early work, in which Dworkin spelt out his anti-positivist theory of law in the context of a challenge to Hart's doctrine of adjudicative discretion, and the model of law as containing nothing but rules, which Dworkin thought lay behind this doctrine. Whereas Fuller's critique of Hart focuses on Hart's claim about easy cases—that the language in which legal rules are cast settles most legal disputes—Dworkin's critique, by contrast, focuses on Hart's claim about *hard* cases. This is the claim that if there is no general agreement that a rule of law applies, judges are in such cases obliged to exercise discretion. By this Hart means, as we saw in 3.8, that the judge has to make a choice unconstrained by legal standards, neither plaintiff nor defendant having a *right* to win. Dworkin calls this kind of discretion 'strong' discretion.[42] Dworkin agrees with Hart that in hard cases judges have to rely on

---

40 P Atiyah, 'Justice and Predictability in the Common Law' (1992) 15 *University of New South Wales Journal* 448, 458.
41 Ibid 460.
42 R Dworkin, *Taking Rights Seriously*, Duckworth, London, 1977, p 32.

controversial moral and political judgments. He disagrees, however, that the *law* is indeterminate in these cases and that judges have the discretion to decide them either way on the basis of what they think the law ought to be.

Dworkin opposes Hart's view about judicial discretion on two grounds, as a descriptive thesis about the practice of adjudication and as a thesis that offers a normative justification for the institution of adjudication.[43] Thus Dworkin argues that judges do not see their task in hard cases as one of exercising strong discretion, and he also argues that Hart's model is morally indefensible and fails to show law in its best moral light. (For further discussion of Dworkin's beliefs about the need to show law in its best moral light, see 6.8.)

Insofar as the first point is concerned, Dworkin claims, against Hart, that judges do not understand their task differently depending on whether the case is easy or hard. Even when the question of whether something is law is controversial, Dworkin maintains that judges see themselves as obliged to make decisions according to their best understanding of what the law requires, rather than as making new law. They do not see themselves as casting aside their law books and they do not describe their task as one of creating new rights. On the contrary, Dworkin thinks that it is clear from the way judges speak and write that they are attempting to *find* the law, that is, to discover which litigant has a *pre-existing* right to win. They may, of course, disagree on this matter. But if so, they disagree about who has the right. They do not take the view that neither party has the right. Dworkin concedes that, in what he calls a 'trivial' sense, judges do 'make new law' every time they decide an important case. They announce 'a rule or principle or qualification or elaboration ... that has never been officially declared before'.[44] But, he says, they 'offer these "new" statements of law as improved reports of what the law, properly understood, already is'.[45]

Insofar as the second point is concerned, Dworkin argues that Hart's views are inconsistent with fairness as well as with democratic values and the separation of powers. He points out that if judges did make new law in hard cases, the new law would be applied retroactively to the case before the judge. Losing parties would be held liable even though they had no duty not to act in that way at the time the events occurred. Dworkin says that this would be unfair. Furthermore, because judges are not elected, and therefore are not accountable

---

43 Ibid p 123.
44 R Dworkin, *Law's Empire*, Belknap Press of Harvard University Press, Cambridge, MA, 1986, p 6.
45 Ibid.

to the electorate for their decisions, they do not, according to Dworkin, have the mandate to determine the political direction of society by making new law.[46]

6.6 Dworkin's distinction between rules and principles

In his early article, 'The Model of Rules I', Dworkin seems to accept Hart's picture of hard cases—that these are cases in which the legal rules fail to provide clear guidance, because they are either silent or lack clear meaning—but rejects Hart's view that judges make new law in such cases. Dworkin's starting point is the claim we encountered in 4.3, that there is more to the law than the explicit rules of law, as found in authoritative sources such as constitutional provisions, statutes and precedents. In particular, Dworkin thinks that there are also moral principles within the law.

Dworkin argues that there are a number of differences between rules and principles. He says that rules either apply or they do not: if it is clear that a situation falls under a valid rule, the legal consequences follow automatically. If, for instance, a rule of law provides that a will must be signed by two witnesses, then a will that has been signed by only one witness will not be valid. If it is not clear whether a case is covered by a rule, either because there seems to be no rule or because the rule does not clearly apply, then the case cannot be decided according to the rule. But principles do not work in this way. A principle can be *relevant* to a situation but not necessarily *decisive* of the answer. Thus, although our law respects the principle that no one should profit from his or her own wrongdoing, there are cases in which this principle does not hold. This is because although relevant principles always have *some* weight, they do not always have *conclusive* weight. In order to decide whether a particular principle applies or not, judges have to weigh up how strong it is in the circumstances of the particular case, a process which may have to take into account the presence of competing principles. But even if the principle does not ultimately prevail, it is not thereby invalidated. Rules, by contrast, cannot be assigned relative weight in this way, according to Dworkin. If two rules conflict, one of them will have to be abandoned.[47]

Dworkin then argues that although *rules* cannot guide a judge in situations where it is unclear whether a case is covered by the rule, *principles* can supply the answers. In his article, 'The Model of Rules II', principles are not merely

---

46 Dworkin, above n 42, p 84.
47 Ibid pp 24–7.

presented as non-rule standards. Instead, they are presented as standards that are only incompletely expressed by the explicit rules of law, which morally justify the explicit rules 'by identifying the political or moral concerns and traditions of the community which ... support the rules'.[48] Hence judges can go beyond established rules while still deciding *according to* law. In effect, judges decide hard cases by *theorising*: they invoke principles that derive their legal authority from the fact that they provide the best moral and political justification for the established legal rules.

Dworkin concedes that reliance on such principles will no doubt be controversial, involving, as it does, complex questions of moral and political theory. Judges who apply principles will therefore have to exercise discretion in one sense of that word—the *weak* sense in which we speak of discretion when the standards to be applied 'cannot be applied mechanically but demand the use of judgment'.[49] Judges are not, however, required to exercise the kind of *strong* discretion postulated by Hart because there is, in Dworkin's view, almost always a uniquely right solution even to such controversial matters. It will, in other words, very rarely be the case that the arguments on both sides are equally good. This is Dworkin's 'right answer' thesis. It will be explained in more detail in 6.11 below.

As we saw in 4.3, Dworkin illustrates his argument about the role played by moral principles in hard cases by referring to the principle invoked in *Riggs v Palmer*,[50] that no one should be permitted to take advantage of his or her own wrongdoing. It is slightly confusing that *Riggs* was not a hard case in Hart's sense: the language of the rule was not, in fact, vague or ambiguous. The murdering grandson was entitled to inherit under the statute and the principle was in fact used to evade the rule's clear meaning. The general point Dworkin wishes to make in 'The Model of Rules I' is nevertheless plain: he believes that when the rules of law are unclear, or when there is no explicit rule on the matter, judges are still bound by law because they are bound by moral principles. Of course, once one has expanded the set of standards for identifying the law in this way, it becomes more plausible to say that all legal disputes can be decided according to the law. If the law extends beyond the agreed meaning of the explicit rules of law and depends in part on moral argument, then, despite the absence of a clear precedent or statutory provision covering an issue, there need be no gap in the law that judges are obliged to fill by the exercise of discretion.

---

48 Ibid p 67.
49 Ibid p 31.
50 *Riggs v Palmer*, 115 NY 506 (1889).

However, Dworkin may have exaggerated the differences between himself and Hart. According to Dworkin, the reason why Hart thinks that judges make new law in hard cases is because Hart thinks that the law consists only of rules. Since the guidance of rules can be indeterminate, Hart is therefore forced to conclude that hard cases cannot be decided legally. But Hart's belief that the law can sometimes fail to supply answers is not based on the view that the law consists only of rules. Hart makes clear in the Postscript to *The Concept of Law* that he agrees with Dworkin that arguments from less conclusive standards than rules (non-rule standards) are an important feature of adjudication and legal reasoning. Hart also argues that the difference between rules and principles is merely one of degree. He says that rules are *more* conclusive than principles but are potentially susceptible to being outweighed by more important rules.[51] Therefore Hart's views about the need for judicial discretion are not based on the claim that the law does not contain non-rule standards.

It is nevertheless true that Hart does believe that there can be gaps in the law, and a crucial point of difference between him and Dworkin therefore remains. Though Hart believes that moral principles may figure in a sound justification of the law, and therefore may be part of a community's law, he also believes that such principles will at some point prove indeterminate, in the same way that authoritative, explicitly formulated rules will prove indeterminate. As Scott Shapiro explains, Hart thinks that it is impossible to eliminate the need for strong discretion because it is impossible to transmit standards that provide for every contingency in advance (see 3.8).[52] Hence, whether judges reason on the basis of rules or moral principles, they will sometimes be engaged in acts of judicial choice or lawmaking. For Dworkin, by contrast, there is *never* a need for the exercise of strong discretion. There is always a right answer to legal questions.

In his later work, Dworkin no longer relies on the supposed logical distinction between rules and principles, and he also distances himself from the idea that the moral principles that (according to him) bear on legal decisions should be counted as belonging to a distinct set of principles called 'legal' principles. Dworkin now makes clear that he does not believe that 'the law' is a set of discrete standards at all. He does not think it makes sense, in other words, to view the law as a collection of special standards and to ask whether

---

51 H L A Hart, *The Concept of Law*, 2nd edn, Clarendon Press, Oxford, 1994, pp 261–3.
52 S Shapiro, 'The "Hart–Dworkin" Debate: A Short Guide for the Perplexed', in A Ripstein (ed), *Ronald Dworkin*, Cambridge University Press, New York, 2007, pp 29–30.

a particular standard is a 'legal' standard, as opposed to some other kind of standard. He is interested in the considerations that legitimately bear on the resolution of legal disputes, not in what he describes as the 'taxonomic' question of whether those considerations should be categorised as belonging to a separate set of standards labelled 'legal'.[53] His main conclusions, however, remain the same and his opposition to positivism is as vigorous as ever, although his arguments are now mainly organised around the claim that positivism cannot account for what he calls 'theoretical disagreements'. Such disagreements are, according to Dworkin, rife in the law. *Riggs v Palmer* (which, as previously noted, is not actually a good example of a hard case in Hart's sense of that phrase, because it is not an example of ambiguous or vague statutory language) is now presented as hard in the sense of being an exemplar of theoretical disagreement. Let us see what Dworkin means by 'theoretical disagreement'.

6.7 Theoretical disagreement

Riggs was not a unanimous opinion. The majority thought that the grandson should not inherit but one of the judges disagreed. The dissenting judge argued that the plain meaning of the New York statute of wills, which did not prevent someone who had murdered the testator from inheriting and did not make provision for courts to alter a will, should be applied. The majority, by contrast, thought that the court should modify the statute by reading an exception for murderers into the clear statutory language. According to Dworkin, the judges in *Riggs* disagreed about the fundamental criteria to be used in ascertaining the law. They all agreed that there was a fact of the matter about what the statute of wills required but they disagreed about the considerations that were relevant to determining the law. The majority thought that the law contains not only the explicit rules of law but also implicit principles of justice, and concluded that courts can alter unambiguous statutory provisions on the basis of the implicit moral principles underlying the legal system. The dissenting judge, by contrast, held that the law had to be determined on the basis of the literal meaning of the enacted provisions.

This, at any rate, Dworkin tells us, is how the judges presented their arguments, and this is the phenomenon that he calls 'theoretical disagreement'. He is keen to distinguish such disagreement from borderline disagreements

---

53 R Dworkin, *Justice in Robes*, Belknap Press of Harvard University Press, Cambridge, MA, 2006, pp 4–5, 234.

about the application of an agreed or shared criterion to particular cases. As we know, positivists see disagreement about the meaning of legal rules as a function of the rules' indeterminacy at their margins, and as calling for a discretionary choice to be made. Dworkin thinks that hard cases such as *Riggs* do not involve disagreements of this kind. He writes:

> The various judges and lawyers who argued our sample cases did not think they were defending marginal or borderline claims. Their disagreements about legislation and precedent were fundamental; their arguments showed that they disagreed not only about whether Elmer should have his inheritance, but about why any legislative act, even traffic codes and rates of taxation, impose the rights and obligations everyone agrees they do ... They disagreed about what makes a proposition of law true not just at the margin but in the core as well. Our sample cases were understood ... as pivotal cases testing fundamental principles, not as borderline cases calling for some more or less arbitrary line to be drawn.[54]

Such assessments by the participants cannot, of course, be accepted by positivists at face value. For positivists, if judges fundamentally disagree about such matters as whether courts can alter unambiguous statutory provisions, they are disagreeing about the content of the rule of recognition and they therefore cannot be disagreeing about *legal* requirements. There cannot be a legally right answer on the matter, since law, according to positivists, consists in shared standards or standards upon which officials generally agree. If there is no settled practice, there is no law. On the positivist view, such disagreements must therefore be non-legal disagreements about what the rule of statutory interpretation *should* be, when, for instance, the plain meaning of a statute leads to a repugnant result. Different opinions about this must therefore be alternative ways of *making* law on the matter. As Brian Leiter explains, if judges talk about the legal correctness of their preferred method of statutory interpretation in such cases, positivists will say that judges are either dressing up their moral views as legal views or simply mistaking the one for the other. In either case, whether they are disingenuous or confused, it is an illusion to suppose that their disagreement is about the law, since there are no shared standards among officials on this matter.[55]

However, Dworkin wants to give an account of disagreement that takes into consideration the way in which participants in legal institutions conceptualise legal practice, and that therefore *does* take at face value the

---

54 Dworkin, above n 44, pp 42–3.
55 B Leiter, 'Explaining Theoretical Disagreement' (2009) 76 *Chicago Law Review* 1215, 1224.

way in which judges describe their task in hard cases. He wants to explain, in other words, how cases in which the criteria of legal validity are not shared can nevertheless involve disagreements about the law.[56] In Dworkin's view, the judges in *Riggs* were attempting 'to construct the "real" statute—a statement of what difference the statute makes to the legal rights of various people—from the text in the statute book'.[57] They agreed on what the printed words said, but they disagreed about what law the words made.

No doubt, Dworkin says, the task of working out what law the words make is a complex one, which cannot be undertaken without relying on controversial moral reasoning. For instance, if judges support a literal reading of statutes, this can only be because they have a moral view about the desirability of identifying the law with the clear dictates of a democratically constituted body. Questions about the applicability of a precedent in a new set of circumstances can be similarly controversial. These may, for instance, involve such fundamental matters as the legitimacy of using policy considerations to distinguish a later case from an earlier one.[58] However, Dworkin continues to insist, against the positivist account, that such disagreements are never resolved by the exercise of strong discretion or judicial choice: there are right answers to such disputes making it possible for judges to decide according to law. Thus although such disagreements are *moral* disagreements, they are disagreements about the *law*. For instance, a disagreement about the application of statutory provisions, as in *Riggs,* is a disagreement about what law the New York legislature made in enacting its statute of wills. Judges are not, in such cases, acting as unelected legislators.

Law's Empire is devoted to showing how theoretical disagreement in this sense is possible. At the heart of Dworkin's revamped attack on positivism is a more sophisticated methodology, based on a new, 'interpretive' approach to understanding the law. The intention is to provide further support for his theory of law by showing, as John Stick says, that '"right" answers are a feature not just of law, but of a much wider set of interpretive practices'.[59] In *Law's Empire*, Dworkin also defends a conception of law which he calls 'law as integrity'. We turn now to the 'interpretive turn' taken by Dworkin in his later work and the way

---

56   Dworkin, above n 44, p 20.
57   Ibid p 17.
58   Ibid pp 28–9.
59   J Stick, 'Literary Imperialism: Assessing the Results of Dworkin's Interpretive Turn in *Law's Empire*' (1986) 34 *UCLA Law Review* 371, 383.

in which it is used by Dworkin to support his view that there is a right answer to all legal disputes.

6.8 Jurisprudence as interpretation

Dworkin focuses on what he calls 'argumentative' social practices. They are argumentative because they are characterised by disagreement or argument about the elements of the practice. He believes that law is such a practice and he describes participants in such practices as taking an interpretive attitude to them. Let us begin by seeing what he means by an 'interpretive attitude'. If you take an interpretive attitude to a practice you assume the practice has a point or has some value, and you try to work out what the practice requires of you by reflecting on this point. According to Dworkin, the interpretation of social practices is therefore like the interpretation of a work of art. Both social practices and works of art are interpreted with the aim of 'imposing purpose on [the object of interpretation] in order to make of it the best possible example of the form or genre to which it is taken to belong'.[60]

Dworkin labels this kind of *value-laden* interpretation 'constructive interpretation' because it aims to show a practice in its best light, and he contrasts it with 'conversational interpretation', in which we assign meaning to sounds on the basis of a *factual* inquiry into the intentions of the speaker. In Dworkin's view, when we interpret social practices and works of art, we interpret something created by people 'as an entity distinct from them, rather than what people say'.[61] The form of interpretation involved is therefore 'creative', rather than 'conversational'.[62]

Dworkin tells us that constructive interpretation of a social practice begins by picking out the 'raw data' to be interpreted. This is the 'pre-interpretive' stage, in which fairly uncontroversial examples of the practice are identified in a rough-and-ready way. As an example, Dworkin uses the convention of courtesy. We can all agree that the practice of courtesy involves such acts as taking off your hat in certain circumstances.[63] Such rules and standards, Dworkin says, are 'taken to provide the tentative content

---

60   Dworkin, above n 44, p 52.
61   Ibid p 50.
62   Ibid.
63   Ibid p 47.

of the practice'.[64] This is a primarily descriptive activity, although Dworkin thinks that some interpretation is required even at this tentative or provisional stage, because '[s]ocial rules do not carry identifying labels.'[65] He signals this by putting the word 'pre-interpretive' in scare quotes.

Then there is an interpretive stage. At this stage, we focus on the point or value of the practice and attempt to provide a justification for it that shows it in its best light: 'A participant interpreting a social practice ... proposes value for the practice by describing some scheme of interests or goals or principles the practice can be taken to serve or express or exemplify.'[66] This enterprise requires moral argument, and participants seeking to follow a practice are likely to differ in their views about which interpretation proposes the most value for the practice. For instance, some participants in the practice of courtesy may think that the point of the practice is to show respect to one's social superiors. Others may disagree.[67] However, if a justification does not fit the bulk of the practice it will not be an interpretation of it, but the invention of a new practice. Notice that there are therefore two kinds of constraints or standards that must be met during the process of interpretation. There is a requirement of 'fit': the interpretation must be consistent with the 'raw data', and not constitute the invention of a new practice. There is also the requirement of 'most value'. This is a substantive standard.

Finally, there is a post-interpretive or reforming stage, in which participants in a practice revisit and revise their views about what the practice requires of them in the light of its best justification. Thus a previously accepted rule of the practice might now come to be seen as a mistake in the light of the justification that does most to enhance the moral attractiveness of the practice.[68] Participants might, for instance, come to the conclusion that the best justification for the practice of courtesy is to show respect for age, not social status, and that previously accepted rules about showing respect for social status are not really requirements of the practice after all. We therefore know what a practice *really* requires of us only when we fully understand its purpose or point.

To come back now to the phenomenon of theoretical disagreement and why it is not an illusion, Dworkin believes that we can explain why judges

---

64 Ibid pp 65–6.
65 Ibid p 66.
66 Ibid p 52.
67 Ibid p 48.
68 Ibid p 99.

in hard cases correctly take themselves to be disagreeing about the law's requirements once we see that law is an argumentative practice like courtesy. When judges, lawyers and other participants seeking to follow the practice of law disagree about the answer to a legal question, this is because they have different, although not necessarily fully articulated, moral views about which way of answering the question would show the practice of law in its best light. For instance, some judges may think that firm adherence to the rules as stated shows law in its best light, while others may think that the point of law requires exceptions to the rules to be made on the basis of the implicit moral principles that underpin the law as a whole.

Furthermore, Dworkin believes that jurisprudence or legal theory involves taking up a view on the very same questions that concern participants in the practice of law. This is because Dworkin believes that theorists cannot understand a practice in which the participants take an interpretive attitude without joining the practice and engaging in a similar process of interpretation for themselves. Thus legal theorists cannot understand the nature of law unless they ask the same kinds of questions as participants ask when they seek to ascertain what the practice requires of them. This being so, Dworkin argues that explicating the nature of law involves arguing for a view about how valid law should be identified, by reference to how that view justifies legal practice or shows it in its best light.

We saw in 4.3 that Dworkin describes accounts of how valid law should be identified as accounts of the 'grounds of law'. The grounds of law 'concern the circumstances in which particular propositions of law should be taken to be sound or true'.[69] Propositions of law are reports of the law's requirements in a particular jurisdiction. Thus propositions of law are statements such as 'It is the law in Australia that citizens have to vote in elections'. For Dworkin, the task of legal theory is therefore to argue for a view about the grounds of law by reference to the way in which the view in question shows law to be a morally attractive institution.

It will be evident that Dworkin dissolves the sharp distinction traditionally drawn between *philosophical* questions about the nature of law, which are answered by a theory of law, and concrete *legal* or *doctrinal* questions about what the law is on a particular matter in a particular jurisdiction. For Hart, these are entirely different questions. As Nigel Simmonds says, for Hart, questions about the nature of law are philosophical questions about the general features that

---

69   Ibid p 110.

characterise all legal systems,[70] whereas questions about the content of law are not philosophical at all but merely involve the application of the rules accepted within a particular system.[71] For Dworkin, by contrast, doing jurisprudence is just a more abstract version of participating in the practice of law. Conversely, judges who disagree about the law in hard cases such as *Riggs* disagree about the tests to be used for determining the law, and are therefore implicitly operating with different jurisprudential theories or different answers to the question 'What is law?' Both enterprises—the jurisprudential and the doctrinal—involve arguments about the moral value of identifying propositions of law in one way rather than another.

Since Dworkin sees jurisprudence as a normative enterprise, it will be clear that he rejects the view that theories about the nature of law can or should be morally neutral or detached. For Dworkin, jurisprudence is not a report on the committed participant's perspective, as Hart, for instance, believes; rather, to engage in jurisprudence is to embrace the participant's perspective. And according to Dworkin, since a theory of law is a morally committed, constructive interpretation of legal practice that attempts to justify it, legal theorists will almost invariably think that what they identify as law should 'normally' be obeyed and enforced.[72]

Deeply sceptical theories, such as Marxism and Critical Legal Studies (see Chapter 9), are, Dworkin says, the only exception to this claim. According to Dworkin, these theories *attempt* to explain why law should be obeyed and enforced, but, finding law to be through and through an instrument of subjugation and exploitation, they conclude that no such explanation is available.[73] He calls these 'internally sceptical' theories because they are willing to engage in interpretation but they come to the conclusion that no constructive interpretation can be provided because there is nothing in the object of interpretation (law) that deserves support. Dworkin does not say that such theories are necessarily wrong, but rather that their diagnosis needs to be backed up by argument and evidence—which he believes they have not provided.[74]

Non-sceptical legal theories, by contrast, will propose an account of the grounds of law with a view to explaining why citizens have a moral obligation,

---

70 N E Simmonds, *Law as a Moral Idea*, Oxford University Press, Oxford, 2007, p 170.
71 Ibid p 23.
72 Dworkin, above n 44, p 111.
73 Ibid pp 78–9, 266–73.
74 Ibid p 274.

even if only a prima facie one, to comply with the requirements contained in propositions of law made true by those grounds. Such an account will also explain why judges have a prima facie obligation to enforce such requirements, for instance by sentencing people to prison or ordering them to pay damages. We first encountered the notion of a prima facie obligation in 3.6. A prima facie obligation is one that has some moral force, although it can be overridden by more powerful moral values in exceptional circumstances. We saw in 3.6 that Hart thinks that there are not necessarily even prima facie moral grounds for the assertion of legal rights and duties. Something can be law without its enforcement being even prima facie morally justifiable. Dworkin takes a different view.

He associates himself with the natural law tradition of theorising about law, which seeks to tie together the nature of law and its ability to justify the ordering of sanctions. Dworkin believes that in very unjust societies, judges may be justified in refusing to enforce the law. However, he insists, against positivism, that at least in general terms, a non-sceptical legal theory has moral implications for what judges and citizens should do. In short: legal theory or jurisprudence, on Dworkin's view, is the enterprise of attempting to give a meaning to 'law' that shows why citizens should in normal circumstances comply with it and courts should in normal circumstances enforce it. Thus Dworkin says that a theory of law 'must explain how what it takes to be law provides a general justification for the exercise of coercive power by the state, a justification that holds except in special cases, when some competing argument is especially powerful'.[75] It therefore follows, for Dworkin, that if a theory of law is unable to show how law justifies the imposition of sanctions and normally provides moral guidance for citizens and officials, then that theory will have given the wrong analysis of the nature of law. In Dworkin's view, determining what law *should* be like helps us to see what it actually *is*.[76] We choose among different *descriptive* senses of 'law' by assigning it the sense that best captures its *value*.[77]

In elaborating on these points, Dworkin proposes as a starting point for jurisprudential inquiry a very abstract statement of the purpose of law, which he thinks is relatively uncontroversial. This is that law exists to guide and constrain the exercise of state power by 'insist[ing] that force not be used or withheld … except as licensed or required by individual rights and responsibilities flowing

---

75   Ibid p 190.
76   Dworkin, above n 53, p145.
77   Ibid p 150.

from past political decisions'.[78] By 'past political decisions', Dworkin means official decisions such as those of courts and legislatures. In later work, he makes much the same point using the vocabulary of 'legality', saying that '[l]egality insists that [the state's coercive] power be exercised only in accordance with standards established in the right way before that exercise'.[79] Thus punishing someone or forcing a person to pay damages is justified if we can point to pre-existing standards that permit or require such sanctions. But what value, if any, is served by requiring that force be used only in ways conforming to rights and responsibilities that flow from past political decisions? And in what sense must rights and responsibilities 'flow from' past decisions if we wish to serve this value? What counts as establishing a standard 'in advance'?[80]

According to Dworkin, these are controversial matters. Different answers to these questions, and therefore rival interpretive theories of law yielding different tests for identifying propositions of law, are possible. Two interpretive theories of law are of particular interest to us here. Dworkin calls the one 'conventionalism' and the other, which is the account he favours, he calls 'law as integrity'. For the moment, we will leave aside his attack on a third interpretive theory, which he calls 'pragmatism'. Pragmatism is an interpretive or prescriptive version of realism. It will be discussed in 7.5.

6.9 Conventionalism

As we have seen, Dworkin thinks that all legal theorists are in the business of attempting to explain why past decisions or pre-established standards, as laid down in cases and statutes, provide legitimate grounds for governmental coercion, and therefore why, in general, we have a duty to obey the law. He says that all theories about the nature of law rest on a view about the value of constraining the use of state force by insisting that its use be sanctioned by rights and responsibilities that are the result of past official acts. Dworkin argues that one such view is that pre-established standards are able to guide conduct *efficiently* and to give *fair warning* to citizens as to the circumstances in which force will be used against them. On this view, the point of insisting that force should be used only as licensed or required by rights and responsibilities flowing from past official acts is to ensure that the use of coercion is predictable.

---

78 Dworkin, above n 44, p 93.
79 Dworkin, above n 53, p 169.
80 Dworkin, above n 44, p 94; Dworkin, above n 53, p 169.

Dworkin then goes on to argue that this view implies a particular account of the way in which rights and responsibilities must 'flow from' past decisions in order to count as legal. In particular, it implies that moral tests should not be included among the tests for law. For 'moral tests allow citizens and officials who disagree, often strenuously, about what morality requires to substitute their own judgment about what standards have been established: the consequent disorganization will produce not utility but chaos'.[81] Likewise, if the decisions of legislatures and courts can be supplemented or qualified by moral considerations, 'citizens cannot as easily or with the same confidence know where they stand'.[82]

By contrast, if rights and responsibilities are viewed as flowing from past decisions and therefore as counting as 'legal' only when they are contained in clear rules explicitly laid down by legislatures or courts, then law becomes certain and predictable. As Dworkin says, legal rights that explicitly flow from past decisions are uncontroversial in terms of 'what everyone knows and expects'.[83] Dworkin concludes that theorists who believe that the point of law is to constrain the use of power by making its use predictable will insist that law should be separated from morality and will see the grounds of law as exclusively a matter of plain or social facts. They will take law to be a matter of plain fact because law thus understood provides clear standards for the guidance of conduct.

This is an interpretive version of positivism, in contrast to the descriptive versions of positivism considered in previous chapters. Dworkin considers this to be a superior way of construing positivist claims because, in contrast to descriptive versions of positivism, it seeks to show what is morally valuable about law. He refers to interpretive positivism as 'conventionalism'. It is interpretive because it justifies a view about the grounds of law by reference to the morally attractive *values* the view serves (efficient guidance of conduct and fair warning), rather than by reference to the view's *descriptive* adequacy. Interpretive positivism claims that tying the 'occasions of coercion' to 'plain facts available to all'[84] shows the practice of law in its best light. As Dworkin explains, it appeals to morality at the jurisprudential level in order to argue for the irrelevance of morality at the doctrinal level.[85] Dworkin believes that it is the implicit acceptance of such a jurisprudential view which explains (and prescribes) the minority's approach in

---

81 Dworkin, above n 53, p 174.
82 Ibid p 175.
83 Dworkin, above n 44, p 118.
84 Ibid p 117.
85 R Dworkin, 'Response' in S Hershowitz (ed), *Exploring Law's Empire: The Jurisprudence of Ronald Dworkin*, Oxford University Press, Oxford, 2006, p 311.

the case of *Riggs*. Accepting a conventionalist theory about the point of law, the minority proceeded to identify the law on the basis of this theory, holding that the plain meaning of the statute of wills should be decisive.

Since it is an interpretive theory, conventionalism, in Dworkin's view, needs to be assessed by reference to the criteria of fit and justification. He finds it unsatisfactory on both counts, mainly because of its implication that, where it is controversial whether a rule of law applies, there is no law either way on the matter and the judge must exercise strong discretion. Dworkin thinks that this does not fit legal practice, making the point referred to in 6.5 that even when judges disagree, they take themselves to be arguing about what the law *is* and they say that theirs is the *correct* reading of a statute or precedent.[86]

Regarding the inability of conventionalism to justify our legal practices, Dworkin argues as follows. As we know, conventionalists draw the line between law and non-law on the basis of a distinction between what is uncontroversial and clear and what is controversial and unclear. Dworkin argues that if we ask why they draw the line in this way, the most plausible answer they can give is that this balances the values of predictability and flexibility in the most efficient way. But Dworkin doubts that conventionalism does achieve the most efficient balance between these values. When the rules are clear, conventionalism serves the value of predictability but entirely ignores the value of flexibility. It protects people's expectations in such cases, no matter how strong the arguments are for changing the law. Conversely, only in cases where the rules are not clear are courts permitted to make new law on the merits. Dworkin argues that if the aim really is to balance predictability and flexibility in the most efficient way, then it would make more sense to adhere to a realist theory of adjudication. On such a theory, as we will see in 7.5, the need for predictability can be balanced even in *clear* cases against the need to change the law, and the law can be set aside if that will yield the optimal outcome.[87] Dworkin concludes that conventionalism is an unsuccessful interpretive account of law. He defends a very different account, which he calls 'law as integrity'. We turn to this account next.

6.10 Law as integrity

Dworkin thinks that integrity is an independent virtue, different from the other political ideals of fairness, justice and procedural due process. Dworkin explains

---

86 Dworkin, above n 44, pp 130–1.
87 Ibid pp 147–50.

these concepts in the following way. Fairness is a matter of finding political procedures, such as methods of electing officials, which distribute political power appropriately. Justice is a matter of distributing resources and liberties in a morally defensible way. Due process relates to the procedures used by institutions such as courts with a view to promoting an appropriate degree of accuracy in findings.[88] Integrity is something different from all of these and can conflict with them.

Dworkin explains the idea of integrity first in individual terms and then in political terms. When we speak of individuals as having integrity, we mean, Dworkin says, that they act 'according to convictions that inform and shape their lives as a whole, rather than capriciously or whimsically'.[89] They do not say one thing one day, and another the next. They are true to their principles. Integrity as a political ideal, says Dworkin, makes an analogous demand on the state. Citizens may disagree about which principles of justice and fairness are correct, but law as integrity requires:

> government to speak with one voice, to act in a principled and coherent manner toward all its citizens, to extend to everyone the substantive standards of justice or fairness it uses for some. If government relies on principles of majoritarian democracy to justify its decisions about who may vote, it must respect the same principles in designing voting districts. If it appeals to the principle that people have a right to compensation from those who injure them carelessly, as its reason why manufacturers are liable for defective automobiles, it must give full effect to that principle in deciding whether accountants are liable for their mistakes as well.[90]

Law as integrity, in other words, strives to 'extend to everyone the same regime of principle'.[91]

So if we return to Dworkin's abstract characterisation of the purpose of law—namely, that law justifies the use of force by insisting that it be used only in ways conforming to rights and responsibilities that flow from past political decisions—law as integrity takes the view that the point of this insistence is to subject everyone to the same standards, thereby ensuring that coercion is not arbitrary.[92] This in turn implies that rights and responsibilities 'flow from' past official decisions and therefore count as legal when they follow from the moral

---

88   Ibid pp 164–5.
89   Ibid p 166.
90   Ibid p 165.
91   Dworkin, above n 53, p 16.
92   Ibid p 176.

principles that underlie and justify these decisions.[93] Dworkin describes this kind of consistency with past decisions as 'consistency in principle' or 'coherence in principle'. Consistency in principle is much more than logical consistency. Consistency in principle requires that 'the various standards governing the state's use of coercion against its citizens ... express a single and comprehensive vision of justice'.[94] The law is consistent in principle when it expresses a unified moral vision.

Law as integrity implies that those who create law by legislation should strive to keep that law consistent in principle and that judges who are responsible for deciding what the law is should prefer interpretations that make it consistent in principle.[95] Dworkin calls the latter tenet the principle of 'integrity in adjudication'. It 'instructs judges to identify legal rights and duties, so far as possible, on the assumption that they were all created by a single author—the community personified—expressing a coherent conception of justice and fairness'.[96]

Let us explore in detail how law as integrity tells judges to decide cases. If judges should strive to interpret the law as speaking with one voice, what does this imply about the tests they should use in identifying true propositions of law? Dworkin argues that, in contrast to conventionalism, law as integrity implies that moral tests are among the tests that judges should use to identify true propositions of law. Law as integrity does not imply that unjust laws cannot be valid, in the simplistic, natural law sense. But it does make the content of law 'depend on justice', albeit 'in less dramatic ways'.[97] This is because law as integrity obliges judges to decide new cases in a way consistent with the moral principles that best justify the previous cases, 'so that each person's situation is fair and just according to the same standards'.[98]

Determining what *the* law is on a particular issue (a doctrinal matter) will therefore be as much of an interpretive and moral exercise as deciding what *law* is in general (a jurisprudential matter). Ordinary legal argument will, in other words, have the same interpretive character as theorising about the concept of law. Dworkin writes: 'Judges who accept the interpretive ideal of integrity decide hard cases by trying to find, in some coherent set of principles about people's

---

93 Dworkin, above n 44, p 96.
94 Ibid p 134.
95 Ibid p 167.
96 Ibid p 225.
97 Dworkin, above n 53, p 5.
98 Dworkin, above n 44, p 243.

rights and duties, the best constructive interpretation of the political structure and legal doctrine of their community.'[99]

Law as integrity is therefore, in Dworkin's words, 'more relentlessly interpretive' than conventionalism.[100] Conventionalism provides an interpretation of legal practice, but unlike law as integrity, it does not tell judges to use the method of constructive interpretation in deciding cases. On the law-as-integrity approach, by contrast, the same methodology is at work in answering both jurisprudential and legal questions. This means that 'morality is implicated in the identification of law not only at the jurisprudential stage of legal theory but at the doctrinal stage as well'.[101] Judges who accept the theory of law as integrity will identify the law's requirements by reference to moral principles that provide the best justification of the body of law considered as a whole. Legal rights are thus seen to be a species of moral rights, not as a contingent possibility by virtue of criteria that happen to be contained in the rule of recognition accepted in particular legal systems, but by virtue of the very nature of law.

In explaining the 'special interpretive challenge'[102] that arises in the adjudicative context when judges accept the theory of law as integrity, Dworkin compares their task to the writing of a 'chain novel'. Suppose a group of people decide to write a novel, with each person contributing a chapter. It must appear at the end as if a single author has written the whole work. Each novelist in the chain must continue the novel by building on what has gone before, with the aim of making the novel the best it can be. In order to continue the novel, all the novelists, except the first, will have to interpret what has gone before. They will, for instance, have to decide what motivates the characters and what the point of the novel is. At the same time, their decisions must continue the novel in the best possible way.[103]

Just as there were two requirements governing the interpretation of a social practice (see 6.8), there will be two requirements governing the activity of the novelists. First, they have to *continue* the novel, not start a new one. This means that each person's chapter will have to be consistent with or fit the material that has been constructed so far. This is not to say that the fit

---

99 Ibid p 255.
100 Ibid p 226.
101 Dworkin, above n 53, p 14.
102 Dworkin, above n 44, p 227.
103 Ibid pp 228–30.

must be perfect. It must, though, fit the bulk of the text. If a new chapter entirely disregards what has gone before, the interpretation will be disqualified. Secondly, in choosing between different interpretations that both meet the criterion of fit, the novelists should choose that interpretation which they believe makes the work in progress the *best* work it can be, judged from the standpoint of aesthetic value. This is the requirement I previously called substantive.[104] Of course, what counts as 'sufficient fit' and what constitutes the ideal mix of 'fit' and 'value' are also interpretive matters.

Interpreting legal data, such as constitutional provisions, statutes and common law precedents, is similar in important ways to the writing of a chain novel, according to Dworkin. It has the same combination of backward-looking and forward-looking aspects.[105] Judges must constructively interpret the data, 'keeping right faith with the past' while also 'show[ing] the best route to a better future'.[106] They should seek to justify what past judges and lawmakers did 'in an overall story worth telling now'.[107] They should therefore think of themselves as authors in the chain of common law.[108] This means that they should think of earlier cases on related matters as part of an ongoing story that requires interpretation and continuation. And when interpreting statutes, judges should likewise think of the legislature as an earlier author in the chain of law, their responsibility being to develop, in the best way, the statutory scheme the legislature began.[109]

In both cases, judges are not entitled to strike off in a new direction: their interpretation of the law must to a significant extent cohere with or fit the 'data'. Judges must weave these into a story that is recognisably continuous with what went before. At the same time, their interpretation must make the story (the legal record) the best story it can be. There may be more than one interpretation that is compatible with the legal record and judges should choose between competing interpretations by considering which one provides the best moral justification for the whole network of legal materials.

The implication of this is that some of the data may need to be rejected as 'mistakes' when they are revisited at the post-interpretive stage. This will be so if they are in conflict with principles that are more fundamental to justifying

---

104 Ibid pp 230–2.
105 Ibid p 225.
106 Ibid p 413.
107 Ibid p 227.
108 Ibid p 239.
109 Ibid p 313.

law as a whole. The legal materials, however plain in meaning they might have seemed to be, may at this stage appear as a pale reflection of the 'real' law. Thus no aspect of legal practice is in principle immune to revision, on Dworkin's account. In the post-interpretive stage, judges must adjust their sense of what the law 'really' requires in the light of the justification they see the legal record as serving, and it is this idealised law that courts are obliged to enforce. On Dworkin's view, the materials that positivists pick out as law are therefore merely 'raw material',[110] which judges fashion and modify in order to present the law as a regime of justified coercion based on the principle of integrity. No wonder, then, that Dworkin calls his ideal judge 'Hercules', for this holistic approach to identifying the law is undoubtedly a Herculean task. Dworkin concedes that real judges decide cases much less holistically. They have discrete problems to resolve and the scope of their inquiry is generally limited. However, he argues that the possibility of reasoning more theoretically about the connection of a particular problem to other areas of the law is always lurking in the background, and that the need to do so may be forced on judges in particular cases.[111]

In *Law's Empire*, the distinction between hard and easy cases recedes in importance. Dworkin tells us that 'hard' is just a label used when people disagree about which reading of the law shows the legal record as a whole in its best light, irrespective of how linguistically clear the words in which the law is couched may be. Thus in the case of *Riggs*, the reason the law was 'unclear' as to whether murderers could inherit was not because the words were unclear, but because some of the judges thought there were good reasons to interpret the statute so as to prevent murderers from inheriting.[112] Conversely, even if the words of a statute are vague or ambiguous, the *law* may nevertheless be clear, because there may be no doubt that one reading of the statute would be 'a better performance of the legislative function'.[113] The same interpretive method is used in both hard and easy cases, but because there is no disagreement about the correct interpretation in an easy case we may not be aware that the theory is at work.[114]

In summary: Dworkin puts forward an integrity-based interpretation of legal practice, which takes the view that the point of requiring power to be exercised in accordance with pre-established standards is to secure consistency

---

110 J Coleman, *The Practice of Principle: In Defence of a Pragmatist Approach to Legal Theory*, Oxford University Press, Oxford, 2001, p 166.
111 Dworkin, above n 53, pp 52–6.
112 Dworkin, above n 44, p 352.
113 Ibid p 353.
114 Ibid p 354.

in principle. This leads him to argue for a particular approach to identifying the law. In particular, he proposes a view of the grounds of law on which moral considerations are relevant to deciding what legal rights and duties people have. This is not for the reason given by inclusive positivists, namely, that it may be the practice of judges in particular legal systems to treat moral facts as grounds of law. Instead, law as integrity instructs judges to interpret the legal materials constructively, and such interpretation, according to Dworkin, is necessarily a moral exercise. It is as a result impossible, on Dworkin's view, to draw a conceptually sharp distinction between the law as it is and the law as it ought to be. We do not know what the law is until we know what interpretation of it would make it morally justifiable: factual and moral reasoning are necessarily interwoven when judges identify the law. 'Justice', says Dworkin, 'plays a role in fixing what the law is'.[115]

Why should we accept Dworkin's account of law? Dworkin argues that the idea of law as promoting integrity provides the best interpretation of legal practice because it both fits the practice of law and shows it in its most attractive light.

Insofar as the question of fit is concerned, Dworkin argues that the value of integrity explains why we reject certain kinds of legislative compromises. He calls these 'checkerboard statutes'. Suppose that the electorate is evenly divided on whether abortion should be permitted. Why would it not be acceptable for parliament to allow access to abortions for women born in even years but not for those born in odd ones?[116]

Dworkin argues that such a checkerboard statute would be *fairer* than a statute either prohibiting abortion for all women or allowing it for all women, because the checkerboard statute allows each half of the electorate to choose half of the law of abortion. By contrast, a law that prohibited abortion for all women or permitted it for all women would allow one half of the electorate to have total influence over the legislative scheme, while the other half would have no influence.[117] The checkerboard statute therefore distributes political power fairly.

Dworkin also argues that there is no argument of *justice* against a checkerboard statute if the only alternative to the statute is a principled statute that you think is wrong. Suppose you think that women are entitled as a matter

---

115 Dworkin, above n 53, p 35.
116 Dworkin, above n 44, p 178.
117 Ibid p 179.

of justice to an abortion and that the only alternative to the checkerboard solution is a statute prohibiting abortion altogether. If so, you will think the checkerboard less unjust because at least it will allow some women access to abortion. Likewise, if you think that as a matter of justice, abortion should be totally prohibited, you will think it better to accept the compromise if, once again, the only alternative to the compromise is a totally permissive law. In other words, if one cannot have all the justice one wants, one would prefer to have less justice in preference to no justice.[118] Why, then, do we find checkerboard statutes unacceptable if they are not unfair and they are less unjust than the alternative? Dworkin's answer is that we find them unacceptable because they violate the independent principle of integrity. They are morally incoherent. He writes:
'[A] state that adopts these internal compromises is acting in an unprincipled way ... The state lacks integrity because it must endorse principles to justify part of what it has done that it must reject to justify the rest.'[119]

Dworkin then explains why integrity is an attractive ideal that we should support. Such an explanation is necessary because integrity or consistency can conflict with justice and fairness in Dworkin's view, as we have seen. Decisions that are consistent in principle with previous decisions are not necessarily the most just decisions. If that is the case, then why is integrity attractive? Although Dworkin does not say that the pursuit of integrity should always triumph over the pursuit of justice, he does say that it is sometimes more important than justice. How can this be? How can it be better for the state to continue to follow an unjust principle for consistency's sake than to change course in the name of justice?

Dworkin's account here is complex (and disputed), but, in brief, he argues that integrity can be defended by reference to the way in which it creates bonds of 'true community', which Dworkin also calls 'fraternity'.[120] It creates such bonds because of its insistence that 'the principles under which we are governed treat us as equals'.[121] Accepting that our fates are linked in this way by the application of common principles to everyone, rather than by 'rules hammered out in political compromise',[122] in turn enhances the legitimacy of law and therefore its ability to impose moral obligations of obedience. Thus Dworkin

---

118 Ibid p 180.
119 Ibid pp 183–4.
120 Ibid p 188.
121 Dworkin, above n 53, p 73.
122 Dworkin, above n 44, p 211.

writes: '[A] political society that accepts integrity as a political virtue thereby becomes a special form of community, special in a way that promotes its moral authority to assume and deploy a monopoly of coercive force.'[123] Dworkin invites us to conclude that law as integrity provides the best justification of the state's exercise of coercive power.

6.11 The objectivity of interpretation

Dworkin seems to have the best of all worlds. He is not guilty of 'mechanical jurisprudence'—the view that judges are 'computers in robes', to borrow a phrase from Martha Minow and Elizabeth Spelman.[124] He does not, in other words, claim that judges are mechanically constrained by rules of law that inexorably dictate the answer to all legal cases. (For discussion of such a view, see 7.2.) On the contrary, like the realists, to whom we turn in the next chapter, Dworkin discounts the role played by narrowly doctrinal rules of law in adjudication. He thinks that judges are required to reflect on moral issues and to make controversial moral judgments, and he likens legal reasoning to an act of creative interpretation.

At the same time, Dworkin also accepts the traditional picture that there are right answers to legal disputes, which judges are under an obligation to find. Indeed, he goes further than Hart, claiming that there are no legal disputes that cannot be resolved according to law. Judges, according to Dworkin, do not have the freedom of legislators and never reach outside the law to make new law: they never create new duties and impose them retrospectively. Thus Hercules is not in the business of lawmaking, which would be an illegitimate exercise of judicial power, in Dworkin's view. There is a difference, Dworkin tells us, between interpretation and invention.

It may be wondered whether it is really possible to incorporate all of these 'desirables' in a single theory. Can law really be, as Dworkin claims, 'deeply and thoroughly political', yet not 'a matter of *personal* or *partisan* politics'?[125] How can judges decide cases on moral grounds without deciding them in a way that reflects the result that, in their opinion, would be the best outcome? Dworkin offers two main arguments in support of his claim that judges are not

---

123 Ibid p 188.
124 M L Minow and E V Spelman, 'Passion for Justice' (1988) 10 *Cardozo Law Review* 37, 53.
125 R Dworkin, 'Law As Interpretation' (1982) 9 *Critical Inquiry* 179, 179, emphasis added.

merely imposing their personal value judgments if they take the approach to adjudication recommended by his theory of law as integrity.

First, he argues that the moral and political reasoning of judges is constrained to some extent by the fact that any satisfactory interpretation will have to fit the pre-interpretive legal materials, as contained, for instance, in precedents and statutes. Judges must be faithful to the object of interpretation. Thus, although judges' moral and political convictions will influence their views as to what rights individuals have under the law, 'the actual political history of [the judge's] community will sometimes check his other political convictions in his overall interpretive judgment'.[126] Dworkin gives the example of a Marxist judge who thinks that the rich should share their wealth with the poor. Such a judge will find that the need to decide cases in a way that fits the bulk of the prior legal record prevents him or her from interpreting the law so as to abolish property rights. In this way, 'the brute facts of political history will ... limit the role any judge's personal convictions of justice can play in his decisions'.[127]

Dworkin makes a related distinction between 'background morality' and 'institutional morality'.[128] Background morality is the morality that judges believe the law ought to reflect, and that they would enact into law if they were legislators. Institutional morality is the scheme of moral rights that best justifies the actual legal record. Judges are in the business of trying to find the best justification of the legal record, not of trying to reach the result they personally think is correct.[129] Dworkin therefore insists that there is a distinction between interpreting the *existing* law and postulating an *ideal* law: the actual legal record may be morally deficient in certain respects, and if so, judges are not entitled to invent a better legal record. He says that something may be the law even if, according to 'some pure objective or natural law',[130] it ought not to be. It is, of course, the possible divergence between the morality that underpins the legal record and perfect political morality, which allows for the possible conflict between integrity and justice, that we noted in 6.10.

Apart from the fact that interpretation needs to fit the pre-existing legal materials, there is also another reason why Dworkin believes that it is possible to

---

126 Dworkin, above n 44, p 225.
127 Ibid p 255.
128 Dworkin, above n 42, pp 112, 128.
129 Dworkin, above n 44, p 338.
130 Dworkin, above n 125, 180.

have the best of both worlds—that adjudication can be based on controversial moral and political views while still remaining a rational and objective enterprise. He believes that there are right and wrong answers to moral questions and that there are therefore objective answers to the interpretive questions that judges are required to consider.

It is not possible to do justice here to Dworkin's account of the objectivity of moral propositions and his attack on what he calls 'external scepticism' (in contrast to the internally sceptical views discussed in 6.8).[131] In outline, however, his position is as follows. External scepticism is the view that value judgments are subjective and that it is therefore impossible for an interpretive view—a claim that a particular interpretation of the law shows it in the best moral light—to be right in some objective sense.[132] External sceptics have moral views and opinions as to which interpretation is the right interpretation. They merely say that their moral opinions are not grounded in reality: they are not 'really' right. This leads them to challenge the distinction between interpretation and invention. Dworkin argues, however, that external scepticism is a confused position.[133] He says that it is a myth to suppose that there could be 'two standpoints, an internal standpoint from which an interpreter has his own answer to interpretive questions, and an external standpoint from which he acknowledges that such questions can have no answers'.[134]

Thus Dworkin argues that it does not make sense for someone to say, for instance, 'I believe slavery is wrong but I do not think that it is "objectively" wrong'. For Dworkin, the statement 'Slavery is wrong' has the same meaning as the statement 'Slavery is objectively wrong'. The latter is just a more emphatic way of making the same point. Likewise, if an external sceptic thinks that a particular interpretation is better than another, then whatever arguments the sceptic offers in support of that view will necessarily be arguments supporting the statement that that view is *correct*. Therefore, in Dworkin's view, after having pronounced jurisprudence 'subjective', external sceptics can do nothing but 'return to their knitting—making, accepting, resisting, rejecting arguments in the normal way, consulting, revising, deploying convictions pertinent to deciding which of competing accounts of legal practice provides the best justification of

---

131 Dworkin sets out his views on this matter in most detail in 'Objectivity and Truth: You'd Better Believe It' (1996) 25 *Philosophy and Public Affairs* 87.
132 Dworkin, above n 44, pp 79–80.
133 Ibid p 85.
134 R Dworkin, *A Matter of Principle*, Harvard University Press, Cambridge, MA, 1985, p 176.

that practice'.[135] He concludes that external scepticism is not a threat to his view about the existence of right answers in hard cases because it is just a 'preliminary dance', which serves no function.[136]

Of course, Dworkin is quick to point out, it may not be possible to *demonstrate* that a particular answer is the right answer. But this does not prevent one answer from *being* the right answer. For, as he says, a proposition can be true even if it is not *uncontroversially* true or cannot be *proved* to be true to everyone's satisfaction. Disagreement about an answer does not show that there is no answer. Dworkin illustrates this point with a literary example. Suppose we are discussing the question of whether David Copperfield had a sexual relationship with Steerforth. Dickens does not directly tell us about this aspect of David's life. There can, nevertheless, be said to be a right answer to this question in the sense that one hypothesis 'provides a more satisfactory explanation of what [David] subsequently did and thought than the [opposite hypothesis]'.[137] The same is true of the law. Propositions of law can be true even if they cannot be conclusively proved to be true.[138]

6.12 Some criticisms of Dworkin

As we have seen, Dworkin attempts to distinguish between the activities of judging and legislating, while simultaneously asserting that judges make controversial moral and political judgments. Many critics argue, however, that in fact Dworkin's ideal judge, Hercules, is exercising exactly the same kind of lawmaking power that Dworkin finds so objectionable in Hart's model of adjudication. The only difference, according to these critics, is that Hercules disguises the fact that he is imposing his own personal views by claiming that they are contained in the law. His claim that the law provides answers for all disputes is therefore just 'rhetoric' or 'ritual language'.[139] These critics point out that it would really make little difference to litigants whether they come before Hercules or whether they come before a judge who sees the judicial task as one of exercising discretion in a hard case. Since Hercules' arguments are not

---

135 Dworkin, above n 44, pp 85–6.
136 Ibid p 86.
137 R Dworkin, 'No Right Answer', in P M S Hacker and J Raz (eds), *Law, Morality and Society: Essays in Honour of H L A Hart*, Clarendon Press, Oxford, 1977, p 78.
138 For further discussion of the difference between indemonstrability and indeterminacy, see M H Kramer, *Objectivity and the Rule of Law*, Cambridge University Press, New York, 2007, pp 17–19.
139 Hart, above n 51, p 274.

guaranteed to persuade and since his decision could not have been predicted in advance, he is exercising power just as unpredictably.[140] These critics conclude that Dworkin's theory is as vulnerable to the charge of retroactive lawmaking as Hart's.

This criticism does not necessarily depend on the assumption that a correct legal answer does not exist in hard cases. Even if, in theory, there is a right answer to the issue in dispute, if two judges conscientiously applying their minds to the problem disagree about the answer, it is hard to deny that they have the discretion to decide the case either way. Kent Greenawalt gives the example of standards of beauty. Suppose a group of judges is told to pick the most beautiful flower. Let us also suppose that there are objective standards of beauty in flowers but no way of telling what they are. Greenawalt writes: 'Then everyone would believe that one choice was "right" but would be unable to ascertain which one. The judges themselves would be thrown back on their own judgments.'[141] If this is not the exercise of discretion, what is? How can judges be said to be under a duty to decide in one way rather than another if no one can say with any confidence which is the correct decision? Greenawalt concludes:

> When authoritative standards yield no clear answers, when a judge must rely on debatable personal assessments to decide a case, and when more than one result will widely be regarded as a satisfactory fulfillment of his judicial responsibilities, then it does not make good sense to say that a judge is under a duty to reach one result rather than another; as far as the law is concerned, he has discretion to decide between them.[142]

A further criticism relates to Dworkin's idea that disagreement is rife in the law. Dworkin believes that 'the more we learn about law, the more we grow convinced that nothing about it is wholly uncontroversial'.[143] His critics argue, however, that this is an exaggeration. They say that the vast majority of cases are easy, not hard, and that it is therefore a mistake to build one's entire theory of law around the small number of controversial cases that raise difficult moral issues and that are contested in the highest courts. They say that there are many potential cases that never reach the courts because the applicability of the legal rules to conduct is obvious. They also point to the numerous cases in which the

---

140 J Bell, *Policy Arguments in Judicial Decisions*, Clarendon Press, Oxford, 1983, pp 213, 222–3.
141 K Greenawalt, 'Discretion and the Judicial Decision' (1975) 65 *Columbia Law Review* 359, 369.
142 Ibid 378.
143 Dworkin, above n 44, p 10.

law guides the behaviour of citizens without any intervention by legal officials. Schauer points to such examples as stopping at stop signs, filing a tax return before the deadline and refraining from infringing water restrictions.[144] Dworkin's critics also claim that the phenomenon of pervasive agreement provides support for positivism because agreement is what one would expect if, as positivists think, the law is fixed by the convergent practices of legal officials and the meaning of precedents and statutory provisions is often plain.[145]

Another criticism relates to Dworkin's views about wicked legal systems. As we know, Dworkin thinks that the value of integrity may conflict with justice and prevail over it. If, however, the conflict between integrity and justice becomes too pronounced, as it does in wicked legal systems, Dworkin thinks that a judge should refuse to enforce the law. Consider, once again, Nazi laws. The only 'principles' that underpin such laws are morally rebarbative. In such cases, Dworkin thinks that a judge should not seek to extend these principles. In the case of wicked legal systems, in other words, justice is more important than keeping the law consistent in principle, and there is no justification for state coercion. Dworkin writes: '[T]he legal practices so condemned yield to no interpretation that can have, in any acceptable political morality, any justifying power at all.'[146]

This solution to the problem of wicked legal systems does, however, create some difficulties. Is Dworkin saying that wicked laws are laws, but they are laws which have no moral force whatsoever? If so, this seems to contradict his claim that all laws, by virtue of being laws, prima facie justify coercion. It also makes his position indistinguishable from positivism, whose central principle is that laws and the use of coercion to enforce them are not necessarily morally justified. Or is Dworkin saying that because wicked 'laws' do not have any moral force and are not able to provide even a prima facie justification for coercion, they are not 'real' laws? If so, he is caught in the difficulties that plague natural law, because even wicked legal systems do seem to have law. Dworkin's solution to this is to say that from one point of view—the pre-interpretive point of view—regimes such as Nazism count as 'legal'. However, from the interpretive point of view, on which law has some ability to justify coercion, they do not count as 'legal'.[147] Many of Dworkin's critics are sceptical about this 'flexible' solution, which they

---

144 Schauer, above n 18, 413.
145 Leiter, above n 55, 1226–8.
146 Dworkin, above n 44, p 102.
147 Ibid pp 101–4.

see as Dworkin attempting to have his cake and eat it too. Waluchow describes some of the problems as follows:

> Dworkin is driven to accommodate [the positivist insight] by creating two senses of 'law', one of which renders legal rights a species of moral rights and explains their nature in those terms, the other of which is left completely unexplained. Instead of recognizing that law sometimes has no moral worth and building this into his explication of its nature, Dworkin simply creates a new category, a second concept of law. This carving off of what is better thought of as part of the domain to be explained is bad enough. One might also ask whether Dworkin has the resources within his theory to deal with it. If law, in this special sense, is not a scheme of moral rights, what exactly is it? ... To these important questions we find answers in legal positivism. Dworkin may still not like those answers, but if legal rights are not to be understood as rights of political morality, he seems to have no better alternative.[148]

Many of Dworkin's critics have disputed his claim that the only plausible legal theories are interpretive and therefore morally committed. As we know, Dworkin thinks that jurisprudence must be built around the organising assumption that the purpose of law is to limit and justify the use of force by the state. He characterises this as an uncontroversial starting point, which is compatible with a great many theories of law.[149] In his view, all plausible legal theories seek to show that their conception of law does the best job of justifying the use of force and therefore of showing why law is legitimate. Since it is impossible to argue for a conception of law with a view to enhancing its legitimacy without engaging in substantive moral argument, Dworkin concludes that jurisprudence is necessarily normative. It is because Dworkin takes this view that he is led to argue that positivistic theories purporting to be descriptive, such as Hart's, are confused and need to be reconceptualised as interpretive versions of positivism if they are to be taken seriously as candidate theories of law.[150] Dworkin therefore reconstructs positivism, as we saw in 6.9. He reads it as asserting that the reason we should accept a plain-fact account of law is that such an account makes law clear and uncontroversial and therefore explains why law morally justifies the use of force.[151] This is the theory Dworkin calls 'conventionalism'. Hart is, however, unconvinced by any of these arguments.

---

148 Waluchow, above n 25, p 63.
149 Dworkin, above n 44, p 93.
150 Dworkin, above n 53, p 165.
151 Ibid.

First, notwithstanding Dworkin's claim that his starting point is uncontroversial, Hart expressly rejects the idea that law has a morally worthy purpose, let alone that its purpose is to justify coercion. Indeed, Hart does not believe that law has a distinctive purpose at all. In his view, there are no purposes that law *uniquely* has. The purpose of guiding conduct, for instance, is shared with other kinds of rules and to say that the law's purpose is to guide conduct is therefore to say something of little interest.[152] The focus of Hart's theory is not on law's functions or goals but rather, as Julie Dickson says, on the *methods* that are distinctive of law. Hart's focus is on the ways in which law works and its special institutions and procedures, such as the role played in legal systems by secondary rules. Dickson writes:

> On such an [institutional] approach, the primary focus of jurisprudential inquiry lies with those distinctive legal institutions and processes which reveal the structure and mode of law's operation ... Many theorists in this tradition do not even accept that law has one overall point or function, let alone that a whole tradition of jurisprudential thought converges upon one view of law's function so as to render it uncontroversial. While such theorists may accept that individual laws or areas of law can have one or more functions, it is not part of their thinking that law as a social institution has one overall function or purpose.[153]

Jules Coleman attacks Dworkin's normative conception of jurisprudence along similar lines to Hart's critique. First, he asks why we should assume that analysis of law must begin by imputing a function or purpose to law. Second, if we should assume this, why should we assume that law's function is a moral function? Third, even supposing that law does function in many communities to justify coercion, why should we assume that this is law's only function or that it is an essential property of law or part of our concept of law? After all, if justifying coercion is not part of our *concept* of law, an analysis of law does not need to show how law serves this function well. According to Coleman, '[a]t each crucial point the inferences seem to come out of thin air'.[154]

Hart also objects to Dworkin's reformulation of positivism in interpretive terms. Hart argues that interpretive issues are not the only proper issues for legal theory.[155] He maintains that it is possible and desirable to give an account of law

---

152 Hart, above n 51, pp 248–9.
153 J Dickson, *Evaluation and Legal Theory*, Hart Publishing, Oxford, 2001, p 112.
154 Coleman, above n 110, p 184.
155 Hart, above n 51, p 243.

that 'is descriptive in that it is morally neutral and has no justificatory aims'.[156] Such an account, he says, 'does not seek to justify or commend on moral or other grounds the forms and structures which appear in [it]'.[157] Hart adds that it is not clear why Dworkin thinks descriptive jurisprudence is impossible. To the extent that this belief is based on Dworkin's view that legal theorists must adopt the participants' perspective if they are to give an adequate account of law, Hart thinks the argument is unsuccessful. Hart does not think jurisprudence must be undertaken from the perspective of committed participants. As we saw in 3.7, he does not even think that committed participants in the legal system must believe that the law's use of coercion is morally justified. Of course, as we know, Hart thinks that legal theorists must *understand* the internal point of view of participants if they are to give an accurate description of the workings of the legal system. To that extent, he thinks that Dworkin is right to stress the participants' point of view. But Hart argues that it is possible for the legal theorist to grasp the participants' perspective without *sharing* or *endorsing* it or 'in any other way ... surrender[ing] his descriptive stance'.[158] Hart adds that even if Dworkin were right that participants in the system must believe that the law's use of coercion is morally justified, the descriptive theorist would merely *record* these moral beliefs as a fact, not adopt them.[159] Since Dworkin has confused *describing* an evaluation with *making* an evaluation, Hart concludes that Dworkin has not shown that jurisprudence is a necessarily moral enterprise.

A similar objection can be made to Finnis's normative conception of jurisprudence. It can be argued that even if Finnis is right that the central case of the participant point of view is the point of view of the person who believes that the law is worth establishing and maintaining (see 5.3), legal theorists would need to take note of this point of view, not take up their own moral stance on it.[160] The issue that divides Hart, on the one hand, and Dworkin and Finnis, on the other, is whether one can understand what moral point others ascribe to law without either agreeing with them or disagreeing with them, and therefore without making one's *own* moral evaluation of the law.

---

156 Ibid p 240.
157 Ibid.
158 Ibid p 242.
159 Ibid p 243.
160 K M Ehrenberg, 'Defending the Possibility of a Neutral Functional Theory of Law' (2009) 29 *Oxford Journal of Legal Studies* 91, 111.

Another criticism of Dworkin, made by Finnis, relates to the 'incommensurability' of the two dimensions—fit and moral value—in terms of which different interpretations must be assessed. When two things are incommensurable, it is impossible to compare them by saying that one is better than the other. One cannot, for instance, normally say that spending the afternoon reading philosophy is better or worse than spending the afternoon going for a walk.[161] Finnis says that judgments of fit and of moral merits may be incommensurable in this way. One solution to a legal problem may be slightly better on the dimension of fit, whereas the other may be slightly better on the dimension of value. In such circumstances, he says, there is an open choice between the two answers: there is no uniquely right way to resolve the dispute.[162]

In recent work, Dworkin has begun to argue against moral pluralism. This is the idea that true values can clash in such a way that protecting one may necessarily involve sacrificing another, and that whatever decision we make will therefore require doing something wrong.[163] Dworkin writes of an ambitious project that 'must find the place of each [political] value in a larger and mutually supporting web of conviction that displays supporting connections among moral and political values generally and then places these in the still larger context of ethics'.[164] However, this is just a start; much work remains to be done in responding to the argument that the values justifying legal practice are deeply conflicting.

Questions

1. Should judges apply the literal meaning of a statutory provision when to do so appears to defeat its purpose or the intentions of those who enacted it? Is there such a thing as literal meaning?
2. What is a 'hard case'? Do judges make new law in hard cases?
3. Do you think that the interpretation of statutes and judicial decisions is analogous to the interpretation of a work of art or literature?
4. Dworkin argues that 'fit' is a constraint on legal interpretation but he also concedes that judgments about fit are a controversial, interpretive matter. Does this threaten his distinction between 'interpretation' and 'invention'?

---

161 B Bix, *Law, Language and Legal Determinacy*, Clarendon Press, Oxford, 1993, p 99.
162 J Finnis, 'On Reason and Authority in *Law's Empire*' (1987) 6 *Law and Philosophy* 357, 371–6; Bix, above n 161, pp 96–101.
163 Dworkin, above n 53, pp 105–16.
164 Ibid p 168.

5   Brian Leiter writes: '[P]ositivists ask Dworkin how he proposes to demarcate those invocations of morality that are supposed to be legally binding from those that are simply cases of judges "legislating from the bench" or exercising discretion. Dworkin ... knows full well that ... lawyers and judges recognize this distinction, and it has been a fundamental difficulty that he has no account of it' ('The End of Empire: Dworkin and Jurisprudence in the 21st Century' (2004) 36 *Rutgers Law Journal* 165, 175). Do you agree with Leiter that Dworkin has no account of this distinction?

6   Why do wicked legal systems pose a problem for Dworkin's theory of law?

Further reading

R Dworkin, *Taking Rights Seriously*, Duckworth, London, 1977, Chapters 2–3.

R Dworkin, *Law's Empire*, Belknap Press of Harvard University Press, Cambridge, MA, 1986.

R Dworkin, *Justice in Robes*, Belknap Press of Harvard University Press, Cambridge, MA, 2006.

S Fish, *Doing What Comes Naturally: Change, Rhetoric, and the Practice of Theory in Literary and Legal Studies*, Duke University Press, Durham, 1989.

L L Fuller, 'Positivism and Fidelity to Law: A Reply to Professor Hart' (1958) 71 *Harvard Law Review* 630.

S Guest, *Ronald Dworkin*, 2nd edn, Edinburgh University Press, Edinburgh, 1997.

S Hershowitz (ed), *Exploring Law's Empire: The Jurisprudence of Ronald Dworkin*, Oxford University Press, Oxford, 2006.

B Leiter, 'Explaining Theoretical Disagreement' (2009) 76 *Chicago Law Review* 1215.

A Marmor, *Interpretation and Legal Theory*, revised 2nd edn, Hart Publishing, Oxford, 2005.

A Marmor (ed), *Law and Interpretation*, Clarendon Press, Oxford, 1995.

D Réaume, 'Is Integrity a Virtue? Dworkin's Theory of Legal Obligation' (1989) 39 *University of Toronto Law Journal* 380.

A Ripstein (ed), *Ronald Dworkin*, Cambridge University Press, Cambridge, 2007.

F Schauer, 'Formalism' (1988) 97 *Yale Law Review* 509.

F Schauer, 'A Critical Guide to Vehicles in the Park' (2008) 83 *New York University Law Review* 1109.

W J Waluchow, *Inclusive Legal Positivism*, Clarendon Press, Oxford, 1994, Chapters 2–3, 6–8.

7

Law as Myth

7.1 Chapter overview

This chapter will deal with American legal realism. The American legal realists were a group of lawyers and legal academics whose heyday was in the 1920s, 1930s and 1940s. Among them were Felix Cohen, Jerome Frank, Karl Llewellyn and Herman Oliphant. Although they were to some extent a disparate group, there are sufficient common themes in their writings to justify regarding them as a movement. In general terms, the realists sought to demythologise law. They were sceptical of the traditional picture of law as consisting in rules. They were also sceptical about the determinacy of the law and the associated view that legal rules are the primary influence on judicial decisions. Instead, they took the view that non-legal and even idiosyncratic factors are the most important influences on judicial decision-making. They thought that this empirical claim could be established by social scientific investigation and they were, in general, attracted to the view that law and legal institutions should be studied empirically or scientifically. Some of the realists also defended the normative view that judges should openly make decisions politically, that is, with an eye on their policy implications and future social consequences.

7.2 The law is what the courts say it is

Oliver Wendell Holmes, Jr, a Justice of the Supreme Court of the United States from 1902 to 1932, was a key influence on the realists. He had talked of the need to 'wash ... with cynical acid'[1] the traditional view of law, on which it consists in

---

1   O W Holmes, 'The Path of the Law' (1897) 10 *Harvard Law Review* 457, 462.

a body of abstract concepts and doctrines developing according to its own inner logic. The realists sought to replace this traditional view with an investigation of how the legal system operates in practice. They focused especially on 'what the courts ... do in fact'[2] and the real reasons for judicial decisions. They believed that this empirical approach to the law would provide a more reliable guide to predicting judicial decisions than the study of legal doctrine. They also thought that this kind of information about the law would be more useful to lawyers and their clients, who are interested in the law only insofar as it has a practical bearing on their conduct and their arrangements. The label 'realism' therefore captures the way in which the realists aimed to bring legal theory down to earth, puncture the illusions in which it trades and describe the practical realities of the legal system in its social context. We might say that the realists wished to describe the law as it *really* is.

At the time the realists were writing, it was widely believed that there were uniquely correct solutions to all legal cases and that judges could arrive at these conclusions by the deductive application of the rules of law to known facts. The judicial task, on this view, was a simple exercise in the mechanical, logical derivation of legal conclusions, with judging entirely insulated from the wider world of morality, politics and practical consequences, and never involving the making of law. The views of Christopher Columbus Langdell, who was Dean of the Harvard Law School at the end of the nineteenth century, were highly influential in the development of this formalist orthodoxy.

This is a different kind of 'formalism' from the kind encountered in 6.4. In 6.4, the word 'formalism' was used to refer to the normative view that judges should always follow clear rules. The view we are now considering maintains that law forms a self-contained system of legal rules and concepts from which legal outcomes can be logically deduced. Langdell was a formalist in this latter sense. He saw legal analysis as like geometry: it involved identifying the principles on which an area of law is based and working out the subordinate principles logically entailed by them. The aim was to construct a logically connected system of rules that would definitively state the law's requirements in a particular area.[3] For obvious reasons, critics described this approach as 'mechanical jurisprudence',[4] and we saw in 3.8 that Hart regarded it as a 'great exaggeration'. In seeking to

---

2   Ibid 461.
3   A T Kronman, *The Lost Lawyer: Failing Ideals of the Legal Profession*, Belknap Press of Harvard University Press, Cambridge, MA, 1993, p 171.
4   R Pound, 'Mechanical Jurisprudence' (1908) 8 *Columbia Law Review* 605.

debunk this view, the realists went even further than Hart, arguing that legal rules are merely 'pretty playthings'[5] and that the notion of legal reasoning is a myth or sham. The realists were, in other words, sceptics about legal rules.

As Hart explains, this scepticism manifested itself in two ways. First, the realists argued that the law should not be identified with the rules of law. This is a theoretical claim about the nature of law and it therefore offers itself as a competitor to other theories about the nature of law, such as positivism and natural law. Secondly, the realists argued that legal rules are of little importance in judicial decision-making.[6] We will deal with the first claim in this section and the second claim in 7.3 and 7.4.

Insofar as the first claim is concerned, the realists argued that the rules enacted by legislatures or declared by courts are not law. These are merely what Karl Llewellyn called the 'paper' rules or 'law in books'. What, then, is the law, if 'talk of rules is a myth'?[7] Law, the realists answered, is 'law in action'. Law is simply what the courts decide or predictions as to what they will decide. Holmes had laid the foundations for this view. He had said that if you want to know what the law is, you must look at it not in terms of idealistic abstractions but as the 'bad man' looks at it. The bad man, Holmes wrote, 'does not care two straws for ... axioms or deductions',[8] but does want to know what conduct is likely to put him in jail or make him liable for damages. This pragmatic focus on the way in which courts affect the lives of those who come before them, and on the consequences courts are likely to attach to our conduct, led the realists to hold that we are under a legal duty if failure to act in a certain way would lead to an adverse court decision. The claim that 'X is under a legal duty' is therefore equivalent to predicting that a court will require certain conduct of X. Furthermore, if the court does not require the conduct, then the claim was false, because the 'law is what the courts say it is'. There is, in other words, no law that exists prior to a court's decision on the matter.

Thus, Llewellyn wrote: 'I should like to begin by distinguishing "real" rules and rights from paper rules and rights. The former are conceived in terms of behaviour; they are but other names, convenient shorthand symbols, for

---

5   K N Llewellyn, *The Bramble Bush*, Oceana Publications Inc, New York, 1930, p 14.
6   Brian Leiter calls these 'conceptual rule-scepticism' and 'empirical rule-scepticism' respectively, although he thinks that the latter kind of scepticism is more central to realism than the former. See B Leiter, 'Legal Realism and Legal Positivism Reconsidered' *Ethics* (2001) 289, 290–3.
7   H L A Hart, *The Concept of Law*, 2nd edn, Clarendon Press, Oxford, 1994, p 136.
8   Holmes, above n 1, 460.

the remedies, the actions of the courts.'[9] They are what the courts will do in a given case.[10] Although Llewellyn calls these the real 'rules', he makes clear that these are not rules in the normative or prescriptive sense of the word—the sense around which Hart's account of law is built—but are merely descriptions of what the courts actually do. He says:

> 'Real rules' ... if I had my way with words, would by legal scientists be called the practices of the courts, and not 'rules' at all. And for such scientists, statements of 'rights' would be statements of likelihood that in a given situation a certain type of court action loomed in the offing. Factual terms. No more ... They are ... on the level of isness and not of oughtness.[11]

Jerome Frank reasoned similarly, saying: 'For any particular lay person, the law, with respect to any particular set of facts, is a decision of a court with respect to those facts so far as that decision affects a particular person. Until a court has passed on those facts no law on that subject is yet in existence.'[12]

It will be evident that this view is similar to Austin's in identifying law with what the sovereign commands. The only difference is that Austin's sovereign lawmaker is the legislature, whereas the realists' sovereign lawmaker is the judiciary. This comes out very clearly in the writings of John Chipman Gray, who made the paradoxical claim that statutes are 'sources of Law ... not part of the Law itself'.[13] In support of this, he quoted from Bishop Hoadly, the seventeenth-century English theologian and political thinker, who had said: 'Whoever hath an *absolute authority* to *interpret* any written or spoken laws, it is *he* who is truly the *Law-giver* to all intents and purposes, and not the person who first wrote or spoke them.'[14]

An obvious objection to the realist account is that predictions are not normative standards for guiding and evaluating conduct. The realists therefore leave out the normativity of law—the fact that legal rules are accepted as guides to conduct, at least by legal officials. We have already seen that Hart criticised Austin's theory for missing this fact about law. And Hart points out that realism is very similar to the command theory in the way in which it seeks to analyse legal concepts such as 'obligation'. Like Austin, the realists take a reductionist approach to defining legal concepts, characterising law as predictions of official behaviour and therefore omitting any reference to the mental states and

---

9   K N Llewellyn, 'A Realistic Jurisprudence—The Next Step' (1930) 30 *Columbia Law Review* 431, 447-8.
10 Ibid 448.
11 Ibid.
12 J Frank, *Law and the Modern Mind*, Brentano's Publishers, New York, 1930, p 46.
13 J C Gray [1909], *The Nature and Sources of the Law*, 2nd edn, Peter Smith, Gloucester, MA, 1972, p 125.
14 Ibid, emphasis in original.

attitudes of those who participate in legal institutions. Yet, as Hart says, law functions in the lives of some people not as the basis for predicting the decisions of courts but rather as a set of accepted standards of behaviour, which they are under an obligation to follow.[15] Such people do not confine themselves to the external point of view but 'continuously express in normative terms their shared acceptance of the law as a guide to conduct'.[16]

Hart also has a further objection to defining the law as whatever the courts decide. He points out that this definition makes it unintelligible to say that a court has made a mistake about the law. Hart argues that realism confuses *finality* with *infallibility*.[17] A court's decision is final when no appeal is possible from it. This does not imply, however, that there was no law on the matter other than the law that the court decided to apply. Hart thinks that, at least in those cases that fall under the central core of meaning of a rule, there are pre-existing standards of correct judicial decision that allow us to describe a particular judicial decision as mistaken, even if it cannot be challenged within the legal system.[18]

Hart gives the analogy of a game. He notes that games can be played without an umpire. In such cases, the players make an honest effort to determine who is winning in terms of the rules. What changes if we add an umpire to this picture? The umpire's determinations may be final, but the rules do not change. It is not as if the umpire has carte blanche to choose the winner of the game: it is the umpire's duty to apply the rules to the best of his or her ability. Suppose that the umpire decides the outcome of the game in favour of someone who did not really win. Is the players' contrary view about who won the game a *prediction* about what the umpire would do—a prediction that turned out to be false? Clearly, says Hart, this is not the case. Rather, the players' view is a competing application of the rules that differs from the umpire's application only in lacking official or authoritative status. The fact that the umpire's application of the rules has official status does not guarantee that the umpire applied them correctly.[19] Hart argues that decisions of courts from which no appeal is possible are just like the decisions of umpires in games: the fact that they are final does not mean that they are infallible, and it is therefore incorrect to identify them with the law on the matter.

---

15 H L A Hart, *The Concept of Law*, 2nd edn, Clarendon Press, Oxford, 1994, p 137.
16 Ibid p 138.
17 Ibid p 141.
18 Ibid p 144.
19 Ibid pp 142–3.

7.3 The indeterminacy of the law

We turn now to the second way in which the realists were sceptics about legal rules. They argued, in particular, that the 'law in books' has little influence on judicial decisions. They therefore believed, as Hart puts it, that 'it is false, if not senseless, to regard judges as themselves subject to rules or "bound" to decide cases as they do'.[20] It follows that judicial decisions are discretionary. The realists were led to this view because they believed that the law is indeterminate—in other words, that legal rules are not capable of yielding uniquely correct answers. By contrast, all of the legal theories that we have considered so far maintain that the law is to some extent or even entirely determinate. They hold that there are standards or norms of legal decision-making that make it possible to arrive at justified legal conclusions. Legal decisions can therefore be right or wrong. Of course, theorists such as Hart and Dworkin do not claim that judges always decide according to the law. They are well aware that judges may fail to apply the law due to prejudice, bias, ideology and other non-legal factors. They say, however, that at least some (and, in the case of Dworkin, all) legal disputes are *capable* of being decided according to law.

The realists offer a radically different account. They maintain not merely that judges do not base their decisions on the legal rules. They believe that the rules are *incapable* of controlling judicial decisions. Judges cannot be criticised for departing from the law, because the law does not provide determinate answers to legal questions. Some of Holmes's statements may have influenced the realists to take this view. He famously remarked that '[g]eneral propositions do not decide concrete cases'.[21] He also said, 'I always say in conference ... that I will admit any general proposition you like and decide the case either way'.[22]

It should be noted that there is some uncertainty about whether the realists' claim about the indeterminacy of the law was meant to apply across the board, or only in cases that reach the stage of being litigated, or perhaps only in cases that reach the stage of appellate review.[23] On the other hand, the more the claim is qualified, the less there is to distinguish realism from positivism, which, as we know, maintains that the law is partially indeterminate.

---

20 Ibid p 138.
21 *Lochner v New York*, 198 US 45, 76 (1905) (Holmes J, dissenting).
22 Quoted in W E Rumble, *American Legal Realism: Skepticism, Reform and the Judicial Process*, Cornell University Press, Ithaca, New York, 1968, pp 39–40.
23 Leiter, above n 6, 298.

In support of their view about indeterminacy, realists argue that there are so many different rules potentially relevant to any legal case that there is virtually always precedential support for both sides in a legal argument. There are also conflicting ways of interpreting precedents. A precedent can be read both narrowly and broadly. It can be confined to its facts or it can be read as standing for a wider proposition. This means that there are different possible and equally justifiable readings of a precedent, some supporting one side and others supporting the other side. The same precedent can, in other words, be used to justify opposing outcomes.[24] And the same, according to the realists, is true of the interpretation of statutes. They too can be read in contradictory ways, in part because the canons of statutory interpretation point in different directions.[25]

Frank, who was a 'fact sceptic' as well as a 'rule sceptic', went even further. He said that even in situations where the rules are clear, it is impossible to predict the factual findings of trial judges and juries. In fact, Frank thought that the 'elusiveness of facts' generates even more unpredictability and uncertainty in the judicial process than the difficulties that attend the application of rules. But, whether in virtue of the indeterminacy of rules or the manipulability of facts, the 'law in books' is, according to the realists, not capable of generating answers to legal problems, or at least the problems that come before the courts. It is therefore not on its own a reliable basis for predicting judicial decisions.

How do the other theorists we have considered thus far respond to these claims? Hart thinks that the realists are right about some legal cases, namely, the hard cases that arise in the penumbra of uncertainty that surrounds legal rules. He denies, however, that 'all legal questions are fundamentally like those of the penumbra'.[26] As we know, Hart thinks that rules have a core of agreed meaning. Thus while 'it is good to be occupied with the penumbra', the realists have, in his view, become 'preoccupied' with it.[27] They have, in other words, exaggerated the indeterminacy of legal rules. Hart's diagnosis is that the realists are 'disappointed absolutists'.[28] By this he means that they share with mechanical jurisprudence the 'absolutist' assumption that for the law to be determinate, legal rules would have to provide answers to all conceivable questions. Since this is obviously not the case, the realists conclude that the rules cannot provide any answers. If, however,

---

24 K N Llewellyn, 'Remarks on the Theory of Appellate Decision and the Rules or Canons about How Statutes Are to Be Construed' (1950) 3 *Vanderbilt Law Review* 395, 395–6.
25 Ibid 399–400, 401–6.
26 H L A Hart, 'Positivism and the Separation of Law and Morals' (1958) 71 *Harvard Law Review* 593, 615.
27 Ibid.
28 Hart, above n 7, p 139.

they had not had such impossibly high expectations of rules, they would have realised that rules which cannot provide answers all of the time can nevertheless provide answers most of the time.

Dworkin believes, as we have seen, that even in hard cases, where a statute is unclear or there is disagreement about whether a precedent is applicable, there are nevertheless right and wrong ways to read the statute and the precedent. He gives the example of a precedent case that awarded compensation to someone who suffered nervous shock on witnessing serious injury to a close relative at the scene of an accident. Subsequently, a later court is presented with slightly different facts: the shock does not occur at the scene of the accident but some hours later and in a hospital, where someone finds out that her daughter is dead and sees the serious condition of her husband and other children. Can she sue the negligent driver for compensation for her emotional injuries? This question was raised in the English case of *McLoughlin v O'Brian*.[29]

The realists would say that there is no *legal* answer to this question because the precedent can be read both narrowly and broadly. It can be confined to situations where someone suffers shock at the scene of the accident or it can be extended to Mrs McLoughlin's situation. Dworkin disagrees. He says that any appearance of indeterminacy disappears once we realise that the law should not be identified with the explicit rules of law. In particular, the answer to the question depends on whether the *moral principles* that justify the earlier decision also apply in the later circumstances. Is there any difference of principle between the case of a mother who suffers emotional injury witnessing her child hit by a car and a mother who suffers identical injury seeing her injured child in hospital? If the damage in both cases is reasonably foreseeable, can the bare fact of suffering the injury later, away from the scene, be a *morally relevant* reason to deny compensation? If not, Dworkin believes that the mother is legally entitled to compensation in both cases and that the precedent cannot be confined to its facts.

7.4 How judges decide cases

We have seen that, for the realists, legal doctrine is indeterminate: it can plausibly support contradictory outcomes. The realists therefore conclude that legal rules cannot be the main factor in the formation of judicial decisions. The real reason for judicial decisions, they tell us, must be something else, no

---

[29] *McLoughlin v O'Brian* [1983] 1 AC 410.

matter what judges may think or say. An understanding of these reasons would therefore enable us to predict judicial decisions in a way that an understanding of the legal rules does not. What, then, really lies behind judicial decisions? If the law in books is incapable of explaining judicial decisions, what does explain them? And if the law does not to any great extent influence or constrain judicial decision-making, how do we explain the fact that there are significant uniformities in judicial behaviour? These are empirical questions and the realists thought that social scientific inquiry would reveal the answers to them.

The key realist claim is that non-legal factors lead judges to have a gut-level response to the facts of cases. These factors may be of a psychological kind, having to do with the personality and attitudes of the judge. Alternatively, they may be of a sociological kind, having to do with a judge's social background, or the institutional environment in which judges operate, or their professional training. Judges may also make decisions in the light of their non-legal views about what is fair, in the public interest or commercially desirable. The central realist point, however, is that judicial decisions are not explained by the legal rules but by non-legal factors of this kind, which operate, whether consciously or unconsciously, on the minds of judges. Once again, Holmes laid the foundation for this approach, saying: 'The felt necessities of the time, the prevalent moral and political theories, intuitions of public policy, avowed or unconscious, even the prejudices which judges share with their fellow men, have had a good deal more to do than the syllogism in determining the rules by which men should be governed.'[30]

Judges, however, are reluctant to acknowledge openly the real reasons behind their decisions, because to do so would subvert the rule of law ideal that judges should be impartial and objective. Instead, taking advantage of the indeterminacy of the legal materials, they trawl through the materials to find principles that support their instinctive view of the case. According to the realists, judges invoke the law after the event to rationalise a decision reached on non-legal grounds, misleadingly presenting it as if it were a deduction 'smoothly made from clear, pre-existing rules without intrusion of the judge's choice'.[31] Judges use the law, in other words, as 'window dressing'. This 'debunking' view of judges' legal arguments can usefully be contrasted with Dworkin's view that we should take the way in which judges present their task at face value (see 6.7).

As indicated above, different realists gave different accounts of the non-legal determinants of judicial decisions. Some put the emphasis on

---

30 O W Holmes, *The Common Law*, Little, Brown and Company, Boston, 1923, p 1.
31 Hart, above n 7, p 12.

idiosyncratic facts about the personality of the judge. Frank, who was heavily influenced by psychoanalysis, put forward this version of realism. In elaborating on his fact scepticism, he stressed the effect of the idiosyncratic prejudices of judges and jurors on their view of the facts of the case, for instance, in according credibility to the accounts of witnesses. Describing some of these prejudices, he said:

> [I]n learning the facts with reference to which one forms an opinion ... these more minute and personal biases are operating constantly ... [The judge's] own past may have created plus or minus reactions to women, or blonde women, or men with beards, or Southerners, or Italians, or Englishmen, or plumbers, or ministers, or college graduates, or Democrats. A certain twang or cough or gesture may start up memories painful or pleasant.[32]

Frank thought that the psychological influences on judges are unconscious and undiscoverable, making it impossible to predict judicial decisions. Other realists were aware, however, that judicial decision-making can often be predicted and that different judges frequently react similarly to the facts of legal disputes. They explained this uniformity by hypothesising that there are common social forces operating on judges and that they share certain background assumptions, leading them to decide in similar ways.[33]

Thus in his book, *The Common Law Tradition*, Llewellyn stressed the institutional setting of judicial decision-making as a sociological factor which 'helps doctrine out' so as to produce predictability (or what he called 'reckonability')[34] in judicial decisions. He discerned various 'steadying factors'[35] in the institutional environment in which courts operate. These are factors that have a stabilising effect on judicial decision-making. One such steadying factor is 'professional judicial office' or the expectations we have of the judicial role. This tradition, Llewellyn said, 'grips [judges], shapes them, limits them, guides them; not for nothing do we speak of *ingrained* ways of work or thought, of men *experienced* or case-hardened, of *habits* of mind'.[36]

Another steadying factor relates to what Llewellyn called the 'period-style',[37] which is the general way of going about the 'job' of judging

---

32   Frank, above n 12, p 106.
33   B Leiter, 'American Legal Realism', in M P Golding and W A Edmundson (eds), *The Blackwell Guide to the Philosophy of Law and Legal Theory*, Blackwell Publishing, Oxford, 2005, pp 54–5.
34   K N Llewellyn, *The Common Law Tradition*, Little, Brown and Company, Boston, 1960, p 6.
35   Ibid p 19.
36   Ibid p 53, Llewellyn's emphasis.
37   Ibid p 36.

at any particular time and place. Llewellyn distinguished two styles that characterise the reasoning of common law judges: the Grand Style and the Formal Style. The latter is in thrall to the mechanical model of law and attempts to deduce the answers from pre-existing rules. The former is more focused on achieving reasonable results that match contemporary needs.[38] The Grand Style is also based on what Llewellyn called 'situation sense'.[39] It seems that by this he meant an approach to the resolution of legal problems that would be broadly thought reasonable. The Grand Style is, according to Llewellyn, more likely to lead to rules that will 'get the same results out of very different judges'.[40]

Whether notions such as 'situation sense', which seems to be a kind of common sense, are compatible with the scientific aspirations of realism is debatable.[41] It nevertheless remains true to say that, in general, with their emphasis on non-legal determinants as the primary explanation of judicial decisions, and on the 'law in action' as opposed to the 'law in books', the realists offered a distinctive account of law. In place of mainstream normative analysis of judicial reasoning in terms of legal rules that justify judicial decisions, they wished to substitute the empirical observation, description and prediction of judicial behaviour, using the scientific model of cause and effect.

This also means that the success of the realist project rests largely on the truth of its empirical claim about the minor role played by legal doctrine in judicial decision-making. At the time the realists were writing, there was no high-level social science available to confirm or disconfirm their hypotheses. Indeed, some of the realists had a rather crude understanding of an empirical approach to the law, favouring a stimulus-response or behaviourist model. They wished to record regularities in judicial 'response' to the 'stimulus' of the facts of a case, in the same way that scientists record the reflex responses of laboratory animals to stimuli. The idea was to discover causal laws that would link particular kinds of factual situations to judicial decisions.[42] In the light of the realist aversion to mechanical jurisprudence, one cannot but be struck by the fact that the influence of behaviourism led some realists to view judges as automata of another kind.

---

38   Ibid pp 36–9.
39   Llewellyn, above n 24, 397–8.
40   Llewellyn, above n 34, p 38.
41   M D A Freeman, *Lloyd's Introduction to Jurisprudence*, 8th edn, Sweet and Maxwell, London, 2008, p 996.
42   Leiter, above n 33, pp 50–1.

More recently, however, social scientists have undertaken sophisticated empirical research with a view to discovering the determinants of judicial decisions. Frederick Schauer discusses some of this research and infers from it that 'it would be plausible to hypothesize that Realist explanations are more often true for ideologically charged issues than otherwise, more often true in high appellate courts than in trial courts, and more often true for the messier common law than for the interpretation of statutes'.[43] He concludes that if this research is sound, it would follow that political and other non-legal factors influence judicial decisions only in specific kinds of circumstances and therefore that realism is 'elevating an occasional feature of legal decision-making into something more than it is'.[44]

7.5 The pragmatic model of adjudication

Some of the realists, such as Felix Cohen, recommended that judges should openly adopt a lawmaking role and address questions of socio-economic policy with the changing needs of society in mind. Instead of pretending that it is possible to do justice 'according to law', judges should, in other words, approach the resolution of disputes in an 'instrumentalist' spirit. Rather than focusing on rights created by past precedents or even by statutory enactments, they should explicitly attend to what Cohen called the 'delicate practical task of social adjustment'.[45] In contrast to traditional views about judging, on which judges are expected to put aside their view of the merits and defer to authority, on Cohen's view the job of judges is to make the choice they think is on balance reasonable, having taken into account all of the relevant moral and political considerations. In effect, they must make law. Dworkin calls this view 'legal pragmatism'.

Before assessing this view, we should note that it is not quite as uninterested in past decisions as it may at first glance seem. This is because judges may follow past decisions for consequentialist or pragmatic reasons. After all, disregarding clearly applicable law can have detrimental social consequences. It can disrupt people's expectations and make it harder to plan one's life. Such considerations of continuity and predictability could, in certain circumstances, make it reasonable for judges to follow a precedent. These would be what Dworkin calls 'strategic' reasons for following a past decision.[46]

---

43 F Schauer, *Thinking Like a Lawyer: A New Introduction to Legal Reasoning*, Harvard University Press, Cambridge, MA, 2009, p 141.
44 Ibid p 145.
45 F Cohen, 'Transcendental Nonsense and the Functional Approach' (1935) 35 *Columbia Law Review* 809, 842.
46 R Dworkin, *Law's Empire*, Belknap Press of Harvard University Press, Cambridge, MA, 1986, p 160.

The real difference between the pragmatic view of judging and the traditional view is not that the pragmatic view ignores past decisions. It is rather that it recommends following them for different reasons. On the traditional view, there is a legal *right* to have a past decision followed, and judges are under a *duty* as a matter of *principle* to follow past decisions. On the pragmatic view, by contrast, past decisions should be followed only if it is on balance reasonable to do so. This means that if following a past decision does not lead to the best social consequences in a particular case, then there is no further, principled reason to follow the decision—no reason, in other words, deriving from anyone's rights.

This point may become clearer if we consider a useful distinction, drawn by Schauer, between 'rule-based' and 'particularistic' decision-making. Rule-based decision-making involves following a rule even if, in the particular circumstances, the decision-maker believes that following the rule will not lead to a reasonable result. Rule-based decision-makers treat rules as precluding an independent evaluation of what to do on the balance of reasons.[47] For instance, when judges regard themselves as *bound* by precedent, they regard themselves as obliged to follow a previous decision even if they would have decided in a different way had there been no precedent (see 4.6).

Particularistic decision-making, by contrast, 'focuses on the particular situation'[48] and is sensitive to the 'needs of the instant'.[49] Particularistic decision-makers attend to all the moral and political considerations that are relevant to achieving the optimal result in each individual case. They are guided by their own assessment of what is reasonable. This is not to say that particularistic decision-makers will always ignore rules when their application to a particular situation appears inappropriate. For instance, as noted earlier, if people are safe in the knowledge that the rules will be applied, even in circumstances where this might be thought to be inappropriate, they will be able to plan their lives more effectively. Particularistic decision-makers can therefore take into account the benefits of rule-following, such as maintaining predictability, reliance and certainty. The key point, however, is that they will factor in these benefits as just some of all the relevant considerations. They will therefore follow rules only if the costs of not following the rule outweigh the advantages. Pragmatic judges are particularistic decision-makers, and it is therefore only in this limited way that they see legal rules as constraints.

---

47   F Schauer, *Playing by the Rules: A Philosophical Examination of Rule-Based Decision-Making in Law and in Life*, Clarendon Press, Oxford, 1991, pp 86–7.
48   Ibid p 77.
49   Ibid p 82.

Let us now return to Dworkin's example of the person who suffers emotional injury away from the scene of an accident (see 7.3) and see how a pragmatic judge would decide the matter. In Dworkin's example, the law provides compensation if a close relative has suffered nervous shock at the scene of an accident. This precedent is firmly established. However, there is no direct precedent governing the situation where a close relative suffers nervous shock a few hours later in the hospital.

Let us suppose that our pragmatic judge believes that there is no difference of principle between suffering nervous shock at the scene of an accident and suffering it a few hours later in the hospital. Let us also suppose that our pragmatic judge believes that the current state of the law is undesirable because it is not in the public interest—that no one should be compensated for nervous shock, even relatives who suffer its effects at the scene of an accident. When confronted with a case in which someone has suffered nervous shock at the scene of an accident involving a family member, our pragmatic judge will nevertheless have a consequentialist reason to apply the undesirable rule, because the harmful consequences of disregarding firmly established law will be greater than the benefits of not applying an undesirable rule.

However, in the new case, where the applicability of the previous decision is unclear, and there are therefore no concerns about predictability and reliance, the pragmatic judge is free to achieve the right result. He or she can refuse to award compensation, despite conceding that there is no difference of principle between the two situations. This is because, as we have seen, the pragmatic judge is guided not by the need to give effect to pre-existing legal rights, but only by the need to make the decision with the best future consequences for the community. As Dworkin puts it, the pragmatist does not allow the past 'some special power of its own in court'.[50] Since refusing to extend the principle will be better, from the perspective of the public interest, than extending it, and since this is the only thing that matters in the view of a pragmatic judge, it is irrelevant that the decision not to award compensation will introduce incoherence into the law.[51]

Dworkin, as one might expect, is highly critical of this results-oriented approach to judging. He describes it as taking 'the bracing view that [people] are never entitled to what would otherwise be worse for the community just because some legislature said so or a long string of judges decided other people were'.[52] He argues that it does not fit our legal practices, because judges do not reason

---

50 Dworkin, above n 46, p 167.
51 Ibid pp 161–3.
52 Ibid p 152.

pragmatically. Furthermore, in rejecting the ideal of consistency in principle as valuable for its own sake, it does not provide a good justification for the exercise of political power. This is because, as we know, Dworkin thinks that legal decisions should exhibit integrity and coherence over time (see 6.10). He believes that to justify state coercion, a conception of law must respect the equal status of citizens. Furthermore, Dworkin argues that only the ideal of government acting in a coherent and principled manner by keeping faith with the principles that justify past political decisions affords such respect. He concludes that the pragmatic approach to judging cannot show why state coercion is legitimate.

For Dworkin, if the law gives the right to compensation in certain circumstances, it should do so in all analogous circumstances, where 'analogous circumstances' means circumstances that are, despite their factual differences, not morally different from the original set of circumstances. They are circumstances that are indistinguishable in principle from the circumstances in which the right was initially granted. Another way of putting this point is to say that, for Dworkin, if the law is to be justifiable it cannot be built on arbitrary distinctions. The pragmatic view of judging, by contrast, rejects the idea that coherence and consistency in legal reasoning are valuable in themselves. Since it focuses only on the social consequences of judicial decisions, it sees nothing wrong with the distinctions that Dworkin regards as 'unprincipled'.

Other critics of the realists' prescriptive views about the judicial task argue that they are an invitation to judicial dictatorship as well as deeply anti-democratic. Thus Geoffrey de Q Walker argues that once we allow judges to 'cast aside the restraining bonds of precedent'[53] and give effect to their own values, two unanswerable questions arise. First, why should we assume that the values that a realist judge injects into the law are acceptable? After all, realism can be a vehicle for a variety of political agendas. Second, how can the realist grant of unlimited power to unelected and unaccountable judges be reconciled with democratic principles? Walker further observes that judges are not equipped to 'perform a feat of perfect social engineering on inadequate information in the individual case'.[54] They do not have the expertise to assess social scientific evidence, nor to predict the social consequences of reforming the law in a particular direction. For these and related reasons, Walker goes so far as to call legal realism in its more extreme forms 'a form of judicial corruption'.[55]

---

53 G de Q Walker, *The Rule of Law: Foundation of Constitutional Democracy*, Melbourne University Press, Carlton, 1988, p 174.
54 Ibid p 194.
55 Ibid p 197.

Questions

1. The realists argue that the rules of law are merely 'pretty playthings' and that judges invoke them only to rationalise decisions made for non-legal reasons and to conceal the fact that judging is not constrained by law. How plausible do you find this form of rule scepticism?

2. Hart argued that 'the claim that talk of rules is a myth ... [if] stated in an unqualified general form, so as to embrace both secondary and primary rules ... is indeed quite incoherent; for the assertion that there are decisions of courts cannot consistently be combined with the denial that there are any rules at all' (H L A Hart, *The Concept of Law*, 2nd edn, Clarendon Press, 1994, p 136). Can the realists respond to this point?

3. Hart argues that if law is nothing more than the prediction of how a court will decide, this makes it unintelligible to say that a court has made a mistake about the law. Hart also argues that the prediction theory implies that judges trying to decide what the law is must be trying to predict what they will decide, which is absurd. Do the realists have any response to these arguments?

4. Do you think that judges should approach their task by attempting to make decisions that have the best social and economic consequences for society?

5. Does realism undermine the legitimacy of the legal system?

Further reading

F Cohen, 'Transcendental Nonsense and the Functional Approach' (1935) 35 *Columbia Law Review* 809.

N Duxbury, *Patterns of American Jurisprudence*, Clarendon Press, Oxford, 1995, Chapters 1–2.

R Dworkin, *Law's Empire*, Belknap Press of Harvard University Press, Cambridge, MA, 1986, Chapter 5.

W W Fisher, M J Horwitz and T A Reed (eds), *American Legal Realism*, Oxford University Press, New York, 1993.

J Frank, *Law and the Modern Mind*, Brentano's, New York, 1930.

M Green, 'Legal Realism as Theory of Law' (2005) 46 *William and Mary Law Review* 1915.

H L A Hart, *The Concept of Law*, 2nd edn, Clarendon Press, Oxford, 1994, Chapter VII.

O W Holmes, 'The Path of the Law' (1897) 10 *Harvard Law Review* 457.

B Leiter, 'American Legal Realism', in M P Golding and W A Edmundson (eds), *The Blackwell Guide to the Philosophy of Law and Legal Theory*, Blackwell Publishing, Oxford, 2005, pp 50–66.

B Leiter, *Naturalizing Jurisprudence: Essays on American Legal Realism and Naturalism in Legal Philosophy*, Oxford University Press, Oxford, 2007.

K N Llewellyn, 'A Realistic Jurisprudence: The Next Step' (1930) 30 *Columbia Law Review* 431.

K N Llewellyn, 'Remarks on the Theory of Appellate Decision and the Rules or Canons about How Statutes Are to Be Construed' (1950) 3 *Vanderbilt Law Review* 395.

F Schauer, *Playing by the Rules: A Philosophical Examination of Rule-Based Decision-Making in Law and in Life*, Clarendon Press, Oxford, 1991.

W Twining, *Karl Llewellyn and the Realist Movement*, Weidenfeld and Nicholson, London, 1973.

8

Law as Wealth-Maximising

8.1 Chapter overview

This chapter will deal with the Law and Economics movement, an approach to law that emerged in the United States in the 1960s and is currently extremely important there. It involves the application of the theory and empirical methods of economics to law. It is now a complex and challenging area of theory that accommodates different schools of thought.

This chapter will concentrate on some main themes, especially as found in the work of Richard Posner, whose work is seminal in the field. Posner is allied to the 'Chicago School' of economics, which is strongly oriented to free-market values and a belief in the ability of market economics to illuminate human behaviour. Posner argues for a combination of empirical and normative claims: that common law rules are on the whole best explained as seeking to maximise wealth and that wealth maximisation is a desirable goal, at least in the common law context. In difficult cases, where the conventional sources of law do not provide clear guidance, Posner therefore believes that judges should look to economics to craft desirable legal rules.

8.2 Posner's pragmatism

Posner's favoured description of his approach is that it is 'pragmatic'. This means, he explains, that his outlook is practical, forward-looking, consequential and empirical.[1] In many ways his approach has affinities with realism. Posner says

---

1   R A Posner, *Overcoming Law*, Harvard University Press, Cambridge, MA, 1995, p 5.

that he is interested in what works and what is useful.[2] Like the realists, he rejects the formalist or Langdellian idea that logical relations between legal concepts should be the focus of legal analysis,[3] believing instead that concepts should be 'subservient to human need'.[4] He tells us that his approach values continuity with the past 'only so far as such continuity can help us cope with the problems of the present and the future'.[5] Thus there may be practical reasons for judges to follow precedents, such as an interest in promoting stability and certainty in the law, but they are under no obligation to do so and they should not hesitate to disregard precedent if there are good reasons to do so.[6] Similarly, there may be practical reasons for judges to defer to statutory language, but these can be balanced against the need to make statutes 'speak intelligently'.[7] Posner's beliefs about adjudication are therefore of the 'balancing' kind held by some realists, and they are susceptible to the same criticisms (see 7.5).

Furthermore, Posner denies the autonomy of law. This is for two reasons. First, he rejects the idea that law develops according to its own inner logic, maintaining instead that it develops in response to social and economic pressures. He therefore shares with the realists a belief that non-legal influences play a much greater role in the development of the law than is commonly acknowledged. Secondly, he believes that it is 'impossible to "do" law without help from other disciplines' because lawyers 'don't know enough about the activities that law regulates and the effects of legal regulation'.[8] The discipline on which Posner draws is, of course, economics. Like some of the realists, Posner therefore takes a social-scientific approach to law. He regards the realists' efforts as doomed, however, because their empirical investigations lacked a theoretical framework.[9]

Posner makes two key claims. First, he makes the empirical claim that economic factors are the underlying explanatory (though not necessarily articulated) determinant of common law judicial decisions: common law rules are a way of efficiently allocating resources. Posner writes: '[T]he logic of the

---

2   Ibid p 4.
3   Ibid p 75.
4   Ibid p 399.
5   Ibid p 4.
6   Ibid p 11.
7   Ibid p 401.
8   R A Posner, *The Problematics of Moral and Legal Theory*, Belknap Press of Harvard University Press, Cambridge, MA, 1999, p viii.
9   Posner, above n 1, p 19.

common law really is economics.'[10] Secondly, he makes the normative claim that efficiency considerations should guide common law decision-making: it is morally desirable for judges to choose legal rules that bring about an efficient allocation of resources.[11]

By 'common law' Posner means law that has been created primarily by judges rather than legislators, or any field of law shaped largely by judicial precedents. Thus common law includes, for him, the law of torts, property, contracts and commercial law, restitution and unjust enrichment, criminal and family law, civil and criminal procedure, conflict of laws and areas of constitutional law.[12] Posner argues, in other words, that the economic approach to law is applicable not only in areas of law where one might expect it to be useful, such as those which regulate market behaviour, but even in areas that do not seem to have an economic dimension, such as family law and criminal law.

By 'efficiency' Posner means something very specific. Efficiency is frequently understood in utilitarian terms, as the maximisation of aggregate happiness, but Posner rejects utilitarianism, as we will see in the next section. By 'efficiency' Posner means 'wealth maximisation', or the achievement of the greatest balance of monetary gains over monetary losses. He explains that maximum social wealth obtains when all goods and resources, including legal entitlements, are held by the individuals who value them most, as measured by their willingness and ability to pay the largest sum of money for them, or by the amount of money they demand in exchange for them, if they already own the goods.

This concept can be illustrated with the following example. Let us suppose that A would be willing to pay up to $100 for a book belonging to B. This means that the book is worth $100 to A. Let us also suppose that B would be willing to sell the book to A for $90. If B then sells the book to A for $100, the wealth of society will have increased by $10, because A has a book worth $100 and B has $100, whereas prior to the transaction A had $100 and B had a book worth $90.[13]

Posner claims that common law rules both tend to and should, as a matter of morality, allocate resources in such a way as to maximise social wealth. It should be noted that the goal of increasing the net wealth of society

---

10 R A Posner, *The Problems of Jurisprudence*, Harvard University Press, Cambridge, MA, 1990, p 362.
11 Ibid p 374.
12 R A Posner, *Economic Analysis of Law*, 6th edn, Aspen Publishers, New York, 2003, pp 31, 249.
13 Posner, above n 10, p 356.

is indifferent to how wealth is distributed. Whitney Cunningham describes wealth maximisation as 'the quintessential economic-based decision-making criterion. It eschews moral judgements, relies on markets wherever possible, and takes wealth as its core value.'[14]

In what follows, I will briefly explain Posner's two claims. The discussion will inevitably be simplified, since it is not possible to discuss the technical details of Posner's views or the subtle shifts in those views over the years. However, it is important to note that in his later work, Posner is careful to say that he does not believe economics 'holds all the keys to legal theory',[15] and he also acknowledges that wealth maximisation as a 'universal social norm' is unsatisfactory.[16] The economic approach is, he says, 'defensible when confined to the common law arena',[17] but it is unsuitable in areas where there is societal agreement on the need to redistribute wealth.[18]

8.3 The normative dimension of law and economics

In order to understand Posner's approach we need to begin with a very influential article written by Ronald Coase in 1960, which provided the inspiration for much of the economic analysis of law. Coase argued that in a situation of zero transaction costs, the rules chosen by courts will be irrelevant because rational, cooperative parties will trade their legal rights for more valued resources and will therefore always negotiate the solution which maximises wealth.[19] Examples of transaction costs are the costs in time and resources of getting together with the other party to trade, as well as the costs of drawing up documents and of enforcing the bargain. It should be noted as a preliminary matter that economists make their predictions on the assumption that we are 'rational utility maximisers', who always act so as to maximise our satisfaction.

Coase's claim can be illustrated using the following example, provided by Dworkin and based on the case of *Sturges v Bridgman*.[20] A candy manufacturer's

---

14 W Cunningham, 'Testing Posner's Strong Theory of Wealth Maximization' (1992) 81 *Georgetown Law Review* 141, 156.
15 Posner, above n 1, p viii.
16 Posner, above n 10, p 373.
17 Ibid.
18 Posner, above n 1, p 404.
19 R Coase, 'The Problem of Social Cost' (1960) 3 *Journal of Law and Economics* 1.
20 *Sturges v Bridgman*, 11 Ch D 852 (1879).

machine is very noisy, making it more difficult for the doctor next door to run his practice. A court has to decide whether the doctor should be able to prevent the manufacturer from running the machine. Let us suppose that the court decides in favour of the doctor. Let us also suppose that this solution does not maximise social wealth, because the candy maker will lose $10 by not running his machine but the doctor would lose only $9 if the machine were run. Coase's argument is that in a world of no transaction costs, the candy manufacturer would purchase the right to make a noise from the doctor for something over $9, because even after compensating the doctor for his lost practice he would still have money left over. In a world of no transaction costs, the initial distribution of legal rights will therefore not affect the final distribution of rights because the party who values the right most will end up with it. If the court gives the right to the doctor, the manufacturer will buy it from him. If the court gives the right to the manufacturer, he will retain it because the doctor will not be willing to pay the $10 the manufacturer would demand to part with it. In either case, regardless of which party owned the rights initially, voluntary market transactions will lead to the efficient result.[21]

In real life, however, there are always transaction costs, such as the cost in time and money of making arrangements with the other party to negotiate an outcome. Let us suppose that in the situation of the doctor and the manufacturer the transaction costs would exceed $1. The consequence is that if the court gives to the doctor a right to practise free of noise, the transaction costs will prevent mutually beneficial trade in the right. The candy manufacturer will not pay more than $10 to purchase a right that is worth only $10 to him. Hence the right will not go to the party who values it most.

Given the transaction cost, the rule the court chooses is therefore of great importance. If the court gives the right to the doctor, the right will remain with the doctor and social wealth will not be maximised: the doctor will have $9 and the manufacturer will have nothing. This is the point at which Posner enters the picture. He extends Coase's theory by arguing that when a consensual or market solution is impossible, the courts should try to mimic or replicate the market by producing the outcome that would have obtained had the transaction costs been zero and had the parties bargained freely. Posner argues, in other words, that when transaction costs are prohibitive, courts should choose legal rules

---

21 R Dworkin, *A Matter of Principle*, Harvard University Press, Cambridge, MA, 1985, pp 237–8.

that maximise social wealth: they should assign legal rights to those who would secure them in a free market by being willing to pay the most for them.[22]

Notice, however, that should the court impose this solution, as recommended by Posner, the doctor will not *actually* receive the amount over $9 that he would have received under the notional bargain. The compensation in question is purely hypothetical, as is any improvement in his welfare. When the court chooses the efficient or wealth-maximising rule, the manufacturer has something worth $10 to him and the doctor has nothing. But this is the desirable outcome in Posner's view, because it produces more wealth than the only *actual* alternative, *given the transaction cost*, which is that the doctor has $9 and the manufacturer has nothing.[23]

The court should therefore, according to Posner, give the candy manufacturer the right to make a noise, because the increase in social wealth is large enough that the candy manufacturer *could* have compensated the doctor and still made a profit in a costless market, and therefore *would* have secured the right to make a noise via negotiations in such a market. The choice of a rule that gives the right to the manufacturer over a rule that gives the right to the doctor is efficient in this sense: the candy manufacturer could compensate the doctor without either of them being worse off than under the alternative rule, and with at least one of them being better off. This is a version of what is known as Kaldor–Hicks efficiency.[24] According to Posner, the increase in wealth to the community justifies the outcome, despite the fact that the doctor receives no actual compensation for his loss. It is sufficient that the candy manufacturer gains more in monetary terms than the doctor loses.

This kind of monetary cost–benefit analysis obviously raises the question: *why* does the increase in wealth to the community justify the outcome? Why should the law impose losses on the doctor in order to increase the size of the pie overall? What reason do we have for thinking this just? This question acquires extra force against the background of the fact that willingness to pay depends on people's ability to pay. There are many goods for which poor people cannot afford to pay, including such necessities as medicine and food. Since their unwillingness to pay is related to their poverty, which in turn is a function of a distribution of wealth that many would argue is unjust (see Chapter 12), it

---

22   Posner, above n 12, pp 15–16.
23   Dworkin, above n 21, pp 239–40.
24   For discussion of Kaldor–Hicks efficiency, see J G Murphy and J L Coleman, *Philosophy of Law: An Introduction to Jurisprudence*, revised edn, Westview Press, Boulder, 1990, pp 186–7.

can be asked why it is just for judges to allocate legal rights to those who have the resources that would enable them to purchase those rights in a free market. Furthermore, is this not a way of increasing the wealth of those who are already wealthy, thereby adding insult to injury? For reasons such as these, Cento Veljanovski believes that the Kaldor–Hicks test is morally unattractive. He writes:

> Losers go uncompensated and hence the wealth maximization principle is consistent with quite drastic, capricious and inequitable actual redistributions of income. Furthermore, it is not obvious why a change in potential welfare is an improvement when there are people suffering uncompensated losses and others reaping windfall gains more than sufficient to compensate the losers ... Moreover Kaldor–Hicks efficiency is not income distribution-neutral, which is to say that it gives priority to those with income and market power. To the extent that the existing distribution of wealth is deemed 'unjust' in society, the ethical appeal of the Kaldor–Hicks test must corresponding [sic] diminish.[25]

In response to points such as these, Posner attempts to demonstrate that wealth maximisation is an ethically attractive principle, at least when confined to the common law. He relies on two arguments. First, he argues that wealth maximisation gives us the advantages of utilitarianism without its disadvantages. We will examine utilitarianism in detail in 10.3. It is the moral theory that in any situation the right thing to do is to maximise happiness. Utilitarianism seems to resolve disputes in an uncontroversial way. After all, do we not all seek to be happy and to avoid unhappiness? If so, is it not rational to act in such a way as to achieve the greatest balance of happiness over unhappiness? Utilitarianism suffers from a number of problems, however. We will canvass some of these in 10.3 and 12.2, but for our immediate purposes it will be sufficient to note the difficulty of measuring people's happiness and unhappiness and therefore of adding up and comparing the amounts of happiness and unhappiness in different situations. Posner therefore describes utilitarianism as a 'spongy' guide for legal decision-making.[26] He says that it is not a source of specific policies or guidelines.[27]

Posner argues that the principle of wealth maximisation does not suffer from this particular problem. He claims that it provides more rigorous and more scientific guidance than utilitarianism. It tells us to determine what people

---

[25] C G Veljanovski, 'Wealth Maximization, Law and Ethics—On the Limits of Economic Efficiency' (1981) 1 *International Review of Law and Economics* 5, 12.
[26] R A Posner, *The Economics of Justice*, Harvard University Press, Cambridge, MA, 1981, p 42.
[27] R A Posner, 'Utilitarianism, Economics and Legal Theory' (1979) 8 *Journal of Legal Studies* 103, 114.

want by investigating what they choose, and to determine how much they want something by investigating how much they are willing to pay for it. If, for instance, A would pay twice as much as B would for a particular book, then A wants the book twice as much as B. Posner says: 'The only kind of preference that counts in a system of wealth maximization is ... one that is backed up by money—in other words, that is registered in a market.'[28] Money is therefore the easily measurable, common currency which allows courts to make comparisons between different people and to calculate which course of action will maximise human satisfaction, as measured by willingness to pay rather than by the 'happiness' different courses of action would generate.

At the same time, Posner argues that wealth maximisation gives us all the benefits of utilitarianism. In comparison to notions such as the fair distribution of wealth, which are, in his view, indeterminate and subjective, Posner thinks that it is relatively uncontroversial to allocate goods and resources to those who value them the most as demonstrated by their willingness to pay the most for them. Just as it seems relatively uncontroversial to give people what makes them happy, what can be wrong with giving people what they value, as determined by what they are willing to trade?

Posner's critics do not find this argument convincing. They argue that, whatever its other defects, at least the claim that happiness is a worthy goal makes sense. But the same is not true of social wealth, which is not a value in itself. Thus Dworkin argues that social wealth might be instrumentally valuable, as a means to other goals. For instance, an increase in social wealth might make it possible to alleviate poverty. But Dworkin says that social wealth is not worth having for its own sake and a society that has more wealth is not, for that reason alone, necessarily better or better off than a society that has less wealth. He asks us to consider the following example:

> Derek has a book Amartya wants. Derek would sell the book to Amartya for $2 and Amartya would pay $3 for it. T (the tyrant in charge) takes the book from Derek and gives it to Amartya, with less waste in money or its equivalent than would be consumed in transaction costs if the two were to haggle over the distribution of the $1 surplus value. The forced transfer from Derek to Amartya produces a gain in social wealth, even though Derek has lost something he values with no compensation. Let us call the situation before the forced transfer takes place 'Society 1' and the situation after it takes place 'Society 2'. Is Society 2 *in any respect* superior to Society 1? I ...

---

28 Ibid 103.

mean whether ... the gain in wealth is, considered in itself, any gain at all. I should say, and I think most people would agree, that Society 2 is not better in any respect.[29]

Dworkin concludes that the fact that goods are in the hands of those who would pay more to have them is of no moral relevance.[30] He says that wealth maximisation makes no sense as a social goal.[31] Notice that it is not open to Posner to say that a society which has more wealth will also have more happiness. This is because Posner distinguishes between wealth maximisation and utility maximisation, and he acknowledges that increases in wealth may bring decreases in utility.[32]

In addition to arguing that wealth maximisation gives us the attractive features of utilitarianism without its defects, Posner also argues for the moral desirability of wealth maximisation on the ground that it respects autonomy. In particular, Posner argues that it is probable that everyone (or almost everyone) can expect to benefit from wealth maximisation in the long run, including those who turn out on occasion to be the unlucky, uncompensated losers as a result of lawsuits decided on wealth-maximising grounds. If this is the case, almost everyone, if asked in advance, would have consented to the principle that judges should maximise social wealth, and the principle consequently respects their autonomy.[33]

Posner illustrates this argument by reference to the negligence system of automobile accident liability. Such a system does not compensate people who are injured in accidents by non-negligent drivers, whereas a strict liability system does compensate such people. Let us assume that the negligence system is wealth-maximising. Posner writes:

> In what sense may the driver injured by another driver in an accident in which neither was at fault be said to have consented to the injury, so as not to be entitled, under a negligence system, to compensation? To answer this question, we must consider the effect on the costs of driving of insisting on ex post compensation, as under a system of strict liability. By hypothesis, they would be higher ... Would drivers be willing to incur higher costs of driving in order to preserve the principle of ex post compensation? They would not.[34]

---

29 Dworkin, above n 21, p 242, Dworkin's emphasis.
30 Ibid p 245.
31 Ibid p 264.
32 Ibid p 244.
33 Posner, above n 26, pp 94–9.
34 R A Posner, 'The Ethical and Political Basis of the Efficiency Norm in Common Law Adjudication' (1980) 8 *Hofstra Law Review* 487, 492-3.

Posner argues, in other words, that if a strict liability system is more expensive than a negligence system, and is therefore not in the interests of most persons, we can infer that almost everyone would have consented to a negligence system if asked in advance of being injured in an accident. More generally, if asked in advance, almost everyone would have consented to the principle that legal rules should be designed to maximise social wealth, because wealth maximisation will benefit almost everyone in the long run.

Dworkin is critical of this argument as well. Dworkin's views on this matter are too complex to summarise here, but it is worth mentioning that he thinks that the mere fact that I would have consented to a system or arrangement had I been asked is not a good reason to enforce such a system against me if I was not asked and therefore did not consent to it.[35] Dworkin is also doubtful about the claim that almost everyone is better off if judges decide common law cases according to wealth-maximising principles.[36]

8.4 The descriptive dimension of law and economics

So far we have been discussing the normative aspects of Posner's theory. But Posner argues not only that courts should decide cases according to wealth-maximising principles, but that they actually do so. He thinks that even if this is not true of every common law rule, traditional common law doctrines tend to be economically efficient.[37] Posner concedes that few judicial decisions explicitly make reference to economic concepts but he says that 'legal education consists primarily of learning to dig beneath the rhetorical surface to find [the true grounds of legal decisions], many of which turn out to have an economic character'.[38] Digging beneath this surface, one finds that:

> [Common law] doctrines form a system for inducing people to behave efficiently, not only in explicit markets, but across the whole range of social interactions. In settings in which the cost of voluntary transactions is low, common law doctrines create incentives for people to channel their transactions through the market ... In settings in which the cost of

---

35 Dworkin, above n 21, p 276.
36 Ibid pp 280–3.
37 Posner, above n 10, p 360.
38 Posner, above n 12, p 25.

allocating resources by voluntary transactions is prohibitively high, making the market an infeasible method of allocating resources, the common law prices behaviour in such a way as to mimic the market. For example, the tort system allocated liability for accidents between railroad and farmer, driver and pedestrian, doctor and patient ... in such a way as to bring about the allocation of resources to safety that the market would bring about if the market could be made to work.[39]

Let us look a little more closely at Posner's view about the way in which the tort system allocates liability for accidents. His starting point is that accidents have social costs. These are the cost to the victim of the accident and the cost to the potential wrongdoer of taking precautions to prevent the accident. Posner's view is that the tort system is structured around rules of liability that minimise the sum of these costs. Consider how the court sets the standard of negligence when drivers are held liable for negligent driving. In setting the standard of negligence, why does the law not insist that drivers of cars should drive at a snail's pace? Posner's answer is that this would be too costly a precaution from the economic point of view when compared to the cost of accidents. The courts, according to him, regard people as negligent only when they fail to take *cost-effective* precautions. Conversely, they regard those who cause accidents but whose behaviour is economically justified as having taken 'reasonable' care. Posner's view, in other words, is that the courts are guided by the need to maximise social wealth when setting the standard of negligence.[40] According to him, their rules achieve what Stephen Bottomley and Simon Bronitt call the '"optimal" accident level; that is, the point beyond which it becomes more expensive to prevent accidents than to allow them to occur'.[41] Posner speculates that judges decide cases in this way because their reputation for impartiality and objectivity is important and it is relatively uncontroversial to seek to maximise wealth (as compared, for instance, with seeking to redistribute wealth, which is more appropriately left to the legislature). Posner says: '[T]here is a broad-based social demand for efficient rules governing safety, property and transactions.'[42]

---

39 Ibid pp 249–50.
40 Ibid pp 167–9.
41 S Bottomley and S Bronitt, *Law in Context*, 3rd edn, Federation Press, Sydney, 2006, p 356.
42 Posner, above n 10, p 360.

Here is another example given by Posner. He discusses the case of *Eckert v Long Island Railroad*.[43] Posner writes:

> The defendant's train was going too fast and without adequate signals in a densely populated area. A small child was sitting on the tracks, oblivious to the oncoming train. Eckert ran to rescue the child and managed to throw it clear but was himself killed. The court held that Eckert had not been contributorily negligent, and therefore his estate could recover damages for the railroad's negligence.[44]

According to Posner, the underlying reasoning of the court was as follows:

> If ... the probability that the child would be killed if the rescue was not attempted was greater than the probability that Eckert would get himself killed saving the child, and if the child's life was at least as valuable as Eckert's life, then the expected benefit of the rescue to the railroad in reducing an expected liability cost to the child's parents was greater than the expected cost of rescue. In that event, but for prohibitive transaction costs, the railroad would have hired Eckert to attempt the rescue, so it should be required to compensate him ex post.[45]

Posner's argument on these matters assumes that judges are able to work out what bargains would be struck by, for instance, those who cause accidents and the victims of accidents if they were able to negotiate under Coasian conditions of zero transaction costs so as to maximise their joint benefits. Thus Posner says: 'I believe that in many cases a court can make a reasonably accurate guess as to the allocation of resources that would maximise wealth.'[46] His critics, however, are sceptical about this. Jon Hanson and Melissa Hart, for instance, argue that it is impossible in practice for courts to take into consideration and weigh all the efficiency effects of a rule and its alternatives. Even economists, they say, cannot answer these questions accurately but resort to 'eyeballing the various efficiency considerations and offering their own view, together with a smattering of contestable empirical support, of how the countervailing efficiency considerations stack up'.[47]

---

43 *Eckert v Long Island Railroad*, 43 NY 502 (1870).
44 Posner, above n 12, p 250.
45 Ibid.
46 Posner, above n 26, p 62.
47 J D Hanson and M R Hart, 'Law and Economics', in D Patterson (ed), *A Companion to Philosophy of Law and Legal Theory*, Blackwell, Oxford, 1996, p 328.

Posner's critics also argue that his theory is almost impossible to test or refute, because when evidence seems to contradict the theory, an appeal is made to factors such as transaction costs in an attempt to save the theory. Thus Veljanovski maintains that 'the law is rationalized as efficient by assuming a configuration of transaction (and other) costs that makes it so without any attempt to investigate whether these costs exist in practice'.[48] Furthermore, although Posner's critics are willing to concede that in market-related areas of law, such as contract law, many existing legal rules may be efficient, they are less convinced that Posner's analysis applies (or should apply) to non-market areas, such as criminal and family law.

Bottomley and Bronitt sum up the numerous criticisms against Posner's descriptive thesis in the following way:

> Posner's arguments about the efficiency of common law are overstated. The methodology by which the theory is purportedly substantiated is dubious, the theory itself may not be testable in any rigorous way, and it lacks an adequate causal basis. Empirical research which *attempts* to test the theory is scanty, and empirical questions are frequently ignored. Finally, much of the empirical evidence which does exist is not supportive of the theory.[49]

It is worth emphasising, however, that although the critics of the economic analysis of law reject its more extreme claims and assumptions, as well as its unattractive and single-minded focus on the value of efficiency at the cost of such values as rights (see Chapter 10) and justice (see Chapter 12), they do not deny that economics has a valuable contribution to make to law. Thus Hanson and Hart, for instance, conclude:

> [W]hile the claim that efficiency should serve as *the* goal of the law might not find much support, many people—perhaps most people—still believe that efficiency should be *a* goal of the legal system. And, where a model's relevant assumptions are plausible, law and economics can contribute in important ways to our understanding of laws' effects, of how those laws might be altered to better serve the goal of efficiency, or, alternatively, of what the efficiency costs of pursuing different policy goals (such as equity) might be.[50]

---

48 C G Veljanovski, *The New Law-and-Economics: A Research Review*, Centre for Socio-Legal Studies, Oxford, 1982, p 96.
49 Bottomley and Bronitt, above n 41, p 367, Bottomley's and Bronitt's emphasis.
50 Hanson and Hart, above n 47, p 330, Hanson's and Hart's emphasis.

Questions

1. Posner argues that wealth maximisation not only gives us all the attractions of utilitarianism without its defects but also that everyone would consent to it if asked in advance. If so, why should wealth maximisation guide the decisions only of judges? Why should it not guide all public decision-making?

2. Some economic historians have argued that American slavery was profitable and wealth-maximising: '[S]laves were a rational way for slave owners to maximize the return on their capital' (W Cunningham, 'Testing Posner's Strong Theory of Wealth Maximization' (1992) 81 *Georgetown Law Review* 141, 154). Assuming that this is correct, does this prove the unacceptability of wealth maximisation as an ethical principle?

3. According to the principle of wealth maximisation, those who value goods most, as determined by willingness to pay, should own them. Consider the following example, provided by Posner. 'Suppose that pituitary extract is ... very expensive. A poor family has a child who will be a dwarf if he does not get some of the extract, but the family cannot afford the price ... A rich family has a child who will grow to normal height, but the extract will add a few inches more, and his parents decide to buy it for him' (R A Posner, *Economic Analysis of Law*, 6th edn, Aspen Publishers, New York, 2003, p 11). Since the pituitary extract is more valuable to the rich family, the principle of wealth maximisation implies that the rich family has the right to the extract. Does this example show that wealth maximisation is biased in favour of the wealthy?

4. Morton Horwitz writes: 'Efficiency has been used in the economic analysis as if it were an independent concept, not entirely relative to whatever distribution of wealth existed. And once it has been realized that efficiency is, by definition, a function of a particular distribution (invariably the status quo), the inherently conservative bias of the definition of efficiency becomes clear' (M Horwitz, 'Law and Economics: Science or Politics?' (1980) 8 *Hofstra Law Review* 905, 911–12). Do you agree?

5. Is social wealth a goal that is worth pursuing?

Further reading

S Bottomley and S Bronitt, *Law in Context*, 3rd edn, Federation Press, Sydney, 2006, Chapters 11–12.

R Coase, 'The Problem of Social Cost' (1960) 3 *Journal of Law and Economics* 1.

R Dworkin, *A Matter of Principle*, Harvard University Press, Cambridge, MA, 1985, Chapters 12–13.

J D Hanson and M R Hart, 'Law and Economics', in D Patterson (ed), *A Companion to Philosophy of Law and Legal Theory*, Blackwell, Oxford, 1996, pp 311–31.

J G Murphy and J L Coleman, *Philosophy of Law*, revised edn, Westview Press, Boulder, 1990, Chapter 5.

R A Posner, 'Utilitarianism, Economics and Legal Theory' (1979) 8 *Journal of Legal Studies* 103.

R A Posner, *The Economics of Justice*, Harvard University Press, Cambridge, MA, 1981, Chapters 3–4.

R A Posner, *The Problems of Jurisprudence*, Harvard University Press, Cambridge, MA, 1990, Chapter 12.

R A Posner, *Economic Analysis of Law*, 6th edn, Aspen Publishers, New York, 2003.

R A Posner, *Law, Pragmatism and Democracy*, Harvard University Press, Cambridge, MA, 2003, Chapter 2.

Symposium, 'Efficiency as a Legal Concern' (1980) 8 *Hofstra Law Review* 485–770.

Symposium, 'Post-Chicago Law and Economics' (1989) 65 *Chicago-Kent Law Review* 3–191.

Symposium, 'The Future of Law and Economics: Looking Forward' (1997) 64 *University of Chicago Law Review* 1129–1224.

C G Veljanovski, *Economic Principles of Law*, Cambridge University Press, Cambridge, 2007.

9

Law as Oppressive

9.1 Chapter overview

This chapter turns to more radical perspectives on the law. A major focus will be on the Critical Legal Studies movement (CLS), which emerged in the United States in the 1970s. It included among its adherents Morton Horwitz, Mark Kelman, Duncan Kennedy, David Trubek, Mark Tushnet and Roberto Unger. CLS theorists were reacting, on the one hand, against views of law as 'above' politics, and on the other hand, against the conservatism of the economic approach to law. Although in some ways sympathetic to realism, especially the realist idea of legal indeterminacy, CLS theorists were also heavily influenced by elements of Marxism and postmodernism. Some key Marxist and postmodernist ideas will be explained in this chapter and the chapter will show how CLS theorists drew on them as the basis for a far-reaching critique of law and liberal legal values, such as the rule of law, rights and legal process. CLS theorists argue that law presents itself as a stable, coherent, neutral and 'natural' system of rules. This, they claim, is an illusion that needs to be stripped away so that law may be seen for what it really is: a deeply contradictory, illegitimate system which excludes and marginalises certain perspectives at the same time as it masks and sustains oppressive social relations.

9.2 The main themes of CLS

An awareness of the eclectic intellectual influences on CLS is essential to understanding it. Like the realists, CLS theorists believe that the law is indeterminate. They believe, in other words, that there are no preordained solutions to legal problems and that the law does not constrain the decisions of judges. Those decisions must therefore be explained by reference to something other than the legal rules.

They also agree with the realists that judges engage in elaborate, post hoc exercises in so-called 'objective legal reasoning' in order to rationalise decisions reached on other grounds. Judges, in other words, conceal the influence of their own views by dressing up their choices in the technical language of precedents and legal concepts. CLS theorists therefore adopt the realist position that legal reasoning is a myth used to assert false claims to objectivity, deny judicial choices and camouflage the realities of adjudication. CLS theorists focus, however, much more strongly than the realists did on the politics, ideology and class interests of judges in explaining why judges make the decisions they do.

The CLS version of indeterminacy is also more radical than that of the realists. This is in part because CLS theorists are influenced by postmodern views in the philosophy of language about the impossibility of words having stable meaning. It is also because CLS theorists see law as an arena in which ideological battles are lost and won. For them, the indeterminacy of the law is a reflection of deep-seated and ongoing social conflict between different ideologies and competing moral and political visions, which has led to contradictions and incoherence in legal doctrine. CLS is therefore much more concerned than realism with the 'politics of law'.[1]

Finally, CLS offers a radical and subversive critique of liberal views about law. Its advocates wish to 'delegitimate' law, which they see as a tool of injustice. The realists, by contrast, tended to be piecemeal reformists and liberals who thought that law should be used as an instrument to advance the values of American liberal democracy. It is true that the realists regarded the idea of the rule of law as a myth, since they thought it was impossible for judges to be constrained by legal rules. The realists tended to assume, however, that social science could make good any deficits in the rule of law by providing a reasonable and objective basis for the resolution of legal problems. Although the realists did not make a serious attempt to translate this idea into practice, some of their successors did, under the description of 'policy science'.[2]

CLS theorists, by contrast, think that policy analysis is just as tainted by subjectivity as legal reasoning. They therefore regard faith in the social sciences'

---

[1] Hence the title of a well-known collection of CLS essays: D Kairys (ed), *The Politics of Law: A Progressive Critique*, Pantheon Books, New York, 1982.
[2] N Duxbury, *Patterns of American Jurisprudence*, Clarendon Press, Oxford, 1995, pp 165-76.

ability to yield objective and uncontroversial conclusions as misplaced. They do not believe that social science has the capacity to deliver a value-free balance of competing interests, and they reject liberal values. Their emphasis is on the ideological nature of law—the powerful interests to which it caters as well as the way in which it obscures relations of power and domination—and they thereby seek to unmask what is, in their view, the merely apparent neutrality of law. CLS is therefore a much more corrosive view than realism.

To understand the more radical approach of CLS theorists to these matters, we need to turn to the influence of Marxist theory on their thought, as well as that of postmodernist theory and deconstruction. It should be noted, though, that the embrace of postmodernism and deconstruction caused controversy within the movement, some CLS theorists preferring the more sociological, Marxist tradition of critique to the language-based approach which characterises postmodernism. Yet, despite the existence of these differences of opinion, there still remains, as Peter Fitzpatrick and Alan Hunt say, a 'significant core of unity ... in opposition to the dominant orthodoxies in legal scholarship and in agreement around a commitment to the necessity and possibility of social transformation'.[3]

9.3 Postmodernism

Postmodernism is impossible to sum up in a few pages. For one thing, the term is used to refer to a variety of theoretical and methodological approaches, not all of them necessarily compatible. In addition, postmodernists write about a wide sweep of phenomena—including 'low culture' phenomena not generally thought to be part of traditional academic territory, such as soap operas and pop culture—and they tend to identify with a range of intellectual disciplines, from literary theory to cultural studies, psychoanalysis, intellectual history and Continental philosophy. Important exponents of these ideas are Jacques Derrida, Michel Foucault, Jacques Lacan and Jean-François Lyotard.

This diversity notwithstanding, some widely shared, interconnected themes of specific relevance to law can be mentioned. First, in art, where the term was initially used, postmodernism was a reaction against modernism, the latter being understood to rest on the belief that art can transcend the particularities of social and historical context. Steven Connor explains that

---

[3] P Fitzpatrick and A Hunt, 'Introduction', in P Fitzpatrick and A Hunt (eds), *Critical Legal Studies*, Basil Blackwell, Oxford, 1987, p 2.

modernist aesthetics prizes purity and unity in works of art. Art should be 'pure', in the sense that it should be absorbed in itself and sealed off from its context, and it should be unified in the sense that it should 'effect reconciliations or unifications out of complex discontinuities'.[4] Postmodernism, by contrast, reacts against modernism by 'stress[ing] the hybridity of the work of art and its complex relatedness to its context'.[5] It embraces 'the disorderliness and complexity of the world'.[6]

Postmodernism in philosophy stands for an analogously destabilising challenge to the rationalist or so-called 'Enlightenment' view that there are objective and universal standards of truth and justice discoverable by human reason. The Enlightenment is associated with eighteenth-century philosophers who believed in the power of human reason to advance knowledge and in the possibility of progress in history and social conditions. They were modernists in the sense that they sought to reorganise society on rational lines, replacing the oppressive hierarchies and corrupt privileges of the past with a better world based on the values of liberty, equality and the pursuit of truth. Postmodernists use the term the 'Enlightenment project' to describe the ideology these rationalist beliefs inspired—the ideology of liberal humanism and the autonomous self that has dominated Western societies in modern times. Postmodernism, by contrast, inspired in part by the political horrors of the twentieth century and the failure of liberal humanism to deliver on its emancipatory promises, regards the idea of objective knowledge in science, morality and politics, and the associated ideas of mastery of the world and social progress, as myths.

Postmodernism is therefore 'anti-foundationalist': it rejects the old certainties of what it calls 'grand theory' or 'grand narratives'.[7] By these terms it means to refer to those general theories, associated with philosophers such as Plato, Aristotle, Descartes, Kant and Marx, which claim to be able to explain everything or to have found an absolute or certain foundation for knowledge and social institutions. Postmodernism rejects as authoritarian any such ambition to be in possession of the truth or to be able to provide criteria for truth. It wishes,

---

4   S Connor, 'Modernism and Postmodernism', in D Cooper (ed), *A Companion to Aesthetics*, Blackwell, Oxford, 1992, p 288.
5   Ibid.
6   Ibid p 291.
7   J-F Lyotard, *The Post Modern Condition: A Report on Knowledge*, G Bennington and B Massumi (trans), Manchester University Press, Manchester, 1984, pp 15, 31–2.

in Lyotard's words, to 'wage a war on totality',[8] whether 'totalising narratives' take the form of religion, science or grand political theories such as Marxism, whose account of the whole of human history is organised around a single, monolithic concept, that of class conflict.

Secondly, postmodernism stresses the socially conditioned nature of all thinking. It is the socially conditioned or contextualised nature of knowledge that makes it impossible, according to postmodernists, to gain access to reality by transcending local or partial apprehensions of the world. They claim that there is no way of ensuring that theories mirror or accurately describe an external reality. Every viewpoint is an experienced viewpoint and experienced viewpoints always *construct* rather than *reflect* how things are. Every perception of the truth is therefore perspectival. Postmodernism consequently constitutes a thoroughgoing attack on the mainstream philosophical tradition, which, though it has grappled with radical forms of scepticism and relativism, has rarely endorsed them.

Foucault's work represents an important inspiration for the development of this set of ideas. Foucault saw power and knowledge as opposite sides of the same coin. What we take to be objective knowledge is just the version of events authorised by those who have power. Though they give it the imprimatur of 'truth', it is merely their interpretation. Foucault uses the concept of 'genealogy' to describe the excavation of the accidental origins of all our concepts and the beliefs we treat as 'knowledge'. The aim is to demonstrate the precariousness and arbitrariness of everything we take to be rationally inevitable and justifiable. Thus, in his first major work, on the history of madness, Foucault argued that the modern concept of mental 'illness' was invented to exclude and marginalise those who defy conventional norms.[9] In later work on the history of sexuality, Foucault likewise argued that the concepts of 'normal' and 'sexually deviant' are invented concepts, not naturally existing categories.[10] Foucault was also very interested in modern methods of exercising power, particularly the way in which earlier, more brutal methods of control have been replaced by the more effective modern techniques of what he called 'disciplinary' power. Foucault argued, for example, that the emphasis on correcting deviance and the constant possibility of being observed, in institutions such as prisons, factories, hospitals

---

8   Ibid p 82.
9   M Foucault, *Madness and Civilization: A History of Insanity in the Age of Reason*, R Howard (trans), Tavistock Publications, London, 1967.
10 M Foucault, *The History of Sexuality*, vol 1, R Hurley (trans), Vintage Books, New York, 1980.

and schools, are highly effective ways of inducing us to conform to and even to internalise what is 'normal'.[11]

A third aspect of much postmodernist scholarship is the way in which it builds on the 'turn towards language'—the idea that philosophy should primarily concern itself with language and with the way in which language influences thought—that characterises much twentieth-century philosophical thought. Postmodernists go further, saying that language constitutes or produces reality. The theory of the Swiss structuralist linguist, Ferdinand de Saussure, was an important influence on the development of these ideas about language.[12] Saussure saw language as a system of signs, a sign being a sound with a meaning. His view of language as a system or a structure led him to argue that no term has meaning in isolation from other terms: meaning is relational in the sense that it is a function of differences between concepts within a system. The concept of 'cat', for instance, has meaning only in relation to other concepts such as 'dog' and 'lion'. This led Saussure to conclude that words do not have meanings fixed by their relationship to objects and that language does not describe pre-existing ideas. On the contrary, different languages constitute different realities. Saussure nevertheless saw the system of signs that constitutes a particular language as coherent, stable and capable of generating meaning in virtue of the rules that govern its operation. In this regard, he compared language to a game of chess.

Derrida, by contrast, rejects the idea of a stable and unified system. For this reason, he is often described as a 'poststructuralist'. Whereas structuralists such as Saussure find order within systems, Stuart Sim explains that '[t]he emphasis in poststructuralist analyses is on the contingent, the different, the unsystematic and the unsystematizable'.[13] Thus Derrida argues that meanings are inherently unstable and contingent and that texts have many, frequently conflicting meanings. There is no single authoritative or correct meaning. Derrida therefore went further than Saussure. Saussure had argued that the meaning of a word is a matter of its relation to other words within the language, rather than a matter of its relation to a non-linguistic reality to which it refers. For Derrida, the meaning of a word is also a function of all the contexts of its use—past, present and future. The idea that the meaning of a text is that which the author intended and hence fixed to a given time is decisively rejected. It is therefore

---

11 M Foucault, *Discipline and Punish: The Birth of the Prison*, A Sheridan (trans), Penguin Books, London, 1991.
12 F de Saussure, *Course in General Linguistics*, W Baskin (trans), McGraw-Hill, New York, 1959.
13 S Sim, 'Structuralism and Poststructuralism', in D Cooper (ed), *A Companion to Aesthetics*, Blackwell, Oxford, 1992, p 402.

impossible, according to Derrida, to achieve finality of interpretation: meaning is endlessly 'deferred' and incapable of being fully determined.

If meaning is so unstable—always in the process of transformation—how, it might be wondered, can we communicate at all? Derrida argues that an illusion of stable meaning is created by binary oppositions. These are natural-seeming conceptual oppositions underlying mainstream philosophy. Examples are male/female, good/evil, reason/emotion, nature/culture, public/private, high culture/low culture. Derrida calls attention to the implicit hierarchy and therefore the hidden politics underlying these linguistic oppositions, the one term carrying positive connotations and the other negative connotations. The privileged term excludes and suppresses the 'other'. Thus men are what women are not. Yet, at the same time, Derrida says, maleness depends for its meaning on the meaning of femaleness, to which it endeavours to define itself in opposition: its superiority is therefore built on sand. Seeing this allows us to 'deconstruct' the way in which the one term in the pair has been privileged and the other suppressed—the way in which one concept is assumed objectively to be the norm while the other is assumed to be the exception or to be marginal. As the dominant discourses and interpretations are destabilised, their contradictions and paradoxes exposed, and the traditional distinctions on which they rely subverted, a space is created for new ways of thinking. Derrida writes: '[I]n a classical philosophical opposition we are not dealing with the peaceful existence of a *vis-à-vis*, but rather with a violent hierarchy. One of the two terms governs the other (axiologically, logically, etc.) or has the upper hand. To deconstruct the opposition, first of all, is to overturn the hierarchy at a given moment.'[14]

Deconstruction is therefore a method or technique of reading texts that is employed by theorists who wish to highlight the impossibility, as they see it, of arriving at a text's true meaning, and that aims to call attention to the way in which alternative interpretations have been suppressed. Derrida further believed that the openness to change entailed by such indeterminacy of meaning should be welcomed, not resisted. Once liberated from the idea that interpretations must conform to constraints to be found in the text, we, as readers, will be free to 'play', as we bring our own contexts to texts and in the process rewrite the texts we read.

One final important postmodernist idea is the 'death of the subject', which is contained in the writings of psychoanalysts such as Lacan,

---

14 J Derrida, *Positions*, A Bass (trans), University of Chicago Press, Chicago, 1981, p 41.

as well as in the work of Foucault and Derrida. Once language came to be seen as constitutive of reality, the modern idea of the choosing, self-determining individual as the driving force of social and cultural developments was correspondingly demoted. For postmodernists, consciousness and subjectivity are the effects of culture and language, not their cause. Margaret Davies explains this view as follows:

> [T]he notion of subjectivity has been questioned in a multitude of ways, the focal point of such controversies being how the subject functions in relation to the systems (of language, law, and society) which surround it. It is no longer possible to theorise the subject as a sovereign entity, since like the sign and, like concepts, it is defined relationally. What I am is a function of what I am not, what I repress, what I exclude, as well as of the various cultural messages which pass through me.[15]

Many of these postmodernist and poststructuralist ideas are crucial to understanding the subversive aspects of the CLS project. As we will see shortly, these include the claim that the law is radically indeterminate, unstable and incoherent; that an illusion of determinacy, stability and coherence is maintained by the suppression and exclusion of alternative solutions; and that exposure of the underlying contradictions and the suppressed alternative solutions will destroy the appearance of necessity associated with the dominant legal categories. At the same time, it will be evident that there are deeply sceptical and relativist aspects to postmodernism, and it can be wondered how well suited it really is to support critical legal theories that seek to transform power relations in the interests of disadvantaged groups. This issue will be deferred until 13.10, where it will be discussed in the context of a consideration of postmodern feminism.

9.4 Marxism and law

We turn now to Marxist theory. Although Karl Marx did not have a developed theory of law, and indeed thought that there would be no need for law in the future classless society that he envisaged, there are important aspects of his work that are relevant to legal theory. For our purposes, we will concentrate on his theory of history, which he called 'historical materialism'. According to historical materialism, changes in the economic system drive all social change. Marx held that in any human society the 'forces of production'—the labour power, the materials, and the instruments and tools used in the process of

---

15 M Davies, *Asking the Law Question*, 3rd edn, Lawbook Co, Sydney, 2008, p 351.

production—are of fundamental importance in explaining everything else about that society, including its law. The forces of production give rise, Marx said, to certain 'relations of production', these being class relationships or relationships of power and control. 'In acquiring new productive forces', Marx said, 'men change their mode of production; and in changing their mode of production, in changing their way of earning a living, they change all their social relations. The hand-mill gives you society with the feudal lord; the steam-mill society with the industrial capitalist.'[16]

Just as the forces of production give rise to this network of social domination and exploitation, which Marx calls the 'base' of society, the base in turn gives rise to the 'superstructure'. The superstructure includes such social practices and institutions as politics, morality, religion, ideology, culture, and most importantly for our purposes, law. Marx says: 'Legal relations ... are to be grasped neither from themselves nor from the so called general development of the human mind, but rather have their roots in the material conditions of life.'[17]

At the same time, although law and the other superstructural practices and institutions derive their character from the character of the base, Marx does not deny that they play an important social role. This is often misunderstood by those who think that Marx was a crude instrumentalist, who saw institutions such as law as mere one-way reflections of the economy, having no causal efficacy of their own. On the contrary, Marx thought that legal, moral, religious and ideological beliefs influence the economy in very important ways. In particular, they help to sustain it by legitimising it. Thus, as G A Cohen shows in his book, *Karl Marx's Theory of History: A Defence*, the superstructure, for Marx, is not merely *explained by* but also *suits* or *sustains* the prevailing class relations in any particular society. One way of putting this is to say that the superstructure is functional for or helps to reproduce the economic relations of society. Thus, in Marx's view, particular superstructural institutions arise in order to serve the economic needs of society. Capitalism, for instance, could not survive without a legal system that serves and legitimises the private ownership of the means of production.[18]

Let us consider in more detail Marx's idea of the functional role played by law. Marx thought that the particular legal rules and doctrines that prevail

---

16 K Marx [1847], 'The Poverty of Philosophy', in K Marx and F Engels, *Collected Works*, vol 6, Lawrence and Wishart, London, 1976, p 166.
17 K Marx [1859], Preface to 'A Contribution to the Critique of Political Economy', in K Marx and F Engels, *Selected Works*, vol 1, Foreign Languages Publishing House, Moscow, 1958, p 362.
18 G A Cohen, *Karl Marx's Theory of History: A Defence*, Clarendon Press, Oxford, 1978, pp 225-34.

in any particular society will be those broadly suited to the economic interests of the dominant class. However, law does not present itself as the instrument of class exploitation and oppression. Instead, Marx thought, it presents itself as an impartial vehicle for serving everyone's interests. In this way, law is deeply 'mystifying'. For instance, in capitalist society, according to Marx, workers are in fact forced to sell their labour power, but the legal 'fiction' of freedom of contract obscures this fact: although the wage-labourer 'is bound to his owner', Marx says this is by 'invisible threads'.[19] Social and economic inequalities are likewise disguised by the legal doctrine of equality. This doctrine leads us to believe that the law extends genuine equality to everyone, disguising the fact that the rights that everyone supposedly enjoys, such as the right to private property, are of benefit only to the wealthy. Every equal right, says Marx, is 'a right of inequality in its content'.[20] Again, law makes the status quo look natural and therefore immutable. The right to private property, for instance, appears inevitable and beyond challenge, whereas in reality, according to Marx, it is merely an institution that serves the economic needs of a dominant class at a particular time.

Marx further maintains that the way in which law obscures reality is critical to its effectiveness in serving the interests of those with economic power. After all, if it were obvious to everyone that the main beneficiary of the law is the dominant class, the members of the exploited classes would be less likely to cooperate. By papering over the cracks or legitimising exploitation, law's falsehoods play a key role in sustaining the system of class domination. Indeed, some Marxist scholars, such as E P Thompson, argue that law not only appears to be non-partisan but is also, on occasion, genuinely non-partisan. According to Thompson, it is 'inherent in the very nature of the medium' that it cannot be 'reserved for the exclusive use only of [the ruling] class'.[21] In thus seeming to represent the requirements of justice, and on occasion by actually being just—by not being a simple or straightforward tool of the ruling class—law enhances the legitimacy of the status quo.

For Marxists, law therefore has an extremely important ideological function, where the term 'ideological' refers to certain ideas' ability to obscure

---

19   K Marx [1867], *Capital*, vol 1, Lawrence and Wishart, London, 1974, p 538.
20   K Marx [1875], 'Critique of the Gotha Program', in K Marx and F Engels, *Selected Works*, vol 2, Foreign Language Publishing House, Moscow, 1958, p 24.
21   E P Thompson, *Whigs and Hunters: The Origin of the Black Act*, Allen Lane, London, 1975, p 264.

and thereby maintain the exploitative relationships on which society is based.[22] In ideology, Marx said, 'men and their circumstances appear upside down'.[23] CLS, as we will shortly see, is heavily influenced by this aspect of Marxist theory. Although CLS theorists do not embrace Marx's economic determinism, they do adopt his views about the way in which law serves the interests of those who have power, whether this be economic or other forms of power. They emphasise the need to penetrate beneath the ideological surface—the distorted way in which things appear in society generally and in legal doctrine specifically—with a view to revealing the underlying relationships of power, which the surface appearances disguise and by disguising, reproduce.

In the light of this sketch of the intellectual currents on which CLS draws, we can now turn to some of its key claims. I will concentrate in what follows on CLS views about legal doctrine and liberal thought, although it should be noted that CLS theorists also devoted considerable critical energy to issues in legal education and the history of legal concepts.

9.5 Contradictions, incoherencies and law as ideology

The realist notion of indeterminacy was relatively superficial, as it was based on the possibility of interpreting statutes and precedents in different ways. This allowed theorists such as Dworkin to respond by saying that there are principles underlying the law that can resolve these difficulties. CLS can be seen as a reply to views such as Dworkin's. A central element of the CLS project is to expose much deeper contradictions and incoherencies, which, in the view of CLS theorists, lie beneath law's surface unity and its appearance of coherence. These contradictions run so deep that it is impossible, according to them, to make coherent sense out of the legal materials. David Howarth summarises this central CLS claim as follows:

> The Critical Legal Studies position is that the law is so full of contradictory values and so obviously the outcome of political conflict that judges can never make fully coherent sense out of it. They may try hard to remove

---

22 D Meyerson, *False Consciousness*, Clarendon Press, Oxford, 1991, pp 2–4.
23 K Marx [1846], 'The German Ideology', in K Marx and F Engels, *Collected Works*, vol 5, Lawrence and Wishart, London, 1976, p 36.

inconsistencies, and to gloss over conflicts of value but, like jelly held in the fingers, the contradictions eventually ooze out somewhere.[24]

Thus, Duncan Kennedy argues in his early writings that the legal system exhibits contradictory commitments. For instance, one such contradiction is between a commitment to mechanically applicable rules as the correct way to resolve disputes, on the one hand, and a commitment to a situation-sensitive, ad hoc approach, on the other. Kennedy claims that this contradiction in turn reflects a more fundamental contradiction between the values of individualism or self-interest and altruism or sharing.[25] This more fundamental contradiction asserts itself, according to Kennedy, in many areas of the law.

In the law of contract, for instance, the concept of freedom of contract favours the individualistic right to drive a hard bargain at the expense of those whose vulnerability may be exploited, whereas concepts such as unconscionability and undue influence favour altruism or a concern for the welfare of the weaker party. Contract law is therefore internally contradictory, as are all the other branches of legal doctrine. Thus the existence of inconsistent legal results equally supported by the legal materials, to which the realists first pointed, is, on the CLS version of this theme, the reflection of much deeper and irreconcilable contradictions between competing social and political ideals in liberal thought and society more generally. According to Mark Kelman, liberal thought contains 'paired rhetorical arguments that both resolve cases in opposite, incompatible ways and correspond to distinct visions of human nature and human fulfillment'.[26] These 'deeply antagonistic ideologies'[27] are reflected within the law, leaving the law so contradictory and unstable that it is impossible to provide a coherent interpretation of it.

If these opposing visions destroy the unity of legal doctrine and liberal theory, making it possible to decide cases either way, how do CLS theorists explain legal cases where the outcome appears to be entirely predictable? Again, they are influenced by the realists, especially the prominence the realists gave to the influence of extra-legal factors on judicial decision-making. For CLS theorists, though, the extra-legal factors are seen through a more radical lens. They argue that the fact that judicial decisions can be predicted and that judges

---

24 D Howarth, 'Making Sense out of Nonsense', in H Gross and R Harrison (eds), *Jurisprudence: Cambridge Essays*, Clarendon Press, Oxford, 1992, p 30.
25 D Kennedy, 'Form and Substance in Private Law Adjudication' (1976) 89 *Harvard Law Review* 1685, 1685–6.
26 M Kelman, *A Guide to Critical Legal Studies*, Harvard University Press, Cambridge, MA, 1987, p 3.
27 R Dworkin, *Law's Empire*, Belknap Press of Harvard University Press, Cambridge, MA, 1986, p 272.

often agree on the answers to legal questions are artefacts of judges' shared political commitment to the status quo. Predictability in the law is therefore the consequence of ideological consensus among the powerful, not a function of the law's 'objective' requirements: 'The judicial emperor, clothed and coifed in appropriately legitimate and vogueish garb by the scholarly rag trader, chooses and acts to protect and preserve the propertied interests of vested white and male power.'[28]

In other words, CLS theorists explain the predictability of judicial decision-making by arguing that due to class and politics, judges will be biased in favour of one of the sides to the political conflicts reflected in the legal materials. The judges therefore fail to notice that the 'repressed contradictory impulse'[29] has as good a claim to resolve the dispute. Blind as they are to the way in which they privilege one of the conflicting interests and marginalise the other, it appears to them that there is just one option, preordained by the law. The appearance of legal coherence and consistency is, however, an illusion, according to CLS theorists. In fact, the outcome reflects an unreasoned, politically motivated affinity for one of the contradictory values and is not predetermined by the inherent logic of the law.

If the law does not constrain judicial decision-making, what is its function? The answer most CLS theorists give to this question is deeply indebted to the Marxist view of law as ideology, which was explained in the previous section: law legitimises the status quo. There is an appearance of naturalness or 'false necessity' attaching to the dominant legal categories, which makes the oppressive power structures of the status quo invisible and gives them the appearance of neutrality and legitimacy. This mystifying façade of legitimacy therefore needs to be stripped off. The contradictions, ideological biases, legitimising functions and injustices of liberal legal thought need to be exposed, to enable us to recognise the contingent and oppressive nature of the choices contained in the law.

This will clear the way, the CLS movement promises, for alternative, more egalitarian ways of thinking about law and its role in society. The ultimate aim of the critical legal approach is therefore social transformation—though, as many critics have pointed out, the critical legal scholars tend to be vague about the nature of the future society they think desirable and how we might get there.

28　A C Hutchinson, 'Introduction', in A C Hutchinson (ed), *Critical Legal Studies*, Rowman and Littlefield Publishers, New Jersey, 1989, p 4.

29　Kelman, above n 26, p 3.

9.6 Rejecting liberal values

As Alan C Hutchinson explains, '[t]he CLS claims of indeterminacy do not simply penetrate legal doctrine and theorizing; they go to the very heart of liberal democratic politics'.[30] Central liberal notions attacked by CLS theorists include the rule of law and rights, understood as protections for individual interests, which the state is bound both to respect and safeguard. In this respect, CLS may once again have been influenced by Marx, who launched a scathing attack on the idea of equal rights in a short piece called 'On the Jewish Question'. Marx thought that rights offer only what he called 'political emancipation', in contrast to real or 'human' emancipation. Rights, he said, exist only to protect those who are motivated by self-interest and who relate to other people in antagonistic ways. They protect those who see others as a threat to themselves and their interests. Rights are therefore 'egoistic' rights—'the rights of man separated from other men and from the community'—and the liberty they protect is the liberty of man viewed as an 'isolated monad, withdrawn into himself'.[31] A society built on respect for rights is therefore not a genuinely cooperative society. Rights are, indeed, an obstacle to cooperation.

Many of these notions resurface in CLS writings on rights. Some CLS writers argue that rights give undue prominence to individuals at the expense of our connections with others and the value of solidarity. They say that those who put their faith in the idea of rights see human beings as isolated individualists. Rights theorists therefore ignore our ties with the culture, traditions and conventions of the community to which we belong. This criticism derives from the 'communitarian' streak in CLS, that is, the idea that we are essentially social creatures, whose sense of identity and whose flourishing depend on a sense of indissoluble connection with our own society and culture. (For further discussion of communitarianism, see 10.8 and 12.8.) It is in this communitarian vein that Kennedy declares: 'The "freedom" of individualism is negative, alienated and arbitrary. It consists in the absence of restraint on the individual's choice of ends, and has no moral content whatever ... We can achieve real freedom only collectively, through *group* self-determination.'[32]

---

30 Hutchinson, above n 28, p 4.
31 K Marx [1843], 'On the Jewish Question', in K Marx and F Engels, *Collected Works*, vol 3, Lawrence and Wishart, London, 1975, p 162.
32 Kennedy, above n 25, 1774, Kennedy's emphasis.

Other CLS theorists claim that a focus on rights masks social and economic inequalities and leads to political paralysis:

> This is the essence of the problem with rights discourse. People don't realize that what they are doing is recasting the real existential feelings that led them to become political people into an ideological framework that coopts them into adopting the very consciousness they want to transform. Without even knowing it, they start talking as if 'we' were rights-bearing citizens who are 'allowed' to do this or that by something called the 'state', which is a passivizing illusion—actually a hallucination which establishes the presumptive political legitimacy of the status quo.[33]

The rule of law is dismissed for similar reasons. Morton Horwitz discusses E P Thompson's view that the rule of law, insofar as it imposes 'effective inhibitions on power' and defends the citizen from 'power's all-intrusive claims', is 'an unqualified good'.[34] Horwitz responds: 'I do not see how a Man of the Left can describe the rule of law as "an unqualified human good"! It undoubtedly restrains power, but it also prevents power's benevolent exercise ... [I]t ratifies and legitimates an adversarial, competitive, and atomistic conception of human relations.'[35] As one CLS theorist put it, 'people do not want just to be beastly to each other'.[36] We will examine the notion of rights in more detail in Chapter 10 and we will also examine criticisms of the CLS position on rights from the perspective of the critical race theorists in 13.14.

9.7 CLS versus constructive interpretation

In rejecting the idea that a constructive interpretation of law is possible, CLS theorists adopt a position that is diametrically opposed to Dworkin's. We know from 6.8 that a constructive interpretation of law is one that shows it in a good light. CLS believes that this is impossible for two reasons, one having to do with the contradictory character of law and the other having to do with its oppressive nature. Let us examine these in turn.

Since CLS theorists believe that law is chaotic and contradictory, they reject Dworkin's claim that it is possible to find a coherent interpretation of the bulk of the legal materials. Roberto Unger, for instance, argues that Dworkin

---

33 P Gabel and D Kennedy, 'Roll Over Beethoven' (1984) 36 *Stanford Law Review* 1, 26.
34 Thompson, above n 21, p 266.
35 M Horwitz, 'The Rule of Law: An Unqualified Human Good?' (1977) 86 *Yale Law Journal* 561, 566.
36 J W Singer, 'The Player and the Cards: Nihilism and Legal Theory' (1984) 94 *Yale Law Journal* 1, 54.

is under the influence of what he calls a 'rationalising spell'[37] in attempting to provide a rational reconstruction of the law, in which 'the stuff of law [is presented] as tied together in a way that justifies most of it'.[38] CLS theorists believe that the principles underlying the law are so conflicting that, for any legal dispute, it is possible to construct an equally convincing principled argument on both sides.[39] Because they challenge the possibility of providing a morally coherent account of the legal materials, CLS theorists are, in Dworkin's terminology, 'internal sceptics' (see 6.8).

Dworkin acknowledges that there is nothing to guarantee the existence of a coherent interpretation of the law. CLS is therefore a serious threat to his theory in 'attack[ing] the feasibility of integrity at its root'.[40] Hercules knows that there are some inconsistencies in the law but 'he assumes that these contradictions are not so pervasive and intractable ... that his task is impossible'.[41] CLS theorists, by contrast, argue that 'our legal culture, far from having any shape amenable to a uniform and coherent justification of principle, can only be grasped through the infertile metric of contradiction'.[42] The CLS critic 'insists that the law ... is so shot through with contradiction that no interpretation can fit more than an arbitrary and limited part of it'.[43] It follows that the CLS approach to law shows law in a bad light. This is so because, according to Dworkin, an interpretation of the law that does not fit the bulk of the legal materials shows 'the record of the community in an irredeemably bad light, because proposing that interpretation suggests that the community has characteristically dishonoured its own principles'.[44]

Dworkin replies to this challenge by saying that the CLS claim is only worth taking seriously if it has tried to find a less sceptical interpretation and failed. Dworkin writes: '[N]othing is easier or more pointless than demonstrating that a flawed and contradictory account fits as well as a smoother and more attractive one. The internal sceptic must show that the flawed and contradictory account is the only one available.'[45]

---

37 R Unger, 'Legal Analysis as Institutional Imagination' (1996) 59 *Modern Law Review* 1, 23.
38 Ibid 22.
39 J Waldron, 'Did Dworkin Ever Answer the Crits?', in S Hershowitz (ed), *Exploring Law's Empire: The Jurisprudence of Ronald Dworkin*, Oxford University Press, Oxford, 2006, p 164.
40 Dworkin, above n 27, p 268.
41 Ibid.
42 Ibid p 270.
43 Ibid p 268.
44 Ibid p 257.
45 Ibid p 274.

In attempting to show that the contradictory account is not the only one available, Dworkin argues that CLS theorists confuse *contradictory* principles with *competing* principles.[46] Dworkin says that the fact that there are competing principles to be found within the law is hardly surprising. In fact, it would be a symptom of failure in a legal system and in liberal political theory if they did not recognise that, for instance, both individual interests and the welfare of others are worth protecting. According to Dworkin, any 'decent response to the world's complexity'[47] would accommodate both principles by recognising each to some extent. The fact that they are both at work in the law shows merely that the law is complex, not that it is contradictory.

Another way of putting this is to say that CLS theorists assume that when principles pull in opposite directions they must be equally weighty and the choice between them must therefore be resolved arbitrarily or on political grounds. Dworkin argues, however, that this overlooks the fact that when principles come into conflict with one another it is usually possible to find a solution that accommodates both principles. Dworkin provides an example of competing principles, both of which can be accommodated. The first principle is a principle of sympathy, which holds that the state should protect people from being ruined by accidents even when the accident is their own fault. The second is a principle of responsibility. It holds that the costs of an accident should be borne by the person at fault. These principles do not contradict each other but they can come into conflict in particular circumstances. For instance, a particular negligent driver might be ruined if held liable for all the damage he or she has caused. One could accommodate both principles by requiring the defendant to compensate the victim to some extent, the balance of the loss to be paid by the state. Alternatively, there could be good reasons for thinking that, in particular circumstances, one of the competing principles is more powerful. For instance, one might think that because the driver could have bought insurance, the principle of responsibility should prevail over the principle of sympathy.[48] In either case, there is a rational resolution to the conflict between the principles, and it would be false to say that the law is contradictory.[49]

---

46 Ibid p 268.
47 Ibid p 443, n 20.
48 Ibid pp 269–71.
49 D Meyerson, 'Contradictions in Critical Legal Studies' (1991) 11 *Oxford Journal of Legal Studies* 439, 443–5.

In addition to seeing law as deeply contradictory and therefore incapable of being interpreted in a coherent way, as demanded by law as integrity, CLS provides a negative interpretation of law as based not on equality of concern, as Dworkin supposes (see 6.10), but rather on the *pretence* of equality—a pretence which hides the reality of domination and oppression. Once again, Dworkin suggests that the onus is on the negative interpreter to justify the negative interpretation. He says that constructive interpretations are the 'normal' or 'paradigm cases'.[50]

But why should the negative interpreter have to show that no more constructive interpretation is possible? It is hard to understand why the odds are stacked against negative interpretations in this way. Why should the constructive interpreter not have to show that the *constructive* interpretation is the only one available? Nigel Simmonds makes this point, suggesting that Dworkin's bias in favour of constructive interpretations is connected with his lack of attention to the history or social context of law. Simmonds argues that even if one accepts Dworkin's starting point, that of the committed participant's perspective on the law, such participants will want to be sure that the practice they are interpreting deserves support. They will therefore need to consider seriously any negative interpretations of the practice, for these may be powerful and enlightening. Furthermore, such evaluation will inevitably require reference to law's social and historical context.

Simmonds refers, by way of analogy, to Dworkin's own example of courtesy (see 6.8). Traditional male practices of courtesy, such as opening doors for women, may appear to be benign. However, when located within the context of a society in which women have traditionally been treated as inferior, we might come to see them as conveying an image of women as weak and in need of support. Likewise, to return to the CLS perspective on law, legal practices that appear to treat people equally, and are therefore superficially amenable to an interpretation that shows law in a good light, may take on a different significance when they are located in the context of a hierarchical and oppressive society. It may now seem much more plausible and enlightening to interpret them as a way of masking domination.[51] It seems fair to say that Dworkin does not really take this idea seriously, notwithstanding his concession that there is no guarantee that a constructive interpretation of legal practice is available.

---

50 Dworkin, above n 27, p 421, n 12.
51 N Simmonds, *Central Issues in Jurisprudence*, 3rd edn, Sweet and Maxwell, London, 2008, pp 224–6; N Simmonds, *Law as a Moral Idea*, Oxford University Press, Oxford, 2007, pp 33–4.

A final point concerns post-CLS developments. Although the CLS movement no longer exists, it inspired and informed other, more recent critical approaches to law, such as feminist legal theory and critical race theory, and in general, critical approaches continue to thrive. Since this more recent critical scholarship tends to be more directly concerned with concrete moral and political issues of a kind that will be examined in a later part of this book, in particular with the way in which law has disempowered women and minority groups, discussion of it will be deferred until Chapter 13.

Questions

1. What does it mean to say that 'law is politics'? Do you think it is true?
2. In the landmark case of *Steel v Houghton* (1788) 126 ER 32, the English Court of Common Pleas found that there was no right to glean. Prior to this decision, it was accepted that the poor could enter the land of farmers to glean any grain that had been left behind after the harvest. The majority judges found, however, that there could not be such a right because it was incompatible with the nature of property, which implies exclusive rights of ownership. How do you think a Marxist scholar would analyse this case?
3. 'CLS is ... trapped in the false dichotomy of thinking that, unless a distinction can be mechanically and uncontroversially delineated, then it is an imposter. The antidote to such thinking is the acceptance of complexity, fallibility, and imprecision as part of human rationality ... CLS has inflated the presence of human internal opposition and disharmony into caricatured claims of logical contradiction ... [T]he dichotomous form of analysis favoured by many in CLS invites hyperbole. It lures CLS into distorting the content of our competing impulses and endowing them with the potency to disable principled rational reflection' (R A Belliotti, *Justifying Law*, Temple University Press, Philadelphia, 1992, pp 165–6). Do you agree?
4. CLS theorists are frequently accused of 'nihilism'. Why do you think this is? Do you think they have a convincing response to this accusation?
5. Do you agree with the postmodern view that the 'modernist' ideas of universal truth, justice, reason, progress and autonomy are suspect?

Further reading

J M Balkin, 'Deconstruction', in D Patterson (ed), *A Companion to Philosophy of Law and Legal Theory*, Blackwell, Oxford, 1996, pp 367–74.

H Collins, *Marxism and Law,* Clarendon Press, Oxford, 1982.

M Davies, *Asking the Law Question*, Lawbook Co, Sydney, 2008, Chapters 5, 8.

C Douzinas, R Warrington and S McVeigh, *Postmodern Jurisprudence: The Law of the Text in the Texts of the Law*, Routledge, London, 1991.

P Fitzpatrick and A Hunt (eds), *Critical Legal Studies,* Basil Blackwell, Oxford, 1987.

A Hunt, 'Marxist Theory of Law', in D Patterson (ed), *A Companion to Philosophy of Law and Legal Theory*, Blackwell, Oxford, 1996, pp 355–66.

A C Hutchinson (ed), *Critical Legal Studies*, Rowman and Littlefield Publishers, New Jersey, 1989.

D Kairys (ed), *The Politics of Law: A Progressive Critique*, Pantheon Books, New York, 1982.

M Kelman, *A Guide to Critical Legal Studies*, Harvard University Press, Cambridge, MA, 1987.

D Kennedy, 'Form and Substance in Private Law Adjudication' (1976) 89 *Harvard Law Review* 1685.

D Patterson, 'Postmodernism', in D Patterson (ed), *A Companion to Philosophy of Law and Legal Theory*, Blackwell, Oxford, 1996, pp 375–84.

Symposium, 'Critical Legal Studies' (1984) 36 *Stanford Law Review* 1–674.

Symposium, 'Postmodernism and Law' (1991) 62 *University of Colorado Law Review* 439–636.

R M Unger, *The Critical Legal Studies Movement*, Harvard University Press, Cambridge, MA, 1986.

I Ward, *An Introduction to Critical Legal Theory*, Cavendish, London, 1998.

Part B
Justice

10

Rights

10.1 Chapter overview

Having considered the nature of law, legal reasoning and adjudication in some detail, this book now turns to the exploration of some important contemporary moral and political issues. The remaining chapters will be concerned, in particular, with questions about the moral and political principles that should govern our laws and legal institutions in the context of a set of related problems about rights, freedom, distributive justice and 'difference'. Answering these questions requires a mixture of conceptual analysis and moral argument. This chapter is concerned with rights and especially with human rights. Although the idea of human rights is currently very popular, as evidenced by the growing number of international, regional and domestic human rights instruments, it is not uncontroversial and there are many theorists who are sceptical about the value of rights. This chapter will analyse the concept of rights, the arguments in favour of and against adopting a rights-based morality, and the particular rights we might be thought to have. It will also consider the desirability of attempting to secure rights via the legal mechanism of a bill of rights.

10.2 The concept of human rights

It is obvious that legal rights exist. Legal rights are those rights, enforceable through the courts, that are granted us by statute, common law and constitutional provisions. But can we talk of the existence of moral rights and, more specifically, of moral rights against the government? If such rights do exist, they are claims that we are justified in making regardless of whether they are legally or socially recognised. They therefore serve as the basis for criticising governments that ignore and neglect them. If people have a moral right not to suffer racial discrimination, for example, they have this right independently of the law, and a society such as apartheid South Africa, where the legal system was built on systematic racial discrimination, violated this right on a daily basis.

In earlier centuries, moral rights of this kind were often called 'natural rights'. This term was used to indicate that the rights in question are not conferred on us as a matter of conventional social or legal arrangements but are possessed simply in virtue of our nature as human beings or in virtue of natural law. Such rights are no longer tied to ideas of nature or natural law and they are now usually referred to as 'human rights'. The term 'human rights' is used, in particular, for the most fundamental moral rights that are possessed by all humans, wherever they live and regardless of the factors that differentiate them, such as race, religion, nationality and so on.

The focus of the human rights tradition has traditionally been on the exercise of state power and this chapter will retain that focus, while noting that other holders of power are increasingly being subjected to human rights scrutiny. Over time, the human rights tradition has also taken an increasingly expansive view of the extent of the state's obligations. The state is now considered to be under an obligation not only to respect human rights (to refrain from violating them), but also to protect them (to prevent others from violating them), and to contribute to their realisation (to take active steps to promote them). Our first task in this chapter will be to examine exactly what is involved in putting rights centre-stage in political decision-making, in the way recommended by the human rights tradition.

10.3 What does respect for rights involve?

In order to understand what is involved when governments are called upon to respect rights, we need to begin by examining the moral theory of utilitarianism, because rights block utilitarian reasoning. Utilitarianism is a type of consequentialist theory. Consequentialist theories determine moral rightness by reference solely to the good consequences or results of, for instance, acting in a certain way, or being guided by certain rules, or having certain motives. Different consequentialist theories place value on promoting different kinds of consequences. For instance, some consequentialist theories value the promotion of goods such as knowledge and beauty. In the case of utilitarianism, which is the best-known form of consequentialism, moral rightness is defined in terms of the production of maximum happiness. In order to understand exactly what is meant by this, let us suppose that we are faced with a conflict of interests between different individuals. Whatever we do, some individuals will gain and others will lose. What is the morally correct way to decide what to do?

Utilitarianism tells us that there is only one principle of morality, namely, to produce the greatest balance of happiness over unhappiness, both in our personal dealings with others and in the context of social decision-making. We will concentrate on social decision-making in this chapter. The early utilitarians tended to understand happiness as a pleasurable state of mind, whereas contemporary utilitarians tend to see it more as a matter of satisfied preferences or desires. They see it, in other words, as a matter of getting what one wants, regardless of whether this is accompanied by the experience of pleasure. I might, for instance, choose to undergo some hardship for the benefit of others, despite the fact that this will not bring me any pleasure, at least not in the ordinary sense of the word. I will ignore these complexities here, and talk interchangeably about 'happiness' and 'preference satisfaction'. I will also use the word 'welfare' as a catch-all word to describe the value that utilitarians believe ought to be promoted.

Jeremy Bentham was one of the earliest utilitarians. It will be remembered from 4.2 that although Bentham insisted on the separability of law and morality, he believed that morality should inform law and it is precisely utilitarian morality that he thought should guide all legislative activity and legal institutions. Bentham described the utilitarian approach like this: 'An action may be said to be conformable to the principle of utility ... when the tendency it has to augment the happiness of the community is greater than any which it has to diminish it.'[1]

Utilitarianism is therefore a *consequentialist* theory: it measures the rightness or wrongness of our actions solely by reference to their consequences and by reference to one particular set of consequences in particular—their effect on human happiness. Furthermore, it is a *maximising* theory, in the sense that it says that the best course of action is the one which achieves either the highest average or the highest total happiness compared to alternative courses of action. Conversely, an act is morally wrong if it does not produce the largest net balance of happiness. One alternative to a theory that tells us to maximise happiness

---

1   J Bentham [1789], 'An Introduction to the Principles of Morals and Legislation', in W Harrison (ed), *A Fragment of Government and an Introduction to the Principles of Morals and Legislation*, Basil Blackwell, Oxford, 1960, p 127.

would be one that tells us to equalise happiness. The latter theory would be sensitive to how happiness is distributed. By contrast, for utilitarians, how happiness is distributed is of no intrinsic concern and whether our actions are intrinsically right or wrong—right or wrong independent of their consequences—is also of no concern. Utilitarianism is also, apparently, a *neutral* theory because it avoids making moral judgments about what makes people happy. It simply puts each person's preferences onto the scales to be weighed against the preferences of everybody else, regardless of the content of those preferences. Finally, this makes it, in one sense of the word, an *egalitarian* theory: the happiness of *everyone* affected must be weighed on the scales when deciding what to do. One person's happiness is just as important as another's, and therefore 'everyone is to count for one, nobody for more than one'.[2]

Utilitarianism looks to be, on the face of it, an attractive and plausible theory. If morality is not about human happiness, what can it be about? Critics of utilitarianism respond that there are problems with the idea that happiness should always be *maximised*. They point out that pursuing maximum happiness can require the violation of rights. In making this argument, the critics identify utilitarianism with the view that on each occasion, decision-makers should decide what to do by calculating the effects on happiness of the different possible actions open to them and choosing the act that produces the most happiness. This version of utilitarianism is called 'act utilitarianism'. We will see in 10.5 that there are other possible versions of utilitarianism but for the moment it is the one on which we will concentrate.

Consider the following examples, which are often used to make the point about the possible conflict between utilitarianism and rights. Suppose the police have captured a terrorist who has planted a bomb in a sports stadium packed to capacity. Let us suppose that there are 100,000 people in the stadium. The terrorist refuses to disclose the location of the bomb and the police know it is about to explode. The terrorist is immune to torture but the police have also captured his small child and they know that if they torture the child the terrorist will disclose the location of the bomb. Clearly, the welfare of the 100,000 people as well as that of their relatives and friends far outweighs the suffering and even the death of the innocent child. Utilitarianism therefore seems to instruct us to torture the child—something most people would intuitively regard as abhorrent and precluded by the child's right not to be tortured.

---

2   This phrase was ascribed to Bentham by J S Mill in 'Utilitarianism' [1861], in M Warnock (ed), *Utilitarianism, On Liberty, Essay on Bentham*, Collins/Fontana, 1962, p 319.

The second example involves the punishment of an innocent person. Suppose that a terrible crime has been committed in a small town and the population is in an inflamed state. They believe that a particular man is responsible for the crime, although the sheriff knows he is innocent. The sheriff also knows, however, that unless the man is arrested and executed, thousands of people will be killed in rioting. Utilitarianism seems to tell the sheriff to make a scapegoat of the innocent man so as to prevent the loss of many lives. After all, the unhappiness caused to the innocent man will be far outweighed by the benefits to all the other inhabitants of the town. But once again this is strongly counter-intuitive insofar as it requires the sheriff to violate the rights of the innocent man.

The third example involves satisfying illegitimate or reprehensible preferences. Suppose that the majority in a society are racists who strongly dislike and wish to persecute a racial minority. Because utilitarians treat all preferences as on a par regardless of their content, utilitarian decision-makers will allow the majority to oppress the minority if the satisfaction this brings the majority outweighs the harm done to the minority. Rights theorists, by contrast, believe that some preferences are illegitimate and should not be taken into account in deciding what to do, no matter how intensely felt or widely shared these preferences may be. They argue that it is not appropriate to balance some people's racist preferences against other people's interest in not being discriminated against. For rights theorists, racist preferences should be given no weight at all in social decision-making. We first need to know whether it is just to satisfy a preference before we can give it weight in social decision-making.

It is against the background of examples such as these that we are able to understand the claims made by those who believe in rights. As we have seen, utilitarians are concerned solely with attempting to maximise welfare. This leads them to balance the interests of different individuals against each other in order to determine which course of action will bring maximum happiness. They take all preferences into account and are indifferent to the content of people's desires and to the nature of the harm that may need to be inflicted on some people in order to increase the general welfare. They approach all moral questions as a matter merely of a 'cost–benefit' analysis.

Those who believe in the importance of rights, by contrast, say that we should recognise that there are limits to utilitarian reasoning, and they use the concept of rights to capture these limits. These theorists say that there is a qualitative distinction between 'ordinary' interests and more fundamental interests. They believe that it is reasonable to balance people's ordinary interests against each other in a utilitarian way, accepting losses for some people in return for greater benefits for others. Dworkin gives the example of a law that forbids motorists to drive up Lexington Avenue: '[T]hough the New York government needs a justification for forbidding motorists to drive up Lexington Avenue, it is sufficient justification if the proper officials believe, on sound evidence, that the gain to the many will outweigh the inconvenience to the few.'[3]

But advocates for rights argue that it is different when it comes to the invasion of more fundamental interests. Such interests, they argue, are too important to be left to the mercy of a cost–benefit utilitarian exercise and we should mark this by giving them a special status—the status of 'rights'. Having a right to something means that the person should not be asked to forgo it merely on the ground that the loss will be outweighed by greater gains to others. A person should not, for instance, be tortured, or punished for a crime that he or she did not commit, or persecuted on racial grounds so as to bring benefits to other people.[4]

Dworkin uses the metaphor of a 'trump' to explain this idea, a trump being a playing card of a suit that outranks the other suits. Dworkin says: 'Individual rights are political trumps held by individuals. Individuals have rights when, for some reason, a collective goal is not a sufficient justification for denying them what they wish, as individuals, to have or to do, or not a sufficient justification for imposing some loss or injury on them.'[5] Rights are therefore a card of a stronger suit than the general interest and '[i]f someone has a right to something, then it is wrong for the government to deny it to him even though it would be in the general interest to do so'.[6]

This is not necessarily to say that theorists who believe in the importance of rights hold that utilitarian considerations can *never* justify the violation of a right. Although some defenders of rights take this view, they do not all do so. For Robert Nozick, as we will see in Chapter 12, rights are absolute and may never be violated, no matter the consequences. Other rights theorists, however, disagree. Thus Schauer uses the metaphor of 'rights as shields'. In Schauer's view, rights

---

3   R Dworkin, *Taking Rights Seriously*, Duckworth, London, 1977, p 191.
4   R Dworkin, *Is Democracy Possible Here? Principles for a New Political Debate*, Princeton University Press, Princeton, 2006, p 31.
5   Dworkin, above n 3, p xi.
6   Ibid p 269.

are like shields or suits of armour against governmental interests. 'Wearing a suit of armor', he says,

> would protect me against arrows, knives, blackjacks, fists and small bullets, and thus it is plain that wearing a suit of armor provides me with a degree of protection I would not otherwise have had. But that suit of armor does not protect me against large bore ammunition, bombs, or artillery fire and is as a result less than totally protective.[7]

Dworkin likewise allows for the possibility that rights, or at least less fundamental rights, may be violated in really exceptional circumstances. Where there is a sufficiently grave and demonstrated threat to society, rights may justifiably be infringed. For instance, freedom of speech might be justifiably infringed during wartime in order to avoid defeat. But since, by definition, rights pick out certain interests for special protection—largely, if not entirely, immunising them against being overridden in the public interest—rights cannot be overridden *merely* because the benefits of doing so would outweigh the costs.[8]

Hence Dworkin rejects the idea that it is permissible to 'balance' rights against the public interest. The metaphor of balance is increasingly used in the context of anti-terrorism measures. Many people believe that it is legitimate to weigh the rights of terrorism suspects against the need for security. Dworkin argues strenuously against this idea. He argues that that the mere fact that measures such as preventive detention and coercive interrogation would make society safer does not justify such policies. Dworkin points out that it would make society much safer if ordinary citizens who pose a risk to other people could be locked up to prevent them from harming others, and if the government could incarcerate people who are thought to have information about the drug trade to get them to reveal the information. But, he says, we do not think it legitimate to sacrifice the rights of these people in order to improve our security and to counter the problem of drug abuse. We are prepared to pay the attendant price in security because we think such measures would be gravely unjust. It cannot therefore be any different in the case of terrorism suspects, unless we are prepared to announce that suspects do not have a right to be treated justly and that we intend to act simply on the basis of our own interests.[9]

We now know what point is being made when it is said that we have rights. The claim is that some of our interests take priority over collective

---

7   F Schauer, 'A Comment on the Structure of Rights' (1993) 27 *Georgia Law Review* 415, 429.
8   Dworkin, above n 3, pp 191–2, 195, 200–4.
9   Dworkin, above n 4, pp 27, 43–4, 47.

goals and that state interference with them or failure to protect them cannot be justified on the basis of a routine utilitarian calculation. Respect for rights therefore involves giving priority to certain interests of individuals at the expense of society. (For further discussion of individualism, see 13.5.)

10.4 Which of our interests deserve the status of rights?

If certain of our interests are so important that they should take priority over the general welfare, which interests might these be? This is obviously a very controversial question, to which there are different possible answers. Different philosophical answers to this question will be considered at various points in this book, but in this section we will consider a well-known legal attempt to formulate a list of our fundamental interests. This is the list contained in the Universal Declaration of Human Rights ('the Declaration'), which was adopted by the General Assembly of the United Nations in 1948 as a response to the atrocities committed during the Second World War. This non-binding declaration and the two treaties that followed in 1966—the International Covenant on Civil and Political Rights and the International Covenant on Economic, Social and Cultural Rights—together constitute what is called the 'International Bill of Rights'.

This is not to say that we should regard these or other human rights instruments, whether international or domestic, as final and definitive statements on human rights. As Tom Campbell says, the United Nations did not invent human rights. It has sought merely to codify them and implement them, and whether it has done so successfully is another matter.[10] This concern about the adequacy of the instruments is, in part, a function of the fact that the international human rights treaties were a product of compromise among different nations with different interests.[11] Quite apart from this, however, the key point is that human rights are *moral* rights and they therefore cannot be identified with attempts to translate them into law, whether international or domestic. If we bear this reservation in mind, the Declaration nevertheless remains useful in picking out a number of rights that are commonly claimed as human rights. The most important of these are the following.

---

10 T Campbell, *Rights: A Critical Introduction*, Routledge, London, 2006, pp 38–9.
11 Dworkin, above n 4, p 29.

Most obviously, the Declaration mentions the rights to life, liberty and security of the person. Particular liberties are also more specifically mentioned. These include the right not to be enslaved; the right to freedom of thought, conscience and religion; the right to freedom of opinion and expression; and the right to freedom of peaceful assembly and association. The Declaration contains a number of rights arising out of the administration of the legal system. These include the right not to be tortured or subjected to cruel, inhuman or degrading treatment or punishment; the right to the equal protection of the law; the right not to be subjected to arbitrary arrest, detention or exile; the right of access to court; and the right to be presumed innocent until proven guilty. There are also rights of political participation, including the right to take part in the government of one's country. The right to property also figures, as do the right to non-discrimination, the right to privacy, the right to marry, and the right to form and join trade unions.

In addition to the rights mentioned in the previous paragraph, which are usually called 'civil and political rights', the Declaration contains rights connected with material well-being. This represents a significant reconceptualisation of the content of human rights and of the state's duties towards its citizens in the twentieth century.

It was previously generally assumed that the function of rights is only to safeguard human freedom or human liberty, such as the freedom to practise one's religion or express one's views. But most contemporary defenders of human rights believe that some degree of material security and welfare is as essential to leading a worthwhile life as the protection of our liberties, and that the role of rights in protecting material well-being is just as important as their role in protecting freedom. Hence they argue for the recognition of so-called 'socio-economic rights'. These are rights that seek to safeguard the satisfaction of our basic needs or welfare. The right to health care, to education and to housing are examples of socio-economic rights. They are sometimes called 'second-generation rights', to distinguish them from the 'first generation' of civil and political rights, which were, as noted, the first rights to be recognised.

The Declaration takes a step down the second-generation path in including such rights as the right 'to just and favourable conditions of work and to protection against unemployment'; to 'rest and leisure'; to education; and to 'a standard of living adequate for the health and well-being' of oneself and one's family, 'including food, clothing, housing and medical care and necessary social services, and the right to security'. Whether we have socio-economic rights and whether they should be contained in a judicially enforceable bill of rights are important and controversial questions, to which we will return at the end of this chapter and again in Chapter 12.

Finally, contemporary human rights law reflects the influence of the idea of a third generation of rights. These confer rights on groups. Such rights include the right of self-determination, language rights for members of cultural minorities and rights to respect for the cultural practices of minorities. Attention is also paid to the rights of the world's indigenous peoples. It should, though, be noted that group rights are more philosophically controversial than individual rights. One obvious source of controversy relates to possible conflicts between cultural rights and the rights of women. This conflict will be discussed in 13.13.

10.5 Why should governments respect rights?

We have seen that the defenders of rights believe that there are limits to the sacrifices that governments can legitimately impose on individuals in the pursuit of collective goals. But why should we accept this view? Why should governmental decision-makers be under an obligation to respect rights? The need to address this question may not be obvious because many people assume that the only people who reject rights are tyrants and sadists who are pursuing reprehensible goals and could not care less about people's suffering.[12] But this assumption is not correct. As we have seen, rights constrain utilitarian reasoning. But this means that they act as a constraint on the pursuit of even *meritorious* or *rational* social goals, preventing measures that would, in the absence of the right, be perfectly legitimate.

Consider the right to freedom of speech. Speech can cause harm in all sorts of ways. It can be used to deceive, to insult, to harass, to threaten, to offend, to provoke violence and to persuade other people to act in undesirable ways. Seeking to avoid these harms is perfectly reasonable. But if we recognise a *right* to freedom of speech, the fact that seeking to avoid these harms is reasonable is not a sufficient justification for interfering with freedom of speech. The right to freedom of speech therefore comes at a considerable price. Interference with it cannot be justified merely on the ground that the benefits of interference will be greater than the costs. Instead, such interference will require a showing of, for instance, serious and imminent danger. Even in the torture

---

12 J Waldron, *The Law*, Routledge, London, 1992, p 93.

and scapegoating cases described above, those who think that the need to respect rights is obvious will need to explain why they are concerned only about the suffering of the person who is tortured or punished, and why they think it justifiable to ignore what J J C Smart describes as the 'greater misery, perhaps the *very much* greater misery, such as that of hundreds of people suffering painful deaths'.[13] As Dworkin observes: 'The institution of rights against the Government is not a gift of God, or an ancient ritual, or a national sport. It is a complex and troublesome practice that makes the Government's job of securing the general benefit more difficult and more expensive, and it would be a frivolous and wrongful practice unless it served some point.'[14]

Why, then, should governments respect our rights? The first point to note is that some (though not all) utilitarians think that there are *utilitarian* reasons for imposing an obligation on government to respect rights. This may seem a strange claim given the fact that, as we have seen, respect for rights requires decision-makers to give priority to individuals over the general welfare, but in fact there are two ways of defending the view that there are utilitarian reasons for governments to respect rights, notwithstanding the fact that the social costs of doing so may outweigh the gains in particular circumstances.

The first theory, which is called 'rule utilitarianism', argues that instead of trying to calculate the effects on the general welfare of particular *acts* (the version of utilitarianism assumed in 10.3), decision-makers should instead decide what to do by applying the test of utility to *rules*.[15] They should, in other words, act in the way prescribed by rules whose adoption would *generally* maximise happiness, ignoring the fact that the rules may fail to maximise happiness in a particular instance. Rule utilitarians then go on to argue that if we adopt rules that require decision-makers to respect rights, such as the right of innocent people not to be punished, we are more likely to maximise happiness than if we adopt rules that allow decision-makers to infringe rights. After all, they say, the latter rules would cause considerable fear and anxiety in the population. Utilitarian decision-makers should therefore respect rights even if doing so will, in a particular instance, fail to maximise happiness.

There is a certain 'hey presto' quality to this argument. How can rule utilitarians be so certain that if we adopt rules that require respect for rights,

---

13   J J C Smart and B Williams, *Utilitarianism: For and Against*, Cambridge University Press, Cambridge, 1973, p 72, Smart's emphasis.
14   Dworkin, above n 3, p 198.
15   See, for instance, J Harsanyi, 'Rule Utilitarianism, Equality, and Justice' (1985) 2 *Social Philosophy and Policy* 115.

we will promote the general welfare? Some theorists also wonder whether this position really makes much sense for a utilitarian to adopt. Why should a happiness-maximising act be avoided by a utilitarian just because it is prohibited by a certain rule? Smart argues along these lines. He claims that it would be irrational for utilitarians to adopt rule utilitarianism. It is, in his view, a form of superstition or 'rule worship'. Why, he asks, should utilitarians follow a rule in circumstances where they know that following the rule will lead to more unhappiness than breaking it? Surely a utilitarian would regard this as irrational?[16]

Rule utilitarianism is not, however, the only basis on which utilitarians attempt to reconcile utilitarianism with our intuitive belief that we should respect rights as constraints on utilitarian reasoning. Some utilitarians argue for the need to respect rights on the basis of a distinction between direct and indirect utilitarianism. Direct utilitarians treat the principle of utility as a way of making moral decisions, that is, as a 'decision procedure'. Both act and rule utilitarianism are direct forms of utilitarianism. Whether decision-makers calculate the effects on happiness of acts or of rules, in both cases they are deciding what to do on the basis of a utilitarian calculation. Indirect utilitarians, by contrast, do not propose the principle of utility as a guide to decision-making, but only as a standard of what is morally right. They say that the important thing is that utility should be maximised. How to maximise it, or the best strategy for maximising it, is a separate question.[17]

Indirect utilitarians then go on to argue that the direct evaluation of the utility of either acts or rules is a poor strategy for maximising utility. This is because, according to the indirect utilitarians, we cannot trust decision-makers to calculate correctly the effects on happiness of different acts or rules. After all, human beings are imperfectly rational, not fully informed, short of time and prone to self-deception and bias. This means that decision-makers who try to determine whether, for instance, torturing someone will maximise happiness will frequently miscalculate. Indirect utilitarians conclude that officials should be prohibited from seeking to maximise utility and required to respect rights instead. This would, no doubt, sometimes have suboptimal consequences from the utilitarian perspective: the costs of respecting rights will sometimes

---

16 J J C Smart, 'Extreme and Restricted Utilitarianism', in P Foot (ed), *Theories of Ethics*, Oxford University Press, Oxford, 1967, p 176.
17 R Railton, 'Alienation, Consequentialism, and the Demands of Morality' (1984) 13 *Philosophy and Public Affairs* 134, 152.

outweigh the gains. But, the indirect utilitarians claim, it would be an even more counterproductive strategy to permit decision-makers to reason in a utilitarian way: the consequences for human happiness would be even worse.

This 'lesser of two evils' argument therefore yields a utilitarian reason for shielding our most fundamental interests from routine balancing against the public interest. In this way, it yields an indirectly utilitarian justification for respecting rights. (It should be plain that there are similarities between this argument and the argument, discussed in 6.4, that the purpose of legislative rules is more likely to be achieved if judges refrain from purposive interpretation.) Jeremy Waldron gives an example of indirect utilitarian reasoning, based explicitly on mistrust of government. He writes:

> Maybe there are times when the suspension of freedom of the press and civil liberties is justified on utilitarian grounds. But we know that these are likely to be tense and dangerous circumstances, and we know also that those in power may be motivated by their resentment of political criticism as much as by any impartial consideration of the general good. We may think it wiser, then, on utilitarian grounds, to lay down rules prohibiting such people from making what purport to be utilitarian decisions about the suspension of these safeguards.[18]

Attractive as this argument may seem, in that it rescues utilitarianism from having to prescribe that, for instance, innocent people should be punished or tortured, it does raise the question as to what is left of utilitarianism as a distinctive position once it has renounced any interest in utilitarianism as a guide to decision-making or as a principle upon which anyone should ever act.

Although some utilitarians try to provide reasons for respecting rights in one of the two ways just discussed, the more usual kind of justification for rights has an entirely different basis, in non-utilitarian moral theory. This way of thinking about rights puts individuals at centre-stage not for strategic or pragmatic reasons but for reasons of justice. On both rule utilitarianism and indirect utilitarianism, maximum happiness is the fundamental goal and rights are valued only derivatively, for their instrumental capacity to serve this goal. But on the non-utilitarian approach, as Dworkin explains, it is *rights* which are taken to be fundamental and the approach is therefore rights-based, not goal-based.[19] It follows that even if the rule utilitarians and indirect utilitarians turn out to be wrong, and there are no instrumental reasons to confer on

---

18   Waldron, above n 12, p 103.
19   Dworkin, above n 3, p 171.

individuals the protection of rights, the rights-based justification for focusing on individuals would be unaffected since it is not tied to the social benefits of giving certain interests special protection.

Rights-based theorists are influenced by the moral philosophy of Immanuel Kant. Kant thought that there is something uniquely precious about human beings, a characteristic that makes us uniquely valuable and confers dignity on us. This is our capacity for rational choice. Kant argued that this capacity gives rise to a special moral status that separates human beings from all other creatures and in virtue of which we are owed a special kind of respect. In particular, we should always be treated as ends in ourselves, and never be used in an instrumental way for someone else's or society's benefit. We should never be used, as he said, as a mere means to someone else's ends. Thus Kant wrote that each rational being 'should treat himself and all others, *never merely as a means*, but always *at the same time as an end in himself*'.[20]

Dworkin, Nozick and John Rawls, who all take the rights-based approach to morality, are influenced in various ways by these Kantian ideas of human dignity, equal worth and respect for persons. We will examine their views in detail in Chapter 12 but it is worth briefly explaining at this point the way in which their defence of rights is influenced by Kantian ideas. Dworkin argues that violating someone's fundamental interests for the good of society denies that person the concern and respect that he or she is owed by virtue of being human.[21] He believes that there are two principles of human dignity that governments must respect. The first is a principle of equal importance; the second is a principle of personal responsibility. The first principle states that it is objectively important that human lives be successful and that this is equally important for all persons, no matter who they are. The second principle states that each of us has a special responsibility for realising the success of our own lives.[22] Dworkin believes that certain rights flow from these principles, and that governments are under an obligation to respect these rights. For instance, Dworkin argues that the right not to suffer discrimination on the basis of race and the traditional liberal rights of free speech, conscience, political activity and religion flow from these principles.[23]

---

20 I Kant [1785], *The Moral Law: Kant's Groundwork of the Metaphysic of Morals*, H J Paton (trans), Hutchinson University Library, London, 1948, p 95, emphasis in original.
21 Dworkin, above n 3, pp 198–9.
22 Dworkin, above n 4, pp 9–10.
23 Ibid pp 32, 37.

Nozick believes that we have rights that protect us against having to make any sacrifices for the sake of others without our consent, no matter what socially beneficial consequences might be achieved. He ties this belief to the Kantian principle that we should be treated as 'inviolate individuals, who may not be used in certain ways by others as means or tools or instruments or resources; [we should be treated] as persons having individual rights with the dignity this constitutes'.[24] According to Nozick, we deserve this special treatment not so much because of our rationality, free will and moral agency, but because we are able to form a conception of the kind of life we wish to lead, a conception that can guide our actions. The moral significance of this ability is that this is how we give meaning to our lives, and Nozick suggests that we would not be able to shape our lives and give meaning to them if others were not prevented from interfering with us without our consent. In other words, it is the valuable ability to guide our own lives in accordance with a chosen conception which gives rise to rights as constraints on how we may be treated.[25]

Rawls's theory of justice as fairness also defends the view that rights take priority over social welfare as a matter of justice, and regardless of whether respecting rights will maximise happiness. He too puts this in Kantian language, saying that '[e]ach member of society is thought to have an inviolability founded on justice or, as some say, on natural right, which even the welfare of everyone else cannot override'.[26] The reason Rawls thinks human beings are owed what he calls 'the guarantees of justice'[27] is because we are 'moral persons'.[28] He tells us that moral persons have two features: they are capable of having a conception of the good and they are capable of having a sense of justice.[29] (For discussion of what Rawls means by a 'conception of the good', see 11.4.) The capacity for moral personality may still have to be developed, as in the case of children, but Rawls thinks that the capacity is sufficient to give rise to the entitlement to be treated justly.[30]

Conversely, Rawls believes that 'we are not required to give strict justice ... to creatures lacking [the] capacity [for a sense of justice]'.[31] The statement that

---

24 R Nozick, *Anarchy, State and Utopia*, Basil Blackwell, Oxford, 1974, pp 333–4.
25 Ibid p 50.
26 J Rawls, *A Theory of Justice*, Oxford University Press, Oxford, 1971, p 28.
27 Ibid p 505.
28 Ibid.
29 Ibid.
30 Ibid p 509.
31 Ibid p 512.

we are not required to give strict justice to creatures lacking the capacity for a sense of justice creates certain problems for Rawls. These problems concern what we owe to persons who are severely mentally impaired and to animals. Rawls concedes that his account has difficulty answering these questions but notes that justice is merely one part of morality. He says that even if we are not required to give strict justice to creatures who lack the capacity for justice, it does not follow that there are no moral requirements with respect to them. As far as animals are concerned, for instance, it is wrong to be cruel to them and we have 'duties of compassion and humanity' to them.[32] It is not possible to examine these issues further here, except to note that some theorists argue that Rawls is wrong to think that these are not matters of justice.[33]

Notwithstanding the fact that Dworkin, Nozick and Rawls all take a rights-based approach, there are important differences between them. In particular, they disagree on whether economic freedoms, such as unrestricted freedom of contract and the freedom to accumulate and dispose of property as we wish, are among our rights and must therefore be given priority over the general welfare. Nozick believes that we do have such rights and that they flow from accepting the Kantian principle that we are ends, not means. By contrast, both Dworkin and Rawls believe that economic freedoms are not among our fundamental interests and that restrictions on them to achieve valuable social goals are consistent with our equal worth. This has important implications for their respective views about the obligation of society to redress social and economic inequality by providing a decent income and services to the poor, as we will see in Chapter 12.

We have considered the reasons that can be given for respecting rights. We turn now to consider the views of the opponents of rights. We have already touched on some of these challenges in discussing the CLS critique of liberal values (see 9.6) but it is now necessary to consider the matter in more detail. I will address the criticisms under four headings, though there is considerable overlap between the various claims and the headings should therefore not be seen as watertight. The criticisms are: rights are selfish; rights are an instrument of oppression; rights are incompatible with the value and importance of community; and rights are ethnocentric.

---

32   Ibid. See also J Rawls, *Political Liberalism*, Columbia University Press, New York, 1993, pp 20–1.
33   For discussion of these issues, see M C Nussbaum, *Frontiers of Justice: Disability, Nationality, Species Membership*, Belknap Press of Harvard University Press, Cambridge, MA, 2006.

10.6 Are rights selfish?

Bentham was deeply hostile to the notion of moral or natural rights, as his scathing attack on the 1789 French Declaration of the Rights of Man and the Citizen demonstrates. Bentham's hostility to the idea of natural rights is explained in part by the fact that he thought it impossible to demonstrate that we have such rights, or what their content might be. He concluded from this that the only rights are legal rights. He said that no one can be said to enjoy a right unless someone else is liable to suffer a legal sanction for failing to respect that right. In the absence of a sanction, according to Bentham, claims of right are mere wishful thinking and, just as 'hunger is not bread', so 'a reason for wishing that a certain right were established, is not that right'.[34]

It is hard to understand why Bentham adopted this position, for he did not take the same view of other moral requirements such as 'duty' and 'obligation'. He thought that these can exist independently of legal recognition. He nevertheless believed that the idea that the law can violate rights is incoherent because there are no rights without law. Thus Bentham pronounced the idea of natural rights 'simple nonsense', going on to quip that 'natural and imprescriptible rights [are] rhetorical nonsense, nonsense upon stilts'.[35]

Bentham's hostility to the notion of natural rights was also a function of his utilitarianism. This led him to argue that those who put their own interests ahead of the general good are egoistic or selfish. Thus he argued that natural rights were not merely nonsense but dangerous nonsense, for they fuel 'the selfish and the hostile passions' which are the 'great enemies of public peace'.[36] Bentham went on to observe:

> Society is held together only by the sacrifices that men can be induced to make of the gratifications they demand: to obtain these sacrifices is the great difficulty, the great task of government. What has been the object, the perpetual and palpable object, of this Declaration of pretended Rights [the Declaration of the Rights of Man and the Citizen]? To add as much force as possible to these passions, already but too strong: to burst the cords that hold them in: to say to the selfish passions, there—everywhere, is your prey: to the

---

34   J Bentham [1795], 'Nonsense upon Stilts', in P Schofield, C Pease-Watkin and C Blamires (eds), *Rights, Representation and Reform: Nonsense Upon Stilts and Other Writings on the French Revolution*, Clarendon Press, Oxford, 2002, p 330.
35   Ibid.
36   Ibid p 321.

angry passions, there, everywhere, is your enemy. Such is the morality of this celebrated composition.[37]

This passage shows that Bentham was opposed to the idea of moral rights precisely because they give priority to individual interests over collective interests, in defiance of the utilitarian injunction to focus only on maximum happiness.

Rights theorists respond to the utilitarian critique by pointing out that rights do not protect all of our interests. They protect only our fundamental interests—our interests, for instance, in bodily integrity, freedom from discrimination, religious freedom and adequate health care. Rights theorists also point out that selfishness is shameful: to be selfish is to care about one's own interests more than one should.[38] They argue that it is not shameful to refuse to surrender one's entire self to society and the interests of other people. They do not, for instance, think it is selfish to claim a right not to be tortured, or a right to practise one's religion or a right to health care.

Most rights theorists also take the view that we can legitimately be asked to do more for other people than merely respect their rights. Nozick is an exception: he thinks, as we will see in 12.11, that the only moral requirement that can legitimately be enforced is to respect rights. But most rights theorists disagree. They say that we are bound to respect rights but that once that baseline is secured we should also care about the general good and collective goals. There is therefore plenty of scope for altruism and cooperation, which is nevertheless consistent with setting limits on the kinds of sacrifices people can legitimately be asked to make in the public interest. Indeed, rights theorists argue that it may be unrealistic to expect people to act altruistically and out of a concern for the community unless their basic interests are first secured.[39]

10.7 Are rights an instrument of oppression?

Marx is perhaps the best-known defender of the view that rights are a way of serving the interests of those who wield power in society and that the promise of freedom and emancipation that they offer is a sham. We already know from 9.6 that he attacked rights in his early essay, 'On the Jewish Question'. In this essay Marx argued that rights are a 'bourgeois' idea, one that creates an illusion

---

37 Ibid.
38 J Waldron, *Nonsense upon Stilts: Bentham, Burke and Marx on the Rights of Man*, Methuen, London, 1987, p 209.
39 Ibid pp 206–7.

of freedom and equality while in fact serving the interests of the dominant, property-owning class by guaranteeing that its acquisitive activity will be unhindered. Marx also believed that rights will not be necessary in a socialist society, in which the private ownership of the means of production will have been eliminated and class divisions will, according to him, have disappeared. He thought that in a harmonious society of this kind, guarantees that our interests will be protected will be unnecessary.

Many commentators have found this picture simplistic, both in its understanding of the interests protected by rights and in its view of the circumstances that make them necessary. Thus Steven Lukes, for instance, argues that Marx had a 'narrow and impoverished' view of human rights.[40] In his view, Marx's interpretation may be a plausible interpretation of some rights, but it it does not apply to all rights. Thus Marx's arguments may seem cogent when applied to an absolute right to private property, such as that argued for by Nozick (see 12.11), which does seem to serve the interests of those with economic power and entrench social and economic inequality. But nowadays, as we have seen, there is a growing emphasis on the importance of socio-economic rights and it is difficult to see why rights that serve basic needs, such as the right to health care, to education and to housing, should be thought to cater only to the self-serving interests of the capitalist class. Furthermore, although socio-economic rights are the most obvious examples of rights that appear to serve the interests of the less powerful members of society, Lukes argues that even the eighteenth-century conception of rights—which was, of course, the conception attacked by Marx—included rights that have little do to with serving the egoistic interests of the capitalist class but are valuable to everyone, no matter what their class. Lukes mentions, for instance, various rights contained in the French Declaration, such as the right to freedom of speech, to be presumed innocent until proven guilty and not to be arbitrarily arrested.[41]

Allen Buchanan argues that even if a society existed in which there were no class conflicts and no class interests, there would still be a need for rights. For even in such a society, it would, for instance, be necessary to protect individual liberties against paternalistic interference, prevent the common good from being pursued in unjustifiable ways, and specify the nature of our obligations to provide or preserve resources for future generations.[42]

---

[40] S Lukes, *Marxism and Morality*, Clarendon Press, Oxford, 1985, p 63.
[41] Ibid p 65.
[42] A E Buchanan, *Marx and Justice: The Radical Critique of Liberalism*, Methuen, London, 1982, p 165.

10.8 Are rights a threat to the value of community?

A contemporary critique of rights can be found in the work of communitarians such as Alasdair MacIntyre, Michael Sandel, Charles Taylor and Michael Walzer. They argue that liberal rights theory assumes a false, individualistic view of the self and wrongly puts individual interests ahead of identification with and participation in community.

We will return to the communitarian critique of the liberal conception of the self in 12.8. For the moment it is enough to note the following. Though liberals do not, contrary to some popular conventional stereotypes, believe that human beings can exist outside society, they do believe that we are able to stand back from our social relationships and social practices, subject them to critical scrutiny and reject them if found wanting. Communitarians take issue with this view. They believe that we are social creatures in a much deeper sense. They think that our identity and our good cannot be divorced from the communities to which we belong and that we can be obliged to pursue ends that we have not chosen, but that have been set by our community.

This philosophical view about the nature of the self leads communitarians to resist the view that the values of justice and rights take priority over the claims of community. In their view, the good for human beings consists in identification with a 'common form of life', an identification which can conflict with and be more important than respect for rights. Taylor makes this point, saying: 'I cannot be too willing to trump the collective decision in the name of individual rights if I haven't already moved some distance from the community which makes these decisions.'[43] In place of rights, with their individualistic focus and their insistence that people should be left free to pursue their own conceptions of the good, communitarians would have us substitute a politics of the common good based on shared objectives. They argue that this will make it possible to enjoy certain communal goods, such as solidarity, fraternity and a sense of belonging, which we will be shut out from if we persist in focusing on what is good for individuals.

Rights theorists respond by pointing out that, historically, shared social practices have been exclusionary: groups such as women, blacks and gays have played little part in defining the common good of the community, and indeed,

---

43 C Taylor, 'Alternative Futures: Legitimacy, Identity and Alienation in Late Twentieth Century Canada', in A Cairns and C William (eds), *Constitutionalism, Citizenship and Society in Canada*, University of Toronto Press, Toronto, 1985, p 211.

these groups have typically been oppressed by those who define the shared communal goals and the social roles that people are expected to play. Thus Will Kymlicka writes:

> Communitarians like to say that political theory should pay more attention to the history of each culture. But it is remarkable how rarely communitarians themselves undertake such an examination of our culture. They wish to use the ends and practices of our cultural tradition as the basis for a politics of the common good, but they do not adequately confront the fact that these practices were defined by a small segment of the population.[44]

In the view of rights theorists, therefore, members of marginalised and disadvantaged social groups are better served by rights which protect them from forced identification with cultural practices than by a politics of the common good which insists that they accept a social identity that has been defined for them by others.

10.9 Are rights ethnocentric?

As we have seen, those who defend human rights believe that they apply to everyone: all people in all social circumstances are morally entitled to their protection. However, many critics of rights are sceptical of such claims to universality. The idea that there are universal principles of political morality is strikingly expressed by Rawls at the end of *A Theory of Justice*. He writes:

> Thus to see our place in society from the perspective of this position is to see it *sub specie aeternitatis*: it is to regard the human condition not only from all social but also from all temporal points of view. The perspective of eternity is not a perspective from a certain place beyond the world, nor the point of view of a transcendent being; rather it is a form of thought and feeling that rational persons can adopt within the world. And having done so, they can, whatever their generation, bring together in one scheme all individual perspectives and arrive together at regulative principles that can be affirmed by everyone as he lives by them, each from his own standpoint.[45]

As we might expect, the idea that we are able to adopt the 'perspective of eternity' in our search for principles of justice is rejected by communitarians, with their emphasis on the importance of culture and shared practices and beliefs in constituting social identity. If what is good for people arises not out

---
44 W Kymlicka, *Contemporary Political Philosophy: An Introduction*, 2nd edn, Oxford University Press, Oxford, 2002, p 260.
45 Rawls, above n 26, p 587.

of universal needs and interests but out of their particular way of life, it will be a mistake to attempt to evaluate such ways of life by reference to external standards that make no sense in the context of particular, local practices. Communitarians argue that the attempt to impose human rights obligations on those who do not understand them represents just such a mistaken attempt to evaluate societies from the outside. Human rights, on their view, do not represent universal values but merely reflect the local practices of contemporary Western societies. Those who deny this are said to be guilty of 'cultural imperialism' or 'ethnocentrism'.

Thus Walzer argues that questions of justice can only be debated within the context of particular communities and their particular traditions. There are no standards of justice that are external to particular communities. Instead, what is just must be measured by reference to the shared perspectives and beliefs of a community as to the value of social goods. Walzer writes:

> We are (all of us) culture-producing creatures; we make and inhabit meaningful worlds. Since there is no way to rank and order these worlds with regard to their understanding of social goods, we do justice to actual men and women by respecting their particular creations. And they claim justice, and resist tyranny, by insisting on the meaning of social goods among themselves. Justice is rooted in the distinct understandings of places, honors, jobs, things of all sorts, that constitute a shared way of life. To override those understandings is (always) to act unjustly.[46]

Rights theorists respond to this kind of cultural relativism in a number of ways. First, they say that they are aware of the dangers of assuming that Western values are the correct values. But, they say, this does not imply that 'anything goes', that everything is 'relative', and that it is impossible to pass moral judgment on people's beliefs and practices. Instead, it should alert us to the possibility of bias in our judgments and lead us to be cautious in criticising other people's beliefs and practices.

Secondly, rights theorists point out that rights set only 'minimum goals': they do not purport to provide a 'complete social programme'.[47] Those who defend rights believe that all human beings have equal moral status and therefore that all governments are obliged to provide their citizens with minimum standards of protection, particularly insofar as their freedom, security and

---

46 M Walzer, *Spheres of Justice: A Defence of Pluralism and Equality*, Basic Books, New York, 1983, p 314.
47 Waldron, above n 38, p 173.

welfare are concerned. They argue that this leaves plenty of room for diversity in cultural practices and moral beliefs once the minimum is secured.

Rights theorists also question why these minimum standards are said to apply only to those in Western societies. How can it be the case—Joel Feinberg asks—that only people living in Western societies are entitled to these privileges?[48] Furthermore, do those who are denied their human rights in totalitarian or discriminatory societies take the view that rights are just a Western invention? Or is it rather the case that communitarians exaggerate the existence of 'shared understandings' in societies in which the idea of human rights is apparently rejected? Thomas Scanlon challenges the argument that rights are ethnocentric along these lines, saying:

> [T]his argument rests on the attribution to 'them' of a unanimity that does not in fact exist. 'They' are said to be different from us and to live by different rules. Such stereotypes are seldom accurate, and the attribution of unanimity is particularly implausible in the case of human rights violations. These actions have victims who generally resent what is done to them and who would rarely concede that, because such behaviour is common in their country, their tormentors are acting quite properly.[49]

Martha Nussbaum makes a similar point in the context of defending the concept of 'international feminism', which assesses how well different nations are doing in promoting women's quality of life and uses certain universal norms, such as human rights, for this purpose. Nussbaum is critical of the idea that these norms are inappropriately imposed on cultures that do not recognise them. She points out that there are feminists who live in these nations who find such notions indispensable. Such feminists are often accused of having become puppets of the West, but Nussbaum wonders whether we should accept this charge or treat it with scepticism, asking whose interests are served by this attempt to discredit women who are fighting for their rights.[50]

10.10 Bills of rights

Supposing that one believes in human rights, how should they be institutionalised or translated into legal form? The strongest form of legal protection involves giving courts the power to strike down legislation that is

---

48 J Feinberg, *Harmless Wrongdoing*, Oxford University Press, Oxford, 1990, p 335.
49 Quoted in J Feinberg, *Harmless Wrongdoing*, Oxford University Press, Oxford, 1990, p 336.
50 M C Nussbaum, *Women and Human Development: The Capabilities Approach*, Cambridge University Press, Cambridge, 2000, pp 34–9.

incompatible with rights, with the only way to reverse such decisions being by constitutional amendment. This is sometimes called 'strong-form judicial review'.[51] We find this mechanism for protecting rights in the United States, where the Supreme Court of the United States has the power to strike down legislation, regardless of the extent of its popular support, if it is in breach of any of the rights protected by the US Bill of Rights and other rights contained in the US Constitution. For instance, in the famous case of *Roe v Wade*, the Supreme Court invalidated Texas criminal abortion laws and declared that women have a constitutionally protected right to abortion.[52]

It is possible, however, to believe that the government ought to respect and protect human rights without believing that it is desirable to place legal limits on the legislative power of parliaments via a judicially enforceable bill of rights.[53] This may seem a strange stance. If someone believes that human rights should be respected and protected, surely he or she will also be in favour of a judicially enforceable bill of rights. If rights are valuable because they protect individuals' interests from being sacrificed in the pursuit of collective goals, does this not imply that majorities should be legally prevented from violating our rights? How are minorities to be protected if the courts cannot invalidate legislation passed by the majority?

In response to this question, the critics of strong-form judicial review argue that giving the courts this kind of power creates a problem of political illegitimacy. They call attention to the fact that rights are inevitably couched in very abstract, moral language—guaranteeing, for instance, 'equality' or 'freedom of speech'. This leads even people who are committed to rights to disagree in good faith about their implications in concrete cases. The example of *Roe v Wade* is a good one for the purpose of illustrating this point. The Supreme Court derived the right to abortion in part from the abstract guarantee of 'due process of law' found in the Fourteenth Amendment, a guarantee not obviously related to a right to abortion. Many people thought that this decision was unwarranted and it has given rise to deep and continuing disagreement in American society.

Concern about these kinds of far-reaching and intractable disagreements is at the heart of Waldron's opposition to rights-based judicial review in his

---

51 M Tushnet, 'Judicial Review of Legislation', in P Cane and M Tushnet (eds), *The Oxford Handbook of Legal Studies*, Oxford University Press, Oxford, 2003, pp 164–5.
52 *Roe v Wade*, 410 US 113 (1973).
53 J Waldron, *Law and Disagreement*, Clarendon Press, Oxford, 1999, p 212.

book, *Law and Disagreement*.[54] He provides a number of reasons for thinking that decisions about rights should not be entrusted to courts. His starting point is the fact that those who believe in rights disagree about what they mean and how they should be weighed against other rights and interests. This leads him to maintain that these decisions should be made through the democratic political process, not handed over to a handful of unelected judges who are thereby given carte blanche to substitute their moral and political opinions for those of the voters.[55] He also argues that to give judges this kind of privileged position is inconsistent with the point of rights, which is to ensure that everyone is afforded equal respect. Waldron thinks that if we really believe in equal respect for individuals, we should allow them to have an equal say in decisions about what rights mean, through their elected representatives in parliament.[56] Judicial review is, in other words, a form of disenfranchisement. Waldron also worries about the ability of the courts to make good decisions about rights, while simultaneously arguing against the low opinion many have of the capacity of legislatures to make such decisions. Thus he believes that there is little need to fear the 'tyranny of the majority', for '[people's] votes and opinions are not always the reflex of their interests'.[57] 'Citizens and representatives', he says, 'often do vote on the basis of good faith and relatively impartial opinions about justice, rights, and the common good'.[58]

There are many ways to respond to these arguments, not all of which can be canvassed here. Some theorists argue that courts are not as out of touch with public opinion as Waldron suggests.[59] Other theorists argue that democracy is not the only value.[60] Yet others, such as John Ely and Dworkin, have provided powerful arguments in favour of the idea that American-style judicial review is, contrary to Waldron's claims, compatible with democracy.

Ely focuses on matters of process. He argues that it is not anti-democratic to give the courts power to invalidate legislation that blocks fair access to political processes, such as laws that deny people the vote without powerful justification, or laws that treat marginalised groups adversely. For without the right to vote or

---

54 Waldron, above n 53. See also J Waldron, 'The Core of the Case against Judicial Review' (2006) 115 *Yale Law Journal* 1346.
55 Waldron, above n 53, p 181.
56 Ibid pp 222–3.
57 Ibid p 14.
58 Ibid.
59 William Eskridge Jr, 'Book Review Essay—The Circumstances of Politics and the Application of Statutes' (2000) 100 *Columbia Law Review* 558, 579.
60 M Moore, 'Natural Rights, Judicial Review and Constitutional Interpretation', in J Goldsworthy and T Campbell (eds), *Legal Interpretation in Democratic States*, Ashgate, Aldershot, 2002.

to be fairly represented in the political process, democracy does not exist. Certain rights are, in other words, constitutive of democracy, in Ely's view.[61]

Dworkin goes further and defends a substantive conception of democracy, which he calls the 'constitutional conception of democracy'[62] or the 'partnership' conception.[63] Dworkin argues that the essence of democracy is not majoritarianism. Instead, the 'defining aim' of democracy, in his view, is that all members of the community must be treated with equal concern and respect.[64] For Dworkin, democracy therefore means majority rule subject to further conditions. These conditions 'protect the status and interests of each citizen as a full partner in [the collective political] enterprise'.[65] In particular, these conditions require the majority to respect a range of substantive and far-reaching rights. This means that when majoritarian institutions disregard these rights, it is not anti-democratic for courts to invalidate their actions.[66]

Of course, these arguments do not convince everyone. Some of those who remain unconvinced reject the idea of bills of rights altogether, taking the view that existing common law and statutory protections are sufficient to protect human rights. Others, however, believe that it is important to improve on existing legal protections while not placing human rights beyond the reach of majorities. They are in favour of bills of rights that provide a weaker form of review. One important type of weak-form review is used by a statutory bill of rights. Such bills can be amended or repealed like any other statute and therefore any protection of rights that they provide can subsequently be taken away, either in whole or in part. Typically, they direct courts and tribunals to interpret law (sometimes only statutory law, sometimes both statutory law and the common law) in a manner that is consistent with the human rights protected by the bill, but only if it is 'possible' to do so. Some statutory bills of rights also allow courts to make a 'declaration of incompatibility'. Such a declaration is to the effect that a challenged law is not consistent with a protected right. The offending legislation remains valid, however, and must be applied to the case at hand, leaving parliament to decide whether to amend it or not.

---

61 J H Ely, *Democracy and Distrust: A Theory of Judicial Review*, Harvard University Press, Cambridge, MA, 1980, pp 102–3.
62 R Dworkin, *Freedom's Law: The Moral Reading of the American Constitution*, Harvard University Press, Cambridge, MA, 1996, p 17.
63 Dworkin, above n 4, p 131.
64 Dworkin, above n 62, p 17.
65 Dworkin, above n 4, p 131.
66 Ibid p 146.

Statutory bills of rights are therefore primarily interpretive instruments, which attempt to accommodate the values of both parliamentary supremacy and judicial supervision of human rights. The underlying philosophy is said to be one of 'dialogue' between the different branches of government.[67] They attempt to strike a balance between the powers of the legislature and the judiciary by allowing each to express its own view as to what human rights require, rather than to give the unelected judiciary the 'monopoly' or 'final say' over human rights issues, a philosophy that some view as undemocratic, divisive and a threat to public confidence in the judiciary. Hence a statutory bill of rights does not empower courts to strike down democratically passed legislation, and the majority is not legally prevented from passing laws that are inconsistent with human rights: in this way, the principle of parliamentary supremacy remains intact.

In Australia, a handful of rights enjoy constitutional protection under the Commonwealth Constitution. They are mainly expressed as restrictions on federal and state powers. The Commonwealth Parliament, for instance, is prohibited from passing any law establishing a religion or preventing the free exercise of religion. The High Court has also to a limited extent found 'implied' rights in the Constitution, such as the right to freedom of political communication.

Furthermore, two Australian legislatures have in recent years adopted statutory bills of rights. The *Human Rights Act 2004* (ACT) and the *Charter of Human Rights and Responsibilities Act 2006* (Vic) incorporate most of the civil and political rights contained in the International Covenant on Civil and Political Rights, including rights to recognition and equality before the law; the right to life; protection from torture and from cruel, inhuman or degrading treatment or punishment; protection of the family and children; the right to privacy; freedom of movement, of thought, conscience, religion and belief, of assembly and association, and of expression; the right to take part in public life; rights to liberty and security of the person; the right to a fair trial and various rights in criminal proceedings; the right to be free from slavery and servitude; and various rights for minorities. Both Acts require those who interpret and apply legislation to do so in a way that is compatible with human rights to the extent

---

67   The metaphor of 'dialogue' has been used by Canadian scholars to describe the way in which legislatures are frequently able to respond to a finding of invalidity by crafting new legislation, which manages to achieve their original objectives. See P Hogg and A Bushell, 'The Charter Dialogue between Courts and Legislatures (Or Perhaps the Charter of Rights Isn't Such a Bad Thing after All)' (1997) 35 *Osgoode Hall Law Journal* 75.

that this is possible, but subject to the proviso that the interpretation must be consistent with the purpose of the legislation.[68] Each also gives the territory or state Supreme Court the power to declare legislation incompatible with human rights,[69] or incapable of being interpreted consistently with human rights,[70] without affecting its validity or enforceability. It is too early to say whether these provisions will prove to be an effective mechanism for the protection of human rights in the Australian Capital Territory and Victoria.

10.11 Socio-economic rights

We have seen that bills of rights are controversial. Even more controversial is the idea of including socio-economic rights, such as rights to health care, housing and social security, in a bill of rights, especially one which is constitutionally entrenched. These objections are based on a range of reasons. Some theorists think that socio-economic rights do not exist. Nozick is a well-known defender of this view. He believes that needy and vulnerable people do not have a moral right to assistance provided by other people or the state. For Nozick, rights exist for one reason only: to protect us from interference with our freedoms. Defenders of socio-economic rights argue, by contrast, that the very same reasons that justify civil and political rights also justify socio-economic rights. How, they ask, can one lead a meaningful and self-determining life if one is starving? This issue will be explored further in Chapter 12, where we will examine issues of socio-economic inequality and the appropriate response to them in more detail.

Some theorists who believe that socio-economic rights exist nevertheless think that they should not be included in a bill of rights. They believe that it is undesirable for courts to be given the power to enforce claims of socio-economic rights because, in their view, this poses an even greater threat to democratic values and the separation of powers than empowering courts to adjudicate civil and political rights claims. It is worth briefly examining this latter issue. Those who take this view argue that the courts do not have the legitimacy or the economic knowledge to make decisions that have implications for the allocation of resources. Such decisions are political ones, which have wide-ranging social

---

68 *Human Rights Act 2004* (ACT) s 30; *Charter of Human Rights and Responsibilities 2006* (Vic) s 32 (1).
69 *Human Rights Act 2004* (ACT) s 32.
70 *Charter of Human Rights and Responsibilities 2006* (Vic) s 36.

and economic consequences. Unelected judges should not have the power to tell the political branches of government how the budget should be spent, in the process diverting funds from other areas of spending. In support of this view, it is often argued that civil and political rights, such as the right to freedom of speech, are merely 'negative' rights, which governments respect simply by not interfering with them. When courts insist that governments should not interfere with these rights, they are therefore not imposing any financial costs on the government. On the other hand, socio-economic rights are 'positive' rights. They are rights to positive assistance from government. And if such rights are regarded as justiciable, then courts are given the power to affect the distribution of resources, a power that they are not entitled to exercise.

In fact, this view of civil and political rights as imposing merely negative or costless obligations on governments is inaccurate. For instance, as David Bilchitz notes:

> recognising a right to a fair trial means imposing on the government the costs of running an effective criminal justice system; similarly the right to vote requires the holding of regular elections. Yet, judges have generally acquitted themselves well in interpreting and enforcing these rights, and their role in this regard has not generally met with accusations that they are unqualified for the job, despite the resource implications of their decisions.[71]

Bilchitz's argument suggests that the difference between the monetary costs associated with the enforcement of civil and political rights and the costs of the enforcement of socio-economic rights is merely one of degree. We may not realise that courts are making decisions with significant resource implications in matters that concern civil and political rights, but that is probably because the costs of institutions and practices we endorse without thinking tend to be invisible to us. At the same time, even if we should not exaggerate the differences between civil and political rights and socio-economic rights insofar as their resource implications are concerned, it would also be wrong to discount the very real concerns about the separation of powers outlined above. These can, perhaps, be addressed if courts charged with adjudicating socio-economic rights claims are relatively deferential when they scrutinise the policies of the democratic branches of government.

---

71   D Bilchitz, *Poverty and Fundamental Rights*, Oxford University Press, Oxford, 2007, p 129. See also S Holmes and C R Sunstein, *The Cost of Rights: Why Liberty Depends on Taxes*, W W Norton & Company, New York, 1999.

Questions

1. The case of *Fardon v Attorney-General (Qld)* (2004) 223 CLR 575 concerned the validity of the *Dangerous Prisoners (Sexual Offenders) Act 2003* (Qld), which authorised the Supreme Court to detain in prison prisoners who had served their sentences on the basis that they posed an unacceptable risk of serious sexual offence. Such laws are sometimes justified on the basis that the right of the person who has served his sentence to be released from prison must be balanced against the rights of the potential victims of his future criminal activity. Do you find this argument convincing?
2. Why do we need to justify the idea that we have rights against the government? Isn't it obvious that the government should respect our rights?
3. How might one attempt to give a utilitarian justification for rights? Do you think that such justifications are plausible?
4. Should there be legal limits on the power of the majority to pass laws that infringe human rights?
5. In the Australian case of *Adelaide Co. of Jehovah's Witnesses, Inc. v Commonwealth* (1943) 67 CLR 116, wartime regulations were challenged by the Jehovah's Witnesses. The Regulations provided for the Governor-General to declare unlawful any associations whose existence, in his opinion, was prejudicial to the war effort. Once declared unlawful, such associations were dissolved and their property could be seized. The Governor-General had made such a declaration in relation to the Jehovah's Witnesses, who refused to bear arms or take sides in the war. The Witnesses argued that the Regulations infringed their constitutionally guaranteed freedom of religion. The Court disagreed. Rich J stated that the constitutional protection is 'not absolute. It is subject to powers and restrictions of government essential to the preservation of the community. Freedom of religion may not be invoked to cloak and dissemble subversive opinions' (at 149). Do you think that the Court was correct to hold that the Regulations were not a violation of religious freedom?
6. Do you think that it is legitimate to criticise cultural practices on the ground that they conflict with human rights?

Further reading

D Bilchitz, *Poverty and Fundamental Rights*, Oxford University Press, Oxford, 2007.

T Campbell, *Prescriptive Legal Positivism: Law, Rights and Democracy*, UCL Press, London, 2004.

T Campbell, *Rights: A Critical Introduction*, Routledge, London, 2006.

R Dworkin, *Taking Rights Seriously*, Duckworth, London, 1977, Chapter 7.

R Dworkin, *Is Democracy Possible Here? Principles for a New Political Debate,* Princeton University Press, Princeton, 2006, Chapter 2.

J Glover (ed), *Utilitarianism and its Critics*, Macmillan, London, 1990.

J Griffin, *Well-Being: Its Meaning, Measurement and Moral Importance*, Oxford University Press, Oxford, 1986.

W Kymlicka, *Contemporary Political Philosophy: An Introduction*, 2nd edn, Oxford University Press, Oxford, 2002, Chapters 1, 6.

M C Nussbaum, *Women and Human Development: The Capabilities Approach*, Cambridge University Press, Cambridge, 2000, Chapter 1.

J J C Smart and B Williams, *Utilitarianism: For and Against*, Cambridge University Press, Cambridge, 1973.

M Tushnet, 'Judicial Review of Legislation', in P Cane and M Tushnet (eds), *The Oxford Handbook of Legal Studies*, Oxford University Press, Oxford, 2003, pp 164–82.

J Waldron (ed), *Theories of Rights*, Oxford University Press, Oxford, 1984.

J Waldron, *Nonsense upon Stilts: Bentham, Burke and Marx on the Rights of Man*, Methuen, London, 1987.

J Waldron, *The Law*, Routledge, London, 1992, Chapter 5.

J Waldron, *Law and Disagreement*, Clarendon Press, Oxford, 1999.

11

Freedom

11.1 Chapter overview

To what extent should we be left at liberty to do as we please, free of state coercion? Are some of our choices not the business of the criminal law? Should we, for instance, be free to engage in conduct that does not cause harm to other people? Or are lawmakers justified in punishing any conduct which they regard as morally unacceptable? These issues are the subject of this chapter. The chapter will examine liberal views on these matters, particularly those of John Stuart Mill, H L A Hart, John Rawls and Joseph Raz. It will also examine the opposing views of the 'legal moralists', particularly the views of Lord Devlin and Robert George. The chapter will also demonstrate the relevance of this theoretical debate to contemporary controversies about pornography, abortion and voluntary euthanasia.

11.2 Possible reasons for state coercion

The threats and punishments of the criminal law interfere with our liberty. Obviously, the more limited the purposes for which the law may legitimately coerce us, the greater will be the area of protected liberty in which we have the right to make our own choices. Joel Feinberg lists four such purposes, which are commonly proposed in support of criminal prohibitions. These are: the prevention of harm to others; the prevention of harm to self; the prevention of offence; and the prevention of immoral conduct quite apart from any harm or offence caused by the conduct.[1] All of these reasons for state intervention are

---

1   J Feinberg, *Harm to Others*, Oxford University Press, New York, 1984, p 12.

based on moral considerations. The prevention of harm to others is, however, quite uncontroversial and everyone will agree that it is a legitimate aim of the state. No one can be left at liberty to assault others or steal from them, to give just two examples of harmful conduct. The other reasons for prohibiting conduct are, by contrast, more controversial. Our focus in this chapter will be on the last ground for legal prohibition, that of preventing immoral conduct quite apart from any harm or offence caused by it. I will call this a 'moralistic' reason, to distinguish it from the other kinds of reasons for state intervention.

Liberals reject the idea that criminal prohibitions can legitimately be based on moralistic reasons. They believe that conduct which does not cause harm—so-called 'victimless' conduct—is not the law's business. Legal moralists disagree. Some legal moralists take the view that *popular* morality is a morally legitimate ground for legal interference with people's choices. They think, in other words, that the mere fact that the majority regards certain conduct as immoral or degrading provides a reason to punish it—not necessarily a decisive reason, since there may be countervailing considerations, but a reason that has at least some weight. Lord Devlin provides a well-known defence of this view. Other legal moralists, such as Robert George, take the view that it is not legitimate to prohibit conduct unless it is really immoral, not merely widely believed to be immoral.[2] It must, in other words, be immoral in terms of the standards of *critical* morality. (For the distinction between popular and critical morality, see 2.5.)

Feinberg gives some examples of conduct that legal moralists would think there is a reason to prohibit just because it is immoral or thought to be immoral. These include sexual activities regarded as 'perversions'; bigamy; prostitution, even when discreetly arranged; and live sex shows or bloody gladiatorial contests presented by voluntary participants to consenting audiences.[3] It should be noted that legal moralists acknowledge that there are *practical* limits to the extent to which the criminal law should be used for moralistic purposes. What they deny is the liberal view that the prevention of immorality in the absence of harm is, *in principle*, not a legitimate reason to limit people's liberty. We turn to explore their disagreement now.

11.3 Mill's harm principle

John Stuart Mill made an influential contribution to our understanding of these matters in his book, *On Liberty*, which was written in 1859. He asked: 'What ...

---

2   R P George, *Making Men Moral: Civil Liberties and Public Morality*, Clarendon Press, Oxford, 1993, p 6.
3   Feinberg, above n 1, p 13.

is the rightful limit to the sovereignty of the individual over himself? Where does the authority of society begin? How much of human life should be assigned to individuality, and how much to society?'[4] And he answered this question in terms of his 'harm' principle, which states that the *only* legitimate use of state power over adult citizens is to prevent harm to others. Mill wrote: '[T]he only purpose for which power can be rightfully exercised over any member of a civilized community, against his will, is to prevent harm to others. His own good, either physical or moral, is not a sufficient warrant.'[5]

Mill made the same point by saying that society may legitimately take an interest in our 'other-regarding' but not our 'self-regarding' behaviour, the latter defined as behaviour that affects only oneself or other adults who have voluntarily consented to be affected.[6] Mill intended his harm principle to limit the exercise of both legal power and what he called the 'moral coercion of public opinion',[7] but in this chapter we will concentrate on the exercise of legal power, and on criminal enforcement in particular. We will also concentrate on laws that seek to enforce morality, leaving aside paternalistic laws that interfere for the sake of the individual's own protection.

It is important to understand that when Mill tells us that the only legitimate ground for legal prohibition is to prevent harm to other people, he is using the word 'harm' in a much narrower sense than we ordinarily use it, thereby placing substantial limitations on the ability of legislators to interfere with conduct. In the ordinary sense of the word, if someone adversely affects my interests, that person has harmed me.[8] Mill concedes that virtually all conduct has the potential to harm someone in this sense. In the ordinary sense of the word 'affect', all of our behaviour also has the capacity to affect others. But Mill tells us that when he talks about conduct that affects only oneself, he means 'directly, and in the first instance'.[9] Likewise, when he talks about harmful behaviour, he does not mean behaviour that causes remote harm, or as he puts it, 'merely contingent' or 'constructive' injury.[10] Instead, he means behaviour that violates a 'specific duty to the public' or causes 'perceptible hurt' to an 'assignable individual'.[11]

---

4   J S Mill [1859], 'On Liberty', in M Warnock (ed), *Utilitarianism, On Liberty, Essays on Bentham,* Collins/Fontana, 1962, p 205.
5   Ibid p 135.
6   Ibid p 137.
7   Ibid p 135.
8   Feinberg, above n 1, p 33.
9   Mill, above n 4, p 137.
10 Ibid p 213.
11 Ibid.

For Mill, causing harm is therefore not simply a matter of adversely affecting another person's interests. It involves infringing interests that we are under a *duty* not to infringe. We cannot say that we have been harmed unless someone has either deprived us of something or failed to provide us with something to which we are *entitled*. This, of course, makes the idea of 'harm' a moral notion, and it must be said that Mill does not explain its contours very clearly. It seems, though, that the harm principle is geared towards the protection of something like the interests we considered in Chapter 10, namely, those interests that we single out as 'rights'. Rights are a narrow subclass of interests, as we have seen. Thus murder, rape, assault and theft are obvious examples of the infringements of rights, whereas the ordinary inconveniences that other people cause us do not infringe our rights. The failure to perform a positive act for the benefit of others is likewise an infringement of their rights only in certain circumstances. We do not, for instance, think of a beggar as having a right to be given money by a passer-by.

It seems clear that Mill wished to confine the notion of harm to injury to a narrow class of interests, or to a definite risk of injury to such interests, because he describes conduct that can be legitimately prohibited as conduct that injures 'certain interests which … ought to be considered as *rights*'.[12] He also talks of '*selfish* abstinence from defending [others] against injury'[13] and of the failure to render to society benefits which 'it has a *right* to exact'.[14] The examples he gives include failing to giving evidence in a court of justice or failing to bear one's fair share in 'any joint work necessary to the interests of … society'.[15] But if our conduct cannot be brought under any of these headings, then however 'foolish, perverse or wrong'[16] other members of society may find it, Mill thinks that we should enjoy perfect freedom to do as we please.

Mill gives a number of examples of laws that are, in his view, illegitimate because they interfere with self-regarding or harmless conduct. Though some of his examples are rather old-fashioned, the underlying point is clear and applicable to many contemporary controversies, as we will see. Mill's examples include laws preventing people from eating certain foods for religious reasons; laws prohibiting 'public amusements', such as music, dancing and the theatre;

---

12 Ibid p 205, emphasis added.
13 Ibid p 209, emphasis added.
14 Ibid p 213, emphasis added.
15 Ibid p 136.
16 Ibid p 138.

laws prohibiting the sale of alcohol; laws preventing people from working or amusing themselves as they please on Sundays; and laws preventing the practice of polygamy.[17]

A difficult issue relates to whether causing offence to others can ever be punishable under the harm principle. Some people, for instance, object to gay and lesbian couples expressing affection for each other in public, and say that the fact that they find it objectionable constitutes harm to them. It is clear, however, that it would make nonsense of Mill's approach to regard this kind of 'harmful' behaviour as falling under the harm principle, precisely because Mill wished to use the principle to ensure a space for individual freedom of action insulated from the public's prejudices and bigotries.

But are there, perhaps, more serious kinds of publicly offensive behaviour which liberals would think it legitimate to punish? Mill did not really confront this issue. Some liberal theorists, such as Feinberg, think that in a very narrow range of circumstances it can be legitimate to criminalise public acts for the reason that they cause emotional distress.[18] On the other hand, some theorists argue that anyone who thinks that moralistic laws are illegitimate must reject such an idea.[19] A fortiori, liberalism rules out legal interference when distress is caused not by public conduct but by the mere thought that people are engaging in behaviour in private that others find offensive. As Hart says, the only liberty that could coexist with such an interpretation of the harm principle 'is liberty to do those things to which no one seriously objects. Such liberty plainly is nugatory.'[20]

It is important to understand that the reason why Mill defends a private sphere of freedom of action is not because he believes that harmless conduct cannot be immoral. Nor is he a relativist who believes that all self-regarding choices are equally valid and that it is therefore not possible to criticise such choices. On the contrary, Mill believes that people may use the liberty to which they are entitled badly. Thus he says: 'There is a degree of folly, and a degree of what may be called ... lowness or depravation of taste, which, though it cannot justify doing harm to the person who manifests it, renders him necessarily and

---

17 Ibid pp 216–24.
18 Feinberg attempts to delineate these circumstances in J Feinberg, *Offense to Others*, Oxford University Press, New York, 1985.
19 See L Alexander, 'The Legal Enforcement of Morality', in R G Frey and C H Wellman (eds), *A Companion to Applied Ethics*, Blackwell Publishing, Oxford, 2003, pp 135–40.
20 H L A Hart, *Law, Liberty and Morality*, Oxford University Press, Oxford, 1963, p 47.

properly a subject of distaste, or, in extreme cases, even of contempt.'[21] Mill thought, however, that we should merely advise such persons of the folly of their ways, not apply legal or social pressure.[22]

It will be clear that Mill's harm principle is highly protective of the value of personal autonomy. It is a radical principle, the effect of which is to carve out a substantial private area in which we are entitled to act freely, immune from state interference, no matter how immoral our conduct may be or may be thought to be. The harm principle therefore insulates our choices from the majority's dislike of them. As Hart says, Mill rejected 'moral populism'.[23] He believed that democratic government is valuable, but rejected the idea that the majority is entitled to do anything it pleases.[24] For Mill, the public sphere, in which state interference is justifiable, should therefore be narrowly defined: conduct should be regarded as public only if rights have been infringed, or are likely to be infringed, or if a duty to perform a beneficial act has been evaded.

On the other hand, because Mill thinks that we can harm people by our omissions and can therefore be compelled to perform positive acts for the benefit of others, his theory should not be confused with libertarianism, a theory which will be discussed in Chapter 12. The libertarian conception of the legitimate functions of the state is much narrower than Mill's. It should also be stressed that the private and public spheres, defined as Mill defines them, do not coincide with the sphere of what takes place *in* private and what takes place *in* public. Conduct that takes place behind closed doors, such as domestic violence, may violate another person's rights, while conduct that takes place in full public view, such as gays expressing affection for each other, may violate no rights.

We turn now to Mill's reasons for defending the harm principle. These are of a broadly utilitarian kind. He argues that the general welfare will be served if the state restricts liberty only in order to prevent harm to others. This may seem hard to understand. Surely a utilitarian would simply weigh up the majority's distaste for certain conduct against the desire of a minority to indulge in it? And surely the majority's desire to restrict the conduct would frequently win out if such an exercise were to be undertaken? The harm principle undoubtedly has the potential to frustrate the majority's wishes and it therefore appears to be in conflict with the general welfare. How, then, can Mill say that it is *required* by the

---

21 Mill, above n 4, p 207.
22 Ibid p 206.
23 H L A Hart, *Law, Liberty and Morality*, Oxford University Press, Oxford, 1963, p 79.
24 Ibid.

general welfare? Mill's answer is that following the harm principle will serve the end of maximum happiness, overall and in the long run. He gives three reasons for this belief.

First, Mill argues that experimentation with different lifestyles is valuable for society. To forbid people from undertaking such 'experiments in living',[25] when they do not harm anyone, makes it difficult to make informed judgments about what is good and bad for human beings and therefore deprives society of valuable knowledge.[26] Second, enjoying and exercising personal freedom is 'one of the principal ingredients of human happiness'.[27] Third, Mill suggests that the principle of maximising happiness is not a reliable basis for decision-making in the area of interference with personal choice, because the majority cannot be trusted to make correct use of the principle. In other words, Mill gives an indirect utilitarian argument for the harm principle: the *end* is maximum happiness but the best *means* to that end is the use of a non-utilitarian principle to decide when limits on liberty are justifiable. (For discussion of indirect utilitarianism, see 10.5.)

Thus Mill argues that if we allow the majority to curtail liberty on utilitarian grounds, rather than on the basis of the harm principle, the majority will quite often make mistakes as to what will maximise human happiness. Mill writes that the opinion of the majority 'on questions of self-regarding conduct, is quite as likely to be wrong as right'.[28] For '[i]n its interferences with personal conduct it is seldom thinking of anything but the enormity of acting or feeling differently from itself'[29] and it ignores 'the pleasure or convenience of those whose conduct [it] censure[s]'.[30] Since the majority's prejudices will prevent its being able to weigh up the costs and benefits of interference accurately, Mill concludes that the only way to maximise human happiness is to prevent the majority from passing moralistic legislation, thereby safeguarding freedom of action in self-regarding matters.

11.4 The concept of state neutrality

An important contemporary liberal approach justifies principled limits on the exercise of state power by means of the idea that the state should be 'neutral'.

---

25 Mill, above n 4, p 185.
26 Ibid.
27 Ibid.
28 Ibid p 215.
29 Ibid.
30 Ibid.

Rawls has defended this idea in detail. He makes a distinction between the 'right' and the 'good'. The right is the sphere of principles of justice, including the protection of rights, whereas the good is the sphere of value. Conceptions of the good life fall within the sphere of value. A view of the good life is a view about what goals it is worthwhile to pursue and about what ways of life are intrinsically worthy. Rawls argues that the state's exercise of power should not be informed by a view about the intrinsic superiority of a particular conception of the good life. The state should, in other words, confine itself to providing a framework of rights and be 'neutral' (in the sense of 'not take sides') on the controversial question of what kind of life it is good to lead. Instead of promoting a particular version of the good, it should allow people to make up their own minds on this matter, freeing them to pursue their own conception of the good.[31]

Of course, Rawls does not say that the state should be neutral on *all* moral questions. Just as Mill argued that the state is entitled to prevent harmful conduct, Rawls argues that the state must insist on the protection of rights and punish those who violate them. Why, then, is it justifiable for the state to 'take sides' on matters of the right, but not on matters of the good? Rawls believes that for the exercise of state power to be legitimate, it must treat all citizens fairly; for Rawls, this means that it must be acceptable to everyone. When the state enforces the principles of justice, it does treat everyone fairly, according to Rawls, because these are principles that all citizens, regardless of their conception of the good, can be reasonably expected to endorse as the basis for social cooperation. The need to enforce the principles of justice therefore provides a morally acceptable justification for state interference with liberty. By contrast, reasonable people disagree about matters of ultimate value and it is unrealistic to expect that these disagreements will ever be resolved. In order to treat everyone fairly, the state must therefore avoid taking a stand on such disputed matters: it must treat such matters as 'private'.

Neutralist liberals therefore conclude that if individuals are not violating anyone's rights, they should be left free to pursue their own conception of the good. This is not to say that all views about the good are equally valid or that all ways of life are equally valuable. Rawls, like Mill, is not a relativist or a sceptic about the possibility of moral truth.[32] He merely says that it is impossible to resolve our disagreements about the good and that they should therefore be

---

31 J Rawls, *Political Liberalism*, Columbia University Press, New York, 1993, pp 190–5.
32 Ibid pp 62–3.

taken off the political agenda. There are obvious difficulties faced by this view. For instance, why should we not expect as much conflict among reasonable people over matters of justice as there is over matters of the good? And is it true that confining the state to the enforcement of a framework of rights is fair to all conceptions of the good? These issues will be pursued further in Chapter 12, where Rawls's theory of justice will be explored in more detail.

11.5 Lord Devlin's conservative version of legal moralism

In his essay, 'Morals and the Criminal Law', Lord Devlin attacked the liberal view of the function of criminal law. His target was the Report of the Committee on Homosexual Offences and Prostitution (the Wolfenden Report), presented to the British government in 1957, which concluded that prostitution should not be punishable and that homosexuality should be decriminalised. The Report clearly adopted the liberal position, stating that a decisive consideration was the importance of individual freedom of choice and action. For this reason, it took the view that sin should not be equated with crime, and that 'there must remain a realm of private morality and immorality which is ... not the law's business'.[33]

Devlin disagreed. He argues that society has the right to use the criminal law to enforce popular morality. There may be various practical reasons why, in particular circumstances, it should not do so, but there are no principled reasons preventing society from using the law to punish immorality as such. For there is no principled distinction—such as the one Mill sought to draw, using the criterion of harm, or the one drawn by Rawls between the right and the good— dividing the private from the public sphere. 'It is not possible', Devlin says, 'to define inflexibly areas of morality into which the law is in no circumstances to be allowed to enter'.[34] Devlin's arguments for this conclusion are not altogether clear, but the following discussion will track the way in which they are usually interpreted.

Devlin begins by pointing out that the criminal law as it stands does not conform to Mill's harm principle. Consider the situation of a doctor who gives a lethal injection to a terminally ill person at that person's request. In terms of Mill's definition of harm, the doctor's conduct is harmless. After all, the patient

---

33 Report of the Committee on Homosexual Offences and Prostitution, Her Majesty's Stationery Office, London, 1957, para 61.
34 P Devlin, *The Enforcement of Morals*, Oxford University Press, Oxford, 1965, p 13.

has voluntarily consented to be killed. No one has been done a tangible injury. But the law does not accept consent as a defence to a charge of murder. The doctor will be found guilty of murder, the patient's consent notwithstanding. It follows that the criminal law punishes some activity that is harmless in Mill's sense. It prohibits voluntary euthanasia not because it violates anyone's rights, but, as Devlin says, because it is thought to be 'an offence against society'.[35] Euthanasia is prohibited because it threatens 'one of the great moral principles upon which society is based, that is, the sanctity of human life'.[36] Devlin concludes that when the criminal law forbids voluntary euthanasia, it is enforcing a moral principle as such.

Devlin next argues that society not only has the right to pass judgment on the personal conduct of its members, but it also has the right to use the law to enforce its judgments, regardless of whether the personal conduct takes place in private and regardless of whether it causes direct harm to a specific person. This is because society is held together by shared moral beliefs. Devlin writes: '[A] recognized morality is as necessary to society as ... a recognized government.'[37] Since Devlin believes that social order would break down without morality, he concludes that the mere practice of immorality is potentially as threatening to society's survival as treason and therefore that '[t]he suppression of vice is as much the law's business as the suppression of subversive activities'.[38]

Of course, having told us that society has the right to enforce popular judgments about morality, Devlin needs to explain how we go about ascertaining the moral judgments of society. He gives a distinctive answer to this question. He says that immorality is what the 'reasonable man' or the 'right-minded man' considers to be immoral. This reasonable man should not, however, be confused with the 'rational man'. For the reasonable man 'is not expected to reason about anything and his judgment may be largely a matter of feeling'.[39] The reasonable man, Devlin tells us, is 'the man in the Clapham omnibus' or 'the man in the jury box'.[40] His judgments are the judgments of 'common sense'.[41]

Having argued that society has the right to use the weapon of the law to enforce the moral 'feelings' of the reasonable man and to prohibit immorality

---

35   Ibid p 6.
36   Ibid.
37   Ibid p 11.
38   Ibid pp 13–14.
39   Ibid p 15.
40   Ibid.
41   Ibid p 17.

as such, Devlin turns at the end of his essay to discuss the circumstances in which society should exercise its right. His view is that the legislature should not necessarily criminalise all actions that the majority regards as immoral, for there may be countervailing considerations. For instance, the legislature should not punish private immorality if the reasonable man does not feel a 'real feeling of reprobation', amounting to 'intolerance, indignation and disgust'.[42] On the other hand, if a vice is regarded as 'so abominable that its mere presence is an offence',[43] then society should legislate against it. If the conduct is consensual and takes place in private, this may be another relevant factor, for the interest in privacy may on occasion outweigh the public interest in preserving the moral order. Furthermore, the standards to which the law holds us are necessarily less demanding than the standards to which morality holds us.

But these are merely relevant, not decisive, factors, according to Devlin. There are no hard and fast principles circumscribing what the legislature may legitimately do and there is certainly no right to be left alone in the area of personal conduct that does not directly harm others. The issue is a practical one, demanding a pragmatic judgment in each case, which takes into account all the relevant factors. For instance, according to Devlin, adultery is just as harmful to the social fabric as bigamy but it would be too difficult to enforce a law that made adultery a crime. Adultery should therefore be tolerated, while bigamy should be prohibited. 'There is', Devlin says, 'no logic to be found in this ... The fact that adultery, fornication and lesbianism are untouched by the criminal law does not prove that homosexuality ought not to be touched.'[44] There is, in other words, no principle that serves to distinguish legitimate legislative aims from illegitimate ones. Instead, it may merely be impractical, in certain circumstances, to punish conduct that the majority regards as immoral—namely, when the costs of doing so are greater than the benefits. It will be evident that Devlin's views on this matter are very different from the views of a theorist like Dworkin, who stresses the need for integrity in the law.

11.6 Some criticisms of Devlin

We have seen that one of Devlin's arguments revolves around the fact that there are circumstances in which the criminal law refuses to accept consent as a

---

42 Ibid.
43 Ibid.
44 Ibid p 22.

defence to a criminal charge. Devlin concludes that the criminal law as it stands does not conform to Mill's harm principle. In response, Feinberg points out that while it may be true that the criminal law punishes some harmless conduct, the harm principle aims to tell us not what conduct the law *does* prohibit but what conduct it may *legitimately* prohibit. Thus, although Devlin is right that the law does not, in fact, always reflect liberal principles, this does not prove that the liberal principles are wrong.[45]

Furthermore, Feinberg goes on to argue, there are some occasions on which the law's refusal to accept consent as a defence can be explained by reference to the harm principle, that is, without recourse to the idea that the law is enforcing a moral principle as such. Consider a case in which someone consents to be maimed or disfigured for the purposes of defrauding an insurance company. The person's conduct harms an identifiable third party and it is therefore possible to justify the law's refusal to accept consent as a defence on perfectly liberal, harm-based grounds. Or again, consider a case where someone in a psychotic state consents to be maimed or disfigured. Again, there are acceptable non-moralistic reasons for not accepting the consent as a defence, namely, that the consent is not genuinely voluntary. But if someone in sound mind and without intent to perpetrate a fraud consents to be maimed, then Feinberg thinks that the law *should* accept the consent as a defence. He gives the example of someone who sells one of his or her kidneys. Provided that the bargain is not exploitative, Feinberg thinks that this is a private choice with which the law should not interfere.[46]

Hart attacks other aspects of Devlin's argument. One focus of his attack is Devlin's conception of morality, namely, popular reactions that may or may not have a rational foundation. Hart points out that most opponents of the liberal point of view have been objectivists about morality. Believing that morality has a rational or (for some theorists) a religious foundation, they see nothing wrong with using the state to enforce it. As we will see in 11.7, this is how George argues. Devlin, however, is not an objectivist about morality and he wishes to translate not reasoned judgments about morality into law but rather gut feelings of indignation, intolerance and disgust. Hart believes that this is an entirely unacceptable justification for legislation. He argues that legislators

---

45   J Feinberg, *Harmless Wrongdoing*, Oxford University Press, New York, 1990, p 165.
46   Ibid pp 170–1.

should subject such feelings to 'critical scrutiny',[47] considering whether they rest on ignorance, superstition or misunderstanding, and whether 'the misery to many parties, the blackmail and the other evil consequences of punishment'[48] have been fully understood. A particular concern for Hart in this regard stems from his belief that laws that require suppression of sexual impulses 'may create misery of a quite special degree'.[49]

Hart also takes issue with Devlin's view that a shared morality is essential to society, and with his related comparison between sexual immorality and treason, a comparison that Hart finds 'absurd'.[50] Hart points out that Devlin's claim that the preservation of a society's morality is necessary for its existence is an empirical one. Devlin does not, however, back up his claim with any evidence and Hart says that '[n]o reputable historian has maintained this thesis and there is indeed much evidence against it'.[51] Hart therefore believes Devlin is wrong in thinking that offences against 'decency' threaten the very fabric of society. Hart says that there must be a consensus of moral opinion on certain matters if society is not to degenerate into anarchy. For instance, it would not be worth living in a society in which people did not agree that murder and theft are morally wrong. But morality is not a 'seamless web',[52] according to Hart, and it is therefore not the case that all of a majority's moral beliefs are of equal importance to social stability and that deviating from society's moral code in any respect will lead to society's disintegration. On the contrary, in Hart's view, 'we have ample evidence for believing that people ... will not think any better of murder, cruelty and dishonesty, merely because some private sexual practice which they abominate is not punished by the law'.[53] If this is the case, what value can be ascribed to preventing such practices? Hart answers that the value is not a moral value. It is merely a 'taboo', belonging to the 'prehistory of morality'.[54]

---

47 H L A Hart, 'Immorality and Treason', in R Dworkin (ed), *The Philosophy of Law*, Oxford University Press, Oxford, 1977, p 87.
48 Ibid.
49 Hart, above n 20, p 22.
50 Hart, above n 47, p 86.
51 Hart, above n 20, p 50.
52 Hart, above n 47, p 85.
53 Ibid p 86.
54 Hart, above n 20, pp 57, 83.

11.7 Perfectionism, liberalism and legal moralism

Some theorists think that it is legitimate to use the law to encourage us to lead lives that are intrinsically worthy and to discourage us from leading lives that are intrinsically unworthy. These theorists are called 'perfectionists'. They have a view about what is objectively good for human beings and what conduces to human flourishing. Furthermore, they believe that the state should support and promote this ideal of the good, while discouraging inferior conceptions of the good. Perfectionists are therefore strongly opposed to Rawls's view, discussed in 11.4, that the state should be neutral on matters of the good life. They believe, on the contrary, that the state should take an interest in our moral well-being. Waldron defines perfectionism as taking the view that 'legislators and officials may consider what is good and valuable in life and what is ignoble and depraved when drafting the laws and setting the framework for social and personal relationships'.[55]

Some perfectionists are nevertheless in favour of an expansive sphere of personal liberty, believing that it is not permissible to use the *criminal* law to achieve perfectionist objectives. They would confine the state's efforts to promote the good to *non-coercive* policies. Raz is an example of such a 'perfectionist liberal'. He thinks that individual autonomy is an essential aspect of a good human life and that government is under a duty to promote it. He writes that the value of autonomy 'requires governments to create morally valuable opportunities, and eliminate repugnant ones'.[56] At the same time, Raz believes that laws that punish immoral but harmless conduct do not respect the value of autonomy. This leads Raz to argue that the only justifiable ground for coercively interfering with a person's choices is to prevent harm to others or to self.[57]

Raz therefore draws a sharp line between coercively promoting the good, which is illegitimate, in his view, and non-coercively promoting it, which he believes is legitimate. Raz gives the following examples of non-coercive promotion of the good: '[c]onferring honours on creative and performing artists, giving grants or loans to people who start community centres, taxing

---

[55] J Waldron, 'Autonomy and Perfectionism in Raz's *Morality of Freedom*' (1989) 62 *Southern California Law Review* 1097, 1102.
[56] J Raz, *The Morality of Freedom*, Clarendon Press, Oxford, 1986, p 417.
[57] Ibid pp 418–19.

one kind of leisure activity, e.g., hunting, more heavily than others'.[58] It can be questioned, however, whether taxes and subsidies are as non-coercive as Raz supposes.[59] A further question relates to the fact that Raz maintains that autonomy has no value when it is used to make bad choices.[60] If so, it can be asked why the value of autonomy should prevent the state from criminalising harmless bad choices.[61]

Raz is a liberal because he opposes the idea of punishing harmless immorality. Other perfectionists, however, reject liberalism. George is an example. He writes in the natural law tradition of Aristotle and Aquinas, whose central claims on this matter he summarises as follows:

> [L]aws forbidding certain powerfully seductive and corrupting vices (some sexual, some not) can help people to establish and preserve a virtuous character by (1) preventing the (further) self-corruption which follows from acting out a choice to indulge in immoral conduct; (2) preventing the bad example by which others are induced to emulate such behaviour; (3) helping to preserve the moral ecology in which people make their morally self-constituting choices; and (4) educating people about moral right and wrong.[62]

George agrees with Devlin that it can be legitimate to punish immoral conduct even if it does not cause direct harm to anyone, but he rejects Devlin's view that the morality which can be criminally enforced is popular morality. For Devlin, as we have seen, whatever threatens to undermine social cohesion can be prohibited. In some societies, polygamy might be generally considered to be wicked, in which case polygamy will undermine social cohesion and it will be legitimate to prohibit it. However, in other societies, polygamy might be necessary for social cohesion, and in such societies it would be wrong to prohibit polygamy. Whether polygamy is objectively right or wrong is irrelevant for Devlin.[63]

By contrast, George argues for the legitimacy of moralistic legislation that enforces *true* morality. Thus he maintains that majorities are not entitled to enact their 'mere prejudices'[64] into law and he argues that preserving social cohesion

---

58 Ibid p 161.
59 Waldron, above n 55, 1141–52.
60 Raz, above n 56, p 380.
61 Waldron, above n 55, 1141.
62 George, above n 2, p 1.
63 Ibid pp 53–5.
64 Ibid p x.

per se does not justify moralistic legislation.[65] George writes: 'A concern for social cohesion around a shared morality can justify some instances of the enforcement of morals but only if that morality is true.'[66] Likewise, he says that 'only real vices may be banned'.[67] In summary, according to George, the criminal law is legitimately used not only to protect us against harm, but to help us to lead 'morally upright lives' and to protect us from 'the corrupting influences of vice',[68] subject to the sorts of pragmatic considerations for tolerating immorality mentioned by Devlin. Liberals, by contrast, will argue that forcing people to lead good lives is oppressive.

11.8 Pornography

Now that we have examined the theoretical considerations relevant to deciding whether it is justifiable to punish harmless immorality, we are in a position to apply our reflections to some controversial topical issues. Let us begin with the issue of pornography, confining our discussion to situations in which children are neither exposed to the materials nor used in their production. Everyone will agree that the making of child pornography should be a crime. It is the prohibition of adult pornography that raises the more difficult issues. What follows is not intended as a full discussion of these issues, but merely aims to highlight the relevance of the debate between liberals and legal moralists to questions about prohibiting the production, distribution and consumption of pornography.

If we examine the law governing the availability of sexually explicit materials (so-called 'obscene' materials) in a number of common law jurisdictions, it is possible to discern two main reasons for which the law has traditionally prohibited their dissemination: either the law relies on the idea of offence to community standards of decency caused by explicit depictions of sexuality, or it relies on the tendency of the materials to deprave and corrupt their users.

Neither of these legal aims would pass Mill's test or Rawls's test, since the materials are prohibited not on the grounds that anyone has been harmed or anyone's rights have been infringed. Rather, they are prohibited on the moralistic grounds of their offensiveness to the community or of their tendency

---

65 Ibid p 53.
66 Ibid p 71.
67 Ibid p 73, n 49.
68 Ibid p 20.

to cause 'moral harm' to their users (a harm which does not, of course, fall under Mill's definition of harm). The first is an aim that Devlin would endorse, the second an aim that natural law perfectionists such as George would endorse. A liberal would also regard the idea that pornography causes harm to society by undermining community values as an impermissible reason to ban it. It seems to follow that if one takes a liberal approach to these matters, insisting that harm or the violation of rights is the only legitimate basis for criminalising conduct, the enjoyment of sexually explicit materials should be regarded as a private matter, outside the legitimate reach of the law.

But before we can come to this conclusion, we need to examine an important contemporary argument made by feminists such as Catharine MacKinnon and Andrea Dworkin. This argument calls for the suppression of certain sexually explicit materials, not, it is claimed, on the traditional moralistic grounds just described, but rather on grounds that even liberal theorists should endorse. These feminists distinguish erotica from pornography. They define erotica as the explicit depiction of sex between equals and they take the view that adults who wish to consume erotica should be free to do so. Pornography, by contrast, depicts sexual violence towards women or depicts women in a degrading or dehumanising way, as sexual objects. On the view of these feminists, it sends the message that women are inferior, and this message is a cause of discriminatory and violent acts directed towards women. They point to cases in which rapists and killers have blamed pornography for their crimes and they conclude that pornography harms women. They also argue that pornography subordinates and silences women and that it therefore infringes women's right to equality of treatment. For both of these reasons, therefore, pornography can legitimately be suppressed.

It will be obvious that the feminist attack on pornography presents itself as very different from the conservative approach of thinkers such as Devlin. It claims that its aim is not to prevent offence or 'moral harm'. After all, it says, it is not opposed to the explicit depiction of sex as such. Its stated aim is rather to protect women against danger and subordination, which are legitimate and non-moralistic concerns. Hence the title of one of MacKinnon's articles on this matter: 'Not a Moral Issue'.[69]

---

69   C A MacKinnon, *Feminism Unmodified: Discourses on Life and Law*, Harvard University Press, Cambridge, MA, 1987, p 146.

This view informed the finding in the Canadian case of *R v Butler*,[70] which upheld the constitutionality of the obscenity provisions of the Canadian Criminal Code in the face of a freedom of speech challenge. The majority—apparently endorsing Mill's approach—said that deviations from society's morals should not be punished if they cause no harm. If the obscenity provisions had aimed to prevent 'dirt for dirt's sake',[71] they would therefore have been invalid. The majority found, however, that this was not the case. On the contrary, the provisions were justified by the need to prevent harm to women and to protect women's right to equality, because sexually explicit materials that depict sex with violence, or that depict sex which is degrading and dehumanising, reinforce male–female stereotypes and make antisocial and unlawful acts against women more likely.

But is this reasoning really an accurate application of Mill's approach? Would someone who adheres to Mill's harm principle accept this argument? It would all depend on the facts. Violence and sexual inequality are major social problems and if exposure to pornography makes violent and discriminatory acts against women probable, the harm principle would certainly require its suppression. Empirical investigation is therefore required, but such research is unfortunately inconclusive, especially given the fact that the message that women are inferior is sent in many ways in our society, not all of them pornographic. It is consequently very difficult to demonstrate a direct link between pornography and violence against women.

Nadine Strossen points out that in many places where pornography is banned there is more violence and discrimination against women than in places where it is openly available.[72] Furthermore, three national commissions that reported on the matter—the 1970 Report of the Commission on Obscenity and Pornography in the US,[73] the 1979 report of the Williams Commission in the UK,[74] and the 1985 Special Committee Report on Pornography and Prostitution in Canada[75]—found that there was no causal link between the consumption of pornography and criminal or antisocial acts. These commissions took the view that the causes of a violent personality lie in childhood, long before any

---

70 *R v Butler* (1982) 89 DLR (4th) 449.
71 *R v Butler* (1982) 89 DLR (4th) 449, 476.
72 N Strossen, *Defending Pornography: Free Speech, Sex, and the Fight for Women's Rights*, Scribner, New York, 1995, pp 253–6.
73 Report of the Committee on Obscenity and Pornography, United States Government Printing Office, Washington, 1970.
74 Report of the Committee on Obscenity and Film Censorship, Her Majesty's Stationery Office, London, 1979.
75 Report of the Special Committee on Pornography and Prostitution, Canadian Government Publishing Centre, Ottawa, 1985.

exposure to pornography, and that the desire to consume violent pornography is a symptom of a violent personality rather than a cause of it.

Even the findings of the US Meese Commission,[76] which are often regarded as supporting the feminist position on pornography, are very weak. The Meese Commission found that sexually violent materials (but not degrading or dehumanising materials) raise the probability of sexually violent behaviour to some extent. The Commission noted, however, that this extent might be very small. It further found that the evidence for even this weak claim was problematic and that it could not be relied on in circumstances where we require great confidence in our empirical findings.[77]

But if the risk to women's rights created by even the most objectionable pornographic materials is as speculative as it seems to be, then it seems that the harm principle would not, after all, support their suppression and that the attempt to invoke it in this context may be misplaced. Mill makes clear that the harm principle is applicable only where there is strong evidence of a definite risk to people's rights—that, as we have seen, is what gives his principle its bite. It has not, however, been shown that even the worst kinds of pornographic materials create such a danger. Consequently, the harm principle cannot be used to justify the outright prohibition of such materials and the feminist argument against pornography would appear to be a moralistic argument in disguise.[78] The same would be true on Rawls's approach. If pornography does not present a real risk of violations of rights, the only argument for prohibiting it would be the argument that consumption of pornography is a degrading activity. If the state were to prohibit it on that basis, it would be doing so on the basis that the choice to consume pornography is intrinsically morally inferior. This, for Rawls, would be an illegitimate reason to ban it.

Of course, women's rights may be violated in the course of producing pornography—women may, for example, be coerced or tricked into making pornography, or assaulted while making it—and the harm principle would certainly demand the criminalisation of such conduct. Furthermore, it could be argued that the harm principle would support regulations that restrict access to pornography, for instance by confining its sale to specialised sex shops. The

---

76 Attorney General's Commission on Pornography: Final Report, United States Government Printing Office, Washington, 1986.
77 F Schauer, 'Causation Theory and the Causes of Sexual Violence' (1987) 4 *American Bar Foundation Research Journal* 737, 753, 767.
78 D Meyerson, *Rights Limited: Freedom of Expression, Religion and the South African Constitution*, Juta, Cape Town, 1997, pp 136-7.

justification would be that people have a right not to have pornography thrust on their attention against their will. At the same time, although some restrictions on access to pornography may be compatible with the liberal rejection of moralistic laws, liberals would insist that these restrictions not be excessive. Liberals would not, for instance, accept the reasoning of the United States Supreme Court in *Paris Adult Theatre I v Slaton*.[79]

This case involved the showing of obscene films by a cinema that refused admission to minors, gave due warning of the nature of the films, and did not use any offensive external advertising. Chief Justice Burger nevertheless held that the films could be banned, saying that the idea of a privacy right and a place of public accommodation were, in this context, mutually exclusive. In this connection, he quoted Alexander Bickel's remark that 'what is commonly read and seen and heard and done intrudes upon us all, want it or not'.[80] Chief Justice Burger then went on to describe as 'morally neutral' the view that the exhibition of obscene material in a public theatre jeopardises the majority's 'right to maintain a decent society'.[81]

Mill would not agree. For Mill, the fact that conduct occurs in a place of 'public accommodation' would not automatically make it public conduct, that is, conduct with which the law may legitimately interfere. Likewise, the fact that the showing of obscene films 'intrudes' on people would not, in itself, convince Mill that the films should be banned. Virtually all activity 'intrudes', for 'no one is an island', as Mill himself conceded. The question, for Mill, would be whether the intrusion violates a right in the sense of a distinct and assignable obligation owed to a definite individual or individuals. Given the fact that the films were inoffensively advertised, that minors were excluded, and that the audience was forewarned, Mill would presumably not find any such violation. Certainly, Mill would not agree with Chief Justice Burger that there is any such thing as 'a right to maintain a decent society'.

11.9 Abortion

Abortion is another issue that can usefully be approached in the light of our discussion of the legitimate reasons for state coercion. What is the aim of laws that criminalise abortion? Is the justification they offer for coercive interference

---

79 *Paris Adult Theatre I v Slaton*, 413 US 49 (1973).
80 *Paris Adult Theatre I v Slaton*, 413 US 49, 59 (1973).
81 *Paris Adult Theatre I v Slaton*, 413 US 49, 69 (1973).

with women's choices legitimate or illegitimate? The following discussion of abortion will be confined to this particular issue.

In answering this question, much depends on how we think of the moral status of the foetus. (I will use the word 'foetus' to refer to the unborn child from the beginning of pregnancy until its end.) What kind of creature is it from the moral point of view? Scientific evidence about conception does not help us to answer this question. We know that within approximately twenty-four hours after the sperm has penetrated the ovum, the forty-six chromosomes that make up a person's unique genetic identity are present. But what *moral* significance should we attach to the start of a new genetic identity? How should we *treat* it? Science cannot answer this question. It is a philosophical question and we therefore need to canvass different philosophical answers to it.

Some people take the view that the foetus is, from the moment of conception, just like a baby in terms of its moral status. It has interests of its own from the moment of conception; it enjoys all the rights that a baby enjoys; and it is entitled to be treated in exactly the same way in which we treat babies. If this view is correct, everyone—not only legal moralists but also liberals—will agree that the state is entitled to prevent abortion. After all, if the foetus from the moment of conception has the same rights as a baby, destroying it would violate its right to life, and abortion would be as serious as murder. There would therefore be a straightforward rights-based or harm-based justification for anti-abortion laws. Indeed, if this view is correct, it would follow that the state not only may but that it *must* prohibit abortion: the state would have a responsibility to forbid all abortions, just as it has a responsibility to forbid the murder of babies.[82] Dworkin calls this a 'derivative' justification for anti-abortion laws, because it is derived from rights and interests that it ascribes to foetuses.[83]

Dworkin argues against the derivative view. First, he claims that although many people espouse the derivative view, they do so only as a matter of rhetoric.[84] He points out that most people who claim to hold the derivative view believe that abortion is morally permissible in certain circumstances. They are likely to believe, for instance, that abortion is permissible to save the mother's life, or to terminate a pregnancy that resulted from rape, or even in cases of severe foetal abnormality. But reasons of this kind would never justify the killing

---

82 R Dworkin, *Life's Dominion: An Argument about Abortion and Euthanasia,* HarperCollins Publishers, London, 1993, pp 109–10.
83 Ibid p 11.
84 Ibid pp 20–1.

of a baby. The same people would undoubtedly regard it as murder if a doctor were to kill a newborn baby in order to save its mother's life. And they would say the same about the killing of a severely disabled baby or a baby that was conceived as the result of a rape. A baby does not forfeit its right to life because its mother was raped or because it is severely disabled.[85]

The fact that most people who say that a foetus has the same moral status as a baby are nevertheless willing to countenance abortion for reasons that would never justify the killing of a baby shows, according to Dworkin, that they do not *really* believe that the foetus has a right to life. Dworkin gives the example of US President George H W Bush and Vice President Dan Quayle—both avowed 'pro-lifers'—who in the 1992 presidential campaign said they would support their own daughters if they wished to have an abortion. Dworkin argues that they would surely not do that if they really thought that abortion meant the murder of their grandchildren.[86]

Having argued that most people do not believe in foetal rights, Dworkin goes on to argue that they are correct. He argues that it is incoherent to ascribe to an early foetus an interest in remaining alive and therefore a right not to be killed, because, according to Dworkin, something has interests of its own only when it has some form of mental life. That is, it must be able to suffer pain and have experiences. In order to have an interest in continuing to live, even more complex capacities are required.[87] Since scientists have shown that the neurological developments that make interests of any kind possible take place only late in pregnancy, abortions in the first two trimesters of pregnancy are not against the interests of the foetuses whose lives they take away.[88] Dworkin concludes that the derivative objection to such abortions does not make sense: it is not possible to object to abortion in the first two trimesters on the basis of the value of its life *to* a foetus.

If Dworkin is right that the advocates of restrictive abortion laws do not really believe the foetus has a right to life, why, then, are they against allowing women the right to choose? According to Dworkin, they believe that there is intrinsic value in human life. They see the foetus as a living human organism, which has 'sacred' or intrinsic value from the moment of its conception, and

---

85 Ibid p 32.
86 Ibid p 20.
87 Ibid pp 16–18.
88 Ibid pp 17–18.

whose destruction is therefore always an intrinsically bad thing.[89] They see the foetus in somewhat the same way that we see artworks or species diversity: as having value in itself. If a species disappears, we see that as objectively bad—bad because the world has been diminished, not because anyone suffers as a result.[90] Likewise, the advocates of restrictive abortion laws believe that it is bad to destroy a foetus, even though it has no interest in surviving. Dworkin calls this a 'detached' argument against abortion, because it is detached from the view that a foetus has rights and interests.[91] It takes the view that human life has intrinsic moral significance and that abortion is therefore always, in itself, a destruction of something valuable. Dworkin thinks that the view that a foetus has rights is wrong. He concedes, however, that the view that a foetus has intrinsic value cannot be refuted.[92]

Let us suppose that Dworkin is right and that the opponents of abortion wish to prohibit it not because the foetus has rights but because abortion is an insult to the intrinsic value of human life. This raises the question whether the protection of the intrinsic value of foetal life is a legitimate reason to criminalise abortion. Dworkin puts the question like this: 'Should any state or nation have [the] power, as a matter of justice and decent government' to 'decide for everyone that abortion insults the intrinsic value of human life and to prohibit it on that ground?'[93] Dworkin answers 'No', thereby safeguarding what he calls 'a woman's sovereignty over the use of her own body for procreation'.[94] His route to this liberal conclusion is, though, quite distinctive.

Dworkin rejects Rawls's 'neutralist' idea that political principles should be insulated from more comprehensive ethical ideals about the nature of the good life.[95] Instead, his liberal conclusions depend on his belief, mentioned in 10.5, that there are principles of human dignity, which governments must respect, and that one of these is the principle of personal responsibility. This principle asserts that 'we have a right and a responsibility to decide for ourselves' about certain matters.[96] These are matters of 'fundamental ethical importance for

---

89 Ibid p 11.
90 Ibid pp 71–2, 75.
91 Ibid p 11.
92 B C Zipursky and J E Fleming, 'Rights, Responsibilities, and Reflections on the Sanctity of Life', in A Ripstein (ed), *Ronald Dworkin*, Cambridge University Press, New York, 2007, p 115.
93 Dworkin, above n 82, p 154.
94 Ibid p 54.
95 R Dworkin, *Sovereign Virtue: The Theory and Practice of Equality*, Harvard University Press, Cambridge, MA, 2000, p 5.
96 R Dworkin, *Is Democracy Possible Here? Principles for a New Political Debate*, Princeton University Press, Princeton, 2006, p 20.

[ourselves]'[97] and among these matters are choices that reflect religious values as well as 'values of the same ethical character and function as the religious values of religious people'.[98] Dworkin writes: 'It is inconsistent with someone's dignity ever to submit to the coercive authority of others in deciding what role religious or comparable ethical values should play in his life.'[99] Furthermore, Dworkin thinks that decisions about abortion fall into this category and are therefore an ethical matter for which we are personally responsible. His arguments for this conclusion are as follows.

Dworkin argues that there are different views about what makes life sacred or intrinsically valuable. Some people value human life primarily because of the biological marvel that it represents, whether they trace this to evolution or God. Others put the emphasis on the way in which human beings consciously confer value on themselves. They emphasise the creative investment humans make in their lives. Those who assign greater importance to the human investment in life will, in most circumstances, find the destruction of a foetus less of an evil than the frustration of a woman's attempt to determine her own fate. By contrast, those who emphasise nature's investment believe that the best way to respect the value of human life is to allow abortion only in the most exceptional of circumstances.[100] Anti-abortion laws in effect take the latter view.

Dworkin then goes on to argue that convictions of this kind—about how and why human life has importance and therefore about what justifies its destruction—are fundamental to our moral personalities, 'touching the ultimate purpose and value of human life itself'.[101] Indeed, Dworkin argues that our disagreements on this matter are so fundamental that they are akin to religious disagreements.[102] Hence, according to him, anti-abortion laws take sides in an essentially religious debate. And since the state is not entitled to prevent people from deciding on a religious matter for themselves, because that would violate their religious liberty, Dworkin concludes that the aim of protecting the intrinsic value of life is likewise an illegitimate basis on which to criminalise abortion. The majority, he tells us, is not entitled to impose its conception of the sacred on everyone but must respect a woman's contrary views on this matter, just as it must show respect for religious beliefs that it does not share. Just as we have

---

97 Ibid p 60.
98 Ibid p 61.
99 Ibid p 146.
100 Dworkin, above n 82, pp 89–94.
101 Ibid p 158.
102 Ibid pp 160–8.

the right to confront religious questions for ourselves, decisions about abortion should be seen as a matter of a woman's private choice, rather than made the subject of majoritarian determinations. Seen in this light, the law ought to make abortion available on demand, as a matter of a woman's rights, at least until the foetus is sufficiently developed to have interests of its own.

Dworkin's stance is quite consistent with believing, as indeed he does, that even early abortion can be an ethical mistake.[103] It will be remembered that Mill made a similar point, when he observed that people may use their liberty badly. Dworkin's view should therefore be distinguished from the view of those who support a right to abortion because they regard abortion as of no moral significance and as raising no moral issues. As we have seen, Dworkin supports a right to abortion for very different reasons and his arguments are consistent with the widely held view that abortion is a morally weighty matter, quite different, for instance, from contraception.

In the United States case of *Roe v Wade*,[104] Justice Rehnquist rejected the view that abortion is a private matter, pointing out that it involves an operation by a physician.[105] It will be clear that he misses the liberal point, just as Chief Justice Burger did in *Paris Adult Theatre*. When liberals call a decision 'private', they mean that it is a decision that individuals are entitled to make for themselves. The fact that they may need the assistance of others in implementing their choices does not make it any less private.

11.10 Voluntary euthanasia and assisted suicide

We have discussed the question whether there are any moral limits on the state's authority to prohibit killing at the one end of life, namely, life in the womb. Now we turn to the question whether there are any moral limits on its authority to interfere with choices at the other end of life, namely, when people wish to die. As with pornography and abortion, the discussion will be confined to investigating the bearing of the debate between liberals and legal moralists on the question whether it is permissible for the state to prohibit euthanasia and assisted suicide.

---

103 R Dworkin, *Freedom's Law: The Moral Reading of the American Constitution*, Harvard University Press, Cambridge, MA, 1996, p 36.
104 *Roe v Wade*, 410 US 113 (1973).
105 *Roe v Wade*, 410 US 113, 172 (1973).

In discussing the issues raised by euthanasia, a distinction is commonly made between voluntary and non-voluntary euthanasia. Voluntary euthanasia is euthanasia carried out at the request of an adult person of sound mind who wishes to die. Non-voluntary euthanasia is performed on someone who is not capable of understanding the choice between life and death. Such a person might, for instance, be permanently comatose, and might not have expressed a preference before becoming comatose as to the preferred course of action in such circumstances.

Non-voluntary euthanasia raises issues that are not relevant to this chapter. We are concerned in this chapter only with delineating the area in which adults should be free to make their own choices, and its focus will therefore be on voluntary euthanasia or the extent to which the law should respect the wish to die. Do we have the right to make decisions about death for ourselves? If so, what sort of assistance in dying should we be able to request? Should we be allowed to refuse life-prolonging treatment? Should doctors be permitted to kill us at our request?

In order to answer these questions, we need to understand the distinction between passive euthanasia and active euthanasia. Passive euthanasia involves intentionally letting someone die or failing to preserve his or her life, whereas active euthanasia involves a positive act of killing. There is some controversy about exactly how this distinction should be drawn, relating to whether withdrawal of life support involves passive or active euthanasia. Some people regard it as passive because the primary cause of death is 'nature' or the patient's illness, not the action of the person who withdraws the support. On the other hand, some regard it as active because something is done when life support is withdrawn.[106] There is no need to enter into this controversy here: for our purposes we can concentrate on cases of euthanasia that are uncontroversially passive because nothing at all is done. For instance, if a doctor accedes to a terminally ill person's request not to be put on a respirator, as a result of which the person dies from respiratory failure, this would be a clear case of passive voluntary euthanasia. By contrast, if the same person were to ask the doctor for a lethal injection, that would be a request for active euthanasia. The doctor would actively be the cause of death, whereas in the respirator case the doctor merely refrains from keeping the patient alive.

---

[106] M Tooley, 'Euthanasia and Assisted Suicide', in R G Frey and C H Wellman (eds), *A Companion to Applied Ethics*, Blackwell Publishing, Oxford, 2003, pp 326–7.

Under Australian law, as under the law of most Western countries, adults who are in full command of their mental capacities have the right to refuse life-sustaining treatment. But they cannot ask to be actively killed and anyone who acquiesced in such a request would be held criminally liable. Nor can they ask their doctor for a prescription for lethal drugs, because assisting a suicide is also a crime. The interesting question for the purposes of this chapter is whether the law on this matter has a legitimate purpose.

Let us begin with the refusal of life-sustaining treatment. Liberal views would support the right to refuse medical treatment, because withholding one's consent to medical treatment is an obvious example of harmless or self-regarding conduct in Mill's sense of the term. It may be morally wrong to want to die—as Kant, for instance, thought—but refusing treatment violates no one's rights. On a liberal view, the state is therefore not entitled to force us to accept medical treatment. The majority may believe that it is wrong to choose a premature death, but to use the law to enforce a moral principle of this kind—a principle that does not seek to prevent harm or the violation of rights—would be to intrude impermissibly into an area of private choice, and to fail to respect personal autonomy.

The fact that the law allows us to refuse medical treatment even though we will die without it therefore demonstrates a clear endorsement of the liberal line of reasoning we find in thinkers such as Mill: if our conduct harms no one, personal autonomy trumps official views about the wrongness of our choices. But the very same line of reasoning seems to support legal acceptance of assisted suicide and active voluntary euthanasia. After all, if people are prevented from being assisted to die in these ways, the damage done to them is as serious as treating them against their wishes. Furthermore, like refusing life-prolonging treatment, assisted suicide and active voluntary euthanasia seem to violate no one's rights, and it therefore appears that they can be forbidden only on the moralistic basis that their immorality is sufficient reason to prohibit them. It seems to follow from this line of reasoning that the law on end-of-life decisions is incoherent—liberal insofar as it allows us to refuse life-prolonging treatment but illiberal when it comes to active voluntary euthanasia and assisted suicide. Liberals conclude that laws prohibiting active voluntary euthanasia and assisted suicide are based on illegitimate, moralistic reasons.

Dworkin agrees with this liberal conclusion, but once again he argues for it via a distinctive route, one which parallels his reasoning in the abortion context. He argues that when the state seeks to prolong human life against the contrary wishes of those who wish to die, the aim is primarily the detached one of preserving human life out of respect for the intrinsic worth of human life.[107] But, he points out, people disagree about what respect for the intrinsic worth of human life requires when it comes to decisions at the end of life, just as they do about such decisions at the beginning of life. Dworkin says that many people believe that choosing premature death is not an insult to the value of life. They believe, in fact, that respect for the intrinsic value of human life speaks in favour of allowing people to choose to die. They think that 'the character of [their] whole life would be compromised'[108] if they were not able to hasten their death in certain circumstances, should they so choose. Finally, Dworkin argues that this is akin to a religious disagreement, and that laws which forbid us from making our own decisions as to when and how to die therefore amount to the illegitimate imposition of a religious view: the majority does not have the right to impose its judgment on such 'spiritual' or life-defining matters. Dworkin writes: 'Making someone die in a way that others approve, but he believes a horrifying contradiction of his life, is a devastating, odious form of tyranny.'[109]

A common response to these and other liberal arguments is to say that legalising active voluntary euthanasia and assisted suicide would not, in fact, be harmless and that laws prohibiting such conduct are not based on the aim of respecting the intrinsic worth of human life, but rather on the need to protect people's rights. Legalising such conduct, it is often said, would present a serious risk of harm because it might lead to vulnerable people being killed against their wishes. For instance, ill people who feel themselves a burden on their relatives might ask to be killed, or might be pressured into making such a request, or might make such a choice when they are in a depressed state of mind. For these and similar reasons, so the argument continues, the law's prohibition of active voluntary euthanasia and assisted suicide does *not* represent an illegitimate intrusion into the realm of private choice and is perfectly justifiable on *liberal* grounds: the state has a legitimate, harm-based interest in preventing people's lives from being ended against their wishes, and the legalisation of assisted suicide and active voluntary euthanasia would create a risk of such unjustified killings.

How do liberals respond to this argument? They take very seriously the risks posed by legalising active voluntary euthanasia and assisted suicide, but they do not agree that total prohibition is the best way to avoid these risks.

---

107 Dworkin, above n 82, p 198.
108 Ibid p 228.
109 Ibid p 217.

They argue that we can protect vulnerable people against abuse while still accommodating the right to die. Liberals point out that there are analogous risks in allowing people to refuse treatment. For instance, patients may become depressed and ask for their life-sustaining machinery to be switched off, or they may be pressured by others into asking for it to be withdrawn. But the law does not treat these risks as a reason to force people to accept medical treatment against their wishes. It deals with the problem by building safeguards into the system: it makes sure that such requests are fully voluntary, fully informed, and made by people in full command of their mental faculties.

Liberals argue that a similar approach could be taken to voluntary euthanasia and assisted suicide. In this way, the risk of harm could be averted, in their view, without undue intrusion into private choices. Since the risks do not speak in favour of total prohibition, the law's prohibitory attitude can therefore be explained only on the basis that its real objection to voluntary euthanasia and assisted suicide is that they are immoral—an objection which, liberals argue, cannot legitimately be translated into law. They maintain that we have a right to personal autonomy in such matters, which the law on voluntary euthanasia and assisted suicide has failed to respect.

Questions

1. What are the legitimate purposes of the criminal law?
2. 'The idea of harm to someone else needs to be clarified and developed. If every unpleasant feeling or negative thought counted as a harm, an act might be prohibited because it made some people envious or disturbed them. With such an expansive notion of harm, enforcement of all aspects of morality could be swallowed up as prevention of harm to others' (K Greenawalt, 'Legal Enforcement of Morality', in D Patterson (ed), *A Companion to Philosophy of Law and Legal Theory*, Blackwell, Oxford, 1996, p 476). In light of this problem, how do you think 'harm' should be defined?
3. Do you agree with Lord Devlin that it is impossible to draw a principled distinction between the private realm and the public realm?
4. The United States case of *National Socialist Party of America v Village of Skokie*, 432 US 43 (1977) concerned a proposed march by the American Nazi Party in the community of Skokie, whose population was 60 per cent Jewish, some of whom were survivors

of the concentration camps and had witnessed relatives being murdered by the Nazis. The Nazis did not propose to speak or to distribute literature. They intended, however, to dress in authentic Nazi uniforms, wear swastikas and carry taunting signs. They gave advance notice of the march. Do you think that they should have been allowed to march?

5   Do you agree with Dworkin that abortion is an ethical matter for which we are personally responsible and that it is therefore illegitimate for the state to restrict access to abortion?

6   Should polygamy be allowed?

Further reading

L Alexander, 'The Legal Enforcement of Morality', in R G Frey and C H Wellman (eds), *A Companion to Applied Ethics*, Blackwell Publishing, Oxford, 2003, pp 128–41.

J Burley (ed), *Dworkin and His Critics*, Blackwell, Oxford, 2004, Chapters 11–13.

P Devlin, *The Enforcement of Morals*, Oxford University Press, Oxford, 1965, Chapter I.

R Dworkin, *Life's Dominion: An Argument about Abortion and Euthanasia*, HarperCollins Publishers, London, 1993.

J Feinberg, *Harm to Others*, Oxford University Press, New York, 1984, Introduction, Chapter 1.

J Feinberg, *Offense to Others*, Oxford University Press, New York, 1985, Chapters 7–9.

J Feinberg, *Harmless Wrongdoing*, Oxford University Press, New York, 1990, Chapters 28–30.

R P George, *Making Men Moral: Civil Liberties and Public Morality*, Clarendon Press, Oxford, 1993.

K Greenawalt, 'Legal Enforcement of Morality', in D Patterson (ed), *A Companion to Philosophy of Law and Legal Theory*, Blackwell, Oxford, 1996, pp 475–87.

H L A Hart, 'Immorality and Treason', in R Dworkin (ed), *The Philosophy of Law*, Oxford University Press, Oxford, 1977, pp 83–8.

C A MacKinnon, *Feminism Unmodified: Discourses on Life and Law*, Harvard University Press, Cambridge, MA, 1987, Part III.

C A MacKinnon, *Only Words*, Harvard University Press, Cambridge, MA, 1993.

J S Mill [1859], 'On Liberty', in M Warnock (ed), *Utilitarianism, On Liberty, Essays on Bentham,* Collins/Fontana, 1962.

J Raz, *The Morality of Freedom*, Clarendon Press, Oxford, 1986, Chapters 14-15.

A Ryan, 'Hart and the Liberalism of Fear', in M H Kramer, C Grant, B Colburn and A Hatzistavrou (eds), *The Legacy of H L A Hart: Legal, Political and Moral Philosophy*, Oxford University Press, Oxford, 2008, pp 315-30.

12

Inequality

12.1 Chapter overview

This chapter is concerned with issues of social and economic inequality. A striking feature of our society is its large disparities in wealth, power and status. Does this matter? Is it just? Is a just distribution of wealth whatever results from voluntary market transactions? Or is the state under an obligation to alleviate poverty by schemes of redistribution, which tax the wealthy so as to improve the situation of the poorer members of society? If the latter, should the state be seeking to improve the welfare or increase the material resources of the poor? And what principle of justice should guide the state in its redistributive endeavours? Should every person be given exactly the same goods? If not, which distributive principle is appropriate? Should we tolerate only those inequalities that can be shown to work to the benefit of the least advantaged members of society? Should benefits be withheld if people are responsible for their impoverished circumstances? This chapter considers the different answers to these questions found in competing liberal theories of distributive justice. After considering utilitarianism, it will turn to the different versions of liberal egalitarianism defended by John Rawls and Ronald Dworkin. Finally, it will examine Robert Nozick's libertarian theory of justice. Feminist views about justice will be explored in the next chapter.

12.2 Utilitarianism and distributive justice

We encountered utilitarianism in 10.3. It is the theory that we should always act in such a way as to maximise happiness or welfare. Insofar as questions of distributive justice are concerned, this means that utilitarians believe that wealth and resources should be distributed in whatever way conduces to maximum welfare. Some factors, such as the diminishing marginal utility of money, may favour equality. In economics, the law of diminishing marginal utility refers to the fact that, generally speaking, as a person is able to obtain more of a good, there is a decline in the utility that person will derive from each additional unit of it. Consequently, those who are poor will derive more utility from a given amount of money than those who are wealthy. On the other hand, there are also factors that may favour inequality, for example, if greater productivity depends on allowing some people to earn much larger amounts of money. Whether utilitarianism will lead to an egalitarian or an inegalitarian distribution therefore depends entirely on the facts. Reducing poverty may be the way to maximise utility. On the other hand, high levels of social and economic inequality may benefit society by creating more wealth. The key point is that if inequalities do maximise happiness, then they cannot be said to be unjust or unfair, for according to utilitarians, there is no *independent* measure of justice in the distribution of wealth and resources: the just distribution is merely whatever distribution happens to maximise happiness. As J J C Smart explains: 'The concept of justice as a fundamental ethical concept is really quite foreign to utilitarianism … [A utilitarian] is concerned with the maximization of happiness and not with the distribution of it … [I]t does not matter in what way happiness is distributed among different persons, provided that the total amount of happiness is maximized.'[1]

Thus, utilitarians offered a choice between the following two societies, in which A, B, C and D are representative members of the different social classes, would pick Society II:

Society I

Individuals	Welfare
A	10
B	10
C	10
D	10

---

[1] J J C Smart, 'Distributive Justice and Utilitarianism', in J Arthur and W H Shaw (eds), *Justice and Economic Distribution*, Prentice Hall, New Jersey, 1978, p 104.

Society II

Individuals	Welfare
A	5
B	5
C	5
D	100

In Society I, welfare is distributed equally and the total amount of welfare is 40 units. In Society II, welfare is distributed very unequally but the total amount is much larger, namely, 115 units. Utilitarians would therefore be bound to say that Society II is more desirable than Society I, despite the fact that the gains in welfare to D, which make Society II desirable from the welfare-maximising perspective, are bought at the cost of the suffering of A, B and C. For the way in which the gains and costs are distributed is irrelevant from the utilitarian point of view. It should be clear that this difficulty is analogous to the difficulty utilitarians face when overall welfare can be increased by torturing or punishing an innocent person.

Rawls objects to utilitarianism on the Kantian ground that, in treating individuals as mere pawns whose interests can be sacrificed in order to achieve maximum happiness (A, B and C in the example above), it does not take seriously our 'plurality and distinctness'.[2] Rawls takes issue with a passage from Smart in which he says:

> [I]f it is rational for me to choose the pain of a visit to the dentist in order to prevent the pain of toothache, why is it not rational of me to choose a pain for Jones, similar to that of my visit to the dentist, if that is the only way in which I can prevent a pain, equal to that of my toothache, for Robinson?[3]

Rawls argues that the analogy is flawed and that it is wrong to extend a form of decision-making that is rational for individuals to society as a whole. We do not think it matters how one person distributes his or her satisfactions over time. That is why we regard it as rational to put up with the pain of the dentist today in order to enjoy greater benefits in the future. But Smart's analogy treats the differences between different *persons* as of no more moral significance than

---

2   J Rawls, *A Theory of Justice*, Oxford University Press, Oxford, 1971, p 29.
3   J J C Smart, *An Outline of a System of Utilitarian Ethics*, Melbourne University Press, Melbourne, 1961, p 26.

the differences between different *times* within *one* person's life. The effect is to treat the desires and interests of different people as if they were the desires and interests of a 'mass person' whose overall good can be maximised by sacrificing some of its constituent parts.[4]

Though Nozick and Rawls disagree on many issues, Nozick agrees with Rawls on this point. He says: '[T]here is no *social entity* with a good that undergoes that sacrifice for its own good. There are only individual people, different individual people, with their own individual lives.'[5] For Rawls and Nozick, individuals are of intrinsic importance—they are of importance in their own right, not merely as interchangeable vessels for happiness—and their interests therefore cannot be sacrificed without limit. As we will see, the rejection of utilitarianism is central to both theorists' conceptions of justice.

12.3 Rawls's two principles of justice

In Rawls's highly influential book, *A Theory of Justice*, published in 1971, he defended a liberal egalitarian conception of justice, which he called 'justice as fairness'. Rawls subsequently came to perceive difficulties in some of his arguments, leading him to shift his emphasis in certain ways. This shift is reflected in *Political Liberalism* (1993) and *Justice as Fairness: A Restatement* (2001). In what follows, it will be simplest to present Rawls's views and the criticisms made of them chronologically, except where it will assist understanding to make reference to his later work.

Rawls believes that there are two principles of justice that govern the basic structure of society, the basic structure being 'the way in which the major social institutions distribute fundamental rights and duties and determine the division of advantages from social cooperation'.[6] The first principle protects traditional civil and political liberties, while the second protects equality.

In *A Theory of Justice*, the first principle reads as follows: 'Each person is to have an equal right to the most extensive total system of equal basic liberties, compatible with a similar system of liberty for all.'[7] Rawls later revised the first principle to read: 'Each person has an equal claim to a fully adequate scheme of equal basic rights and liberties, which scheme is compatible with the same

---

4   Rawls, above n 2, pp 23–4, 26–7, 188.
5   R Nozick, *Anarchy, State and Utopia*, Basil Blackwell, Oxford, 1974, pp 32–3, Nozick's emphasis.
6   Rawls, above n 2, p 7.
7   Ibid p 302.

scheme for all; and in this scheme the equal political liberties, and only those liberties, are to be guaranteed their fair value.'[8] The political liberties include such rights as the right to vote, to hold public office, to oppose the government and to join and form political parties. Ensuring their fair value means that measures must be taken to prevent those who have more wealth and power from exerting a disproportionate influence on the democratic process.

The second principle, which has not undergone much change over the years, states that '[s]ocial and economic inequalities are to be arranged so that they are both: (a) to the greatest benefit of the least advantaged, consistent with the just savings principle, and (b) attached to offices and positions open to all under conditions of fair equality of opportunity'.[9] The 'just savings principle' is the principle that resources must be left for future generations, and 'fair equality of opportunity' means that there must be equal opportunities of education for all. Furthermore, Rawls tells us that the first principle takes priority over the second, except in societies where economic development is at a very low level. This means that the basic liberties cannot be sacrificed for social and economic gains: balancing liberty against equality is entirely ruled out.[10]

Rawls does not provide much detail about the 'basic liberties' protected by his first principle but he does provide the following list of basic liberties: 'freedom of thought and liberty of conscience; the political liberties and freedom of association, as well as the freedoms specified by the liberty and integrity of the person; and finally, the rights and liberties covered by the rule of law'.[11] Rawls thinks that many more specific rights and liberties would fall under these rather abstractly stated liberties. He also makes clear that among the basic liberties of the person is the right to hold personal property.[12] This is a right to hold personal belongings. However, as Samuel Freeman explains, 'rights to unlimited accumulation, absolute ownership of the means of production, and unregulated use and transfer of economic resources are not among the basic rights to hold personal property'.[13] Nor could they be, given the fact that which economic liberties we have and how far they extend are determined by the need

---

8   J Rawls, *Political Liberalism*, Columbia University Press, New York, 1993, p 5. This revision was made to accommodate criticisms made by H L A Hart in 'Rawls on Liberty and Its Priority', in his *Essays in Jurisprudence and Philosophy*, Clarendon Press, Oxford, 1983.
9   Rawls, above n 2, p 302.
10 Ibid p 63.
11 Rawls, above n 8, p 291.
12 Ibid p 298.
13 S Freeman, *Rawls*, Routledge, London, 2007, p 50.

to maximise the position of the least advantaged in society,[14] as will become clear in due course.

It is clear from the first principle and its priority over the second that Rawls believes that the basic liberties cannot be infringed, either to secure the general good or even to reduce inequality. Respect for the basic liberties also precludes restrictions on liberty based on perfectionist policies that aim to promote or discourage a particular conception of the good life.[15] It is in this sense that, for Rawls, the 'right' is prior to the 'good'.

The most important part of the second principle for our purposes is the principle that social and economic inequalities are just only if they improve the situation of the least advantaged members of society. Rawls calls this the 'Difference Principle'. Rawls tells us that the Difference Principle applies to the basic structure of society. This means that the Difference Principle is intended to apply to the design of all the major social institutions within which economic transactions take place, such as the rules governing ownership and property rights and permissible market transactions.

Let us suppose that these institutions can be designed in three different ways, giving rise to three different distributions. It should be noted at this point that, in contrast to utilitarians, Rawls believes that distributive justice is concerned with the resources to which individuals have access, not the welfare or satisfaction they derive from their use of resources. More particularly, it is concerned with the distribution of what Rawls calls 'primary goods'. These include goods such as rights and liberties, powers and opportunities, income and wealth, and the social bases of self-respect.[16] The three distributions we will consider distribute these economic and social advantages as follows:

Society I *egalitarianism.*

Individuals	Primary goods
A	10
B	10
C	10
D	10

---

14 Ibid pp 58–9.
15 Rawls, above n 8, p 295.
16 Rawls, above n 2, p 62.

Society II

Individuals	Primary goods
A	20
B	30
C	40
D	50

Society III *Utilitarianism*

Individuals	Primary goods
A	5
B	60
C	70
D	80

Someone who believes that justice requires strict equality would choose Society I because everybody gets the same. A utilitarian, who believes that justice is synonymous with maximising welfare, would choose Society III because Society III offers the greatest average and total welfare (on the assumption that primary goods translate into welfare). Rawls, who believes that a just society must satisfy the Difference Principle, would think Society II is most just, because A, who is a representative member of the worst-off class in society, does best in Society II. The inequalities in Society II make *everyone* better off than they would be in a society of pure equality. By contrast, the inequalities in Society III are not to the advantage of the members of the worst-off class. The best-off are made better off at the expense of those who are worst-off.

The Difference Principle is therefore a strongly egalitarian principle. It requires any inequalities to be justified to those who are worst-off by showing that they benefit from them. This means that social institutions should be designed to equalise everyone's share of the primary goods, until the point is reached at which any further equalisation would harm the prospects of even the members of the worst-off class. It reduces social inequality to the greatest extent that is consistent with making the prospects of the members of the worst-off class as good as possible.

How might inequalities make everyone better off? Rawls explains that this would be so if incentives are needed to encourage people of ability to develop their talents and exert themselves in socially valuable ways, thereby increasing the wealth of society. If this is the case, allowing talented people to earn more would benefit the least advantaged. Rawls describes this possibility as follows: '[T]he greater expectations allowed to entrepreneurs encourages [sic] them to do things which raise the long-term prospects of [the] laboring class. Their better prospects act as incentives so that the economic process is more efficient, innovation proceeds at a faster pace, and so on. Eventually the resulting material benefits spread throughout the system and to the least advantaged.'[17] Rawls does not express any opinion as to whether these empirical claims are true. He says merely: 'The point is that something of this kind must be argued if these inequalities are to be just by the difference principle.'[18]

Notice that although the Difference Principle does allow inequalities, those who profit from their abilities do so only on terms that benefit the least fortunate. They are therefore not being rewarded on the basis that their talent and hard work give them a *right* to be rewarded. Instead, they are being rewarded only to the extent necessary in order to improve the situation of the least advantaged. In effect, on the Difference Principle, some people's superior abilities and talents are treated as collective assets, which are available to be exploited for the good of everyone.[19] As we will see, Nozick objects strenuously to this idea (see 12.5 and 12.13).

Are the inequalities found in our society to the advantage of the least advantaged, and therefore just in terms of the Difference Principle? In other words, would the poor be worse off in a more egalitarian society than they are in our society? If not, the inequalities in our society would not be just under the Difference Principle. David Lyons argues that the inequalities in societies such as ours are not to the benefit of the least advantaged. He writes:

> The occupants of some social positions receive enormous shares of primary goods without performing any useful social functions at all. And, while some of the special benefits enjoyed by those in the highly paid professions, such as law and medicine, may be needed to attract competent individuals to those jobs, it is arguable that the benefits actually received exceed the level required to ensure that those tasks are performed well. Such inequalities as these

---

17 Ibid p 78.
18 Ibid. For a challenge to the idea that incentive-based inequality can be a feature of a just society, see G A Cohen, *Rescuing Justice and Equality*, Harvard University Press, Cambridge, MA, 2008, Part I.
19 Rawls, above n 2, p 101.

that flow from basic institutions could not be justified under the difference principle. Our system also seems to require that there be a permanent pool of unemployed as well as low-paid laborers, and individuals within these groups may well be worse off than they would be under egalitarian arrangements. That too would violate the difference principle.[20]

12.4 The original position

We now know what a just society would look like, according to Rawls. But why does he think this? Why does justice require respect for our basic rights and liberties and why would it allow only those inequalities that benefit the worst-off individuals? In order to understand Rawls's arguments for his two principles of justice, we need to understand that his approach to matters of justice is 'contractarian'. The contractarian tradition in political philosophy seeks to derive principles to govern the exercise of state power from the consent or voluntary agreement of the governed. The idea of a social contract has its origins in the seventeenth and eighteenth century, some of its most important exponents being Hobbes, Locke and Rousseau. There is, however, an important difference between the approach of these thinkers and Rawls's approach.

The early contract theorists tended to think of the contract as an actual contract, whereby individuals in a pre-political 'state of nature' negotiated the terms of their obedience to the state. This supposition is open to the obvious objection that no such state of nature has ever existed and no actual contract has ever been negotiated. Furthermore, even if such a contract had been negotiated, one could hardly expect the outcome to be just, given the likely differences in bargaining power between the parties to the contract. Rawls's contract is not, however, undermined by either of these criticisms, because his contract is not an actual contract but a hypothetical one. Rawls argues that the way to ascertain the correct principles of justice is to ask what principles *would* be agreed to by rational individuals concerned to advance their own interests if they were forced to deliberate impartially and without personal bias, in a context in which differences in bargaining power have been negated. To this end, he constructs an imaginary situation, which he calls the 'original position', and he asks what principles would be chosen in this situation.

I will shortly explain the features of this imaginary situation but it is important to understand that the function of the original position is merely to

---

20 D Lyons, *Ethics and the Rule of Law*, Cambridge University Press, Cambridge, 1984, p 134.

assist us in imagining a situation of deliberation that is, according to Rawls, fair to all the parties and that neutralises or filters out the distorting influence of self-interest. It is merely a way of making the requirements of impartiality, as he sees them, more vivid. Thus Rawls writes: 'The idea here is simply to make vivid to ourselves the restrictions that it seems reasonable to impose on arguments for principles of justice, and therefore on these principles themselves.'[21]

At the heart of Rawls's theory is a simple idea, namely, that justice is a matter of what people would choose if they did not know facts about their own particular situation that would bias them to make a choice in their own interests. If a child is given a cake and told to share it fairly with her sister and she wants to know what is fair, we might answer: cut it on the assumption that you could end up with either piece. Rawls believes that if we want to arrive at principles of justice to govern the basic structure of society, we should reason similarly. We should ask ourselves what principles people would choose on the basis of rational self-interest if they were not able to favour their own interests. Some theorists criticise Rawls's contract on the basis that it is 'fantastic', or that people are not like this in 'real life', or that we do not always reason on the basis of rational self-interest. It should be clear that these criticisms miss the point of the contract. The aim of the contract is simply to make it easier for us to think about justice from what Rawls regards as a genuinely impartial perspective.

Let us turn, then, to the features of the original position, in which rational persons are required to choose principles of justice to govern their life prospects and the rights and liberties they will enjoy. In the original position, they are behind a 'veil of ignorance'. They are ignorant of features of themselves such as their social class and their natural talents and abilities. They do not know whether their family circumstances are privileged or impoverished. They do not know how intelligent, strong or talented they are. Nor do they know the probability of finding themselves in any particular social position. Furthermore, although they know that they have a conception of the good life—they know, for instance, that they have views about religion, politics and philosophy—they do not know what actual beliefs they hold and they therefore do not know their actual values. They may, for instance, be atheists or they may be fundamentalist Christians.[22]

---

21 Rawls, above n 2, p 18.
22 Ibid pp 12, 137.

They are therefore required to choose principles of justice knowing nothing about what distinguishes them in real life from other individuals. They must make a choice that will be of most advantage to themselves, but they do not know what social position they will occupy, or what natural abilities they will have, or what their personal values are. Their choice will therefore not be influenced by their particular situation and their personal conception of the good life. They will have no reason to make a choice that is biased in favour of a particular social position or a particular conception of the good life, because they will not know whether such a choice will benefit them.

Of course, in order to make such a choice, they must have some information and must know something about what matters to them. Rawls says that the choice must be made on the assumption that they are concerned only to advance their own interests and therefore that they wish neither harm nor good to others.[23] They also know 'the general facts about human society'.[24] They understand, for instance, political affairs and the principles of economic theory. They know, in addition, that they prefer more rather than fewer primary goods.[25] Furthermore, since a just society is a stable society, the people in the original position also know they must make a choice that they would be prepared to honour in real life, not one they would immediately want to renege on when the time comes to implement it. Rawls calls this last condition the 'strains of commitment': the parties cannot enter into agreements that may have consequences they cannot accept. Thus 'they must weigh with care whether they will be able to stick by their commitment in all circumstances'.[26]

Rawls thinks that if individuals were to be placed in the original position and asked to choose principles of justice to govern their society, they would choose the two principles set out in 12.3. He also thinks that they would want the first principle to take priority over the second. Let us begin with the reasoning that would lead them to choose the first principle, the principle that protects the basic liberties. Rawls argues that individuals who know nothing about their conception of the good would choose a society that does not take sides on what kind of life it is worthwhile to lead, but leaves its citizens maximally free to pursue their own goals, provided they do not interfere with the similar freedom of others. No one would choose a society in which, say, atheists are not tolerated,

---

23 Ibid p 141.
24 Ibid p 137.
25 Ibid p 93.
26 Ibid p 176.

because when the veil is removed they might find that they themselves embrace atheism. Hence they would choose a society that respects the basic liberties.

In later work, Rawls expands on this by saying that the basic liberties would be chosen because they are essential for the development and exercise of the capacity for a sense of justice and the capacity to have, revise and pursue a conception of the good. He calls these the 'moral powers'[27] and he says that the parties in the original position have a 'higher-order interest' in the exercise and development of these powers, an interest that motivates them in the original position.[28] This leads them to choose, for instance, freedom of thought and the equal political liberties, such as the right to vote, hold public office and join and form political parties, because these ensure the opportunity to apply the principles of justice to the basic structure. And it leads them to choose liberty of conscience and freedom of association because these ensure the opportunity to pursue a conception of the good.[29]

Let us now turn to the second principle. Given that the parties in the original position know nothing about their natural talents and social position or the probability of finding themselves in a particular social position, Rawls thinks that they would choose the Difference Principle to govern the distribution of wealth in their society. It is worth examining in a little more detail the reasoning that would lead them, according to Rawls, to choose the Difference Principle. Let us return to the three societies described in 12.3. According to Rawls, individuals behind the veil of ignorance, not knowing whether they will be A, B, C or D, or the probability of finding themselves in these social positions, would choose to 'maximin', that is, to maximise what they will receive should they land up in the minimum (worst-off) position, namely, that of A.[30] They will therefore choose Society II.

They will not choose Society I, the society of pure equality, because everyone is worse off in that society than in Society II. And they will not make the utilitarian choice of Society III because Rawls thinks that behind the veil of ignorance, the parties would not choose to risk lower prospects for themselves in order to make it possible for others to be better off. This is because it would be irrational to gamble with something as important as one's life prospects,

---

27 Rawls, above n 8, p 19.
28 Ibid p 74.
29 J Rawls, *Justice as Fairness: A Restatement*, E Kelly (ed), Belknap Press of Harvard University Press, Cambridge, MA, 2001, pp 112–13.
30 Rawls, above n 2, pp 152–3.

forgoing the guarantee of a satisfactory minimum and taking the chance of an intolerable outcome in the hope of finding oneself in one of the better-off classes. There are also the strains of commitment to be taken into account. This is the fact that the parties must make a choice they could live with in real life, whatever position they subsequently turn out to occupy. Since the person who turns out to be A would find it very difficult to accept his or her position in Society III, it is not a choice the parties would make.[31]

For all these reasons, according to Rawls, individuals behind the veil of ignorance would not choose Society III. They would not, in other words, take the view that A's sacrifice in Society III is compensated by the greater sum of benefits enjoyed by B, C and D. Instead, they would allow inequalities only if these inequalities make all individuals better off than they would be in a society of pure equality. They would, in other words, choose the Difference Principle. In effect, as Rawls explains, the parties in the original position would agree 'to regard the distribution of talents as a common asset and to share in the benefits of this distribution whatever it turns out to be'.[32]

The final point to note is that Rawls thinks it would be rational for the parties in the original position to give priority to the first principle, except where resources are very scarce. They would not, in other words, choose to sacrifice their basic rights and liberties for an increase in income, wealth or power.[33] Rawls argues that they would rank the principles in this way because, once our most urgent wants are fulfilled, our interest in determining and pursuing our own plan of life becomes of fundamental importance to us. Thus, unless economic development is at a very low level, the parties in the original position would not choose an authoritarian society, even if everyone would be economically better off in such a society than in a free society.[34]

12.5 Are the conditions of choice in the original position justifiable?

We have examined Rawls's reasons for believing that his two principles would be chosen in the original position. In 12.6, we will examine the views of theorists who doubt that the parties *would* choose the Difference Principle. However,

---

31 Ibid p 154.
32 Ibid p 101.
33 Ibid p 151.
34 Ibid pp 542–3.

accepting for the moment that Rawls is right that his principles would be chosen, this still leaves a gap to be filled. After all, why should we care which principles would be chosen in the original position? We have no reason to take any interest in Rawls's principles unless the conditions of the original position are justifiable. If the conditions are not justifiable, Rawls's principles would not be principles of justice and we would have been given no reason to accept them. This means that Rawls needs to defend the conditions of choice built into the original position. In particular, he needs to demonstrate that the restrictions on people's knowledge imposed by the veil of ignorance and the motivational assumptions built into the original position are fair to everyone. Let us therefore examine the reasons Rawls gives for constructing the original position in the way he does.

Consider, for instance, the fact that the parties in the original position know that they want more rather than less of the primary goods. Rawls argues that this element of the original position is fair to everyone because everyone wants the primary goods, whatever their conception of the good may happen to be. These goods, Rawls says, assist in the pursuit of all conceptions of the good. They are all-purpose means to any goals.[35] This being the case, the theory of the good which underpins the original position is a suitably 'thin theory', by which Rawls means that it treats all conceptions of the good fairly.[36] Rawls's critics argue, however, that the primary goods are not equally valuable to everyone and therefore that the conditions of choice in the original position put some people at a disadvantage. Jonathan Wolff describes the criticism like this:

> [I]t has been said that these goods are not neutral. These goods are particularly suitable for life in modern capitalist economies, built on profit, wages, and exchange. Yet surely there could be non-commercial, more communal forms of existence, and hence conceptions of the good in which wealth and income—even liberty and opportunity—have lesser roles to play. So, runs the criticism, Rawls's original position is biased in favour of a commercial, individualist organization of society, ignoring the importance that non-commercial, communal goods could have in people's lives.[37]

Let us also consider the fact that the parties in the original position are deprived of knowledge of their natural talents and their class position. This leads them, as we have seen, to regard any inequality as unfair unless everyone can be shown to benefit from it. But why does Rawls think that it is justifiable to deprive

---

35 Ibid p 62.
36 Ibid p 396.
37 J Wolff, *An Introduction to Political Philosophy*, Oxford University Press, Oxford, 1996, p 188.

the parties of their knowledge of their natural talents and social circumstances? His starting point in answering this question is the fact that children born to wealthier parents have access to better education and greater resources, both of which give them a head start in the competition for society's rewards. Likewise, those who have talents and skills that are in social demand have better life prospects than those who do not have such skills and talents. But, Rawls goes on to argue, no one *deserves* to be born to wealthy parents or with greater natural abilities, any more than anyone deserves to be born to poor parents or with lesser natural abilities. One's social position and natural abilities are a mere matter of *luck*.[38] These characteristics are, as Rawls puts it, 'arbitrary from a moral point of view'.[39] Even the capacity to put effort into developing one's talents will be influenced by 'fortunate family and social circumstances for which [one] can claim no credit'.[40]

Natural talents and social circumstances are therefore undeserved, which, according to Rawls, justifies the use of the veil of ignorance to deprive people of knowledge of these facts. Because they are undeserved they are, as he puts it, morally irrelevant or irrelevant from the standpoint of justice. Hence, if we wish to deliberate impartially about principles of justice, we need to do so in ignorance of our social position and natural talents. This prevents us from making a choice tailored to our interests as someone holding a particular, undeserved ticket in the natural and social lottery of life.

Should we accept Rawls's argument? Is he right that the veil of ignorance deprives the parties only of morally relevant information and is therefore a justifiable restriction on their knowledge? Nozick thinks not. He argues that the original position suppresses morally relevant information at the expense of people who are talented. It is therefore biased against the talented. Nozick concedes that our natural talents are arbitrary from the moral point of view and that we therefore do not *deserve* them. But this does not mean, he says, that we are not *entitled* to them and to whatever property flows from our use of them. If so, we should not be kept ignorant of them when asked to choose principles to govern the distribution of wealth—an ignorance which, as we have seen, makes it rational for the more talented to refrain from demanding larger shares. Nozick writes:

> It is not true ... that a person earns Y ([such as] a right to keep a painting he's made ...) only if he's earned (or otherwise *deserves*) whatever he used

---

[38] Rawls, above n 2, pp 74–5.
[39] Ibid p 72.
[40] Ibid p 104.

(including natural assets) in the process of earning Y. Some of the things he uses he just may *have*, not illegitimately. It needn't be that the foundations underlying desert are themselves deserved, *all the way down*.[41]

Nozick gives the analogy of a group of students who have taken an examination but not yet received their grades. Let us suppose that there are three students, who received 30, 50 and 70 out of 100 respectively, but have not yet been told their marks. They are now told to allocate marks among themselves so that the marks total to 150. If the students had to decide unanimously on a particular allocation of marks not knowing what mark they have actually received, no doubt they would agree that each person should receive 50 marks.[42] But this is absurd, says Nozick, because it ignores the fact that grades do not fall out of the sky. Those who have earned a high grade have a *right* to the grade, even if they do not deserve the intelligence which is part of the reason why they were able to earn it.

The same applies to wealth, according to Nozick. Rawls deprives the people in the original position of knowledge of their natural advantages. This leads them to treat wealth as 'falling from heaven like manna'[43] and therefore available to be divided up in a way which benefits everyone. But wealth, according to Nozick, is not a social pie which comes into the world unencumbered by prior claims. Wealth comes into the world already belonging to particular individuals by virtue of the fact that they created it using their natural talents. And it is therefore as unfair to expect individuals to choose principles for the distribution of wealth in ignorance of their talents as to ask students to agree on a distribution of marks. We are entitled to our talents and the fruits of them, regardless of the fact that our having them is a matter of luck. We will examine Nozick's own theory of distributive justice later in this chapter.

12.6 Would it be rational to choose Rawls's principles in the original position?

Let us now pursue a different line of criticism and assume, for the sake of argument, that the original position is a fair position from which to make choices about the basic structure of society. We now need to ask whether Rawls is correct that his principles would be chosen in the original position as the basis

---

41   Nozick, above n 5, p 225, Nozick's emphasis.
42   Ibid p 199.
43   Ibid p 198.

for distributing the benefits and burdens of social cooperation. In particular, would it be rational to choose the Difference Principle?

This question relates to the fact that the Difference Principle represents a very cautious, risk-averse choice. As we have seen, it focuses only on improving the position of the least advantaged. In saying that the parties in the original position would choose the Difference Principle, Rawls is implying that they would not choose even a massive increase in the resources of the more advantaged if this were to cause the position of the least advantaged to deteriorate by the smallest amount. The parties would, in other words, choose always to sacrifice the interests of the more advantaged to the interests of the least advantaged. Rawls attempts to justify the choice of the Difference Principle by saying that it would be rational to be very cautious in the special circumstances of the original position. As we saw in 12.4, he argues that the parties are making an irreversible choice of principles to govern their entire life prospects, and they also know that they must choose principles with which they are prepared to comply if they turn out to be in the worst-off class.[44] His critics, however, argue that it would not be rational to be this cautious.

Some theorists argue that Rawls might be right that the parties in the original position would find utilitarianism (Society III in 12.3) too risky a strategy. For if they end up in A's position, they will have to make intolerable sacrifices to bring gains to others, an outcome which they could not willingly accept. But is there not, perhaps, a strategy which is less risk-averse than the Difference Principle but not as risky as utilitarianism? R M Hare suggests that there is such a strategy. He calls it an 'insurance strategy'.

In order to understand the insurance strategy, let us add a fourth society to the three societies described previously. In this society, the primary goods are distributed in the following way:

Society IV

Individuals	Primary goods
A	15
B	80
C	90
D	100

---

44 Rawls, above n 2, p 154.

Let us suppose that the situation of A in Society IV, though not quite as good as in Society II, is nevertheless tolerable. By contrast, let us suppose that the situation of A in Society III is intolerable. Hare concedes that individuals in the original position might not be willing to take the risks inherent in choosing Society III. But he suggests that they might well choose Society IV over Society II. In Society IV, the average position is much better than in Society II and no one is in intolerable circumstances. Hare's suggestion is therefore that individuals in the original position might be inclined to insure against calamity, by fixing a social minimum or safety net below which no one in their society is allowed to fall, thus ruling out the choice of Society III. But, provided that everyone enjoys the social minimum, they might well be prepared to trade off some relatively small losses for the disadvantaged, in exchange for large gains for the more advantaged.[45]

12.7 Does the Difference Principle unfairly subsidise people's choices?

At points in his work, Rawls suggests that we are responsible for our choices.[46] It can, however, be argued that the Difference Principle is inconsistent with recognising such responsibility. Dworkin objects to the Difference Principle on these grounds. He agrees with Rawls, against Nozick, that the factors of social circumstance and natural endowment are morally arbitrary because they are due to luck and he thinks that insofar as inequality is caused by these undeserved factors it should be redressed. Dworkin argues, however, that the Difference Principle is insensitive to the fact that some inequality is caused not by bad luck but by choices for which people are responsible. People's choices are, according to Dworkin, not a morally arbitrary source of social and economic inequality and an adequate theory of distributive justice should reflect this fact. In this way, Dworkin accommodates, to some extent, Nozick's point that wealth does not fall from heaven like manna.

Will Kymlicka illustrates Dworkin's argument with the following example. Consider two people who are alike in their social background and their natural talents and who start off with equal resources. One chooses to live a life of leisure, playing tennis, whereas the other is a hard-working gardener.

---

[45] R M Hare, 'Rawls' Theory of Justice', in N Daniels (ed), *Reading Rawls: Critical Studies of* A Theory of Justice, Basil Blackwell, Oxford, 1975, pp 104-6.

[46] J Rawls, 'Social Unity and Primary Goods', in A Sen and B Williams (eds), *Utilitarianism and Beyond*, Cambridge University Press, Cambridge, 1982, pp 168-9.

Soon their initial equality in resources will be replaced by striking inequality. The Difference Principle tells us that if the tennis player does not benefit from the inequality, then the state should redistribute resources from the gardener to the tennis player.[47] But is such a transfer really just? Should one person's leisure be subsidised by another's hard work?

Dworkin argues that it should not, because the inequality in income is the result of a free choice. It is a function of the gardener and tennis player having different preferences and ambitions. Dworkin describes Rawls's notion of equality as 'flat'.[48] He is referring to the fact that the Difference Principle seeks to equalise primary goods, without regard to whether inequality in primary goods is the result of different 'endowments' (such as natural talents) or of different 'ambitions'. For Dworkin, a just redistributive scheme should be endowment-insensitive but ambition-sensitive.[49] It should, in other words, distribute resources in a way that compensates for involuntary disadvantages, such as disability or lack of talent, while holding us responsible for our choices. We will examine Dworkin's theory of distributive justice in 12.9. It represents another version of liberal egalitarianism.

12.8 Political liberalism

In the three decades that followed the publication of *A Theory of Justice*, Rawls significantly restated his views. This shift in his approach is documented in most detail in his 1993 book, *Political Liberalism*. Rawls is still in search of fair terms of social cooperation and he does not retract his principles of justice. However, he argues for them differently. In particular, *Political Liberalism* is intended to cure a problem with the way in which Rawls previously defended the first principle.

As we know, individuals in the original position choose principles of justice in ignorance of the ends that they think it worthwhile to pursue. Given this restriction on their knowledge, it is plausible to suppose that they will choose an anti-perfectionist framework of basic rights and liberties—that is, one that is neutral as to which ends it is worthwhile to choose and that therefore gives them maximum freedom to pursue their ends, whatever these may turn out to be. They are hardly likely to choose a society that, for instance, persecutes a certain

---

47 W Kymlicka, *Contemporary Political Philosophy: An Introduction*, 2nd edn, Oxford University Press, Oxford, 2002, pp 72–3.
48 R Dworkin, *Sovereign Virtue: The Theory and Practice of Equality*, Harvard University Press, Cambridge, MA, 2000, p 116.
49 Ibid p 89.

religion if they do not know whether they will be adherents of this religion. They are much more likely to choose a neutral state that does not attempt to force a particular religion or any other conception of the good life on its citizens. Depriving the people in the original position of knowledge of their conception of the good life therefore leads them to give priority to the basic liberties. But why does Rawls restrict their knowledge in this way?

In his early work Rawls argued that this aspect of the original position reflects our nature as rational beings with the capacity to critically form, revise, pursue and take responsibility for our conceptions of the good. This characterisation of humans as rationally autonomous and self-determining is drawn from Kant. Rawls writes that '[i]t is not our aims that primarily reveal our nature but rather the principles that we would acknowledge to govern the background conditions under which these aims are to be formed and the manner in which they are to be pursued. For the self is prior to the ends which are affirmed by it.'[50] Rawls means by this that we are not locked in to any particular conception of the good but are able to adjust our goals and aims in the light of our critical reflections on the good. Our ends are not set in stone. This being the case, we need the basic liberties so as to develop and exercise our capacity for working out which conception of the good suits us best. It is therefore, for Rawls, our capacity for choosing our own ends, and for changing our minds about what sort of life we find worthwhile, that ultimately explains why we should be deprived of knowledge of our conception of the good, behind the veil of ignorance. This is a justifiable restriction, according to Rawls, because it speaks to the interest everyone has, as a rational being, in living in a society which, by remaining neutral on matters of the good, provides the conditions necessary for self-determination.

Communitarians strongly oppose this idea. They believe that it is incoherent to suppose that we are autonomous or self-determining selves who formulate, pursue and revise our own conceptions of the good in abstraction from our social and cultural context. We first encountered communitarianism in 10.8. Communitarians argue that the self is not 'unencumbered', but is rather 'embedded' or 'situated' in existing social, cultural and linguistic practices from which it cannot detach itself but must accept as setting the parameters for its choices. According to communitarians, our communal attachments play a role in defining or constituting who we are. It is therefore impossible for us to reflect in

---

50 Rawls, above n 2, p 560.

a thoroughgoing way on everything we value, changing our identifications, aims and goals at will and rejecting social and cultural practices as we please. On the contrary, our ends are at least in part a function of the social context in which we find ourselves: our unchosen attachments and loyalties to families, religious groups, ethnic affiliations, and so on. Thus Michael Sandel writes: 'Certain moral and political obligations that we commonly recognize—such as obligations of solidarity, for example, or religious duties—may claim us for reasons unrelated to a choice. Such obligations are ... difficult to account for if we understand ourselves as free and independent selves, unbound by moral ties we have not chosen.'[51]

Communitarians conclude that Rawls's liberalism reflects a conception of the self that is deeply flawed, and that consequently there is no reason to accept the anti-perfectionist view about justice to which it leads—the view that a just society does not promote or discourage any particular version of the good but is neutral about such matters. Why, Sandel asks, 'should we not base the principles of justice ... on our best understanding of the highest human ends?'[52] For communitarians, the state should not be neutral, but rather should encourage us to identify with whatever traditional conception of the good life is endorsed by our community, so that we may 'know a good in common that we cannot know alone'.[53]

In *Political Liberalism*, the claim that free choice of our ends is desirable and defines us as human beings no longer plays a central role in the argument for the principles of justice. This is not because Rawls has come to accept the communitarian picture of the self or to agree with the communitarians that the liberal belief in 'critical revisability'[54] is incoherent. Rawls does not renounce the idea that we have an interest as rationally autonomous agents in being able to revise our conception of the good, but he now thinks that it is too controversial to form the basis for agreement on a liberal conception of justice. As a result, he aims to show that that there is a way of justifying such a liberal conception, and especially the primacy it gives to securing the basic liberties, which does not 'take sides' on the issue of whether it is desirable to choose and revise one's own ends. Hence this justification should appeal to 'communitarian' groups in society who

---

51 M J Sandel, 'Book Review of *Political Liberalism*' (1994) 107 *Harvard Law Review* 1765, 1770.
52 Ibid 1773.
53 M J Sandel, *Liberalism and the Limits of Justice*, Cambridge University Press, Cambridge, 1982, p 183.
54 This is Allen Buchanan's phrase. See A Buchanan, 'Revisability and Rational Choice' (1975) 5 *Canadian Journal of Philosophy* 395, 399.

do not place value on freely choosing one's way of life. Let us examine Rawls's arguments in more detail.

Rawls now claims that he was not sufficiently mindful in *A Theory of Justice* of the fact that modern democratic societies are characterised by the permanent fact of 'reasonable pluralism'.[55] This is the fact, according to Rawls, that in modern democratic societies there is a diversity of incompatible but reasonable religious, moral and philosophical doctrines about such issues as the meaning of life and the nature of the self.[56] Rawls calls such doctrines 'comprehensive', saying that a comprehensive doctrine is one that 'includes conceptions of what is of value in human life, and ideals of personal character, as well as ideals of friendship and of familial and associational relationships, and much else that is to inform our conduct, and in the limit to our life as a whole'.[57] Comprehensive doctrines therefore attempt to provide answers to the deepest questions about philosophy, religion and morality. Examples of such doctrines are Christianity, Marxism and Kantian liberalism. There are many hazards involved in the conscientious exercise of the powers of reason, according to Rawls, and achieving general agreement on such doctrines is not practically possible. Rawls now sees this fact as the central problem for political theory.

Rawls thinks that, given the fact of reasonable pluralism, no comprehensive doctrine is capable of serving as the basis of general agreement about the principles that should govern the structure of society, and any attempt to found political community on such a doctrine could only be maintained by oppression.[58] It was, however, a comprehensive doctrine that Rawls offered as part of the justification for liberal institutions in *A Theory of Justice*. He defended the basic liberties and the neutral state on the ground that they allow us to develop and exercise our capacity to evaluate our goals and to change our minds about what way of life is best for us. Rawls now thinks that the value of autonomously choosing how to live one's life is too controversial to serve as the basis for agreement on the principles that should govern the basic structure of society, because many people reject the liberal ideal that we should treat all our ends as open to revision in the light of critical reflection. Consider, for example, religious fundamentalist groups who seek to protect their children from exposure to views that threaten their way of life, and to restrict the ability of

---

55 Rawls, above n 8, p 36.
56 Ibid p xvi.
57 Ibid p 13.
58 Ibid p 37.

their members to reject traditional practices and to leave the group. Such people reject the ideal of choosing one's way of life in favour of unreflective immersion in inherited practices.[59]

Rawls therefore concludes that the neutral state should not be justified by reference to 'comprehensive' liberal views, which rely on the controversial value of autonomy. Rawls now seeks to provide a less controversial justification of the neutral state. Hence he defends a more modest, 'political' form of liberalism, which 'aims for a political conception of justice as a free standing view'.[60] Such a political conception of justice 'is neither presented as, nor as derived from ... a [comprehensive] doctrine applied to the basic structure of society'.[61] It therefore presents the principles of justice without reference to disputable moral views about the value of autonomy, or to philosophical views about the nature of human agency, or to any other comprehensive doctrine. Instead, 'justification ... proceeds from what is, or can be, held in common; and so we begin from shared fundamental ideas implicit in the public political culture'.[62] Rawls mentions three such shared fundamental ideas: the idea of society as a fair system of cooperation, the idea of citizens as free and equal persons, and the idea of a well-ordered society.[63]

Once the focus is on the shared notions implicit in a democratic political culture, it is possible to narrow the scope of the theory of justice to apply only to the political sphere and not to the whole of life.[64] Rawls tells us that the liberal political conception of justice applies only to citizens in their political relations to one another and it concerns itself only with their interests *as citizens*. Thus, in a contemporary democratic regime, citizens conceive of themselves as free in the sense that they claim the right to 'view their persons as independent from and not identified with any particular [conception of the good] with its scheme of final ends'.[65] This is, however, compatible with the fact that, in their *personal* lives, people may regard it as 'unthinkable to view themselves apart from certain religious, philosophical and moral convictions, or from certain enduring attachments and loyalties'.[66] In their personal lives, citizens are at liberty to see

---

59 Kymlicka, above n 47, pp 228–9.
60 Rawls, above n 8, p 10.
61 Ibid p 12.
62 Ibid p 100.
63 Ibid p 14.
64 Ibid p 13.
65 Ibid p 30.
66 Ibid p 31.

their attachments as constitutive of themselves and to reject the ideal of critical revisability. In contrast to the conception of the person found in *A Theory of Justice*, which aims to capture the essential nature of a person by reference to the capacity to choose our ends without limit, this is a purely 'political conception of the person'.[67] This political conception conceives of persons as free to affirm whatever ends they please solely for the purpose of determining rights and responsibilities in the political sphere, while allowing individuals to see their way of life as fixed and beyond revision in their personal lives.

Rawls then goes on to argue that the liberal political conception of justice is compatible with all reasonable comprehensive doctrines and can be affirmed by them from their own point of view. The political conception of justice can therefore gain the support of what Rawls calls an 'overlapping consensus'. An overlapping consensus 'consists of all the reasonable opposing religious, philosophical, and moral doctrines likely to persist over generations and to gain a sizable body of adherents in a more or less just constitutional regime'.[68]

This is part of Rawls's answer to the problem of 'stability'—the problem of why citizens should voluntarily abide by the liberal conception of justice in a world of permanent moral disagreement. Rawls wants to show that people can commit to a liberal conception of justice in the real world, and moreover, that they can commit to it for the 'right reasons'. The right reasons are moral reasons, not pragmatic ones. For instance, according to Rawls, it would not be sufficient for people to accept the political conception of justice as a compromise of expediency, struck between different groups of society who would prefer to impose their views on others if they had the power to do so but realise that this is not currently feasible. Stability of this kind would be threatened if the balance of power were to shift.[69] How, then, can stability for the right reasons be secured? Rawls's answer is that the political conception of justice can be given both public and non-public justifications. It can be presented by drawing only on shared ideas, but it is also independently supported by all reasonable comprehensive doctrines.[70] Some people will, for instance, endorse freedom of religion because they believe that being guided by one's own freely chosen values is part of the good life for human beings, while believers may endorse it because they see

---

67 Ibid p 29.
68 Ibid p 15.
69 Ibid pp 147–8.
70 Ibid pp 12, 140.

free faith as the route to salvation.[71] In this way, a consensus can develop on a broadly liberal conception of justice, which secures civil and political rights, meaningful equality of opportunity and a social minimum or minimum standard of living. This, according to Rawls, is the route to social unity.

Finally, Rawls emphasises the role played by what he calls 'public reason' in securing stability. Rawls ties the concept of public reason to the 'liberal principle of legitimacy'. This principle states that 'our exercise of political power is proper and hence justifiable only when it is exercised in accordance with a constitution the essentials of which all citizens may reasonably be expected to endorse in the light of principles and ideals acceptable to them as reasonable and rational'.[72] Rawls argues that when questions about the interpretation of the political conception of justice arise in public life, the principle of legitimacy imposes a moral duty of 'civility' on citizens and officials. They must be able to explain how their views are supported by reasons not derived from the particular comprehensive doctrine to which they adhere.[73] Rawls thinks that it is not reasonable to justify one's views in terms that cannot be accepted by citizens who do not share one's comprehensive doctrines. For instance, one should not justify opposition to same-sex marriage on the ground that homosexuality is a sin, because this is not a view that everyone can reasonably be expected to endorse. Instead, a person's views should be supported by reasons that are accessible to everyone. One should appeal 'only to presently accepted general beliefs and forms of reasoning found in common sense, and the methods and conclusions of science when these are not controversial'.[74]

It may be wondered whether Rawls's new arguments for the basic liberties will be any more acceptable to religious fundamentalists and other people who reject the value of autonomy than his previous arguments. On this issue Rawls thinks that the views of all reasonable people would converge, regardless of their underlying philosophical disagreements about the characteristics that define us as human beings. Kymlicka disagrees. He points out that, insofar as its conclusions are concerned, political liberalism is no different from comprehensive liberalism.[75] There are groups who wish to restrict the liberty of their members to question their practices, renounce their religion and leave

---

71 Ibid p 145.
72 Ibid p 217.
73 Ibid.
74 Ibid p 224.
75 Kymlicka, above n 47, p 232.

the group. In a society that accepts the basic liberties, these groups will be prevented from interfering in this way with their members' choices, whether those liberties are justified on the basis of the value of autonomy or in terms of the ideas implicit in a democratic culture, as proposed by Rawls in *Political Liberalism*. Kymlicka thinks that there is no overlapping consensus on these matters of individual rights. He therefore finds implausible Rawls's idea that, as Kymlicka puts it, 'people can be communitarians in private life, and liberals in public life'.[76] A liberal state, in Kymlicka's view, inevitably affects the private life of communitarian groups by restricting their freedom in certain ways, and there is no reason to think that such groups have reason from within their own perspectives to endorse liberal institutions. Indeed, a common response on the part of communitarian groups to the way in which the liberal state affects their way of life is to ask to be exempted from the regime of rights and liberties that applies to everyone else. This has caused particular problems in the context of women's rights, and it will be considered in the next chapter (see 13.13).

12.9 Dworkin's equality of resources theory

Dworkin believes, as we saw in 10.5, that there are two dimensions of human dignity: the first is a principle of equal importance; the second is a principle of personal responsibility.[77] Dworkin builds his theory of distributive justice around respect for these two principles, which reflect the value of equality, on the one hand, and liberty on the other. Dworkin insists that we do not have to arrive at a compromise between these values or make a choice between them. On the contrary, he thinks it is possible to give a unified account that respects both of them. Dworkin's account is very complex and it will not be possible to do more here than capture some of its key elements.

Dworkin is an egalitarian but he favours equality of resources, as opposed to equality of welfare. The ideal of equality of welfare states that 'so far as is possible, no one should have less welfare than anyone else'.[78] The idea is therefore that everyone's well-being should be as nearly as possible the same. Although the ideal of equality of welfare is like utilitarianism in being welfare-based, utilitarianism seeks to *maximise* welfare, whereas the ideal of equality of

---

76 Ibid p 236.
77 R Dworkin, *Is Democracy Possible Here? Principles for a New Political Debate,* Princeton University Press, Princeton, 2006, pp 9–10.
78 Dworkin, above n 48, p 16.

welfare seeks to *equalise* welfare. Of course, the difficulties with defining 'welfare' are common to both theories. In discussing utilitarianism, we canvassed different conceptions of welfare. We referred in particular to a conception on which welfare consists in the experience of pleasure, and another conception on which it consists in the satisfaction of preferences (see 10.3). Welfare egalitarians might therefore seek to satisfy people's preferences equally or to ensure that people have equal amounts of pleasure.

Apart from the difficulties involved in giving a satisfactory account of welfare, Dworkin objects to equality of welfare on the ground that it costs more to provide people with expensive tastes (defined broadly to include, for instance, expensive ambitions) the same level of welfare as is enjoyed by people with less expensive tastes. Dworkin does not think that this is justifiable from an egalitarian point of view.[79] For instance, if I prefer to drink champagne, while someone else is happy to drink water, then equality of welfare requires that I be given more money to achieve the same level of welfare as the person who drinks water. According to Dworkin, this subsidy ignores my individual responsibility for the choices I have made. We have already seen that Dworkin thinks the Difference Principle makes the same mistake (see 12.7).

Dworkin's own theory of distributive justice unfolds as follows. He asks us to imagine a situation in which a group of people are shipwrecked on an island and they want to divide up the available resources. We are also to suppose that their natural talents are more or less equal, natural talents being, in Dworkin's view, a kind of resource, namely, 'personal resources'.[80] According to Dworkin, the fair way of dividing up the resources on the island is to give everyone equal purchasing power—an equal number of clamshells, for instance—and to hold an auction, letting everyone bid for the resources that suit their tastes, life plans and ambitions. In effect, the islanders pay the market price for the life they want to lead.[81]

The auction will lead to differences in income among the islanders because some people will, for instance, choose to work harder, while others will choose a life of leisure. Choosing a less productive occupation is an expensive choice, which will lead to less income. However, on the assumption that everyone starts off with equal purchasing power and that everyone has the same natural talents, the differences in income are fair, according to Dworkin. For they reflect

---

79 Ibid pp 48–59.
80 Ibid pp 286, 300.
81 Ibid pp 68–70.

the islanders' different values and priorities and the requirement that people take personal responsibility for and pay the financial cost of their choices in relation to such matters as work, leisure, consumption and investment. In this way, the auction has achieved equality in resources.[82] People who have expensive tastes cannot be said to have fewer resources, because if they had preferred another person's bundle of resources they could have bid for it.[83] Redistribution in such circumstances is therefore not justifiable.

Of course, the real world is not like this. In the real world, some inequalities of income are due not to choice but to unchosen disadvantages, such as illness and disability, and to genetic differences in natural talents and the ability to acquire the skills that allow people to earn a satisfactory income. Dworkin writes that differences in natural talents are due to 'genetic luck, to talents that make some people prosperous but are denied to others who would exploit them to the full if they had them'.[84] The differences in income to which such 'inequality of circumstances' leads are not consistent with equality of resources. How, then, would a just society respond to inequality caused by factors such as disability and lack of talent, which limit people's ability to lead the lives they would otherwise lead?

It is obviously impossible to equalise personal resources, such as health and talent, by transferring them. Dworkin also argues that it is not possible to transfer extra money to those who are disadvantaged before the auction begins and then to give everyone an equal share of the remaining money to spend as they please. This is because some people would require so much by way of compensation that nothing would be left over for anyone else.[85] The best we can do to compensate for undeserved inequalities, according to Dworkin, is to allow the level of compensation to be determined by a hypothetical insurance market. We should ask how much of their initial equal allotment of resources the islanders would have been prepared to spend on insuring themselves against such bad luck in the 'natural lottery', if they did not know whether they would turn out to be naturally disadvantaged. We need to ask, in Dworkin's words:

> what level of insurance of different kinds we can safely assume that most reasonable people would have bought if the wealth of the community had been equally divided among them and if, though everyone knew the overall

---

82 Ibid p 81.
83 Ibid p 68.
84 Ibid p 92.
85 Ibid p 80.

odds of different forms of bad luck, no one had any reason to think that he himself had already had that bad luck or had better or worse odds of suffering it than anyone else.[86]

It would be irrational not to spend any resources on such insurance. It would, though, be equally irrational to spend all of one's resources on such insurance, since one would have no resources left to pursue one's ambitions or even to lead a comfortable life if it were to turn out that one drew a 'good ticket' in the natural lottery. Dworkin argues that people would choose to insure against disaster (such as very low income due to natural disadvantages) but not against all undesirable outcomes (such as an income that is merely less than average). The tax system can then be seen as a way of collecting the hypothetical 'insurance premiums' the islanders would have chosen to pay if they were equal in their opportunity to insure against bad luck. Furthermore, social security benefits can be seen as insurance pay-outs from this insurance pool to those who turn out to be disadvantaged, or suffer accidents, or become ill.[87] In summary, then, the hypothetical insurance mechanism is a way of equalising personal resources by compensating those who 'draw' disability or low talents in the lottery for the personal resources.[88]

Dworkin believes that although it may be difficult to arrive at the exact answer as to how much insurance people would buy if they were equal in their ability to insure, we 'should tax ourselves at least to the level below which it would be wholly implausible to suppose people would not insure'.[89] He also thinks that it is obvious that the level of taxation in the United States does not provide the minimum in health care and unemployment benefits that we can safely assume people would have sought to provide for themselves via insurance if they were equal in their ability to insure. He concludes that the American tax system does not show equal concern for the poor.[90]

12.10 Some criticisms of Dworkin's theory

The attraction of Dworkin's mechanism for achieving equality of resources (markets constrained by compulsory insurance) is that it respects the values of

---

86   Dworkin, above n 77, p 115.
87   Dworkin, above n 48, pp 77–80, 92–6, 99–100.
88   J E Roemer, 'Equality of Talent' (1985) 1 *Economics and Philosophy* 151, 157–8, 178.
89   Dworkin, above n 77, p 122.
90   Ibid pp 118, 146.

free choice and responsibility while also accommodating the intuition that it is just to redistribute income to those whose poverty is due to bad luck. In this way it appears to accommodate both the value of liberty (via markets) and the value of equal concern (via redistribution). Dworkin's critics wonder, however, whether it is possible to translate this idea into practice.

Joseph Carens argues that an ideal such as Dworkin's cannot be institutionalised, and that if one wants to compensate people for bad luck there is no alternative to 'indiscriminate taxation and redistribution'.[91] Such an undiscriminating system would sometimes tax people who deserve to be compensated and it would sometimes transfer income to people who do not deserve it. But it is impossible, in practice, to determine whether a person's poverty is due to the influence of his or her choices or to genetically determined talents. Therefore even if Dworkin's theory is superior in theory to the Difference Principle, Carens suggests that it is no different in its practical implications.[92]

Kymlicka argues that Dworkin has played into the hands of the New Right opponents of the welfare state by emphasising the moral importance of not subsidising those who have had the same opportunities to acquire resources as the wealthy but who have chosen not to do so. The New Right is, in Kymlicka's view, 'obsessed with identifying and punishing the irresponsible and indolent. According to the New Right, the welfare state wrongly limits the choices of the well off in order to subsidize the irresponsible behaviour of welfare dependants.'[93] Kymlicka notes that Dworkin does not intend to add fuel to this fire, but Kymlicka says that a theory of justice emphasising the need to be ambition-sensitive may inadvertently strengthen 'stereotypes of the "undeserving poor"'.[94]

Jonathan Wolff makes the related point that a theory such as Dworkin's overemphasises the injustice of subsidising choices for which people are responsible and neglects the value of showing respect for everyone. Wolff argues that any attempt to implement the idea of conditional welfare benefits would encourage the state to view its citizens as potential free-riders and therefore as 'object[s] of suspicion'.[95] It would lead to a system in which 'the poor are singled out for insulting levels of scrutiny'.[96] Wolff also argues that collecting the necessary data would be humiliating because it would require people to prove

---

91 J Carens, 'Compensatory Justice and Social Institutions' (1985) 1 *Economics and Philosophy* 39, 66.
92 Ibid 66–7.
93 Kymlicka, above n 47, p 93.
94 Ibid.
95 J Wolff, 'Fairness, Respect and the Egalitarian Ethos' (1998) 27 *Philosophy and Public Affairs* 97, 111.
96 Ibid 112.

that the reason they have not secured a job is because they are entirely lacking in talent. It would force them to admit to things about themselves of which they may feel ashamed.[97] Thus, although Wolff agrees that it is unjust to subsidise choices for which people are responsible (or, as he puts it, unjust to redistribute resources from one person to another if they are both equally talented and have therefore had the same opportunity to acquire resources),[98] he concludes that the need to show respect is sometimes more important than the need to be just.[99]

A different view, sometimes called 'sufficientarianism', maintains that people are entitled to 'enough' or to sufficient goods as a matter of justice, whether they are responsible for their plight or not.[100] Elizabeth Anderson develops a position of this kind. Her argument is rich in detail and it will not be possible to do more than mention some key points here. Anderson argues against the view, which she ascribes to Dworkin among others, that people should be compensated for undeserved misfortune. In part, this is because she thinks this view, which she calls 'luck egalitarianism',[101] is too harsh.

Luck egalitarians refuse to help people if the consequences of their choices could reasonably have been foreseen. Anderson argues that this view has a number of troubling implications. For instance, suppose that a negligent, uninsured driver has caused an accident. According to Anderson, luck egalitarianism implies that the driver has no right to medical care.[102] Or suppose that someone cares for a dependant, thereby becoming poor and vulnerable to exploitation. Luck egalitarianism implies that such a person—who, as Anderson points out, is highly likely to be a woman—has an 'expensive taste for charity'.[103] Or suppose that someone else has risked his or her wealth, lost it and is now destitute. Luck egalitarianism implies that the person should not be aided.[104] For Anderson, by contrast, 'justice does not permit the exploitation or abandonment of anyone, even the imprudent'.[105]

---

97 Ibid 113–14.
98 Ibid 101.
99 Ibid 122.
100 R J Arneson, 'Why Justice Requires Transfers to Offset Income and Wealth Inequalities', in E F Paul, F D Miller and J Paul (eds), *Should Differences in Income and Wealth Matter?*, Cambridge University Press, Cambridge, 2002, pp 173, 192.
101 E Anderson, 'What is the Point of Equality?' (1999) 109 *Ethics* 287, 289.
102 Ibid 296.
103 Ibid 297.
104 Ibid 298.
105 Ibid.

Anderson also has a further objection to luck egalitarianism, namely, that it insults and stigmatises those whom it is willing to aid, namely, the 'blamelessly' unfortunate. She writes: '[Luck egalitarianism] makes the basis for citizens' claims on one another the fact that some are inferior to others in the worth of their lives, talents, and personal qualities. Thus, its principles express contemptuous pity for those the state stamps as sadly inferior.'[106]

For Anderson, the luck egalitarians have missed the point of equality. The point of equality is to abolish socially created oppression—the way in which some people dominate, marginalise and exploit others—and to create a society in which people live together in a democratic community as equals. She calls this a 'democratic conception of equality'.[107] To this end, she believes that everyone should be guaranteed a package of 'capabilities'.

This idea is associated with the important work of Amartya Sen. Sen believes that quality of life is measured by the capability (by which he means real freedom or real opportunities) to function in ways that are valuable. A capabilities approach focuses on what people are able to do and to be. The functions may include such things as adequate nutrition, taking part in the life of the community and having self-respect. For instance, providing a wheelchair to someone who is disabled affords the person the capability or freedom to get around, which is one kind of functioning. Sen thinks that egalitarians should be seeking to equalise capabilities to engage in various activities, not to equalise resources, for some people may require more resources to enjoy the same capabilities. For instance, sick or disabled people may need more income to achieve the same capabilities.[108] Anderson draws on these ideas to argue that people are entitled to whatever capabilities are necessary to avoid being entangled in oppressive relationships and to function as equal citizens in a democratic society.[109]

12.11 Nozick's libertarianism

We turn now to Nozick's very different view of distributive justice, which represents a forceful and provocative challenge to liberal egalitarian views. In his important book, *Anarchy, State and Utopia*, Nozick defends a free-market

---

106 Ibid 289.
107 Ibid 313.
108 A Sen, *Development as Freedom*, Oxford University Press, Oxford, 1999, pp 74–5, 88.
109 Anderson explains the nature of these capabilities in detail: Anderson, above n 101, 316–20.

distribution of resources and opposes taxation for the purposes of redistributing wealth and resources. It is important to understand, though, that Nozick defends the free market not on the grounds that it maximises a society's wealth (as Posner, for instance, would argue), but rather because it is, in his view, the only *just* system. As far as Nozick is concerned, even if the market were grossly inefficient, it would still be required as a matter of justice. Let us see why he believes this.

According to Nozick, the just distribution of goods is not independent of how these goods came to be in people's hands, and justice should therefore not be seen as a matter of carving up a social pie over which no one has any antecedent claims. Liberal egalitarians, who think that wealth can simply be redistributed by a central planning mechanism, ignore the fact that this wealth already belongs to certain people. Nozick therefore rejects principles of justice that are 'patterned'. Patterned principles specify a desirable pattern to which a distribution should conform, and coercively transfer money from some to others, so as to achieve conformity to the pattern. For instance, Nozick gives the example of 'distribute according to need' as an example of a patterned principle.[110] Rawls's Difference Principle is another example of a patterned principle. By contrast, Nozick's own theory of justice, which he calls an 'entitlement theory of justice', is 'historical' and 'unpatterned'. An unpatterned, historical theory focuses on how people come to hold their property. It is uninterested in who gets what, and how much or how little they get. Whether a distribution is just depends simply on how it came about. On Nozick's theory, we are entitled to our property if we came to possess it justly and we can come to possess property justly in one of three ways.

First, the 'principle of just acquisition' states that holdings over something that was previously unowned must have been acquired in a just way. Nozick says that this condition will be fulfilled if the overall position of those who are no longer at liberty to use the thing—since it now has an owner—is not thereby worsened.[111] Nozick believes that this condition is easy to fulfil. For even though appropriation of a previously unowned resource leaves less of that resource for others, they are likely to benefit in other ways. If, for instance, they work for those who have appropriated the resource, they will probably be better off financially than they were when the resource was not privately owned.

---

110 Nozick, above n 5, p 156.
111 Ibid p 178.

Thus Nozick asks: 'Is the situation of persons who are unable to appropriate (there being no more accessible and useful unowned objects) worsened by a system allowing appropriation and permanent property?'[112] And he answers: 'Here enter the various familiar social considerations favoring private property.'[113] Among these, according to Nozick, are the fact that private property 'increases the social product by putting means of production in the hands of those who can use them most efficiently (profitably)'; that private property encourages 'experimentation'; and that it 'enables people to decide on the pattern and types of risks they wish to bear'.[114] Nozick's views on this matter have attracted considerable criticism on the basis, inter alia, that he assumes that the world is initially unowned rather than jointly owned, and that his test is far too weak and allows people to acquire absolute rights too easily over large shares of the world's resources.[115]

Nozick's second principle, the 'principle of transfer', describes how property that is already owned can be justly transferred from one person to another. This is, for Nozick, by the exercise of free choice. Thus donating property, bequeathing it and selling it are all examples of just transfer, whereas compulsory transfers from one person to another are unjust. The principle of transfer will be considered in more detail in 12.12.

Finally, the third principle, the 'principle of rectification', states that if a person acquires property unjustly—by force or fraud, for instance—then the property can be taken from that person and returned to the rightful owner. The third principle is the source of potential difficulties for Nozick, insofar as inquiry into the origins of current holdings in property may reveal that these holdings rest on historical force and fraud. In such cases, which are all too likely, Nozick is committed to maintaining that current holdings are tainted because justice is, for him, solely a function of 'history'. If so, this could well require considerable redistribution of wealth at least in the short term, as Nozick himself concedes.[116] Indeed, the difficulties of proving and the consequences of rectifying all historical injustices could, as Jonathan Wolff says, be 'mind-boggling'.[117] I will put this point aside, however, and focus on Nozick's claim that if a distribution is the

---

112 Ibid p 177.
113 Ibid.
114 Ibid.
115 For criticism of Nozick's views about just appropriation, see G A Cohen, *Self-Ownership, Freedom, and Equality*, Cambridge University Press, Cambridge, 1995, Chapters 3-4. For further discussion of these issues, see Kymlicka, above n 47, pp 116-121.
116 Nozick, above n 5, pp 230-1.
117 J Wolff, *Robert Nozick: Property, Justice and the Minimal State*, Polity Press, Cambridge, 1991, p 115.

consequence of the free transfer of justly acquired resources, people are entitled to their holdings under the distribution and the distribution is just.

This entitlement is unqualified, according to Nozick. Our property rights are absolute. We own ourselves and our possessions and the only moral requirement that can legitimately be enforced (other than voluntarily undertaken duties) is to respect these rights. There may be moral values other than respect for property rights, such as the value of a heritage site or social utility, but it is not legitimate for the state to enforce these values and it is never permissible to override rights in order to protect such values.[118] Provided we respect the rights of others, we may therefore do with our holdings exactly as we please, using them and disposing of them as we see fit. We may not be interfered with unless we are interfering or threatening to interfere with other people's rights. We will examine the philosophical arguments underpinning this view in 12.13.

The unrestrained capitalism licensed by Nozick's entitlement theory would no doubt lead to massive inequalities in society, as the talented and those born to privileged families prosper, while those who lack skills and are born to poor families suffer. However, taxation to relieve poverty or to provide goods such as public education or public health care would violate people's rights over their property and would therefore be unjust, according to Nozick. The only legitimate use of tax money is to protect individuals in the enjoyment of their rights to person and property, and the state's role is therefore the minimal one of 'nightwatchman'. It is confined to ensuring that there is no force, theft, fraud or breach of contract. Thus tax money may be used to provide goods such as a defence force, a police force and a legal system, but a state that is any more extensive is morally illegitimate. In particular, a state that provides public services for everyone, such as roads, libraries, and social security benefits, is morally illegitimate. People can and should help the poor by private acts of charity, but it is not permissible for the state to force them to do so.

It may be wondered why it is permissible to tax citizens to fund the army, the police and the courts. Nozick thinks that this is legitimate because the state legitimately prohibits people from enforcing their rights privately and so it must compensate them by protecting them in the enjoyment of their rights.[119] Nozick's arguments on this point are very complicated and for the purposes of this discussion, which is concerned with the illegitimacy of taxation for redistributive

---

118 Ibid pp 4, 22–3.
119 Nozick, above n 5, pp 82–3.

purposes, they can be set aside. We will focus instead on Nozick's arguments for the existence of absolute rights over property.

12.12 Liberty and patterns

Why should we accept the entitlement theory of justice? One of Nozick's arguments is intended to show that patterned theories of justice are inconsistent with our intuitions about the right to transfer property. This is the so-called 'Wilt Chamberlain' argument. Nozick asks defenders of a patterned conception of justice to imagine that their favoured pattern has been realised. Perhaps they believe that everyone should have an equal share of society's resources. They are therefore to imagine that they are living in a society in which everyone has been given an equal share. Call this distribution D1. Now suppose that all the people in this society very much want to watch Wilt Chamberlain play basketball and are prepared to pay $1 each to do so. At the end of the season, the pattern will have been disrupted by these voluntary transfers. Resources will no longer be distributed equally: Wilt will be a multimillionaire and everyone else will be $1 poorer. Call this distribution D2.[120]

Nozick argues that D2 must be just because people voluntarily moved to it from D1.[121] Nozick also argues that any attempt to maintain D1, the favoured pattern, would involve interference with liberty. Either people would have to be forbidden from transferring money to Wilt or their free choices would have to be reversed by forcing Wilt to pay the money back. To maintain the pattern, one would have to 'forbid capitalist acts between consenting adults'.[122] Patterned conceptions therefore give with one hand and take back with the other: they give people property and then forbid them to use it in the ways they prefer. Nozick concludes that patterned conceptions are incompatible with liberty. Hence anyone who accepts the value of liberty must accept the entitlement theory and reject the idea of redistribution.

There are numerous criticisms of this argument. One criticism relates to Nozick's claim that the move from D1 to D2 is voluntary. Another criticism relates to his claim that voluntary transfers are necessarily just. Wolff points out that the Wilt Chamberlain example is a clear-cut case of voluntary transfer, but the voluntariness of other market transactions may be less clear-cut. For instance, if someone accepts a very poorly paid job in order to avoid starvation,

---

120 Ibid pp 160–1.
121 Ibid p 161.
122 Ibid p 163.

is this a free choice or a forced choice?[123] Wolff also argues that even voluntary transfers are not necessarily just:

> Justice in transfer is not simply a matter of the agreement of the parties making the transfer. Aside from the point that the parties might not have agreed had they appreciated all the consequences of their trade, the effects of an exchange on third parties, and future generations, also need to be considered. The easy intuition that of course a transaction is just if it is voluntary, conflicts with the equally obvious thought that voluntary transfers can lead to a situation of manifest unfairness. Transfers require more supervision from the state than Nozick allows, perhaps even to the point where a pattern is thought desirable.[124]

12.13 The principle of self-ownership

It might seem that Nozick gives pride of place in his philosophy to liberty. In fact, however, as G A Cohen points out, Nozick is unconcerned about the lack of freedom of the propertyless poor, and the real reason why Nozick defends a libertarian society is not because it is the most free society. Nozick defends libertarianism because he believes that it respects the 'principle of self-ownership'. Equality can, in Nozick's view, be achieved only at the cost of injustice, since the achievement of equality requires violating people's rights of self-ownership.[125] This is, for Nozick, the most fundamental right, and it is at the heart of his belief that the functions of government are limited to the protection of life, liberty and property.

We saw in 12.2 that Nozick, like Rawls, adheres to the Kantian principle that we are all ends in ourselves: we are all separate individuals, leading separate lives, and we therefore have rights that protect us against being used merely as a means to the ends of others. We also saw in 10.5 that Nozick thinks that such rights are a precondition for leading a meaningful life. Unlike Rawls, however, Nozick thinks that respect for our separateness as persons makes it illegitimate to force the wealthy to contribute to the welfare of the poor. This is because the Kantian principle implies, according to Nozick, that we have absolute rights *over ourselves*. We 'own' ourselves. This might seem a relatively uncontroversial claim. Nozick, however, draws a striking implication from it. He says that if we own ourselves, then we must own our talents and whatever we can produce

---

123 Wolff, above n 117, pp 83–4.
124 Ibid p 88.
125 Cohen, above n 115, pp 13, 67–8.

with them.[126] Hence Rawls's theory of justice, which does not recognise a right to profit from one's talents but instead treats them as a collective resource to be used for the benefit of everyone, violates the principle of self-ownership and fails to respect the distinctness of individuals. It uses the talented as a resource for those who are in need. Cohen sums up Nozick's principle of self-ownership as follows: '[E]ach person enjoys, over herself and her powers, full and exclusive rights of control and use, and therefore owes no service or product to anyone else that she has not contracted to supply.'[127]

In explaining how redistributive taxation violates the principle of self-ownership, Nozick writes:

> Seizing the results of someone's labor is equivalent to seizing hours from him and directing him to carry on various activities. If people force you to do certain work, or unrewarded work, for a certain period of time, they decide what you are to do and what purposes your work is to serve apart from your decisions. This process ... makes them a *part-owner* of you; it gives them a property right in you.[128]

Taxing of earnings from labour is therefore, in Nozick's view, the equivalent of forced labour. It is like 'forcing unemployed hippies to work for the benefit of the needy'.[129]

If talents are a collective resource to be used for the benefit of everyone, surely—Nozick goes on to suggest—the logic of this approach also requires that we should treat bodily organs in the same way. If one person has two healthy kidneys, why should we not force her to give up one of them to someone who is suffering kidney failure? After all, she does not deserve to have two healthy kidneys. It is a matter of mere good luck. If we object to this idea because we believe we are not resources for the benefit of others, then we should also object, according to Nozick, to the idea of using people's talents as resources for the benefit of others.

Nozick concludes that if we are to respect the Kantian principle that we are ends, not means, we need to recognise the principle of self-ownership; this implies, in turn, that any forcible redistribution from the wealthy to the needy is totally illegitimate. The needy cannot claim that they have a 'right' to assistance because '[n]o one has a right to something whose realization requires certain uses of things and activities that other people have rights and entitlements

---

126 Kymlicka, above n 47, p 109.
127 Cohen, above n 115, p 12.
128 Nozick, above n 5, p 172, Nozick's emphasis.
129 Ibid p 169.

over'.[130] Or, as Nozick also writes: '[A] right to life is not a right to whatever one needs to live; other people may have rights over those things.'[131]

Nozick's arguments on these matters have been heavily criticised. Some theorists argue that the principle of self-ownership does not rule out forcing one person to assist another and therefore does not rule out redistributive taxation.[132] Other theorists agree with Nozick that the principle of self-ownership rules out forcing one person to help another, but they reject the principle of self-ownership. Cohen argues along these lines. He maintains that rejection of the principle does not have the morally unacceptable consequences that Nozick claims it has. Rejecting the principle does not, for instance, amount to endorsing slavery or using people merely as a means.

One of Cohen's arguments is as follows. He asks us to imagine that someone forcibly detains an innocent person for five minutes because of a temporary need for social order. Although this can be called 'imprisonment', Cohen argues that there is a vast difference, morally speaking, between forcibly detaining an innocent person for five minutes and forcibly detaining him or her for a lifetime. The latter could never be justified but the former could be. Analogously, even if Nozick is right that redistributive taxation can be called the imposition of 'slavery', small amounts of forced labour are very different from the lifelong forced labour of a slave.[133] Cohen also argues that forcing some people to help others does not necessarily involve using them merely as a means. We do not treat them merely as a means if forcing them to help others does not 'blight their lives'.[134]

Hart makes a similar point. He argues that some forcible sacrifices violate people's autonomy and deprive their lives of meaning. Others, such as taxation, do not have this effect. Hart asks:

> How can it be right to lump together, and ban as equally illegitimate, things so different in their impact on individual life as taking some of a man's income to save others from great suffering and killing him or taking one of his vital organs for the same purpose? ... Is taxing a man's earnings or income, which leaves him free to choose whether to work and to choose what work to do, not altogether different in terms of the burden it imposes from forcing him to labour?[135]

---

130 Ibid p 238.
131 Ibid p 179.
132 See D Gauthier, *Morals by Agreement*, Oxford University Press, Oxford, 1986, pp 273-6.
133 Cohen, above n 115, p 231.
134 Ibid p 240.
135 H L A Hart, *Essays in Jurisprudence and Philosophy*, Clarendon Press, Oxford, 1983, p 206.

Questions

1. Rawls argues that deliberating about questions of justice behind the veil of ignorance forces us to reason impartially. Do you agree? Would you choose Rawls's principles of justice if you were behind the veil of ignorance?
2. Do you think people who have superior natural talents and abilities should be able to benefit from those talents and abilities by earning more income and wealth than other people?
3. Do you think people who are responsible for their impoverished circumstances should be entitled to receive welfare benefits?
4. Why does Nozick think people in need do not have a right to state assistance? Do you agree with him?
5. The South African case of *Soobramoney v Minister of Health, Kwazulu-Natal* 1998 (1) SA 765 (CC) concerned an unemployed man in a state of chronic renal failure, who could not survive without renal dialysis. The hospital did not have sufficient resources to provide dialysis to everyone suffering from chronic renal failure. Its policy was to provide dialysis for such patients only if they were eligible for a kidney transplant. Mr Soobramoney was not eligible for a transplant and was therefore denied dialysis. He asked the court to compel the hospital to provide dialysis for him, relying on the right to health care, which is contained in the Constitution of South Africa. The relevant section provides that '[e]veryone has the right to have access to health care services' and that '[t]he state must take reasonable legislative and other measures, within its available resources, to achieve the progressive realisation of [this right]'. The court held that, given the scarcity of resources and the reasonableness of the hospital's policy, it was not for the court to interfere with the hospital's decision. Mr Soobramoney died a few days later. Do you think that the court gave sufficient recognition to the fact that the Constitution of South Africa attempts to translate moral ideals of socio-economic justice into legal rights?

Further reading

E Anderson, 'What is the Point of Equality?' (1999) 109 *Ethics* 287.

S Avineri and A de-Shalit (eds), *Communitarianism and Individualism*, Oxford University Press, Oxford, 1992.

G A Cohen, *Self-Ownership, Freedom and Equality*, Cambridge University Press, Cambridge, 1995.

R Dworkin, *Sovereign Virtue: The Theory and Practice of Equality*, Harvard University Press, Cambridge, MA, 2000, Chapters 1-2.

S Freeman (ed), *The Cambridge Companion to Rawls*, Cambridge University Press, Cambridge, 2003.

S Freeman, *Rawls*, Routledge, London, 2007.

W Kymlicka, *Contemporary Political Philosophy: An Introduction*, 2nd edn, Oxford University Press, Oxford, 2002, Chapters 2-4, 6.

L Murphy and T Nagel, *The Myth of Ownership: Taxes and Justice*, Oxford University Press, New York, 2002.

R Nozick, *Anarchy, State and Utopia*, Basil Blackwell, Oxford, 1974.

M Nussbaum and A Sen (eds), *The Quality of Life*, Oxford University Press, Oxford, 1993.

J Rawls, *A Theory of Justice*, Oxford University Press, Oxford, 1971.

J Rawls, *Political Liberalism*, Columbia University Press, New York, 1993.

J Wolff, *Robert Nozick: Property, Justice and the Minimal State*, Polity Press, Cambridge, 1991.

13

Difference

13.1 Chapter overview

This chapter explores approaches that can be loosely linked under the heading of 'outsider jurisprudence'. They all emphasise the way in which the law reflects and perpetuates a dominant perspective, which is systematically biased against and devalues those who are 'different', whether in terms of their gender, race, culture or sexuality. These approaches therefore offer another kind of critical perspective on the law, one that is frequently accompanied by a practical and political concern with social and legal transformation. It is because of their practical concern with overcoming the disadvantage and disempowerment suffered by members of marginalised social groups that these theories are dealt with in this part of the book, which is concerned with the justice of our laws and legal institutions. This chapter will mainly focus on feminist legal theory but it will also explore some issues concerning culture, race and sexuality.

13.2 Feminist legal theory

Feminist legal theorists believe that women are subordinated through the law. They maintain that, although it pretends otherwise, the law is not neutral or impartial in its treatment of men and women. Instead, it systematically reflects, maintains and legitimises 'patriarchy', that is, a social structure in which men hold the power. In addition to providing an analysis of law as reflecting and perpetuating male values and male interests, thereby oppressing and excluding women, feminism is also a political movement that aims to challenge male power and eliminate women's subordination.

Notwithstanding the shared beliefs and political commitments mentioned above, feminists do not all adopt the same theoretical approach. In fact, feminist legal scholarship is characterised by a diversity of theoretical views about, for instance, the causes of women's subordination and the best strategies for addressing it, the significance that should be attached to the differences between men and women, and the possibility and desirability of theorising about the position of women as such. Moreover, feminism continues to develop in new and interesting ways. There are different ways of categorising the different 'feminisms', but one frequently used set of categories distinguishes four broad schools of feminist thought: liberal feminism, cultural feminism (or difference feminism, as it is also sometimes called), radical feminism and postmodern feminism.[1] These categories are inevitably simplistic and their importance should not be exaggerated. They do, however, provide a useful starting point for thinking about the issues. This chapter will explain the concerns of these different theoretical approaches and will also explore feminist views about issues such as rights, justice, multiculturalism and the reform of the family.

13.3 Formal equality

It is only in about the last hundred years that women have had the right to vote, to own and manage property after marriage, to enjoy the same educational opportunities as men, and to be admitted to professions, such as medicine and law. The law took even longer to recognise women's right to be paid the same as men for doing the same job. These benefits and opportunities were withheld from women on the basis of stereotyped beliefs about their innate differences from and inferiority to men. It was believed that women were emotional, weak creatures, suited only to a life of domesticity and looking after children, which, however taxing that may have been, was not accorded the same significance as men's work. Men and women, so it was said, naturally inhabited 'separate spheres'. The separation of society into two spheres was elaborated upon in the United States case of *Bradwell v Illinois*.[2] The case involved a challenge to the refusal to admit a woman to the Illinois bar because she was a woman. In rejecting Bradwell's challenge, Justice Joseph P Bradley remarked as follows:

---

1 These categories are used by P A Cain in 'Feminism and the Limits of Equality' (1990) 24 *Georgia Law Review* 803.
2 *Bradwell v Illinois*, 83 US 130 (1873).

The civil law, as well as nature herself, has always recognized a wide difference in the respective spheres and destinies of man and woman. Man is, or should be, woman's protector and defender. The natural and proper timidity and delicacy which belongs to the female sex evidently unfits it for many of the occupations of civil life. The constitution of the family organization, which is founded in the divine ordinance, as well as in the nature of things, indicates the domestic sphere as that which properly belongs to the domain and functions of womanhood. The harmony, not to say identity, of interests and views which belong or should belong to the family institution, is repugnant to the idea of a woman adopting a distinct and independent career from that of her husband.[3]

Even after the elimination of the most obvious forms of discrimination against women, the law continued to treat women less favourably than men in more subtle ways. Such different treatment—particularly in the public sphere of employment, education and access to goods, services and accommodation—was the focus of so-called 'liberal feminism', which came to prominence during the 1960s and 1970s. Although there are reasons, as we will see, for thinking that the label is inappropriate, for there are many liberals who do not endorse the approach of so-called 'liberal feminism', the phrase is so entrenched that I will continue to use it to describe a particular approach to sexual equality.

Liberal feminism is premised on the assumption that women are similar to men in their ability to operate in the public world, and its primary focus is on the securing of equal opportunity (understood as the absence of legal barriers to advancement) and equal rights for women within the established framework of society. It insists that individuals should be assessed on the basis of their individual merits, not their membership in a group. Thus whether a particular applicant gets a job should not depend on the irrelevant characteristic of sex but only on his or her ability to do the job well. I will call this the 'formal equality' model of sexual equality, meaning by this a model on which sexual equality is guaranteed when the law treats men and women in a formally identical way. On this view, sex-blind or gender-neutral laws are sufficient for sexual equality.

The equal opportunity goals of liberal feminism were encapsulated in anti-discrimination statutes such as the *Sex Discrimination Act 1975* in the United Kingdom and the *Sex Discrimination Act 1984* (Cth) in Australia. Such statutes rule out less favourable treatment on the ground of sex in a limited number of public areas of activity, such as employment, education, housing and the provision of

---

3   *Bradwell v Illinois*, 83 US 130, 141–2 (1873).

goods and services. Less favourable treatment of this kind is often called 'direct discrimination' on the ground of sex.

In fact, anti-discrimination legislation goes further than liberal feminism, typically also ruling out conduct which, though formally treating men and women in the same way, unreasonably and disproportionately affects members of one sex more than the other. This kind of conduct is usually called 'indirect discrimination'. The focus here is on different *impact*, not different *treatment*. Suppose, for instance, that an employer makes it a condition of employment that an employee not be the primary caregiver for small children. This could amount to indirect discrimination against women, since more women than men are primary caregivers for small children within their families. The employer's condition is sex-blind, since both men and women need to comply with the condition. The *effect* of such formally equal treatment, however, would be (whether intentionally or not) to discriminate against women. It should be clear that legislation that prohibits indirect discrimination goes beyond 'liberal feminism' and its belief that sexual equality is merely a matter of eliminating direct sex discrimination or gender-based classifications. Indirect discrimination is a concept with considerable potential to redress sex inequality, though much depends on how the courts approach it. We will return to the concept of indirect discrimination in the next section.

13.4 Formal equality and the male norm

The formal equality approach to the problem of sexual inequality came under attack relatively quickly. One problem with it, demonstrated in numerous legal cases, is its apparent difficulty in showing why discrimination on the ground of characteristics that are *unique* to women, such as pregnancy, should be seen as a form of sex-based discrimination. This is because the formal equality approach relies on *comparisons* between the treatment of men and women: it insists that the treatment received by members of one sex should be the same as the treatment received by members of the other sex who are in similar circumstances. But men cannot become pregnant. How, then, can women discriminated against on the ground of pregnancy (by being dismissed from their jobs, for instance) argue that they have been treated less favourably than similarly situated men? Since there appears to be no right extended to a man which they have been denied, it seems that on the formal equality approach they cannot complain of sex-based discrimination.

A more general problem with the formal equality approach is that most of the inequalities of prestige, wealth and power that characterise the relative positions of men and women in our society have little to do with sex-based exclusionary treatment in the public world. The ideal of equal access to educational and economic institutions has no doubt been important in opening up opportunities for women that they were previously denied. Most women continue, nevertheless, to be found in the lower-paying, less influential, less valued and less secure occupations, and even those who have high-status positions frequently fail to achieve the top positions in their professions, companies or political organisations. Furthermore, many more women suffer from poverty, unemployment and violence than men.

Feminist opponents of the formal equality approach argue that the reason why equal rights to education and employment within the existing system cannot on their own address these sex-based disparities is because it is not public discrimination which is the primary cause of sexual inequality. Instead, the cause is disadvantages suffered by women in areas of life that the formal equality approach tends to ignore. These are the so-called 'private' areas of life. One major source of disadvantage, on this analysis, is the fact that for whatever reasons, women continue to bear the brunt of child-rearing and domestic responsibilities. These are tasks that our society has historically undervalued and failed to reward. Furthermore, the burden of this unpaid form of labour, the inadequacy of child-care facilities, and employers' expectations that employees should have no family commitments that would interfere with full-time work make it much more difficult for women to compete for the positions that society does reward. The conclusion drawn is that the kind of neutrality offered by liberal feminism—the right to compete on the same terms as men in a male-dominated world—is of benefit only to a minority of economically and socially privileged women, a group of women whose lives approximate the male norm.

On the formal equality approach, as Christine Littleton explains:

> [T]he law should require social institutions to treat women as they already treat men—requiring, for example, that the professions admit women to the extent that they are 'qualified', but also insisting that women who enter time-demanding professions such as the practice of law sacrifice relationships (especially with their children) to the same extent that male lawyers have been forced to do.[4]

---

4 C Littleton, 'Reconstructing Sexual Equality' (1987) 75 *California Law Review* 1279, 1292.

But—the feminist critics of formal equality ask—why *should* women have to meet workplace standards which have been designed for the benefit of men in order to claim the protection of the law? Why should sexual equality be a matter of integrating women into a male world? Thus Catharine MacKinnon asks:

> Why should you have to be the same as a man to get what a man gets simply because he is one? Why does maleness provide an original entitlement, not questioned on the basis of *its* gender, so that it is women—women who want to make a case of unequal treatment in a world men have made in their image...— who have to show in effect that they are men in every relevant respect, unfortunately mistaken for women on the basis of an accident of birth?[5]

This is an example of what feminists call 'asking the woman question'. As Katherine Bartlett explains, asking the woman question involves looking beneath the surface of the law, so as to expose how the law fails to take into account the perspectives of women or how it is used to maintain structures and practices that disadvantage women.[6] Thus feminists ask the woman question when they ask why satisfying, well-paid jobs should be the preserve of workers who are able to work full-time in virtue of having minimal domestic responsibilities. In showing how certain apparently neutral and unavoidable practices, which seem to treat men and women equally, are really only of advantage to women who are like men—to whose situation and characteristics the rules are in fact tailored— feminists reveal that men are the assumed subject of the law.

If we now return to the concept of indirect discrimination, it will be clear that its function is precisely to focus attention on practices that are formally neutral but in effect based on a male norm. The formal equality approach regards gender-neutral rules as a guarantee of sexual equality. It thereby ignores the differences between men and women and their different situations and characteristics. The concept of indirect discrimination, by contrast, allows women to argue that they are disproportionately susceptible to the impact of certain gender-neutral rules. Furthermore, laws that prohibit indirect discrimination force employers either to justify formally neutral practices whose effect is to exclude women, or to substitute new practices that do not unfairly subject women to male standards. For instance, employers may be required to redesign job requirements so that they do not constitute barriers to women's participation in the workplace. More generally, the concept of indirect

---

5   C A MacKinnon, *Feminism Unmodified: Discourses on Life and Law*, Harvard University Press, Cambridge, MA, 1987, p 37, MacKinnon's emphasis.
6   K Bartlett, 'Feminist Legal Methods' (1990) 103 *Harvard Law Review* 829, 837.

discrimination requires unjustifiable workplace norms to be changed so that men and women can compete on genuinely equal terms. In this way, many feminist theorists believe that indirect discrimination provides a legal tool 'with which to begin to squeeze the male tilt out of a purportedly neutral legal structure and thus substitute genuine for merely formal gender neutrality'.[7]

13.5 Formal equality, liberalism and individualism

We have seen that the critics of the formal equality approach maintain that equal rights, although important, are not the complete answer to sexual inequality, for not all women have the ability to take advantage of their equal rights. The problem with the formal equality model, on their view, is that it does not challenge the entrenched injustice and unequal power structures that are built into the status quo. Though it claims to offer neutrality as between men and women, it does not challenge the prevailing male standards, and is therefore incapable of delivering on the promise of equality.

Those who criticise the formal equality model hold a conception of equality on which the aim should be to improve women's social and material circumstances, not merely to ensure that they are afforded the same opportunities as men within the status quo. On this view, if men and women are to be truly equal, it is not enough to make place for a handful of 'honorary men' in the boardroom. The deeper social and material disadvantages of women need to be redressed. Laws that are genuinely aimed at overcoming inequality will therefore be laws that aim to deliver equality of *results* or *outcomes*. They will deliver 'substantive' equality, not merely 'formal' equality.

As noted in 13.3, it is common to describe the pursuit of formal equality as a 'liberal' form of feminism, a description which suggests that liberals are uninterested in the issue of substantive inequality. This is, however, a misconception. As we know from the discussion of justice in Chapter 12, many liberal theorists are not indifferent to matters of social and material disadvantage. It is, in fact, difficult to define liberalism in a way that does not caricature it or obscure the differences among liberal theorists. Though most liberals believe in rights as a desirable constraint on government power, they have

---

[7] W Williams, 'Equality's Riddle: Pregnancy and the Equal Treatment/Special Treatment Debate' (1984–85) 13 *New York University Review of Law and Social Change* 325, 331.

different views about what should be done about the fact that poverty and other factors may make it difficult to take advantage of one's rights. For libertarians such as Nozick, the answer is that nothing need be done. Most liberals, however, take a different view. Thus Hart says:

> Except for a few privileged and lucky persons, the ability to shape life for oneself and lead a meaningful life is something to be constructed by positive marshalling of social and economic resources. It is not something automatically guaranteed by a structure of negative rights. Nothing is more likely to bring freedom into contempt and so endanger it than failure to support those who lack, through no fault of their own, the material and social conditions and opportunities which are needed if a man's freedom is to contribute to his welfare.[8]

Rawls and Dworkin are likewise liberal egalitarians, who believe that society has an obligation to provide the material preconditions for the effective exercise of rights, thus ensuring that rights are of use to everyone. As we saw in Chapter 12, they are sensitive to the moral 'arbitrariness' of unequal starting points in life and they believe that social arrangements should be geared towards improving the position of those who are disadvantaged.

Martha Nussbaum draws on liberal ideas to defend a liberal form of feminism that provides, in her view, the foundation for a radical critique of society. According to Nussbaum, this critique is crucial to improving women's quality of life, not only in Western societies, but even more importantly, in developing countries, where women's second-class status is even more deeply entrenched.[9] Nussbaum identifies the core of the liberal tradition as consisting in the idea that everyone—whether rich or poor, female or male, black or white—is of equal worth and equally deserving of respect, and that this requires society to provide not merely formal equality of opportunity but positive, material support to individuals so that they may pursue their own goals according to their own views about what matters in life.[10]

It is often said to be a defect of liberalism that it is 'individualistic', and feminists often argue that individualism is a value associated with men and masculinity. Nussbaum disagrees on both counts. She thinks that the individualism that is built into liberalism is valuable, and she also thinks that its individualism is precisely what makes liberalism good for women. In her view,

---

8   H L A Hart, *Essays in Jurisprudence and Philosophy*, Clarendon Press, Oxford, 1983, pp 207–8.
9   M C Nussbaum, *Sex and Social Justice*, Oxford University Press, New York, 1999, p 56.
10 Ibid pp 5, 9.

individualism stresses 'the basic fact that each person has a course from birth to death that is not precisely the same as any other person; that each person is one and not more than one, that each feels pain in his or her own body, that the food given to A does not arrive in the stomach of B'.[11]

Another way of putting this is to say that, on an individualistic view, the basic units of moral concern are individual human beings, not larger groups such as families, communities or states. On such a view, the flourishing of individuals should never be subordinated to the flourishing of groups: the goal of politics should be to improve the lives of individuals, each and every one of them considered as a separate individual. This view is connected with the Kantian approach to rights discussed in 10.5. Nussbaum argues that an individualistic view of this kind is in the interests of women because women's individual well-being has too often been ignored in the service of the goals of others. She writes:

> Women have very often been treated as parts of a larger unit, especially the family, and valued primarily for their contribution as reproducers and caregivers rather than as sources of agency and worth in their own right. In connection with this non-individualistic way of valuing women, questions about families have been asked without asking how well each of its individual members are doing.[12]

This is even more obvious in poor countries, where it is the female members of the family who suffer most from lack of resources. In these countries, statistics show that it is the girls and women who are most often malnourished, whose educational and health needs are most often neglected, and who are most often the victims of violence within the family. Nussbaum concludes that liberalism properly understood is a theory with radical aspirations, focused not only on providing equal opportunities but also on more fundamental changes geared to remedying the structural and institutional sources of women's disadvantage. We will return to some of these issues in 13.11, where we will examine in more detail the way in which the family contributes to sexual inequality and Nussbaum's views about how this should be countered.

13.6 Difference feminism

We turn now to difference or cultural feminism, which focuses on and embraces women's differences from men. Difference feminism is against the idea of

---

11 Ibid p 62.
12 Ibid p 63.

assimilating women into a system that it sees as patriarchal. Assimilation, according to these feminists, forces women to act like men. The work of the psychologist Carol Gilligan has been influential in the elaboration of difference feminism. She argues that women see themselves as connected with others, whereas men see themselves as separate from others. This difference, according to her, leads men and women to reason in a different way or to speak in a different voice. When confronted with moral dilemmas, women are more concerned about relationships, needs and responsibilities and the context in which the dilemma arises. Men are more concerned about abstract, rigid rules and adversarial and individualistic concepts such as rights and justice. Women tend to take an 'ethic of care' approach, whereas men tend to take an 'ethic of justice' approach.

Gilligan explains how she posed a moral dilemma to a group of children and asked them how they would deal with it. In the scenario, Heinz's wife is dying and needs a drug, which he cannot afford. Should Heinz steal the drug from the pharmacy? Jake, an eleven-year-old boy, sees the problem as a clash of rights. He weighs up life against property, finds life more valuable, and concludes that Heinz should steal the drug. He deals with the situation as one would deal with a mathematical problem. Amy, an eleven-year-old girl, wonders why Heinz does not discuss the problem with the pharmacist. For surely he will then give Heinz the drug or at least arrive at a compromise, such as a loan. Amy does not see the dilemma in universal terms, as a clash between property and life, but focuses instead on the particular persons, their relationships and needs, and seeks a solution that will satisfy everyone. According to Gilligan, the ethic of justice is commonly thought to represent a 'higher' or more sophisticated stage of moral development, and the feminine point of view has been correspondingly marginalised and devalued. She wishes to replace the traditional approach with an approach that calls attention to the distinctive virtues of the feminine point of view.[13]

Drawing on these ideas, some feminist legal scholars have argued that the law reflects male values and that it needs to incorporate the ignored values associated with 'woman's voice'. Robin West, for instance, argues that law is built on the masculine idea that the individual is physically separate and apart from others. This is, in her view, untrue of women, who are connected to others through experiences such as pregnancy and activities such as breastfeeding.

---

13 C Gilligan, *In a Different Voice: Psychological Theory and Women's Development*, Harvard University Press, Cambridge, MA, 1982, pp 25–32.

Women see separation as a threat and intimacy as the most important value. In this, they are entirely unlike men. West writes:

> We need to flood the market with our own stories until we get one simple point across: men's narrative story and phenomenological description of law is not women's story and phenomenology of law. We need to dislodge legal theorists' confidence that they speak for women, and we need to fill the gap that will develop when we succeed in doing so.[14]

The French feminist and psychoanalyst Luce Irigaray goes even further. Instead of arguing that law should be more inclusive and incorporate the values of care and connection, she makes the controversial argument that the difference between men and women is the most fundamental difference and that there should be a separate law for men and women, which she describes as 'a law of persons appropriate to their natural reality, that is, to their sexed identity'.[15] Sexual difference should, in Irigaray's view, be accentuated, not minimised. She argues that the law must recognise rights appropriate to women's sexed bodies if women are to achieve self-realisation. Among the sexed rights for which Irigaray argues are the right to realise sexual difference by participating in traditions and practices that are culturally specific to women; the right to dignity (which requires an end to the commercial use of women's bodies and the right to positive representations of women in public places); a right to bodily and moral integrity, which for girls is a right to virginity; and a right to choose motherhood freely.[16]

13.7 Criticisms of difference feminism

Difference feminism is controversial because its picture of women's separate identity is so close to the stereotyped views about women contained in the hierarchical 'separate spheres' ideology, which have traditionally been used to subordinate women, as we have seen. Many feminists also worry that women's propensity to care for others and discount their own needs may simply be an artefact of male domination. John Stuart Mill made this point in his essay 'The Subjection of Women'. He wrote:

---

14   R West, 'Jurisprudence and Gender' (1988) 55 *Chicago University Law Review* 1, 65.
15   L Irigaray, *I Love to You: Sketch for a Felicity within History*, A Martin (trans), New York, Routledge, 1996, p 51.
16   L Irigaray, 'How to Define Sexuate Rights?', in M Whitford (ed), *The Irigaray Reader*, Basil Blackwell, Oxford, 1991, p 208. See also A Stone, 'The Sex of Nature: A Reinterpretation of Irigaray's Metaphysics and Political Thought' (2003) 18 *Hypatia* 60.

> All women are brought up from the very earliest years in the belief that their ideal of character is ... submission and yielding to the control of others. All the moralities tell them that it is the duty of women ... to live for others; to make complete abnegation of themselves, and to have no life but in their affections. And by their affections are meant the only ones they are allowed to have—those to the men with whom they are connected, or to the children who constitute an additional and indefeasible tie between them and a man.[17]

Mill therefore believes that men hold women in subjection by imposing on them the voice of care. MacKinnon provides a contemporary formulation of the same point, when she says: 'Women value care because men have valued us according to the care we give them.'[18] If you want to know in what tongue women speak, she adds: 'Take your foot off our necks.'[19]

The fear that difference feminism might be used to rationalise the second-class treatment of women was borne out by a United States employment discrimination case, *EEOC v Sears, Roebuck & Co.*,[20] in which an expert witness cited Gilligan's work to support the arguments of the company. The Equal Employment Opportunity Commission had brought charges of sex discrimination against Sears, Roebuck & Co. The basis for the complaint was that women accounted for only one-quarter of the employees hired to work in commission sales positions. Employees in these positions made more money than salaried employees. Sears justified the imbalance by explaining that the company was looking for specific personality traits in commission sales employees. These included being 'aggressive', 'outgoing and good with people', 'highly motivated' and 'leaders'. An expert witness for Sears, relying in part on Gilligan's work, testified that because women have traditionally put their families above their careers, they were unsuited to commission sales work and had less interest in it. Sears was therefore not, in her view, responsible for the low number of women in commission sales work. The court was convinced by these arguments and ruled that the EEOC had not proved its charges against Sears.

Difference feminism is also controversial insofar as it argues for 'special' treatment of women as a way of accommodating their particular needs. Charles Taylor writes illuminatingly on the radical shift from a 'politics of universalism' to a 'politics of difference' (sometimes also called 'identity politics') that underlies

---

17 J S Mill [1869], 'The Subjection of Women' in *Three Essays: On Liberty, Representative Government, The Subjection of Women*, M G Fawcett (ed), Oxford University Press, London, 1912, p 444.
18 MacKinnon, above n 5, p 39.
19 Ibid p 45.
20 *EEOC v Sears, Roebuck & Co.*, 839 F 2d 302 (7th Cir 1988).

the demand for these kinds of measures. The politics of universalism insists that we should all have the same rights, based on our identical human worth and common human needs. The politics of difference, by contrast, seeks rights for specific groups on the basis that the members of the group have a shared, distinctive identity. It identifies discrimination and second-class citizenship not with exclusion from a common citizenship, but rather with assimilation, uniformity and the ignoring of difference. It maintains that equality for minority groups and vulnerable groups may require different treatment, not identical treatment.[21] Furthermore, this is not just a matter of levelling the playing field so that difference can eventually be left behind. Instead, as Taylor says, the claim is that the search for genuinely universal or neutral principles is an impossible aspiration. It is said that difference-blind principles are necessarily exclusionary.[22] The idea is therefore 'to maintain and cherish distinctness, not just now but forever'.[23] The opponents of difference feminism fear, however, that 'cherishing distinctness' will reinforce and perpetuate the traditional stereotypes about women's role that have been such an obstacle to their fight for equality.

This debate raises what Martha Minow calls the dilemma of difference. The dilemma is that 'we may recreate difference either by noticing it or ignoring it'.[24] Margaret Radin talks in similar terms of the 'double bind', which, according to her, is at the heart of the problem of sexual inequality. The 'double bind' refers to the fact that '[f]or a group subject to structures of domination, all roads thought to be progressive can pack a backlash'.[25]

Suppose, for instance, that pregnant employees are given advantages that are denied to other workers. An employer might, for example, guarantee reinstatement in the job after childbirth, but not reinstatement for those who have taken time off from work due to illness. It can be argued that this perpetuates the traditional view about women's natural 'destiny' as mothers, a view which is one of the causes of their subordinate position in society. On the other hand, if pregnant women are not given pregnancy-specific benefits, then women are penalised in the workplace because of their biological differences: men can have a family without losing their jobs but women cannot. And this is another kind of obstacle to the goal of sexual equality.

---

21   C Taylor, 'The Politics of Recognition', in A Gutmann (ed), *Multiculturalism*, Princeton University Press, Princeton, New Jersey, 1994, pp 37–40.
22   Ibid pp 43–4.
23   Ibid p 40.
24   M L Minow, 'Justice Engendered' (1987) 101 *Harvard Law Review* 10, 12.
25   M Radin, 'The Pragmatist and the Feminist' (1990) 63 *Southern California Law Review* 1669, 1701.

One response to this double bind, made by feminists who are opposed to the use of gender-based classifications in the law, is to say that feminists should concentrate on improving workplace protection for *everyone*. Feminists should work for fundamental legislative change that makes adequate provision for parental leave, not maternity leave, and that provides proper protection for those who are disabled. Employers should therefore be required to extend benefits to pregnant employees as well as to non-pregnant employees, both male and female, who need time off work because of physical conditions and other characteristics that affect their workplace participation. Thus Wendy Williams writes:

> Pregnancy creates not 'special' needs, but rather exemplifies typical basic needs. If these particular typical needs are not met, then pregnant workers simply become part of a larger class of male and female workers, for whom the basic fringe benefit structure is inadequate. The solution ... is to solve the underlying problem of inadequate fringe benefits rather than to respond with measures designed especially for pregnant workers.[26]

The controversial nature of the special treatment approach was highlighted in a South African case, *President of the Republic of South Africa v Hugo*.[27] In this case, the Constitutional Court of South Africa was faced with a challenge to a Presidential Act, in terms of which President Mandela had exercised his power to pardon convicted prisoners. The Act provided for special remission to be granted to all mothers in prison who had children younger than 12 years old on the day of President Mandela's inauguration. The Constitution of South Africa forbids unfair discrimination on the ground of sex. Hugo was a male prisoner whose wife had died, and he had a child younger than 12 years old at the relevant date. He claimed that the Act unfairly discriminated against him on the ground of his sex by treating him less favourably than a similarly situated female prisoner.

The majority rejected his challenge. Goldstone J, who wrote the majority judgment, said that the group of mothers with young children was a vulnerable group, which had been the victim of discrimination in the past. Furthermore, the point of releasing the female prisoners was to protect the well-being of children. Since women are in general responsible for the care of small children in South African society, the release of male prisoners would not have served the purpose as effectively. Finally, the male prisoners had no legal entitlement to an

---

26 Williams, above n 7, 327.
27 *President of the Republic of South Africa v Hugo* 1997 (4) SA 1 (CC).

early release. Goldstone J concluded that for all these reasons the discrimination against the male prisoners was not unfair.[28]

Kriegler J, however, dissented, voicing the concerns alluded to above about the dangers of using the law to reinforce the traditional 'separate sphere' stereotypes, which paint men as breadwinners and women as mothers and homemakers. Accepting that the less favourable treatment of members of one sex is not necessarily unfair, he nevertheless said that a statute which is likely to promote the continuation of deeply entrenched patterns of inequality is unlikely to be defensible. It might seem that the president had used gender stereotypes to the advantage of women, but Kriegler J, on looking more deeply, found that the imposition of roles on the basis of 'predetermined ... gender scripts'[29] is not in the interests of women and will lead only to more inequality in the long run.

Kriegler J therefore called attention to the complexities involved in deciding whether special treatment, which appears to favour women, is really of benefit to them. He might have noted, in this connection, that a justification for the oppressive labour laws of the past, which, among other restrictions, limited the hours that women could work and prohibited them from working at night, was that they were necessary in order to 'protect' women and were therefore in their interests.

13.8 Dominance and subordination

We turn now to radical feminism, which focuses on dominance and power, not difference. The most influential exponent of radical feminism is MacKinnon. She argues that women do not so much speak with a different voice as have no voice at all. The domination of women as a class by men as a class is fundamental to the legal system, and indeed, to the whole of society. Oppression on the basis of sex is, in fact, the most fundamental kind of social oppression, and the sexual abuse of women is the indispensable mechanism by which women are subjugated. Power and sexuality are therefore central to the radical feminist analysis.

MacKinnon rejects both the 'sameness' approach and the 'difference' approach. Whether women are taken to be similar to or different from men, in both cases men provide the standard against which women are judged. MacKinnon, by contrast, takes up the perspective of women. Her feminism is

---

28 *President of the Republic of South Africa v Hugo* 1997 (4) SA 1 (CC) [47].
29 *President of the Republic of South Africa v Hugo* 1997 (4) SA 1 (CC) [83].

therefore 'feminism unmodified': feminism unaffected by anything except the subordination of women to men. She asks not whether women are relevantly like or relevantly unlike men, but whether their treatment perpetuates their inferiority. Sex equality will be achieved only when male power over women has been eliminated.

According to MacKinnon, gender difference is just 'the velvet glove on the iron fist of domination'.[30] It is a socially constructed concept that 'obscures and legitimizes the way gender is imposed by force'.[31] It is, in other words, men's power that constructs the idea of femininity, in the process ensuring the continuation of that power. For MacKinnon, gender would have no social meaning in the absence of male domination: 'what a woman "is" is what [men] have *made* women "be"'.[32]

Much of MacKinnon's work has a strongly practical focus on the way in which male sexuality is expressed in ways that objectify and subjugate women, especially through violence, rape, sexual harassment, prostitution and pornography. All are forms of sexual subordination and therefore, in MacKinnon's view, should be seen as sex discrimination. Her account of pornography is particularly well known, because it led her to draft legislation allowing anyone who had been harmed by pornography, broadly defined, to sue for damages. This legislation was adopted by the city of Indianapolis in 1984 but subsequently struck down by the Supreme Court of the United States on the ground that it infringed the right to freedom of speech.

MacKinnon argues that pornography eroticises inequality and the exercise of male power:

> [P]ornography is neither harmless fantasy nor a corrupt and confused misrepresentation of an otherwise natural and healthy sexual situation. It institutionalizes the sexuality of male supremacy, fusing the eroticization of dominance and submission with the social construction of male and female ... Men treat women as who they see women as being. Pornography constructs who that is.[33]

MacKinnon argues, in other words, that pornography is an issue of men's power and women's lack of it. Its consumption is a political issue, not a matter of men's personal sexual preferences and choices.

About rape MacKinnon writes: 'Perhaps the wrong of rape has proved so difficult to define because the unquestionable starting point has been that

---

30 MacKinnon, above n 5, p 8.
31 Ibid p 3.
32 Ibid p 59, MacKinnon's emphasis.
33 C A MacKinnon, 'Pornography, Civil Rights and Speech', in C Itzen (ed), *Pornography: Women, Violence and Civil Liberties*, Oxford University Press, Oxford, 1992, p 462.

rape is defined as distinct from intercourse, while for women it is difficult to distinguish the two under conditions of male dominance.'[34] On MacKinnon's analysis, all heterosexual relations are coercive in a society characterised by male supremacy: there is no clear way of distinguishing between consensual heterosexual sex and rape.

The bleakness of this picture has led some feminists to challenge MacKinnon's view of women as incapable of anything but helpless, silenced victimhood and as beings whose sexuality is entirely defined in terms of male power—the power, as MacKinnon puts it, 'to make us make the world of their sexual interaction with us the way they want it'.[35] MacKinnon's views about pornography have also proved controversial among feminists, some of whom are opposed to restricting pornography, notwithstanding their strong dislike of it due to the demeaning stereotypes about women that it conveys. This is because they do not accept that pornography is a root cause of women's oppression. Many feminists are also worried that laws restricting pornography would be hijacked by conservative groups wishing to suppress all forms of sexually explicit material, including feminist and lesbian art. Thus Gillian Rodgerson and Elizabeth Wilson argue that:

> [n]o matter how confident feminists may be that they know what they mean, there are those who consider any depiction of women as sexual beings, especially women enjoying being sexual, as degrading; any depiction of homosexuality as degrading; any depiction of women participating in sexual acts as necessarily objectifying them.[36]

Rodgerson and Wilson also argue that the message of pornography is much more complex and ambiguous than MacKinnon suggests.[37]

13.9 Postmodern feminism, essentialism and intersectionality

The 1990s saw the increasing influence of postmodern feminism. The main ideas of postmodernism will be recalled from 9.3. For our purposes, the most

---

34 C A MacKinnon, *Toward a Feminist Theory of the State*, Harvard University Press, Cambridge, MA, 1980, p 174.
35 MacKinnon, above n 5, p 58. For some criticisms of MacKinnon's view, see D Cornell, 'Sexual Difference, The Feminine, and Equivalency: A Critique of MacKinnon's *Toward A Feminist Theory of the State*' (1991) 100 *Yale Law Journal* 2247.
36 G Rodgerson and E Wilson, *Pornography and Feminism: The Case against Censorship*, Lawrence and Wishart, London, 1991, p 69.
37 Ibid p 72.

important of these are the following. First, there is postmodernism's distrust of grand, general theories aiming to tell the whole, objective truth. In place of such theories, postmodernism wishes to substitute a plurality of small-scale, partial, perspectival accounts. According to postmodernists, there are no objective and universal standards of truth and justice discoverable by human reason. There are only different, socially conditioned, subjective interpretations. Second, postmodernism seeks to deconstruct binary oppositions such as male/female, reason/emotion, nature/culture, with the aim of showing how these traditional distinctions of Western thought have developed and then subverting them. Deconstruction reveals how one of the concepts in each pair has been privileged and the other suppressed, thereby making space for previously excluded and marginalised views.

We see the same emphasis on partial perspectives, as well as a similar attempt to destabilise traditional categories and identities, in the case of postmodern feminism. Whereas all of the feminist views canvassed so far make generalisations, in one way or another, about women, and contrast the situation of women as such with that of men as such, postmodern feminism emphasises the differences *among* women. It criticises the other theories for what it calls their 'essentialism'. This is the assumption that all women, regardless of their other differences, such as race, ethnicity, class, age and sexual orientation, share a common experience of oppression and have common interests. MacKinnon, for instance, seems to make this assumption when she states: 'Inequality because of sex defines and situates women as women.'[38] And Gilligan makes essentialist assumptions in postulating a distinctively female kind of moral reasoning. For postmodernist feminists, by contrast, essential 'woman' does not exist.

Postmodern feminists argue that earlier feminist theories were the theories of privileged, middle-class, white women. Perhaps, for these women, sex oppression appears as the most fundamental form of oppression, but the experiences of women oppressed on the basis of other characteristics, such as their class, race or sexual orientation, will be different. Theories which stress the uniqueness of the disadvantage suffered by those who are subject to more than one system of subordination are called theories of 'intersectionality' because they hold that different bases of subordination intersect to produce a distinctive kind of disadvantage and a distinctive experience of oppression. Intersectional approaches therefore highlight the complex nature of inequality.

---

38   MacKinnon, above n 34, p 215.

The idea of intersectionality is central to Critical Race Theory, which will be discussed in 13.14. The critical race theorists argue that black women are not merely more oppressed than white women but *differently* oppressed. Kimberlé Crenshaw, for instance, argues that race affects the kinds of gender subordination that black women experience. She gives the example of sexual harassment: black women who complain of sexual harassment come up not only against stereotypes that are faced by white women and black men but also against the stereotype of black women as sexually promiscuous and unlikely to tell the truth. They also face the commonly held belief that sexually abusive behaviour directed towards black women is less abusive than the same behaviour directed towards white women. They are therefore *uniquely* disadvantaged as black women.[39]

A similar position has been adopted by Indigenous women in Australia. Larissa Behrendt remarks:

> The experiences of minority women have as much to do with racism as sexism. For Aboriginal women, this is illustrated by the experience of rape. When an Aboriginal woman is the victim of a sexual assault, how, as a black woman, does she know whether it is because she is hated as a woman and is perceived as inferior or if she is hated because she is Aboriginal, considered inferior and promiscuous by nature?[40]

Theorists such as Crenshaw and Behrendt argue that the failure to recognise the uniqueness of the experiences of black women silences and excludes them. In this case, however, the silencing and exclusion is not at the hands of men but at the hands of white women: though they claim to speak for all women, white feminists assume an implicit female norm analogous to the male norm they are at such pains to expose. They take their particular, partial perspective to be the whole truth. For instance, the picture feminists paint of women trapped within the home is, in reality, a picture of the predicament of *white* women: black women have generally worked outside the home. Lesbian theorists make a similar complaint. They say that feminist theory has spoken only for heterosexual women.

Elizabeth Spelman sums up the argument against essentialism as follows: 'Essentialism invites me to take what I understand to be true of me "as a woman" for some golden nugget of womanness all women have as women; and it makes

---

39   K Crenshaw, 'Race, Gender and Sexual Harassment' (1992) 65 *Southern California Law Review* 1467, 1470.
40   L Behrendt, 'Aboriginal Women and the White Lies of the Feminist Movement: Implications for Aboriginal Women in Rights Discourse' (1993) 1 *Australian Feminist Law Journal* 27, 35.

the participation of other women inessential to the production of the story. How lovely: the many turn out to be one, and the one that they are is me.'[41]

Postmodern feminism therefore wishes to make feminist jurisprudence more inclusive and pluralistic. It renounces the aspiration to general theorising about women, regarding this as impossible, and it pays attention instead to the different forms that oppression takes in different women's lives and therefore to the highly specific ways in which 'difference' manifests itself. This emphasis on 'fragmentation' is, of course, distinctively postmodern. Patricia Cain sums up the focus of postmodern feminism like this:

> [P]ostmodern feminism tells us to beware of searching for a new truth to replace the old ... There is no such thing as the woman's point of view. There is no single theory of equality that will work for the benefit of all women. Indeed, there is probably no single change or goal that is in the best interest of all women.[42]

13.10 Postmodernism and feminist politics

The developments in feminist theory described in the previous section raise troubling questions about feminism as a political movement. If theorists cease to use the category 'woman', can they still be said to be offering a form of *feminist* jurisprudence? How will feminists be able to critique the gender bias of the law and pursue their political goals if the category 'woman' disintegrates into multiple perspectives and points of view, based not only on the gender of those whose perspective it is, but also on their other characteristics, such as race, religion, sexual orientation and class? Must a feminist politics not presuppose that women have common interests if it is to speak for them?

Furthermore, acceptance of the postmodernist view that there is no such thing as objective truth and justice seems to make it more difficult to launch a compelling attack on sexual inequality. For this reason, feminist opponents of postmodernism argue that the cause of sexual equality is better served by the Enlightenment belief that all social arrangements should be scrutinised and rejected if found to be incapable of rational justification, than by the postmodernist belief that there are no universal standards of cognitive and normative legitimacy.

---

41 E V Spelman, *Inessential Woman: Problems of Exclusion in Feminist Thought*, Beacon Press, Boston, 1988, p 159.
42 Cain, above n 1, 838.

Sabina Lovibond, for instance, argues that, historically, feminism is a modern movement. One distinguishing feature of modern movements, according to Lovibond, is that they endorse the Enlightenment rejection of traditional practices and seek to eliminate the exercise of arbitrary power. Modern movements therefore make the liberating demand that traditional and arbitrary hierarchies of power based on criteria such as race, sex and class should be abolished and replaced by social arrangements organised on rational, egalitarian lines. Lovibond argues that this egalitarian project of emancipation for women has not yet been concluded and that it is therefore not in the interests of feminists to give up on it.[43] She argues that once feminists reject the Enlightenment agenda of a rational reconstruction of society, it becomes impossible to mount an effective challenge to a social order that systematically discriminates against women.[44] She also argues that the fact that mainstream feminism has denied the experiences of black women does not disprove the 'ideal unity' of feminism as a movement constituted by the 'single aim of ending sexual oppression'.[45] Instead, what black feminists have shown, in Lovibond's view, is that feminism has failed to live up to its own ideals.

MacKinnon also attacks postmodern feminism. She argues that as feminists make the description of particular women's experiences more and more detailed, the more they approach 'liberal feminism', with its emphasis on individuals, rather than group disadvantage. Thus, MacKinnon has this to say about the postmodern view that because sex always intersects with other bases for oppression, there is no such thing as 'woman':

> [I]f women don't exist, because there are only particular women, maybe Black people don't exist either, because they are divided by sex. Probably lesbians can't exist either, because they are divided by race and class; if women don't exist, woman-identified women surely don't exist, except in their heads. We are reduced to individuals, which, of all coincidences, is where liberalism places us.[46]

---

43 S Lovibond, 'Feminism and Post Modernism' (1989) 178 *New Left Review* 5, 11–12.
44 Ibid 22. For an alternative view, which argues that Derrida's concept of deconstruction helps us to think about justice and is conducive to legal transformation, see D Cornell, *The Philosophy of the Limit*, Routledge, New York, 1992.
45 Lovibond, above n 43, 28.
46 C A MacKinnon, 'Points against Postmodernism' (2000) 75 *Chicago-Kent Law Review* 687, 698.

MacKinnon believes that the postmodern feminists whose analyses lead to these sorts of conclusions have turned their backs on the reality of women's subordination and the practical struggle to improve the lives of women.[47]

13.11 The family as a political institution

A critique of the public–private distinction is an important theme in the works of feminist legal scholars. We have already taken note of the 'separate spheres' ideology and the distinction it draws between the public sphere of male governance and the private, domestic sphere of women and children. Feminist legal scholars argue that the relegation of women to the so-called 'private' realm is one of the most important causes of their subordinate position in society. For one thing, it is the reason why they are expected to bear the brunt of the responsibility for the unpaid and undervalued work of the home, which, many feminists argue, is one of the main causes of women's low employment status, economic dependence on men and inability to participate fully in the public world. Thus women's relegation to the private realm is a primary cause of their second-class status and any attack on women's inequality must involve an attack on their traditional role within the family.

Secondly, feminists point out that the law has seen fit to regulate the public domain, understood as encompassing state and market institutions, while traditionally regarding it as inappropriate to interfere in the 'loving' or 'intimate' area of family relationships and the home. This has led the law to ignore the way in which women are treated within the home. There are many examples of the law's failures in this area. Probably the best known is the fact that until very recently women were denied a remedy for rape within marriage. At one time, husbands also had the right to beat their wives and even now law enforcement agencies often turn a blind eye to domestic violence, something that does not happen in the context of violence outside the home. The upshot of this hands-off attitude is that male power in the domestic sphere is in practice supported at the same time as its exercise is concealed. Thus MacKinnon writes:

> When the law of privacy restricts intrusions into intimacy, it bars change in control over that intimacy ... It is probably not coincidence that the very things feminism regards as central to the subjection of women—the very place, the body; the very relations, heterosexual; the very activities, intercourse and reproduction; and the very feelings, intimate—form the core of what

---

47 Ibid 702.

is covered by privacy doctrine. From this perspective, the legal concept of privacy can and has shielded the place of battery, marital rape, and women's exploited labor.[48]

This kind of analysis underlies the feminist slogan 'the personal is the political'. The slogan is a way of calling attention to the following points. First, there is the point, made above, that private inequality is the source of public disadvantage. Second, it is argued that the world of private relationships is not a world of free choice and maximum autonomy, but a world imbued with the politics of power. Third, the slogan suggests that problems faced by women that might seem to be a matter of their individual, personal circumstances are in fact a function of systemic injustice against women as a group and therefore need to be addressed as matters of public concern. Some feminists emphasise 'consciousness-raising' as a method for reaching these insights. This involves the use of shared experience in groups as a way of enabling women to identify and understand the forces that oppress them. It is thought that when women share their experiences of subordination, it will become clear that they are not dealing with personal problems but systemic problems; not isolated problems but connected problems. It will become clear, in other words, that 'the personal is the political'.

There are further aspects to the feminist critique of the public–private distinction. Some feminists point out that it is a public decision to treat family life as a private matter. It was, after all, the law that allowed husbands to rape their wives. Others point out that the domestic sphere is, in fact, regulated in many ways that belie the law's official attitude to it. As Nicola Lacey observes, 'in spite of a great deal of rhetoric about privacy in the family sphere, a moment's thought reveals that many aspects of family life are hedged around with legal regulation—marriage, divorce, child custody, social welfare rules, to name but the most obviously relevant areas of law'.[49]

Many feminists also make the point that the law's decision not to regulate an area of life has political consequences, in just the same way as a decision to regulate has political consequences. Thus Katherine O'Donovan writes: 'Not legislating contains a value-judgement just as legislating does. Law cannot be neutral; non-intervention is as potent an ideology as regulation.'[50] Thus when

---

48 MacKinnon, above n 5, p 101.
49 N Lacey, *Unspeakable Subjects: Feminist Essays in Legal and Social Theory*, Hart Publishing, Oxford, 1998, p 74.
50 K O'Donovan, *Sexual Divisions in Law*, Weidenfeld and Nicolson, London, 1985, p 184.

the law refuses to intervene in the domestic sphere, the effect is to entrench and give legitimacy to the status quo. A connected claim is that the state should be held responsible for its hands-off approach to the domestic sphere and the inequalities and violence that flow from this indifference.

The feminist attack on the public–private distinction is widely accepted, as is the associated claim that the family is a political institution. But many feminist theorists go further, saying that liberals ignore and even help to create the injustices to which women are subjected in the family, because they defend the idea of a private sphere of freedom of action. Hilaire Barnett puts the point like this: '[L]iberalism ... contributes to the problem which women face. By distinguishing between the public sphere of life, which is legally regulated, and the private sphere of life, which is largely legally unregulated, liberalism carves out a haven for domestic violence.'[51]

But is it true that liberals who emphasise freedom of choice in the 'private sphere' wish to insulate the family from the principles of justice? As we know, Mill was a strenuous defender of the private realm, meaning by this a realm in which the law should not interfere and in which we should enjoy perfect freedom of action (see 11.3). At the same time, in 'The Subjection of Women', Mill vigorously objected to the way in which the law sanctions inequality and violence within the family. He observed that 'the wife's position under the common law of England is worse than that of slaves in the laws of many countries',[52] and he listed all the ways in which the life of a married woman amounts to servitude under the law. He especially stressed the law's acceptance of marital rape. In this connection he wrote:

> [N]o slave is a slave to the same lengths, and in so full a sense of the word, as a wife is. Hardly any slave ... is a slave at all hours and all minutes ... Above all, a female slave has (in Christian countries) an admitted right ... to refuse to her master the last familiarity. Not so the wife: however brutal a tyrant she may unfortunately be chained to ... he can claim from her and enforce the lowest degradation of a human being, that of being made the instrument of an animal function contrary to her inclinations.[53]

How could Mill defend the idea of a private realm while also criticising the way in which men exercise power in the domestic sphere? The answer to this is that the private realm that Mill and other liberals defend is not the domestic realm.

---

51 H Barnett, *Introduction to Feminist Jurisprudence*, Cavendish Publishing, London, 1998, p 258.
52 Mill, above n 17, p 462.
53 Ibid p 463.

Liberals do not identify the private realm with a place, such as the home. For liberals the private realm is the realm in which the law ought not to interfere. For Mill, if we are not violating anyone's rights or failing to perform our positive obligations, the law should leave us alone. 'Private' is therefore just a label liberals apply to conduct in which we are morally entitled to engage without interference. This does not coincide with the realm of family or domestic relationships, which are often characterised by harmful conduct, especially to women and children. Liberals therefore do not say that the realm of the family is a realm of freedom or that the law should treat it as such. On the contrary, they say that the state is obliged to protect us from harmful conduct, regardless of whether it occurs in public or private. Liberals can therefore agree with feminists that when the state refuses to protect women against injustice in the domestic realm, this is a political choice and an abdication of responsibility. They can also agree with feminists that when the domestic sphere is wrongly described as 'private', the label serves to mask the oppression and exploitation of women and children.

Liberals may also go on to argue that their defence of a private realm, understood as a defence of the right to make decisions that ought to be ours alone, serves the interests of women by granting them the right to make decisions about their own bodies—something frequently denied them by the law. Consider, for instance, the issue of abortion. As we saw in 11.9, Dworkin argues that women are entitled to choose whether to have an abortion because it is a personal choice. Indeed, it was precisely on this basis that the United States Supreme Court struck down anti-abortion laws in the case of *Roe v Wade*.[54] On the other hand, some feminists think that it is a mistake to defend the right to abortion on the ground that it is a personal or private choice. MacKinnon, for instance, claims that it was because the Supreme Court saw abortion as a private choice in *Roe v Wade* that it was willing to uphold a law that prohibited the use of government funds to finance abortions for poor women in the later case of *Harris v McRae*.[55] MacKinnon writes: 'Freedom from public intervention coexists uneasily with any right that requires social preconditions to be meaningfully delivered.'[56] She suggests, in other words, that if we understand the right to abortion in negative terms, as a right to choose abortion free of state

---

54 *Roe v Wade*, 410 (US) 113 (1973).
55 *Harris v McRae*, 488 (US) 297 (1980).
56 MacKinnon, above n 5, p 100.

interference, then we will be less inclined to believe there is a positive obligation on the state to fund abortions for those who cannot afford them.

Is MacKinnon's argument correct? Dworkin argues that it is not. He agrees with MacKinnon that it is not enough that abortion should be legal. Women must also be able to exercise their right to abortion and the state should therefore, in Dworkin's view, finance abortions for poor women. But, according to Dworkin, this is not incompatible with seeing abortion as a matter of 'sovereignty over personal decisions'. On the contrary, he thinks that 'recognizing that women have a ... right to determine how their own bodies are to be used is a prerequisite, not a barrier, to the further claim that the government must ensure that the right is not illusory'.[57]

We have seen that liberalism's private sphere of freedom is not the same as the domestic sphere, and that nothing in the liberal defence of the right to make certain decisions free of state interference implies that the state should not intervene in the family. It is nevertheless true that the major liberal theorists, such as Rawls, have tended to be relatively uninterested in the systemic subordination of women and the role played by the family in the creation of gender roles and sexual inequality. Rawls attempts to rectify this in his later writings, in which he argues that the family is part of the basic structure of society and that the principles of justice therefore apply to the family and, indeed, require its reform.[58] Rawls now writes: 'The equal rights of women ... are inalienable and protect them wherever they are. Gender distinctions limiting those rights and liberties are excluded ... If the so-called private sphere is alleged to be a space exempt from justice, then there is no such thing.'[59] Thus Rawls insists, for instance, that 'a long and historic injustice to women is that they have borne, and continue to bear, an unjust share of the task of raising, nurturing, and caring for their children'.[60] This leads him to argue that the law should count a woman's economic contribution in staying home to look after children as entitling her to an equal share in the income earned by her husband.[61]

Other liberals, such as Nussbaum, would go further. Nussbaum stresses the way in which the family is constructed or defined by the state and she insists

---

57 R Dworkin, *Life's Dominion: An Argument about Abortion and Euthanasia*, HarperCollins Publishers, London, 1993, p 54.
58 J Rawls, 'The Idea of Public Reason Revisited' (1997) 64 *University of Chicago Law Review* 765, 788, 791, 792-3.
59 Ibid 791.
60 Ibid 790.
61 Ibid 793.

that the state should conform to the standards of justice when it shapes family relationships. Whereas Rawls accepts the family as a given and seeks to police it from the outside, Nussbaum thinks that the state should consider which groupings it should protect, and on what basis.[62] She argues, for instance, that the Indian government was right to outlaw the dowry system because it was a major contribution to the unequal capabilities of Indian women. (For discussion of the notion of capabilities, see 12.10.) Nussbaum thinks, however, that Rawls would find it difficult to justify this government decision because he still thinks of the family as to some extent pre-political, and would therefore think of dowry as a choice made by the family. On Nussbaum's approach, by contrast, 'permitting dowry is not neutral state inaction toward an autonomous private entity; it is another (alternative) way of constituting a part of the public sphere'.[63] Likewise, she advocates changes to property rights in countries that give women no control over land. She says that control over property is one of the central capabilities, which cannot be denied on the basis of sex. No doubt giving women such control would profoundly alter family governance but Nussbaum would justify this by saying: 'You didn't just find the family lying around, you constituted it in one way, through the tradition of property law; now we shall constitute it in another way, one that protects women's capabilities.'[64]

13.12 Rights, justice and care

Feminist scholarship is characterised by ambivalence about the notions of rights and justice, which are said by some feminists to be gendered concepts. Feminists influenced by the CLS view that rights are too individualistic, as well as by the claims of writers such as Gilligan, argue that the notions of rights and justice reflect a competitive, male perspective on the world. They say that instead of pressing our own individual claims, we should accept our responsibilities and care about other people. As Deborah Rhode explains, these feminists believe that:

> [a] preoccupation with personal entitlements can divert concern from collective responsibilities. Rights rhetoric too often channels individuals' aspirations into demands for their own share of protected opportunities and fails to address more fundamental issues about what ought to be protected.

---

62 M C Nussbaum, *Women and Human Development: The Capabilities Approach*, Cambridge University Press, Cambridge, 2000, p 278.
63 Ibid p 280.
64 Ibid p 282.

Such an individualistic framework ill serves the values of cooperation and empathy that feminists find lacking in our current legal culture.[65]

On the other hand, as Rhode also points out, other feminists believe that rights have an empowering aspect, especially for members of disadvantaged groups. They may argue that the law's failure to protect women in the domestic sphere suggests that what women need is not fewer 'personal entitlements' or rights, but more. Consider, for instance, the importance to women of the recent recognition that married women have the right to refuse to have sex with their husbands. And consider the way in which the ability of women to control their own fertility depends on the right to abortion. On the basis of these and similar examples, many feminists are loath to give up on the language of rights, which they see as a necessary protection for members of subordinate groups.[66]

Defenders of rights also argue that rights have other functions besides protecting us against interference from other people. As we saw in Chapter 12, it is only libertarians who argue that we do not have a right to positive assistance from other people. Most contemporary rights theorists reject libertarianism and believe that rights have just as important a role to play in protecting material well-being as in protecting freedom. Kymlicka argues that once we realise that there are rights to positive assistance, it is very hard to make sense of the idea that rights and responsibilities, or justice and care, are incompatible. After all, positive rights clearly reflect the importance of assuming responsibility for the fulfilment of other people's needs.[67]

13.13 Feminism and multiculturalism

An important issue for contemporary feminists is the potential clash between cultural rights and women's rights. This has arisen because the same impulse that led some feminists to insist on the recognition of women's distinctive identity has led certain minority ethnic and religious groups to reject the 'homogenising' idea of conforming to majority norms.[68] They, too, have pursued 'identity politics' (see 13.7). Arguing that they are marginalised and excluded, and mobilising on the basis of their minority identity, these groups have claimed

---

65 D Rhode, 'Feminist Critical Theories' (1990) 42 *Stanford Law Review* 617, 633.
66 Ibid 634–5.
67 W Kymlicka, *Contemporary Political Philosophy: An Introduction*, 2nd edn, Oxford University Press, Oxford, 2002, p 410.
68 For a sympathetic account of these developments, see I M Young, *Justice and the Politics of Difference*, Princeton University Press, Princeton, 1990, pp 163–6.

the right to recognition and accommodation of their differences under the banner of group rights or multiculturalism. Instead of equal rights, in other words, they ask for special rights. They may, for instance, seek exemptions from laws that apply to other citizens. Or they may seek to rely on cultural defences as an excuse for conduct that would otherwise be criminal.[69] There is considerable controversy about the legitimacy of the legal recognition of cultural differences. Paul Kelly puts the issue like this: 'Is being in favour of multicultural policies the natural response to rejecting group discrimination, racism and bigotry, or is it to fall prey to a subversive conservatism that endorses hierarchy, tradition and the denial of opportunity?'[70]

The worry that cultural rights are conservative has particularly exercised feminists who note that the groups in question frequently seek to restrict the freedom and equality of women within the group. They also observe that a double standard operates when cultural practices disadvantage women: many defenders of cultural group rights draw the line at the accommodation of racist practices, but are willing to accommodate practices that harm women.[71] Susan Okin discusses this tension between feminism and the multiculturalist ideal of respecting cultural diversity. She argues that there are two important connections between culture and gender. First, religious and cultural groups tend to be particularly concerned with the sphere of personal, sexual and reproductive life. This means that respect for cultural practices is likely to have a much greater impact on the lives of women and girls than on those of men and boys.[72] Secondly, Okin argues that one of the principal aims of most religious and cultural groups is the control of women's sexuality and their reproductive capabilities by men. She mentions some controversial examples of such customs: clitoridectomy, polygamy and forced marriage.[73] Such control over women is typically exerted informally in the 'private' sphere of the family, but it substantially limits the ability of women to lead the lives they would like to lead.[74]

---

69 For discussion of cultural defences, see D L Coleman, 'Individualizing Justice through Multiculturalism: The Liberals' Dilemma' (1996) 96 *Columbia Law Review* 1093; S Bronitt and K Amirthalingam, 'Cultural Blindness: Criminal Law in Multicultural Australia' (1996) 21 *Alternative Law Journal* 58.
70 P Kelly, 'Introduction: Between Culture and Equality', in P Kelly (ed), *Multiculturalism Reconsidered*, Polity, Cambridge, 2002, p 4.
71 S Okin, '"Mistresses of Their Own Destiny?" Group Rights, Gender, and Realistic Rights of Exit' (2002) 112 *Ethics* 205, 213, 216.
72 S Okin, 'Is Multiculturalism Bad for Women?', in J Cohen, M Howard and M C Nussbaum (eds), *Is Multiculturalism Bad for Women?*, Princeton University Press, Princeton, 1999, pp 12-13.
73 Ibid pp 13-14.
74 Ibid p 12.

Okin thinks that those who defend group rights are too willing to overlook these private kinds of abuse.

Although Okin does not deny that Western liberal democracies practise sex discrimination, she says that they have made efforts to depart from patriarchal practices. Thus, she remarks, most families in Western liberal cultures 'do not communicate to their daughters that they are of less value than boys, that their lives are to be confined to domesticity and service to men and children, and that their sexuality is of value only in marriage, in the service of men, and for reproductive ends'.[75] It is different for women in many of the minority cultures that ask for legal recognition and accommodation of their customs. How, then, should the law respond when women claim that their rights are being infringed by the 'private' practices of the cultural groups to which they belong? Should women from a patriarchal minority culture who live in a Western liberal democracy enjoy less protection than other women? Okin's answer is 'no'. It is the male members of the group who demand group rights and they generally do not speak for the whole group. Minority cultural practices that subordinate women should therefore not be tolerated.[76]

On the other hand, Okin's opponents argue that she has dogmatically assumed that liberal values are universally valid. Thus Bhikhu Parekh argues that '[t]o insist that [nonliberals] must abide by our fundamentals is to expose ourselves to the same charge of fundamentalism that we make against them, and to rely solely on our superior coercive power to get our way'.[77] Parekh describes the 'feminist sensibility' as 'parochial' and suggests that it could benefit from the 'radically novel ways of conceptualizing and structuring intergender relations' that multiculturalism would generate.[78] This returns us to the questions, discussed in 10.9 and 12.8, as to whether liberal rights are a Western imposition and whether they can be justified in a way that can appeal to people who have different conceptions of the good life and do not place value on autonomy.

13.14 Critical race theory

We turn now to Critical Race Theory (CRT). This movement originated in the United States in the 1970s with the writings of Derrick Bell, an African American

---

75 Ibid p 17.
76 Ibid pp 23–4.
77 B Parekh, 'A Varied Moral World', in J Cohen, M Howard and M C Nussbaum (eds), *Is Multiculturalism Bad for Women?*, Princeton University Press, Princeton, 1999, p 72.
78 Ibid p 75.

lawyer, who argued that racism and white dominance will never disappear. He maintained that the apparent progress in race relations in the United States is a short-term phenomenon, to be explained by the self-interest of white elites.[79] CRT subsequently gained momentum in the 1990s, via the work of theorists such as Richard Delgado, Mari Matsuda and Patricia Williams. Although CRT is an American development, and its concerns are therefore influenced by slavery and the civil rights movement, many of the points it makes about the inadequacy of current legal approaches to race are more general and can be extended outside the US context. For instance, it has obvious relevance to Indigenous critiques of law in Australia.

There are a number of themes in CRT. One is the contingency of 'race' as a category of identity. What is meant by this is that 'race' is a socially and legally constructed category. Richard Delgado and Jean Stefanic explain this as follows:

> [G]roups of people are physically different ... but the differences between groups are swamped by their similarities and by the range of differences existing within groups themselves. Races exist, then, because we pick out certain features, such as skin colour, decide to notice them and not others, and ascribe importance to them, usually in a negative way, notwithstanding that the construction of different groups occurs in different ways, and one group can be constructed more or less negatively or positively at different times.[80]

Second, CRT attacks the idea of colour-blindness, that is, the idea that race is an irrelevant category, which the law should ignore, and that racial equality involves extending identical treatment to members of different races. Critical race theorists, like many feminist legal theorists, believe that this is merely a way of requiring those who are different to conform to an unstated and unthinkingly accepted 'norm'—in this case, the white norm. CRT therefore holds that the law's official blindness to racial difference is, in reality, a way of privileging and perpetuating practices that were designed for the benefit of whites and that reflect their interests. In short, in the same way that feminists argue that law has a gender—namely male—CRT theorists argue that it has a colour—namely white: everything about the law reflects and perpetuates the perspective of whites. In place of the law's pretence to neutrality, CRT wishes to highlight the pervasive presence of racism in the legal system and to give voice

---

79 D Bell, '*Brown v Board of Education* and the Interest Convergence Dilemma' (1980) 93 *Harvard Law Review* 518.
80 R Delgado and J Stefanic, 'Critical Race Theory: Past, Present and Future' (1998) 51 *Current Legal Problems* 467, 476.

to the 'outsider' perspectives on law of those who have suffered from racial oppression. Angela Harris writes:

> [P]art of the reason why race-crits have tried to distance themselves from traditional civil rights scholarship is precisely that the old verities, the old optimistic faith in reason, truth, blind justice, and neutrality, have not brought us to racial justice but have rather left us 'stirring the ashes'. History has shown that racism can coexist happily with formal commitments to objectivity, neutrality, and color-blindness.[81]

Third, CRT scholarship is committed to analysis employing the concept of intersectionality, as described in 13.9, with the aim of showing how race intersects with other characteristics to produce a distinctive kind of oppression. Black feminist analysis, for instance, explores such matters as the extent to which the interests of black women are marginalised in mainstream feminist movements, thus exposing injustices to which mainstream feminism is blind.

Fourth, CRT places great emphasis on the role of storytelling and narratives in exposing racism. Critical race theorists tell their own stories as a way of challenging mainstream legal assumptions and prejudices. In part, these stories seek to make the postmodernist point that 'what you see depends on where you stand'.[82] Storytelling is also a way of building identity and new communities.[83] Adoption of a narrative style is also intended to give us a concrete understanding of how the law affects minorities.[84] Matsuda, for instance, relies on such a style to attack the legal protection of racist hate speech in the United States. The US position is that hate speech cannot be legally restricted because of the very strong protection for freedom of speech granted under the US Constitution by the First Amendment. Matsuda observes that the First Amendment has not prevented other forms of offensive speech from being made illegal, such as child pornography and defamation. This is because, according to her, the 'legal imagination' is able to comprehend the harms done by child pornography and defamation.[85] When it comes to hate speech, by contrast, the harms are trivialised and discounted as 'pranks'.[86] Matsuda uses concrete, detailed stories to counter this failure of the legal imagination, evoking

---

81   A Harris, 'The Jurisprudence of Reconstruction' (1994) 82 *California Law Review* 741, 759.
82   Ibid 756.
83   Ibid 764.
84   Ibid 757.
85   M Matsuda, 'Public Response to Racist Speech: Considering the Victim's Story' (1989) 87 *Michigan Law Review* 2320, 2375.
86   Ibid 2327.

the lived experience of the victims of hate speech in order to sensitise lawmakers and judges to the reality of racism and the harms it causes. She writes: 'We are a legalized culture. If law is where racism is, then law is where we must confront it.'[87]

Finally, in developing a race-conscious form of legal theory, CRT emphasises the value of rights to members of minority groups. This aspect of CRT scholarship represents a response to the perceived elitism of Critical Legal Studies and its failure to understand what oppression and domination in real life are actually like. It will be remembered that CLS theorists attacked rights and the rule of law on the basis that they are unnecessary, since 'people do not want just to be beastly to each other'.[88] Furthermore, according to CLS theorists, rights serve only to protect the selfish interests of isolated individualists.

CRT, which has a much more practically oriented focus on achieving justice and abolishing oppression than CLS, counters these arguments by saying that they are a luxury that black people cannot afford. Thus Williams, for instance, points out that at one time, African American slaves were not regarded as legal subjects who were capable of enjoying rights. Now that that is no longer the case, she says that it would be hard to persuade African Americans to surrender their rights on the basis of the theoretical reflections and experiences of mainly privileged white men, who are able to take rights for granted. Williams writes: '"Rights" feels so new in the mouths of most black people. It is still so deliciously empowering to say. It is a sign for and a gift of selfhood that is very hard to contemplate restructuring ... at this point in history.'[89] Writing from the perspective of a black woman in the United States, Williams therefore refuses to dispense with such 'reformist' and liberal notions as rights and the rule of law in the hope of more far-reaching but vaguely described forms of social transformation.

Delgado argues along similar lines that '[o]ne explanation for the CLS position on rights may be that the average Crit, a white male teaching at a major law school, has little use for rights. Those with whom he comes in contact in his daily life—landlords, employers, public authorities—generally treat him with respect and deference.'[90] For black people, however, it is different.

---

87 Ibid 2381.
88 J W Singer, 'The Player and the Cards: Nihilism and Legal Theory' (1984) 94 *Yale Law Journal* 1, 54.
89 P Williams, 'Alchemical Notes: Reconstructing Ideals from Reconstructed Rights' (1987) 22 *Harvard Civil Rights- Civil Liberties Law Review* 401, 431.
90 R Delgado, 'The Ethereal Scholar: Does Critical Legal Studies Have What Minorities Want?' (1987) 22 *Harvard Civil Rights—Civil Liberties Law Review* 301, 305-6.

Williams describes an arrangement to lease property and recalls that she was 'acutely conscious of the likelihood that, no matter what degree of professional or professor I became, people would greet and dismiss my black femaleness as unreliable, untrustworthy, hostile, angry, powerless, irrational and probably destitute'.[91]

13.15 Sexuality and the law

Lesbian and gay legal theorists are concerned with the oppression of lesbians and gay men and the privileging of heterosexual norms. In many ways, lesbian and gay legal theory has developed along similar lines to feminist legal theory. Early lesbian and gay activists took the view that there is an essential lesbian or gay identity and that there are distinctively lesbian or gay experiences. This gave rise to criticisms alleging essentialism—that a very specific conception of lesbian and gay identity had been assumed and that, for instance, white lesbians had claimed to speak for all lesbians, or that those lesbians whose sexuality fell outside the lesbian 'norm' of sexuality, such as non-monogamous lesbians, had been marginalised.

Queer theory responds to these concerns. It is a theoretical development influenced, like postmodern feminism, by poststructuralism and its rejection of stable, unitary categories, including its suspicion of the idea of a self-determining and unified subject (see 9.3). It rejects the notion of an essential identity, whether gay, lesbian or heterosexual. All identities are seen as shifting, contingent and socially constructed. Queer theory points to the fact that same-sex practices have been understood differently and have taken different forms in different cultures and times. It concludes from this that there is no such thing as 'natural' sexuality. Sexuality, on this view, is a function of the variable cultural resources available for self-understanding.[92] These claims owe an obvious debt to Foucault's work on sexuality (see 9.3).

Furthermore, queer theory takes the view that the way to reverse homophobia is not to say that 'gay is good' but to occupy the 'deviant' position created by homophobic discourse.[93] 'Queer' therefore amounts to the adoption of a transgressive position, which can be occupied by anyone whose sexual activities challenge the idea of normal behaviour. It is said that queer is not

---

91 Williams, above n 89, 407.
92 D M Halperin, *One Hundred Years of Homosexuality and Other Essays on Greek Love*, Routledge, New York, 1990, pp 41–53.
93 D M Halperin, *Saint Foucault: Towards a Gay Hagiography*, Oxford University Press, New York, 1995, p 61.

subject to the complaint of essentialism because 'queer' does not refer to any particular identity category. It is simply that which transgresses the norm, whatever the norm may be. David Halperin writes: 'Queer is by definition *whatever is at odds with the normal, the legitimate, the dominant. There is nothing in particular to which it necessarily refers*. It is an identity without an essence.'[94]

Queer theory poses a philosophical challenge to identity politics by questioning the very idea of stable identities. A different concern about identity politics is that it is ultimately repressive, in dictating that members of groups play certain defined roles, which, even if they are not the same as the negative roles of the past, are nevertheless inhibiting and constraining. K Anthony Appiah writes as follows about the tyranny of collective identities:

> I think we need to go on to the next necessary step, which is to ask whether the identities constructed in this way are ones we—I speak here as someone who counts in America as a gay black man—can be happy with in the longer run. Demanding respect for people as blacks and as gays requires that there are some scripts that go with being an African-American or having same-sex desires. There will be proper ways of being black and gay, there will be expectations to be met, demands will be made. It is at this point that someone who takes autonomy seriously will ask whether we have not replaced one kind of tyranny with another.[95]

There is no space to pursue these various issues about identity and their possible connections here.[96] Instead, I will focus on a controversial issue of current legal interest, the issue of same-sex marriage. Many people resist legalising same-sex marriage on the ground that same-sex relationships are intrinsically wrong and that they are inconsistent with the nature of marriage. For instance, John Finnis and Robert George argue from a natural law perspective that marriage must be between a man and a woman because procreation is essential to marriage.[97] Other opponents of same-sex marriage argue that it is damaging to children and to society more generally.[98] More interesting for our purposes, however, is the fact that there is disagreement among lesbians and

---

94 Ibid, Halperin's emphasis.
95 K Anthony Appiah, 'Identity, Authenticity, Survival', in A Gutmann (ed), *Multiculturalism*, Princeton University Press, Princeton, New Jersey, 1994, pp 162-3.
96 For a detailed argument connecting queer theory's suspicion of gender and sexuality identity categories with the value of autonomy, see A Zanghellini, 'Queer, Antinormativity, Counter-Normativity and Abjection' (2009) 18 *Griffith Law Review* 1, 6-8.
97 J Finnis, 'The Good of Marriage and the Morality of Sexual Relations: Some Philosophical and Historical Observations' (1997) 42 *American Journal of Jurisprudence* 97; R P George and G V Bradley, 'Marriage and the Liberal Imagination' (1995) 84 *Georgetown Law Journal* 301.
98 For discussion, see A Koppelman, 'The Decline and Fall of the Case against Same-Sex Marriage' (2004) 2 *University of St Thomas Law Journal* 5, 25-32.

gay men themselves about the desirability of marriage rights. Let us examine the nature of their disagreement.

The primary argument for the right to marry is an equality argument. Marriage is a very important institution in our society, which makes it possible for people to demonstrate a distinctive kind of commitment to each other, and lesbians and gay men who seek marriage rights argue that denying them access to the institution is discriminatory and stigmatising. They also say that they are entitled to have the legitimacy of their relationships publicly accepted and acknowledged. Exclusion from marriage, they say, treats them as second-class citizens. Furthermore, they reject the idea that same-sex civil unions, which provide the legal advantages of marriage without its name, and therefore without its symbolic status, are sufficient to meet these concerns. They argue that creating a special category of civil unions for same-sex couples treats them as inferior in the same way that 'separate but equal' schools treated black children as inferiors. These arguments invoke the values of equal rights and equal respect.[99] A related argument, made by Cheshire Calhoun, claims that painting lesbians and gay men as unfit for family life and as bad influences for children has been a central cause of their subordination. Same-sex marriage should therefore, in her view, be placed at the centre of lesbian and gay politics as an indispensable means to the achievement of equal citizenship.[100]

On the other hand, lesbians and gay men who are opposed to seeking the right to marry make two main points. First, they argue that marriage is an oppressive institution, especially for women (see 13.11). Secondly, they argue that pursuing same-sex marriage is an assimilationist strategy with conservative implications. They believe that marriage is 'heteronormative'. In other words, it has a built-in bias towards heterosexual values. For instance, it assumes that the ideal relationship is monogamous and emotionally intimate. Many lesbians and gay men, however, do not wish to pursue relationships of this kind. The goal of legalising same-sex marriage therefore implies that lesbian and gay relationships should conform to mainstream, heterosexual norms, thereby erasing their differences. Furthermore, in the view of the opponents of same-sex marriage, if lesbians and gay men were allowed to marry this would lead to a new division,

---

99 A A Wellington, 'Why Liberals Should Support Same Sex Marriage' (1995) 26 *Journal of Social Philosophy* 5; A Rajczi, 'A Populist Argument for Same-Sex Marriage' (2008) 91 *The Monist* 475.
100 C Calhoun, *Feminism, the Family, and the Politics of the Closet: Lesbian and Gay Displacement*, Oxford University Press, Oxford, 2000, pp 140–60.

between 'respectable' married and 'deviant' unmarried lesbians and gay men, leading the latter to become even more stigmatised and marginalised.

Nancy Polikoff argues along these lines, writing: 'I believe that the desire to marry in the lesbian and gay community is an attempt to mimic the worst of mainstream society, an effort to fit into an inherently problematic institution that betrays the promise of both lesbian and gay liberation and radical feminism.'[101] Likewise, in the context of discussing the legal struggle in Canada for family benefits for same-sex couples, which used the slogan 'We Are Family', Brenda Cossman writes: 'While the claim that We Are Family pushes at the margins of family by challenging its exclusive and restrictive borders, and the ostensible "naturalness" of its heterosexual form, the claim has not challenged the hierarchical opposition between family and not family. On the contrary, family remains the dominant and positive social value.'[102]

William Eskridge, who is a well-known advocate of legalising same-sex marriage, writes sympathetically of these arguments but ultimately rejects them. He believes that for an earlier generation of lesbian and gay activists, who grew up in a more anti-homosexual environment, difference was more important. For them it was important to fight 'the hard battles against a compulsory heterosexuality whose hallmark is the wedding photo'.[103] But separatism is no longer, in his view, so attractive. Other lesbians and gay men respond to the worry about assimilation by arguing that same-sex marriage would have radical consequences, not conservative ones. It would help, in their view, to counter damaging stereotypes of lesbians and gay men, and to transform the family and its associated gendered division of labour.[104] Although it is not possible to pursue these matters further here, it is worth mentioning that there are some deep philosophical questions underlying this debate, to do with the nature of marriage, whether it is a good, and what its purpose is. One can, indeed, ask whether there should be a law of marriage at all or whether people should be left free to enter into whatever contracts they please to govern the terms of their relationships.[105]

---

101 N D Polikoff, 'We Will Get What We Ask for: Why Legalizing Gay and Lesbian Marriage Will Not "Dismantle the Legal Structure of Gender in Every Marriage"' (1993) 79 *Virginia Law Review* 1535, 1536.
102 B Cossman, 'Family Inside/Out' (1994) 44 *University of Toronto Law Journal* 1, 28.
103 W N Eskridge, Jr, 'A History of Same-Sex Marriage' (1993) 79 *Virginia Law Review* 1434, 1490.
104 N D Hunter, 'Marriage, Law, and Gender: A Feminist Inquiry' (1991) 1 *Law and Sexuality* 9, 13–19.
105 See C R Sunstein and R H Thaler, 'Privatizing Marriage' (2008) 91 *The Monist* 377.

Questions

1. Do you think the law reflects a male point of view?
2. Is 'gender-neutral' law possible? Is it desirable?
3. Consider the following problem. The Commonwealth Parliament passes the *Protection against Pregnancy Discrimination Act* (Cth). This Act requires employers to treat pregnancy the same as any other disability. The Parliament of New South Wales subsequently passes the *Pregnant Employees Leave Act* (NSW), which requires employers to give pregnant employees three months' paid maternity leave. There are no NSW laws requiring employers to provide paid leave to other employees who are temporarily unable to work. An employer challenges the state Act on the ground that it gives pregnancy preferential treatment and is therefore inconsistent with the Commonwealth Act. Do you think the Acts are inconsistent? How might different feminist theories support different answers to this question?
4. An employer wants to revitalise the workforce by employing younger people and stipulates that, in addition to meeting all the other requirements for the job, the applicants must be under the age of 28. Do you think the employer's requirement discriminates on the ground of sex/gender?
5. Although women constitute 40% of an area's labour market, they constitute only 20% of a particular employer's workforce. Furthermore, they are mainly employed in non-skilled positions. The employer wishes to counteract the under-representation of women in skilled positions and designs a plan with the aim of eventually attaining a balanced workforce. In terms of the plan, the number of women in skilled positions should increase by a certain percentage annually. When a vacancy for a skilled position becomes available, the employer advertises for new employees, stating that preference will be given to women. He subsequently passes over a male applicant with more experience and higher test scores in favour of a less qualified female applicant. Do you think that the employer unfairly discriminated against the male applicant?
6. The Victorian case of *R v Dincer* [1983] VR 460 concerned a man, described as a conservative Muslim of Turkish origin, who stabbed and killed his 16-year-old daughter because she had had premarital sex. The court heard evidence that in the accused's culture, an

unmarried daughter's loss of virginity is a matter of great shame and disgrace to the parents. Lush J stated that in determining what an ordinary man might have done under the same provocation, 'the jury must consider an ordinary man who has the same characteristics as the man in the dock. In this case it has been put to you from the outset that you have to take into consideration the fact that Dincer is Turkish by birth, the fact that he is Muslim by religion, the fact that he is ... a traditionalist, the picture painted of him that he was a conservative Muslim, and as part of the consequences of those characteristics ... there are the social practices which are assessed by him as desirable or undesirable, permissible or not permissible, by reference to those essential background aspects of his character. The problem becomes what would an ordinary man whose make-up included these components ... have possibly done in these circumstances' (at 466). Do you think the accused should have been judged by a culturally relative test of self-control?

Further reading

J Cohen, M Howard and M C Nussbaum (eds), *Is Multiculturalism Bad for Women?*, Princeton University Press, Princeton, 1999.

K Crenshaw, 'Demarginalizing the Intersection of Race and Sex: A Black Feminist Critique of Anti-Discrimination Doctrine, Feminist Theory and Antiracist Politics' (1989) *University of Chicago Legal Forum* 139.

C Gilligan, *In a Different Voice: Psychological Theory and Women's Development*, Harvard University Press, Cambridge, MA, 1982.

R Graycar and J Morgan, *The Hidden Gender of Law*, 2nd edn, Federation Press, Sydney, 2002.

N Lacey, *Unspeakable Subjects: Feminist Essays in Legal and Social Theory*, Hart Publishing, Oxford, 1998.

C A MacKinnon, *Feminism Unmodified: Discourses on Life and Law*, Harvard University Press, Cambridge, MA, 1987.

C A MacKinnon, *Toward a Feminist Theory of the State*, Harvard University Press, Cambridge, MA, 1989.

M L Minow, *Making All the Difference: Inclusion, Exclusion and American Law*, Harvard University Press, Cambridge, MA, 1991.

N Naffine, 'In Praise of Legal Feminism' (2002) 22 *Legal Studies* 71.

M C Nussbaum, *Sex and Social Justice*, Oxford University Press, New York, 1999.

M C Nussbaum, *Women and Human Development: The Capabilities Approach*, Cambridge University Press, Cambridge, 2000.

S Okin, *Justice, Gender and the Family*, Basic Books, New York, 1989.

D Rhode, *Speaking of Sex: The Denial of Gender Inequality*, Harvard University Press, Cambridge, MA, 1997.

P Smith, 'Domesticity and Denial', in M Golding and W Edmundson (eds), *The Blackwell Guide to the Philosophy of Law and Legal Theory*, Blackwell Publishing, Oxford, 2005, pp 90–104.

N Sullivan, *A Critical Introduction to Queer Theory*, Edinburgh University Press, Edinburgh, 2003.

Symposium, 'Critical Race Theory' (1994) 82 *California Law Review* 741–1125.

Index

A page reference followed by 'n' refers to footnotes on that page.

Aboriginal land claims   9, 15
abortion, right to   262, 290–5, 369
adjudication *see* judicial decision-making
Alexander, Larry   275n
Alexy, Robert   9n, 115, 129, 131n
American Declaration of Independence   113
American legal realism *see* realism
American Revolution   113
Anderson, Elizabeth   333–4
Appiah, K Anthony   379
Aquinas, Thomas   110–12, 113, 114, 120, 285
    four types of law   110
Aristotle   108, 220, 285
Arneson, Richard   333n
assisted suicide *see* euthanasia
Atiyah, Patrick   148
Augustine   110, 114
Austin, J L   37
Austin, John   13–33, 35–7, 40, 42, 48–50, 54, 55, 56, 59, 70, 71, 186
    command theory of law   13–33
        criticisms of   13, 17–23
Australian constitution   22, 131–2, 140, 265
authority
    Finnis's account of   120–1
    notion of   17–18
    Raz's account of   90–6
        criticisms of   98–101
    realist rejection of   98, 146, 194
    theoretical versus practical   88–9
Ayer, Alfred   70n

Barnett, Hilaire   368
Bartlett, Katherine   350
Behrendt, Larissa   363
Bell, Derrick   374–5
Bell, John   7, 175n
Bentham, Jeremy   13, 14, 28, 71, 74, 103, 241, 255
    hostility to notion of moral rights   255–6

Bickel, Alexander   290
Bilchitz, David   267
bill of rights   261–6
    applying moral standards in   81, 97, 98–9, 101
    Canada, in   87
    International Bill of Rights   246
    invalidation of legislation under   81–2
    South African bill of rights   9
    statutory   264–5
        in Australia   265–6
    strong-form judicial review   262
        critics of   262–3
    US Bill of Rights   81, 262
    weak-form judicial review   264
Bix, Brian   5n, 180n
Black, Donald   32
Blackstone, William   14
Bottomley, Stephen   211, 213
Bronitt, Simon   211, 213, 373n
Buchanan, Allen   257, 323n
Burger, Chief Justice   290, 295
Bush, US President George H W   292

Cain, Patricia   346n, 364
Calhoun, Cheshire   380
Campbell, Tom   69, 102, 103n, 246
Carens, Joseph   332
'checkerboard statutes'   169–70
Christian thought   110
Cicero, Marcus Tullius   109, 110
Coase, Ronald   204
cognitivism   24, 70–1
Cohen, Felix   183, 194
Cohen, G A   225, 310n, 336n, 339, 340, 341
Coke, Chief Justice   98, 131
Coleman, Jules   6, 25n, 41, 45n, 69, 79n, 80, 82, 83n, 85n, 87n, 89n, 168n, 178, 206n
command theory of law   13–17
    criticisms of   13, 17–23

Commonwealth Constitution *see* Australian Constitution
communitarianism   322–3, 328
   rights, critique of   258–61
Connor, Steven   219
consequentialism   240–1
constructive interpretation
   Critical Legal Studies (CLS) scepticism about   231–5
   Dworkin's notion of   156–7, 166, 167, 169, 231–4
   internal scepticism   159, 232
conventionalism   161–3, 166, 177
conventions   25, 44–6, 92
coordination problem   44–5, 92, 119
Cornell, Drucilla   361n, 365n
Cossman, Brenda   381
courtesy, convention of   156–7
courts
   natural law in   129–32
Crenshaw, Kimberlé   363
criminal prohibitions
   moralistic reasons, whether should be based on   272
Critical Legal Studies (CLS)   159, 217, 227–9, 377
   constructive interpretation, impossibility of   231–5
   contradictions, incoherencies and law as ideology   227–9
   liberal values, rejection of   230–1
   main themes of   217–19
   post-CLS developments   235
Critical Race Theory (CRT)   363, 374–8
Crowe, Jonathan   112
Cunningham, Whitney   204

Davies, Margaret   224
de Saussure, Ferdinand   222
Delgado, Richard   375, 377
democracy, concept of   31, 263–4
Denning, Alfred   145
Derrida, Jacques   219, 222–4
Descartes, René   220

Devlin, Patrick   272, 279–81, 285–6, 287
   legal moralism, conservative version of   279–81
   criticism of   281–3
   'reasonable man'   280
Dickson, Julie   30, 45, 117n, 121n, 123, 178
discrimination
   anti-discrimination legislation   347–8
   indirect   348, 350–1
distributive justice
   capabilities approach   334, 371
   contractarian tradition   311
   Dworkin's equality of resources approach   328–31
      criticisms of   331–4
   equality of welfare approach   328–9
   liberty and patterns   338–9
      Wilt Chamberlain argument   338
   luck egalitarianism   333–4
   Nozick's libertarianism   334–8
   Rawls's principles of *see* Rawls's two principles of justice
   self-ownership, principle of   339–41
   sufficientarianism   333
   utilitarianism and   303–6
Duxbury, Neil   218n
Dworkin, Andrea   287
Dworkin, Ronald   31, 55, 61, 65–7, 76, 81–4, 95, 96, 98, 101, 135, 190, 194, 209–10, 231–4, 281, 291–5, 297, 298, 320–1, 352, 370
   abortion, view on   291–5
   'argumentative' social practices   156–8
   conception of democracy   264
   constructive interpretation *see* constructive interpretation
   conventionalism   161–3, 166, 177
   criticisms of   174–80
   Difference Principle, objection to   320–1
   equality of resources theory   328–31
      criticisms of   331–4
   euthanasia, view on   297–8
   external scepticism   173–4

Dworkin, Ronald (cont.)
   Hart's doctrine of discretion, challenge to 148–50
   indeterminacy, criticism of 190
   internal scepticism 159, 232
   interpretation, objectivity of 171–4
   law as integrity 163–71
   legal pragmatism, attack on 194–7
   normative conception of jurisprudence 31, 158–61, 177
   point of law, account of 31, 161, 164, 177
   positivism, attack on 76–80, 84–7, 98–9, 148–56
   principle of equal importance 252, 328
   principle of personal responsibility 252, 293–4, 328
   rights, advocate of 244, 245, 249, 251, 252, 263–4
   rules and principles, distinction between 150–3
   wicked legal systems, view on 176–7
Dyzenhaus, David 102, 130n

East German Border Guards cases 9–10, 130–1
economics
   diminishing marginal utility, law of 304
   efficiency considerations 212
   judicial decisions, as underlying explanatory determinant of 202
   law and economics
      descriptive dimension of 210–13
         criticisms of 213
      normative dimension of 204–10
         criticisms of 206–7, 208–9, 210
   Law and Economics movement 201
efficiency
   Posner's views on 203
Ehrenberg, Kenneth 179n
Ely, John 263–4
equal rights 226, 230, 347, 349, 351
Eskridge, William 381
eternal law 110

euthanasia 280, 295–9
   liberal view on 298–9
   medical treatment, right to refuse 297
   passive and active, distinction between 296–7
   voluntary and non-voluntary, distinction between 296
exclusionary reason 90–1, 94, 99–100

Feinberg, Joel 261, 271–2, 275, 282
feminism
   abortion see abortion, right to
   categorising 346
   Critical Race Theory 363
   difference or cultural 353–5
      criticisms of 355–9
   equality, formal 346–8, 351
      male norm, and the 348–51
      problems with 348–51
   ethic of care versus ethic of justice 345, 371–2
   family as a political institution 366–71
   feminist legal theory 345–6
   international, defending concept of 261
   liberal 346, 347–8, 351–3
      equal opportunity goals of 347–8
      individualism in 352–3
   multiculturalism and 372–4
   pornography, views on 287–90, 360–1
   postmodern 361–6, 364–6
      criticisms of 364–6
      essentialism 362–4
      intersectionality 362–3
   public-private distinction 366–71
   radical 359–61
   rights and justice
      ambivalence concerning 371
      empowering aspect 372
   sexual harassment 363
   sexual subordination 360
   special treatment approach 358–9

Finnis, John   31, 55, 107, 112, 179–80, 379
   authority of law, account of   120–1
   basic human goods   118–19
   central case of law   113–22
      criticisms of   122–4
   normative conception of
      jurisprudence   31, 116–18, 179
Fitzpatrick, Peter   219
Fleming, James   293n
foetus, moral status of   291
formalism   144–8, 184–5
Foucault, Michel   219, 221, 378
Frank, Jerome   183, 186, 189, 192
freedom of choice
   Devlin's conservative view on   279–81
   George's natural law view on   285–6, 287
   Mill's harm principle   272–7, 279, 282, 287–8, 289–90, 297
   prevention of offence   275
   Rawls's neutralist view on   277–9, 286, 289
   Raz's liberal perfectionist view on 284–5
   state coercion, reasons for   271–2
   state neutrality, concept of   277–9
   see also criminal prohibitions
Freeman, Michael   193n
Freeman, Samuel   307
French Declaration of the Rights of Man and the Citizen 1789   255, 257
French Revolution   113
Fuller, Lon   25n, 74, 107, 124–7, 129, 135–41
   internal morality of law   124–7
      criticisms of   127–8
   'The Case of the Speluncean Explorers'   144
   theory of adjudication   141–4
      criticisms of   145–8
   theory of meaning   136–41

Gabel, Peter   231n
Gardner, John   26n, 28n, 73
Gauthier, David   341n
George, Robert   272, 282, 285–6, 287, 379
Gilligan, Carol   354, 371
Glorious Revolution   131

Goldsworthy, Jeffrey   83n, 88n
Gray, John Chipman   186
Greek philosophers   108
Green, Leslie   5, 23, 29, 44, 45n, 52, 71
Greenawalt, Kent   175
Greenberg, Mark   23n
Grotius, Hugo   112

Halperin, David   378n, 379
Hanson, Jon   212
Hare, R M   319
Harris, Angela   376
Harsanyi, John   249n
Hart, H L A   13, 14n, 15, 17–19, 23, 24, 25n, 28n, 70, 72–5, 80, 85–7, 88–9, 90, 101, 103, 116–18, 121, 123, 128, 129, 152, 177–9, 186–7, 189, 275, 282, 307n, 341, 352
   being obliged versus being under an obligation   17, 38, 40, 48
   core versus penumbra   62–4, 101, 136–7, 189
   criticisms of   55–60, 117–18
   Fuller and, debates between   74, 127–8, 136–8, 142–3
   habit and social rule, distinction between   38
   hermeneutic approach   36–7
   internal point of view   36, 38–9, 40, 43, 46–7, 48, 50, 54–6, 116–17, 179
   judicial discretion   72–5
      Dworkin's challenge to   148–50
   law as a 'remedy'   50–2
   law, normativity of   35, 36, 40, 43, 48, 54
   legal obligations, Hart's analysis of 40, 48, 52–3
   legal theory as morally neutral   32–3, 51–2, 54–5, 178–9
   legal validity, Hart's analysis of   36, 41–2, 43, 48
   'no vehicles in the park' rule   62–7, 136–8
   preconditions for the existence of law, Hart's account of   46–8
   recognition, rule of   24, 40, 41–2, 43–8, 53, 57–8, 69, 76, 77, 79, 80–3, 84–6, 154

Hart, H L A (cont.)
    statements of legal obligation, Hart's analysis of   54, 57–60
        criticisms of   56–57
    see also legal rule; social rule
Hart, Melissa   212
Himma, Kenneth   38, 60n, 88n
Hoadly, Bishop   186
Hobbes, Thomas   13, 73, 311
Hogg, Peter   265n
Holmes Jr, Oliver Wendell   183, 185, 188, 191
Holmes, Stephen   267n
Homosexual Offences and Prostitution, Report of the Committee on   279
Horwitz, Morton   217, 231
Howarth, David   227–8
human rights see rights
Hume, David   70
Hunt, Alan   219
Hunter, Nan   381n
Hutchinson, Alan C   229n, 230

identity politics   356, 372–3, 379
ideology   218, 226–7, 228, 229
indeterminacy
    CLS version of   218, 230
    Dworkin's view on   61, 62–3, 151, 171, 174
    Hart's view on   61–4, 65, 101, 152
    'mechanical jurisprudence'   66, 184–5
    realists' view on   188–90
        criticisms of   189–90
    traditional view   60–1
individualism   230, 352–3, 371
integrity, law as   163–71
internal morality of law   126–7
International Bill of Rights see bill of rights
International Covenant on Civil and Political Rights   246, 265
International Covenant on Economic, Social and Cultural Rights   246
interpretation
    clear meaning   62, 63, 136–7, 138, 140–1, 142, 162–3, 168, 176, 222–3
    Dworkin's interpretive approach   135–6, 155, 156–9, 165–9

interpretation (cont.)
    Fuller's purposive approach   136, 137–9, 141–4
    legislative intentions, relevance to   138–9
    objectivity of   171–4
        external scepticism   173–4
    see also constructive interpretation
intersectionality   362–3, 376
Irigaray, Luce   355

judicial decision-making
    adjudication, pragmatic model of   194–7, 202
    clear rules, should judges follow   144–8
    CLS view of   228–9
    conventionalism and plain meaning approach to   162–3
    economic determinants of   202–3, 210–12
    formalism   144–8
    Fuller's theory of adjudication   141–4
    Fuller's theory of meaning   136–41
    Hart's account of   60–7
        Dworkin's challenge to   148–50
    integrity, law as   163–71
    interpretation, objectivity of   171–4
    judicial discretion   65
        Dworkin's challenge to   148–50
    legally unregulated cases   66, 101
    non-legal determinants of   190–4
    theoretical disagreement   153–6
jurisprudence
    interpretation, as   156–61
    labels, categories and schools of thought   4–7
    point of studying   7–10
    what is   1–3
    whether analytical or normative   5, 29–32, 51–2, 54–5, 116–18, 158, 159–60, 177–9
justice see distributive justice

Kairys, David   218n
Kaldor-Hicks efficiency   206–7
Kant, Immanuel   220, 252, 297
Kantian ideas   252–4, 305, 322, 339, 340, 353

Kelly, Paul 373
Kelman, Mark 217, 228
Kelsen, Hans 117
Kennedy, Duncan 217, 228, 230, 231n
Koppelman, Andrew 379n
Kramer, Matthew 26n, 28n, 60n, 72n, 82, 83, 123, 174n
Kronman, Anthony 184n
Kymlicka, Will 259, 320–1, 325n, 336n, 327–8, 332, 340n, 372

Lacan, Jacques 219, 223–4
Lacey, Nicola 367
Langdell, Christopher Columbus 184
Law and Economics movement 201
legal moralism 272, 284–6
    Devlin's conservative version of 279–81
    criticisms of 281–3
    George's perfectionist version of 285–6
legal pragmatism 194, 201–2
legal rule
    duty-imposing rules 20, 50
    power-conferring rules 20, 49, 51, 117–18
    primary and secondary rules, law as union of 41, 47, 50–2
    primary rules 41, 48, 50–3
    principles, difference between, and 150–3
    rules of change 42
    rule of recognition *see* rule of recognition
    rules of adjudication 42
    secondary rules, concept of 41, 42–3, 47, 48–52, 59
Leiter, Brian 154, 176n, 185n, 188n, 192n, 193n
Lewis, David 44n
lex iniusta non est lex 110, 114, 116
liberal egalitarianism 303, 306, 321, 334, 352
liberalism
    consent as a defence, acceptance of 282
    family, attitudes to intervention in 368–9, 370–1

liberalism (cont.)
    feminism and 351–3, 368–71
    inequality, attitudes to 254, 351–2
    political versus comprehensive 321–8
    prevention of offence, whether legitimate aim 275
    private realm, protection of 275–6, 368–70
    punishing harmless immorality, illegitimacy of 272, 273–5, 284
    Rawls's neutralist version of 277–9
    Raz's perfectionist version of 284–5
    see also abortion, right to; euthanasia; freedom of choice; liberal egalitarianism; libertarianism; pornography, prohibition of
libertarianism 276, 303, 372
    Nozick's libertarianism 334–8
liberty *see* freedom of choice
liberties, Rawls's list of basic 307
    personal property, right to hold, extent of 307
Littleton, Christine 349
Llewellyn, Karl 183, 185–6, 192–3
Locke, John 112–13, 311
Lovibond, Sabina 365
Lukes, Steven 257
Lyons, David 24n, 63, 80, 139n, 310–11
Lyotard, Jean-Francois 219, 221

MacCormick, Neil 26n, 37n, 57
MacIntyre, Alasdair 258
MacKinnon, Catharine 287, 350, 356, 359–61, 365–6, 369–70
Mandela, President Nelson 9, 358
Marmor, Andrei 45n, 75n, 88
marriage *see* same-sex marriage
Marx, Karl 220, 224–7, 230, 256–7
Marxism 159, 172, 220, 221, 224–7
materialism, historical 224
Matsuda, Mari 375, 376–7
Meese Commission, US 289
methodological positivism 29–32, 51–2
Meyerson, Denise 227n, 233n, 289n
Mill, John Stuart 272–7, 278, 279, 287–8, 289–90, 295, 355–6, 368–9

Minow, Martha   171, 357
Moore, Michael   263n
morality, critical versus popular   26, 53, 72
multiculturalism
    feminism and   372–4
Murphy, Jeffrie   206n
Murphy, Liam   75
Murphy, Mark   18–19, 23n, 112n, 114–15, 116

natural law   107–32
    common good   111, 112, 119, 121
    courts, in the   129–32
    Finnis's central case approach   113–22
        criticisms of   122–4
    Fuller and the internal morality of
        law   124–7
        criticisms of   127–8
    legal theory   108
    'Moral Reading'   114–15
    morality as necessary influence on
        law-identification   135–6, 139, 144,
        165–6, 169
    positivism and, debate between   4–7,
        25, 108
    procedural theories   107, 124–7
    'Strong Natural Law Thesis'   115–16, 121
    substantive theories   107, 113
    tradition   108–13
    'Weak Natural Law Thesis'   115–16
Nazi regime   74, 115, 127, 129–30, 131, 176
non-cognitivism   70–1
Nozick, Robert   244, 252, 253, 256, 266,
    306, 317–18, 334–41, 352
Nussbaum, Martha   254n, 261, 352–3,
    370–1

Obscenity and Pornography in the US, 1970
    Report of the Commission on   288
O'Donovan, Katherine   367
Okin, Susan   373–4
Oliphant, Herman   183

Pappe, H O   130n
Parekh, Bhikhu   374
Paulson, Stanley   74n

Penner, James   92n
perfectionism   284
    George's defence of   285–6
    Rawls's rejection of   308, 321–2, 323
    Raz's defence of   284–5
    Sandel's defence of   323
Perry, Stephen   29n, 51–2, 99–100
Plato   108, 220
Polikoff, Nancy   381
pornography
    MacKinnon's account of   360
        criticisms of   361
    prohibition of   286–90
Pornography and Prostitution in Canada,
    1985 Special Committee Report on 288
positivism
    Dworkin's attack on   76–80, 84–6,
        98–9, 148–56
    ethical   69, 101–3, 147
    exclusive   27, 69, 79–80
        Raz's   87–98
            criticisms of   98–101
    inclusive   27, 69, 75–6, 79, 80–4, 87, 95,
        96, 101, 102, 169
        acceptable theory of law,
            whether   84–7
    interpretive version of   161–3, 177,
        178–9
    key ideas of   23–33
    law's function, view of   85–6, 100, 178
    legal versus logical   70–1
    methodological positivism   29–32, 51–2
    misconceptions about separability
        thesis   70–6
    natural law and, debate between   4–7,
        25, 108
    separability thesis   25–8, 53–4, 56, 72,
        74, 75, 79, 83, 84, 87
    social construction, law as   23–5, 83
    sociological positivism   32–3
    substantive legal positivism   23–9
    see also social facts
Posner, Richard   201–13
Postema, Gerald   45, 103n
postmodernism   219–24
poststructuralism   222

Pound, Roscoe   184n
precedent
   doctrine of   63
   sense in which authoritative   99–100
principles
   distinction between rules and   150–3
private–public distinction   366–71
property
   just acquisition, Nozick's principle of   335–6
   rectification, Nozick's principle of   336
   rights, Nozick's absolute conception of   337–8
   transfer, Nozick's principle of   336

Quayle, Vice president Dan   292

racism *see* Critical Race Theory (CRT)
Radbruch, Gustav   115, 129
Radin, Margaret   357
Railton, Peter   250n
Rajczi, Alex   380n
rape
   MacKinnon's account of   360–1
   marital   366, 368
Rawls, John   252–4, 259, 278, 293, 305–6, 339–40, 352, 370, 371
   criticisms of   316–17, 318–20, 320–1, 322–3, 327–8
Rawls's two principles of justice
   basic liberties, principle that protects   306–8, 313–14, 324
      Difference Principle   308–11, 314–15
         Hare's insurance strategy   319–20
         rational to choose, whether   318–20
         unfairly subsidises people's choices, whether   320–1, 329
   distributive justice   308–9
   liberties, list of basic   307
   original position   311–15, 321–2
      justifiable, whether conditions of choice in   315–18
      veil of ignorance, justification in using   317

Rawls's two principles of justice (cont.)
   political liberalism, defence of   321–8
   state neutrality   277–9, 313–4, 321–2, 324–5
   to whom owed   253–4
Raz, Joseph   16n, 17n, 18, 29–30, 39, 41n, 54n, 56, 61, 65, 66, 69, 79n, 284–5
   exclusive positivism   87–98
      criticisms of   98–101
   law's claim to legitimate authority   18, 93–4
   perfectionist liberal   284–5
   service conception of authority   91–2, 93, 95
   statements of legal obligation, account of   56–7
realism   183–97
   adjudication, pragmatic model of   194–7
      criticism of   196–7
   American legal realism   183
   indeterminacy of law   188–90
      criticisms of   189–90
   judicial decisions, determinants of   190–4
   law is what courts say it is   185–6
      criticisms of   186–7
   'paper' rules   185–6
recognition, rule of *see* rule of recognition
Rhode, Deborah   371–2
Riggs and *Henningsen* principles   78–80
rights
   bill of rights *see* bill of rights
   civil and political   247, 265, 266–7
   CLS views on   230–1
   communitarian critique of   258–61
   conflict between utilitarianism and   242–3
   constitutional protection of   81, 87, 262, 265
   ethnocentric, whether   259–61
   feminist views on   371–2
   freedom of speech, right to   248
   fundamental interests, list of   246–8
   group   248

rights (cont.)
   human rights
      concept of   239–40
      state's obligations, extent of   240
      interests deserving status of   246–8
      Kantian justification for   252–4
      legal versus moral   239–40
      natural rights   112–3, 240
      opponents of   255–61
      oppression, whether instrument of   256–7
      respect for   240–6
      why governments should   248–54
      selfish, whether   255–6
      socio-economic   247, 257, 266–7
      terrorism suspects, rights of   245
      theorists   243–5, 252–4, 256, 258–9, 260–1, 266–7
      threat to value of community, whether   258–9
Rodgerson, Gillian   361
Roemer, John   331n
Rousseau, Jean-Jacques   311
rule *see* legal rule; rule of recognition; social rule
rule-based decision-making   32, 39, 103, 144–8, 195
rule of law   28, 125, 128, 230, 231
rule of recognition   24, 40, 41–2, 43–8, 53, 57–8, 69, 76, 77, 79, 80–3, 84–6, 154
Ryle, Gilbert   37

same-sex marriage   379–81
Sandel, Michael   258, 323
Sayre-McCord, Geoffrey   24n
Scanlon, Thomas   261
Schauer, Frederick   37n, 62, 63, 64n, 87, 98, 99, 101, 139–41, 142n, 144, 147, 176, 194, 195, 244–5, 289n
   rights as shields   244–5
   rule-based versus particularistic decision-making   195
   semantic autonomy of language   140
self-ownership, principle of   339–41
Sen, Amartya   334

sexual inequality *see* feminism
sexuality and the law
   lesbian and gay legal theory   378
      essentialism, complaint of   378–9
      queer theory   378–9
   same-sex marriage   379–81
Shapiro, Scott   39n, 43n, 45n, 65, 88, 92, 152
Shiner, Roger   32, 55
Sim, Stuart   222
Simmonds, Nigel   43n, 57n, 58n, 128, 158–9, 234
Singer, Joseph   231n, 377n
Smart, J J C   249, 250, 304, 305
Smith, Matthew Noah   24, 39n
social facts   23–4, 25, 26–7, 43, 53, 79, 83, 88
social rule
   compatible with moral tests for law, whether   84–5
   concept of   36–40
   distinction between habit and   38
   internal aspects of   38
   reasons for accepting   58
   rule of recognition *see* rule of recognition
   social practice, created by form of   24–5, 38–9
Socrates   8
Soper, Philip   115
Sophocles   109
sovereignty   15, 19–23, 49, 81
   Austin's account of   15, 49
   criticisms of   20–3
   Hart's account of   49–50
   legal source of   49
   parliamentary   21, 81
Spelman, Elizabeth   171, 363–4
state neutrality *see* perfectionism
Stavropoulos, Nicos   60n
Stefanic, Jean   375
Stick, John   155
Stoics, writings of   108, 109
Strossen, Nadine   288
suicide, assisted *see* euthanasia
Sunstein, Cass   147n, 267n, 381n

taxation, redistributive   331, 335, 337, 338, 340, 341
Taylor, Charles   258, 356–7
Thaler, Richard   381n
theoretical disagreement   153–6
Thompson, E P   226, 231
Tooley, Michael   106n
tort system
    allocation of liability for accidents   211
totalitarian regimes, collapse of   129
transaction costs   204, 205, 206, 212, 213
Trubek, David   217
Tushnet, Mark   217, 262n
Twining, William   37n

Unger, Roberto   217, 231
US Constitution   21, 81, 262
Universal Declaration of Human Rights   246–8
utilitarianism   207
    act utilitarianism   242
    Bentham's view on   71, 103, 241, 255–6
    conflict between rights and   242–3
    criticisms of   207, 242–4, 249–50, 251, 256, 305–6
    distributive justice and   303–6
    happiness, maximisation of   241–2, 303–5
    harm principle and   276–7
    indirect   250–1
    moral theory of   240–6
    rule utilitarianism   249–51
    wealth maximisation, difference between, and   207–8
    welfare, maximisation of   243, 328–9

Veljanovski, Cento   207, 213
voluntary euthanasia *see* euthanasia

Waismann, Friedrich   63
Waldron, Jeremy   69, 102, 125–6, 232n, 248n, 251, 256n, 260n, 262–3, 284
Walker, Geoffrey de Q   197
Waluchow, Wilfred   29n, 30n, 69, 75, 80, 86, 87, 97n, 99n, 100n, 142, 146n, 177
Walzer, Michael   258, 260
wealth, distribution of *see* distributive justice
wealth maximisation   203–4
    ethically attractive, whether   205–10
Weinreb, Lloyd   109n, 110
welfare
    definition of   241, 329
    equality of   328–9
        Dworkin's objection to   329
    maximisation of   243, 328–9
Wellington, Adrian   380n
Wellman, Vincent   93
West, Robin   354–5
Williams, Patricia   375, 377–8
Williams, Wendy   351n, 358
Williams Commission in the UK, 1979 report of the   288
Wilson, Elizabeth   361
Wolfenden Report *see* Homosexual Offences and Prostitution, Report of the Committee on
Wolff, Jonathan   316, 332–3, 336, 338–9
World War II   113, 129, 246

Young, Iris   372n

Zanghellini, Aleardo   379n
Zines, Leslie   132
Zipursky, Benjamin   293n